THE
ARCTIC HOME IN THE VEDAS

THE

ARCTIC HOME IN THE VEDAS,

BEING ALSO A NEW KEY TO THE INTERPRETATION
OF MANY VEDIC TEXTS AND LEGENDS,

BY

LOKAMANYA

BAL GANGADHAR TILAK B. A., LL. B.

GYAN

Published by

GYAN

Gyan Publishing House
5, Ansari Road
Daryaganj, New Delhi-110002
Phone: 011-47034999, 9811692060
E-mail: books@gyanbooks.com

Distribution Network
gyanbooks.com
India, USA, Canada, UK, Australia, France

ISBN: 978-81-212-8248-2 (PB)
First Published, 1903

2nd Impression 2023

Printed at: Gyan Press, Delhi.

THE ARCTIC HOME IN THE VEDAS
Author: LOKAMANYA BAL GANGADHAR TILAK

THE

ARCTIC HOME IN THE VEDAS.

THE

ARCTIC HOME IN THE VEDAS,

BEING ALSO A NEW KEY TO THE INTERPRETATION OF MANY VEDIC TEXTS AND LEGENDS,

BY

LOKAMANYA

BĀL GANGADHAR TILAK B. A., LL. B.

THE PROPRIETOR OF THE '*Kesari*' & THE '*Maratha*' NEWSPAPERS, THE AUTHOR OF THE '*Orion*' OR *Researches into the Antiquity of the Vedas*, THE '*Gita Rahasya*' (*a Book on Hindu Philosophy*) etc. etc.

1925.

PREFACE.

THE present volume is a sequel to my *Orion or Researches into the Antiquity of the Vedas,* published in 1893. The estimate of Vedic antiquity then generally current amongst Vedic scholars was based on the assignment of arbitrary periods of time to the different strata into which the Vedic literature is divided ; and it was believed that the oldest of these strata could not, at the best, be older than 2400 B. C. In my *Orion*, however, I tried to shew that all such estimates, besides being too modest, were vague and uncertain, and that the astronomical statements found in the Vedic literature supplied us with far more reliable data for correctly ascertaining the ages of the different periods of Vedic literature. These astronomical statements, it was further shewn, unmistakably pointed out that the Vernal equinox was in the constellation of Mṛiga or Orion (about 4500 B. C.) during the period of the Vedic hymns, and that it had receded to the constellation of the Kṛittikâs, or the Pleiades (about 2500 B. C.) in the days of the Brâhmaṇas. Naturally enough these results were, at first, received by scholars in a sceptical spirit. But my position was strengthened when it was found that Dr. Jacobi, of Bonn, had independently arrived at the same conclusion, and soon after scholars like Prof. Bloomfield, M. Barth, the late Dr. Bulher and others more or less freely acknowledged the force of my arguments. Dr. Thibaut, the late Dr. Whitney and a few others were, however, of opinion that the evidence adduced by me was not conclusive. But the subsequent discovery, by my friend the late Mr. S. B. Dixit, of a passage in the Shatapatha Brâhmaṇa, plainly stating that the Kṛittikâs never swerved, in those days, from the *due east*, *i. e.*, the Vernal equinox, has served to dispel all lingering doubts regarding the age of the Bâhmaṇas; while another Indian astronomer, Mr. V. B. Ketkar, in a recent number of the Journal of the Bombay Branch of the Royal Asiatic Society, has mathematically worked out the statement in the Taittirîya Brâhmaṇa (iii, 1, 1, 5), that Bṛihaspati, or the planet Jupiter, was first discovered when confronting or nearly occulting the star Tiṣhya, and shewn that the observation was possible only at about 4650 B. C., thereby remarkably confirming my estimate of the oldest period of Vedic literature. After this, the high antiquity of the oldest Vedic period may, I think, be now taken as fairly established.

But if the age of the oldest Vedic period was thus carried back to 4500 B. C., one was still tempted to ask whether we had, in that limit, reached the *ultima Thule* of the Aryan antiquity. For, as stated by Prof. Bloomfield, while noticing my *Orion* in his address on the occasion of the eighteenth anniversary of John Hopkin's University, "the language and literature of the Vedas is, by no means, so primitive as to place with it the real beginnings of Aryan life." "These in all probability and in all due moderation," he rightly observed, "reach back several thousands of years more," and it was, he said, therefore "needless to point out that this curtain, which seems to shut off our vision at 4500 B. C., may prove in the end a veil of thin gauze." I myself held the same view, and much of my spare time during the last ten years has been devoted to the search of evidence which would lift up this curtain and reveal to us the long vista of primitive Aryan antiquity. How I first worked on the lines followed up in *Orion*, how in the light of latest researches in geology and archæology bearing on the primitive history of man, I was gradually led to a different line of search, and finally how the conclusion, that the ancestors of the Vedic Rishis lived in an Arctic home in inter-glacial times, was forced on me by the slowly accumulating mass of Vedic and Avestic evidence, is fully narrated in the book, and need not, therefore, be repeated in this place. I desire, however, to take this opportunity of gratefully acknowledging the generous sympathy shewn to me at a critical time by that venerable scholar Prof. F. Max Muller, whose recent death was mourned as a personal loss by his numerous admirers throughout India. This is not the place where we may, with propriety, discuss the merits of the policy adopted by the Bombay Government in 1897. Suffice it to say that in order to put down certain public excitement, caused by its own famine and plague policy, the Government of the day deemed it prudent to prosecute some Vernacular papers in the province, and prominently amongst them the *Kesari*, edited by me, for writings which were held to be seditious, and I was awarded eighteen months' rigorous imprisonment. But political offenders in India are not treated better than ordinary convicts, and had it not been for the sympathy and interest taken by Prof. Max Muller, who knew me only as the author of *Orion*, and other friends, I should have been deprived of the pleasure,—then the only pleasure,—of following up my studies in these days. Prof. Max Muller was kind enough to send me a copy of his second edition of the Ṛig-Veda, and the Government was pleased to allow me the use of these and other books, and also of light to read for a few hours at night. Some of the passages from the Ṛig-Veda, quoted in support of the Arctic theory in the following pages, were collected during such leisure as I could get in these times. It was mainly through the efforts of Prof. Max Muller, backed by the whole Indian press, that I was released after twelve months; and in the very first letter I wrote to Prof. Max Muller after my release, I thanked him sincerely for his disinterested kindness, and also gave him a brief summary of my new theory regarding the primitive Aryan home as disclosed by Vedic evidence. It was, of course, not to be expected that a scholar, who had worked all his life on a different line, would accept the new view at once, and that too on reading a bare outline of the evidence in its support. Still it was encouraging to hear from him that though the interpretations of Vedic passages proposed by me were probable, yet my theory appeared to be in conflict with the established geological facts. I wrote in reply that I had already examined the question from that stand-point, and expected soon to place before him the whole evidence in support of my view. But, unfortunately, I have been deprived of this pleasure by his deeply mourned death which occurred soon after.

The first manuscript of the book was written at the end of 1898, and since then I have had the advantage of discussing the question with many scholars in Madras, Calcutta, Lahore, Benares and other places during my travels in the different parts of India. But I hesitated to publish the book for a long time,—a part of the delay is due to other causes,—because the lines of investigation had ramified into many allied sciences such as geology, archæology, comparative mythology and so on; and, as I was a mere layman in these, I felt some diffidence as to whether I had correctly grasped the bearing of the latest researches in these sciences. The difficulty is well described by Prof. Max Muller in his review of the *Prehistoric Antiquities of Indo-Europeans*, published in the volume of his *Last Essays*. "The ever-increasing division and sub-division," observes the learned Professor,' 'of almost every branch of human knowledge into more special branches of study make the specialist, whether he likes it or not, more and more dependent on the judgment and the help of his fellow-workers. A geologist in our day has often to deal with questions that concern the minerologist, the chemist, the archæologist, the philologist, nay, the astronomer, rather than the geologist *pur et simple*, and, as life is too short for all this, nothing is left to him but to appeal to his colleagues for counsel and help. It is one of the great advantages of University life, that any one, who is in trouble about some question outside his own domain, can at once get the very best information from his colleagues, and many of the happiest views and brightest solutions of complicated problems are due, as is well-known, to this free intercourse, this scientific give and take in our academic centres." And again, "Unless a student can appeal for help to recognised authorities on all these subjects, he is apt to make brilliant discoveries, which explode at the slightest touch of the specialist, and, on the other hand, to pass by facts which have only to be pointed out in order to disclose their significance and far-reaching importance. People are hardly aware of the benefit which every branch of science derives from the free and generous exchange of ideas, particularly in our Universities, where every body may avail himself of the advice and help of his colleagues, whether they warn him against yet impossible theories, or call his attention to a book or an article, where the very point that interests him, has been fully worked out and settled once for all." But alas! it is not given to us to move in an atmosphere like this, and small wonder if Indian students are not found to go beyond the stage of passing the examinations. There is not a single institution in India, nor, despite the University Commission, can we hope to have any before long, where one can get all up-to-date information on *any* desired subject, so easily obtainable at a seat of learning in the West; and in its absence the only course open to a person, investigating a particular subject, is, in the words of the same learned scholar, "to step boldly out of his own domain, and take an independent survey of the preserves of his neighbours," even at the risk of being called "an interloper, an ignoramus, a mere dilettante," for, "whatever accidents he may meet with himself, the subject itself is sure to be benefited." Working under such disadvantages, I was, therefore, glad, when, on turning the pages of the first volume of the tenth edition of the Encyclopædia Britannica, recently received, I found that Prof. Geikie, in his article on geology, took the same view of Dr. Croll's calculations, as summarised at the end of the second chapter of this book. After stating that Croll's doctrine did not make way amongst physicists and astronomers, the eminent geologist says that more recently (1895) it has been critically examined by Mr. E. P. Culverwell, who regards it as "a vague speculation, clothed indeed with delusive semblance of severe numerical accuracy, but having no foundation in physical fact, and built up of parts which do not dovetail one into the other." If Dr. Croll's calculations are disposed of in this way, there remains nothing to prevent us from accepting the view of the American geologists that the commencement of the Post-glacial period can not be placed at a date earlier than 8000 B. C.

It has been already stated that the beginnings of Aryan civilisation must be supposed to date back several thousand years before the oldest Vedic period; and when the commencement of the Post-glacial epoch is brought down to 8000 B. C., it is not at all surprising if the date of primitive Aryan life is found to go back to it from 4500 B. C., the age of the oldest Vedic period. In fact, it is the main point sought to be established in the present volume. There are many passages in the Ṛig-Veda, which, though hitherto looked upon as obscure and unintelligible, do, when interpreted in the light of recent scientific researches, plainly disclose the Polar attributes of the Vedic deities, or the traces of an ancient Arctic calendar; while the Avesta expressly tells us that the happy land of Airyana Vaêjo, or the Aryan Paradise, was located in a region where the sun shone but once a year, and that it was destroyed by the invasion of snow and ice, which rendered its climate inclement and necessitated a migration southward. These are plain and simple statements, and when we put them side by side with what we know of the Glacial and the Post-glacial epoch from the latest geological researches, we cannot avoid the conclusion that the primitive Aryan home was both Arctic and inter-glacial. I have often asked myself, why the real bearing of these plain and simple statements should have so long remained undiscovered; and let me assure the reader that it was not until I was convinced that the discovery was due solely to the recent progress in our knowledge regarding the primitive history of the human race and the planet it inhabits, that I ventured to publish the present volume. Some Zend scholars have narrowly missed the truth, simply because 40 or 50 years ago they were unable to understand how a *happy* home could be located in the ice-bound regions near the North Pole. The progress of geological science in the latter half of the last century has, however, now solved the difficulty by proving that the climate at the Pole during the interglacial times was mild, and consequently not unsuited for human habitation. There is, therefore, nothing extraordinary, if it be left to us to find out the real import of these passages in the Veda and the Avesta. It is true that if the theory of an Arctic and inter-glacial primitive Aryan home is proved, many a chapter in Vedic exegetics, comparative mythology, or primitive Aryan history, will have to be revised or re-written, and in the last chapter of this book I have myself discussed a few important points which will be affected by the new theory. But as remarked by me at the end of the book, considerations like these, howsoever useful they may be in inducing caution in our investigations, ought not to deter us from accepting the results of an inquiry conducted on strictly scientific lines. It is very hard, I know, to give up theories upon which one has worked all his life. But, as Mr. Andrew Lang has put it, it should always be borne in mind that "Our little systems have their day, or their hour: as knowledge advances they pass into the history of the efforts of pioneers." Nor is the theory of the Arctic home so new and startling as it appears to be at the first sight. Several scientific men have already declared their belief that the original home of man must be sought for in the Arctic regions; and Dr. Warren, the President of the Boston University, has anticipated me, to a certain extent, in his learned and suggestive work, the *Paradise Found or the Cradle of the Human Race at the North Pole*, the tenth edition of which was published in America in 1893. Even on strict philological grounds the theory of a primitive Aryan home in Central Asia has been now almost abandoned in favour of North Germany or Scandinavia; while Prof. Rhys, in his *Hibbert Lectures* on Celtic Heathendom, is led to suggest "some spot within the Arctic circle" on purely mythological considerations. I go only a step further, and show that the theory, so far as the primitive Aryan home is concerned, is fully borne out by Vedic and Avestic traditions, and, what is still more important, the latest geological researches not only corroborate the Avestic description of the destruction of the Aryan Paradise, but enable us to place its existence in times before the last Glacial epoch. The evidence on which I rely is fully set forth in the following pages; and, though the question is thus brought for the first time within the arena of Vedic and Avestic scholarship, I trust that my critics will not prejudge me in any way, but give their judgment, not on a passage here or an argument there,—for, taken singly, it may not sometimes be found to be conclusive,—but on the whole mass of evidence collected in the book, irrespective of how far-reaching the ultimate effects of such a theory may be.

In conclusion, I desire to express my obligations to my friend and old teacher Prof. S. G. Jinsivâle, M. A., who carefully went through the whole manuscript, except the last chapter which was subsequently written, verified all references, pointed out a few inaccuracies, and made some valuable suggestions. I have also to acknowledge with thanks the ready assistance rendered to me by Dr. Râmkṛishṇa Gopâl Bhâṇḍârkar, C. I. E., and Khân Bahâdur Dr. Dastur Hoshang Jamâspji, the High Priest of the Parsis in the Deccan, whenever I had an occasion to consult them. Indeed, it would have been impossible to criticise the Avestic passage so fully without the willing co-operation of the learned High Priest and his obliging Deputy Dastur Kaikobâd. I am also indebted to Prof. M. Raṅgâchârya M. A., of Madras, with whom I had an opportunity of discussing the subject, for some critical suggestions, to Mr. Shrinivâs Iyengar, B. A., B. L., of the Madras High Court Bar, for a translation of Lignana's Essay, to Mr. G. R. Gogte, B. A., LL. B., for preparing the manuscript for the press, and to my friend Mr. K. G. Oka, who helped me in reading the proof-sheets, and but for whose care many errors would have escaped my attention. My thanks are similarly due to the Managers of the Ânandâshrama and the Fergusson College for free access to their libraries and to the Manager of the Ârya-Bhûshaṇa Press for the care bestowed on the printing of this volume. It is needless to add that I am alone responsible for the views embodied in the book. When I published my *Orion* I little thought that I could bring to this stage my investigation into the antiquity of the Vedas; but it has pleased Providence to grant me strength amidst troubles and difficulties to do the work, and, with humble remembrance of the same, I conclude in the words of the well-known consecratory formula,—

ॐ तत् सत् ब्रह्मार्पणमस्तु ।

POONA: *March, 1903.* B. G. TILAK.

CONTENTS.

CHAPTER I.

PREHISTORIC TIMES.

CHAPTER V.

The Vedic Dawns.

Appendix to Chapter V.

PAGE

CHAPTER VI.

Long Day and Long Night.

CHAPTER VII.

Months and Seasons.

CHAPTER VIII.

The Cows' Walk.

CHAPTER IX.

VEDIC MYTHS—THE CAPTIVE WATERS.

CHAPTER XI.

The Avestic Evidence.

PAGE

CHAPTER XII.

Comparative Mythology.

THE ARCTIC HOME IN THE VEDAS.

CHAPTER I.

PREHISTORIC TIMES.

The Historic Period —Preceded by myths and traditions —The Science of Mythology —Fresh impulse given to it by Comparative Philology —Unity of Aryan races and languages —The system of interpreting myths, and the theory of Asiatic Home —Recent discoveries in Geology and Archæology —Requiring revision of old theories —The Vedas still partially unintelligible —New key to their interpretation supplied by recent discoveries —The Ages of Iron, Bronze and Stone—Represent different stages of civilization in Prehistoric times —The Ages not necessarily synchronous in different countries —Distinction between Neolithic and Palæolithic or new and old Stone Age —The Geological eras and periods —Their correlation with the three Ages of Iron, Bronze and Stone —Palæolithic Age probably inter-glacial—Man in Quaternary and Tertiary eras —Date of the Neolithic Age —5000 B. C. from lake-dwellings—Peat-mosses of Denmark—Ages of Beach, Oak and Fir —Date of the Palæolithic or the commencement of the Post-Glacial period —Different estimates of European and American geologists—Freshness of fossil deposits in Siberia —Favours American estimate of 8000 years —Neolithic races —Dolicho-cephalic and Brachy-cephalic —Modern European races descended from them —Controversy as to which of these represent the Primitive Aryans in Europe —Different views of German and French writers —Social condition of the Neolithic races and the primitive Aryans —Dr. Schrader's view—Neolithic Aryan race in Europe cannot be regarded as autochthonous —Nor descended from the Palæolithic man —The question of the original Aryan home still unsettled.

If we trace the history of any nation backwards into the past, we come at last to a period of myths and traditions which eventually fade away into impenetrable darkness.

In some cases, as in that of Greece, the historic period goes back to 1000 B. C., while in the case of Egypt the contemporaneous records, recently unearthed from ancient tombs and monuments, carry back its history upto about 5000 B. C. But in either case the historic period, the oldest limit of which may be taken to be 5000 or 6000 B. C., is preceded by a period of myths and traditions; and as these were the only materials available for the study of prehistoric man up to the middle of the nineteenth century, various attempts were made to systematise these myths, to explain them rationally and see if they shed any light on the early history of man. But, as observed by Prof. Max Muller, "it was felt by all unprejudiced scholars that none of these systems of interpretation was in the least satisfactory." "The first impulse to a new consideration of the mythological problem" observes the same learned author "came from the study of comparative philology." Through the discovery of the ancient language and sacred books of India—a discovery, which the Professor compares with the discovery of the new world, and through the discovery of the intimate relationship between Sanskrit and Zend on the one hand and the languages of the principal races of Europe on the other, a complete revolution took place in the views commonly entertained of the ancient history of the world.[1] It was perceived that the languages of the principal European nations—ancient and modern—bore a close resemblance to the languages spoken by the Brahmans of India and the followers of Zoroaster; and from this affinity of the Indo-Germanic languages it followed inevitably that all these languages must be the off-shoots or dialects of a single primitive tongue, and the assumption of such a primitive language further implied the existence of a primitive Aryan people. The study of Vedic literature and classical Sanskrit by Western scholars thus gradually effected

1. See Lectures on the Science of Language, Vol. II, pp. 445 6.

a revolution in their ideas regarding the history and culture of man in ancient times. Dr. Schrader in his work on the *Prehistoric Antiquities of the Aryan Peoples* gives an exhaustive summary of the conclusions arrived at by the methods of comparative philology regarding the primitive culture of the Aryan people, and those that desire to have further information on the subject must refer to that interesting book. For our present purpose it is sufficient to state that comparative mythologists and philologists were in the sole possession of this field, until the researches of the latter half of the nineteenth century placed within our reach new materials for the study of man not only in prehistoric times but in such remote ages that compared with them the prehistoric period appeared to be quite recent.

The mythologists carried on their researches at a time when man was believed to be post-glacial, and when the physical and geographical surroundings of the ancient man were *assumed* not to have been materially different from those of the present day. All ancient myths were, therefore, interpreted on the assumption that they were formed and developed in countries, the climatic or other conditions of which varied very little, if at all, from those by which we are now surrounded. Thus every Vedic myth or legend was explained either on the Storm or the Dawn theory, though in some cases it was felt that the explanation was not at all satisfactory. Indra was only a Storm-God and Vṛitra the demon of drought or darkness brought on by the *daily* setting of the sun. This system of interpretation was first put forward by the Indian Etymologists; and though it has been improved upon by Western Vedic scholars, yet upto now it has remained practically unchanged in character. It was again believed that we must look for the original home of the Aryan race somewhere in Central Asia, and that the Vedic hymns, which were supposed to be composed after the separation of the

Indian Aryans from the common stock, contained the ideas only of that branch of the Aryan race which lived in the Temperate zone. The scientific researches of the latter half of the nineteenth century have, however, given a rude shock to these theories. From hundreds of stone and bronze implements found buried in the various places in Europe the archæologists have now established the chronological sequence of the Iron, the Bronze and the Stone age in times preceding the historic period. But the most important event of the latter half of the last century, so far as it concerns our subject, was the discovery of the evidence proving the existence of the Glacial period at the close of Quarternary era, and the high antiquity of man, who was shown to have lived not only throughout the Quarternary but also in the Tertiary era, when the climatic conditions of the globe were quite different from those in the present or the Post-Glacial period. The remains of animals and men found in the Neolithic or Palæolithic strata also threw new light on the ancient races inhabiting the countries where these remains were found; and it soon became evident that the time-telescope set up by the mythologists must be adjusted to a wider range, and the results previously arrived at by the study of myths and legends must be checked in the light of the facts disclosed by these scientific discoveries. The philologists had now to be more cautious in formulating their views, and some of them soon realised the force of the arguments advanced on the strength of these scientific discoveries. The works of German scholars, like Posche and Penka, freely challenged the Asiatic theory regarding the original home of the Aryan race, and it is now generally recognised that we must give up that theory and seek for the original home of the Aryans somewhere else in the further north. Canon Taylor in his *Origin of the Aryans* has summed up the work done during the last few years in this direction. "It was" he says "mainly a destructive work," and concludes his book with the observation that "the whilom tyranny of the Sanskritists is happily overpast, and it is seen that hasty philological deductions require to be systematically checked by the conclusions of prehistoric archæology, craniology, anthropology, geology, and common-sense." Had the remark not been used as a peroration at the end of the book, it would certainly be open to the objection that it unnecessarily deprecates the labours of the comparative mythologists and philologists. In every department of human knowledge old conclusions have always to be revised in the light of new discoveries, but for that reason it would never be just to find fault with those whose lot it was to work earlier in the same field with scanty and insufficient materials.

But whilst the conclusions of the philologists and mythologists are thus being revised in the light of new scientific discoveries, an equally important work yet remains to be done. It has been stated above that the discovery of the Vedic literature imparted a fresh impulse to the study of myths and legends. But the Vedas themselves, which admittedly form the oldest records of the Aryan race, are as yet imperfectly understood. They had already grown unintelligible to a certain extent even in the days of the *Brâhmaṇas* several centuries before Christ, and had it not been for the labours of Indian Etymologists and Grammarians, they would have remained a sealed book upto the present time. The Western Scholars have indeed developed, to a certain extent, these Native methods of interpretation with the aid of facts brought to light by comparative philology and mythology. But no etymological or philological analysis can help us in thoroughly understanding a passage which contains ideas and sentiments foreign or unfamiliar to us. This is one of the principal difficulties of Vedic interpretation. The Storm or the Dawn theory may help us in understanding some of the legends in this ancient book. But there are passages, which, in spite of their simple diction, are quite unintelligible on any of these theories, and in such cases Native scholars, like Sâyaṇa, are either content with simply paraphrasing the words, or have recourse to distortion of words and phrases in order to make the passages yield a sense intelligible to them; while some of the Western scholars are apt to regard such texts as corrupt or imperfect. In either case, however, it is an undoubted fact that some Vedic texts are yet unintelligible, and, therefore, untranslatable. Prof. Max Muller was fully alive to these difficulties. "A translation of the Ṛig-Veda," he observes in his introduction to the translation of the Vedic hymns in the Sacred Books of the East series, "is a task for the next century,"[1] and the only duty of the present scholars is to "reduce the untranslatable portion to a narrower and narrower limit," as has been done by Yâska and other Native scholars. But if the scientific discoveries of the last century have thrown a new light on the history and culture of man in primitive times, we may as well expect to find in them a new key to the interpretation of the Vedic myths and passages, which admittedly preserve for us the oldest beliefs of the Aryan race. If man existed before the last Glacial period and witnessed the gigantic changes which brought on the Ice Age, it is not unnatural to expect that a reference, howsoever concealed and distant, to these events would be found in the oldest traditionary beliefs and memories of mankind. Dr. Warren in his interesting and highly suggestive work the *Paradise Found* or the *Cradle of the Human Race at the North Pole* has attempted to interpret ancient myths and legends in the light of modern scientific discoveries, and has come to the conclusion that the original home of the *whole human race* must be sought for in regions near the North Pole. My object

1. See S. B. E. Series, Vol. XXXII, p. xi.

is not so comprehensive. I intend to confine myself only to the Vedic literature and show that if we read some of the passages in the Vedas, which have hitherto been considered incomprehensible, in the light of the new scientific discoveries, we are forced to the conclusion that the home of the ancestors of the Vedic people was somewhere near the North Pole before the last Glacial epoch. The task is not an easy one, considering the fact that the Vedic passages, on which I rely, had to be, and have been, hitherto either ignored or explained away somehow, or misinterpreted one way or another by Native and European scholars alike. But I hope to show that these interpretations, though they have been provisionally accepted, are not satisfactory, and that new discoveries in archæology and geology provide us with a better key for the interpretation of these passages. Thus if some of the conclusions of the mythologist and the philologist are overthrown by these discoveries, they have rendered a still greater service by furnishing us with a better key for the interpretation of the most ancient Aryan legends, and the results obtained by using the new key cannot, in their turn, fail to throw further light on the primitive history of the Aryan race, and thus supplement or modify the conclusions now arrived at by the archæologist and the geologist.

But before proceeding to discuss the Vedic texts which point out to a Polar home, it is necessary to briefly state the results of recent discoveries in archæology, geology and palæontology. My summary must necessarily be very short, for I propose to note down only such facts as will establish the probability of my theory from the geological and palæontological point of view ; and for this purpose I have freely drawn upon the works of such well-known writers as Lyell, Geikie, Evans, Lubbock, Croll, Taylor and others. I have also utilised the excellent popular summary of the latest results of these researches in Samuel Laing's *Human Origins* and other works. The belief, that man is post-glacial and that the Polar regions were never suited for human habitation, still lingers in some quarters, and to those who still hold this view any theory regarding the Polar home of the Aryan race may naturally seem to be *a priori* impossible. It is better, therefore, to begin with a short statement of the latest scientific conclusions on these points.

Human races of earlier times have left ample evidence of their existence on the surface of this globe; but like the records of the historic period this evidence does not consist of stately tombs and pyramids, or inscriptions and documents. It is of a humbler kind, and consists of hundreds and thousands of rude or polished instruments of stone and metal recently dug out from old camps, fortifications, burial grounds (tumuli), temples, lake-dwellings, &c. of early times spread over the whole of Europe; and in the hands of the archæologist these have been found to give the same results as the hieroglyphics in the hands of the Egyptologist. These early implements of stone and metals were not previously unknown, but they had not attracted the notice of scientific experts till recently; and the peasants in Asia and Europe, when they found them in their fields, could hardly make any better use of them than that of worshipping the implements so found as thunderbolts or fairy arrows shot down from the sky. But now after a careful study of these remains, archæologists have come to the conclusion that these implements, whose human origin is now undoubtedly established, can be classified into those of Stone (including horn, wood or bone), those of Bronze, and those of Iron, representing three different stages of civilization in the progress of man in prehistoric times. Thus the implements of stone, wood, or bone, such as chisels, scrapers, arrow-heads, hatchets, daggers, etc. were used when the use of metal was yet unknown, and they were gradually supplanted first by the implements of bronze and then of iron, when the ancient man discovered the use of these metals. It is not to be supposed, however, that these three different periods of early human civilization were divided by any hard and fast line of division. They represent only a rough classification, the passage from one period into another being slow and gradual. Thus the implements of stone must have continued to be used for a long time after the use of bronze became known to the ancient man, and the same thing must have occurred as he passed from the Bronze to the Iron age. The age of bronze, which is a compound of copper and tin in a definite proportion, requires an antecedent age of copper; but sufficient evidence is not yet found to prove the separate existence of copper and tin ages, and hence it is considered probable that the art of making bronze was not invented in Europe, but was introduced there from other countries either by commerce or by the Indo-European race going there from outside.[1] Another fact which requires to be noted in connection with these ages is that the Stone or the Bronze age in one country was not necessarily synchronous with the same age in another country. Thus we find a high state of civilization in Egypt at about 6000 B. C., when the inhabitants of Europe were in the early stages of the Stone age. Similarly Greece had advanced to the Iron age, while Italy was still in the Bronze period, and the West of Europe in the age of Stone. This shows that the progress of civilization was slow in some and rapid in other places, the rate of progress varying according to the local circumstances of each place. Broadly speaking, however, the three periods of Stone, Bronze and Iron may be taken to represent the three stages of civilization anterior to the historic period.

Of these three different ages the oldest or the Stone age is further divided into the Palæolithic and the Neolithic period, or the old and the new Stone age. The distinction is

1. Lubbock's Prehistoric Times, 1890 Ed., pp. 4 and 64.

based upon the fact that the stone implements of the Palæolithic age are found to be very rudely fashioned, being merely chipped into shape and never ground or polished as is the case with the implements of the new Stone age. Another characteristic of the Palæolithic period is that the implements of the period are found in places which plainly show a much greater antiquity than can be assigned to the remains of the Neolithic age, the relics of the two ages being hardly, if ever, found together. The third distinction between the Palæolithic and the Neolithic age is that the remains of the Palæolithic man are found associated with those of many great mammals, such as the cave bear, the mammoth and woolly-haired rhinoceros, that became either locally or wholly extinct before the appearance of the Neolithic man on the stage. In short, there is a kind of hiatus or break between the Palæolithic and Neolithic man requiring a separate classification and treatment for each. It may also be noted that the climatic conditions and the distribution of land and water in the Palæolithic period were different from those in the Neolithic period; while from the beginning of the Neolithic period the modern conditions, both geographical and climatic, have prevailed almost unaltered up to the present time.

To understand the relation of these three ages with the geological periods into which the history of the earth is divided we must briefly consider the geological classification. The geologist takes up the history of the earth at the point where the archæologist leaves it, and carries it further back into remote antiquity. His classification is based upon an examination of the whole system of stratified rocks, and not on mere relics found in the surface strata. These stratified rocks have been divided into five principal classes according to the character of the fossils found in them, and they represent five different periods in the history of our planet. These geological eras, like the three ages of Stone,

Bronze and Iron, cannot be separated very sharply from each other. But taken as a whole we can clearly distinguish one era from another by its characteristic fossil remains. Each of these geological ages or eras is again subdivided into a number of different periods. The order of these Eras and Periods, beginning with the newest, is as follows :—

Eras.	*Periods.*
Post-Tertiary or Quarternary ...	Recent (Post-Glacial). Pleistocene (Glacial).
Tertiary or Cainozoic	Pliocene. Miocene. Oligocene. Eocene.
Secondary or Mesozoic	Cretaceon. Jurassic. T riassic.
Primary or Palæozoic	Permian. Carboniferous. Devonian, and Old Red Sandstone. Silurian. Cambrian.
Archæan or Eozoic	Fundamental Gneiss.

Thus the oldest of the stratified rocks at present known is the Archæan or Eozoic. Next in chronological order come the Primary or the Palæozoic, the Secondary or the Mesozoic, the Tertiary or Cainozoic, and last the Quarternary. The Quarternary era, with which alone we are here concerned, is subdivided into the Pleistocene or the Glacial, and the Recent or the Post-Glacial period ; the close of the first and the beginning of the second being marked by the last Glacial epoch, or the Ice Age, during which the greater portion of northern Europe and America was covered with an ice-cap several thousand feet in thickness. The Iron age, the Bronze age and the Neolithic age come under the Recent or the

Post-Glacial period, while the Palæolithic age is supposed to fall in the Pleistocene period, though some of the palæolithic remains are post-glacial, showing that the palæolithic man must have survived the Ice Age for some time. Latest discoveries and researches enable us to carry the antiquity of man still further by establishing the fact that man existed even in the Tertiary era. But apart from it, there is, now, at any rate, overwhelming evidence to conclusively prove the wide-spread existence of man throughout the Quarternary era, even before the last Glacial period.

Various estimates have been made regarding the time of the commencement of the Neolithic age, but the oldest date assigned does not exceed 5000 B. C., a time when flourishing empires existed in Egypt and Chaldea. These estimates are based on the amount of silt which has been found accumulated in some of the smaller lakes in Switzerland since the lake-dwellers of the Neolithic period built their piled villages therein. The peat-mosses of Denmark afford means for another estimate of the early Neolithic period in that country. These mosses are formed in the hollows of the glacial drift into which trees have fallen and become gradually converted into peat in course of time. There are three successive periods of vegetation in these peat-beds, the upper one of beech, the middle one of oak, and the lowest of all, one of fir. These changes in the vegetation are attributed to slow changes in the climate and it is ascertained from implements and remains found in these beds, that the Stone age corresponds mainly with that of Fir and partly with that of Oak, while the Bronze age agrees mainly with the period of Oak, and the Iron with that of Beech. It has been calculated that about 16,000 years will be required for the formation of these peat-mosses, and according to this estimate we shall have to place the commencement of the Neolithic age in Denmark, at the lowest, not later than 10,000 years ago.

But these estimates are not better than mere approximations, and generally speaking we may take the Neolithic age in Europe as commencing not later than 5000 B. C.

But when we pass from the Neolithic to the Palæolithic period the difficulty of ascertaining the commencement of the latter becomes still greater. In fact we have here to ascertain the time when the Post-Glacial period commenced. The Palæolithic man must have occupied parts of Western Europe shortly after the disappearance of the Ice Age and Prof. Geikie considers that there are reasons for supposing that he was inter-glacial. The Glacial period was characterised by geographical and climatic changes on an extensive scale. These changes and the theories regarding the cause or the causes of the Ice Age will be briefly stated in the next chapter. We are here concerned with the date of the commencement of the Post-Glacial period, and there are two different views entertained by geologists on the subject. European geologists think that as the beginning of the Post-Glacial period was marked with great movements of elevation and depression of land, and as these movements take place very slowly, the commencement of the Post-Glacial period cannot be placed earlier than 50 or 60 thousand years ago. Many American geologists, on the other hand, are of opinion that the close of the last Glacial period must have taken place at a much more recent date. They draw this inference from the various estimates of time required for the erosion of valleys and accumulation of alluvial deposits since the last Glacial period. Thus according to Gilbert, the post-glacial gore of Niagara at the present rate of erosion must have been excavated within 7000 years.[1] Other American geologists from similar obervations at various other places have arrived at the conclusion that not more than about 8000 years have

1. See Geikie's Fragments of Earth Lore, p. 286; also Dr. Bonney's Story of our Planet, p. 560.

elapsed since the close of the last Glacial period. This estimate agrees very well with the approximate date of the Neolithic period ascertained from the amount of silt in some of the lakes in Switzerland. But it differs materially from the estimate of the European geologists. It is difficult to decide, in the present state of our knowledge, which of these estimates is correct. Probably the Glacial and the Post-Glacial period may not, owing to local causes, have commenced or ended at one and the same time in different places, just as the ages of Stone and Bronze were not synchronous in different countries. Prof. Geikie does not accept the American estimate on the ground that it is inconsistent with the high antiquity of the Egyptian civilisation, as ascertained by recent researches. But if no traces of glaciation are yet found in Africa this objection loses its force, while the arguments by which the American view is supported remain uncontradicted.

There are other reasons which go to support the same view. All the evidence regarding the existence of the Glacial period comes from the North of Europe and America; but no traces of glaciation have been yet discovered in the Northern Asia or North Alaska. It is not to be supposed, however, that the northern part of Asia did not enjoy a genial climate in early times. As observed by Prof. Geikie "everywhere throughout this vast region alluvial deposits are found packed up with the remains of mammoth, woolly rhinoceros, bison, and horse;" and "the fossils are usually so well preserved that on one occasion the actual carcass of a mammoth was exposed in so fresh a state that dogs ate the flesh thereof."[1] These and other equally indisputable facts clearly indicate the existence in Siberia of a mild and genial climate at a time, which, from the freshness of the fossil remains, cannot be supposed to be removed from the present by several

1. See Geikie's Great Ice Age, 1st Ed., p. 495; Dr. Croll's Climate and Cosmology, p. 179.

thousands of years. Again in North Africa and Syria we find in dry regions wide-spread fluviatile accumulations which are believed to be indications of rainy seasons, contemporaneous with the Glacial period of Europe.[1] If this contemporaneity can be established, the high estimate of time for the commencement of the Post-Glacial period in Europe will have to be given up, or at any rate much curtailed.

As regards the races which inhabited Europe in these early ages, the evidence furnished by human remains or skulls shows that they were the direct ancestors of the races now living in the different parts of Europe. The current classification of the human races into Aryan, Semetic, Mongolian, &c. is based upon the linguistic principle ; but it is evident that in dealing with ancient races the archæologist and the geologist cannot adopt this principle of division, inasmuch as their evidence consists of relics from which no inference can be drawn as to the language used by the ancient man. The shape and the size of the skull have, therefore, been taken as the chief distinguishing marks to classify the different races of prehistoric times. Thus if the extreme breadth of a skull is three-fourths, or 75 per cent., of its length or lower, it is classed as long-headed or dolicho-cephalic, while if the breadth is higher than 83 per cent. of the length, the skull is said to be brachy-cephalic or broad-headed ; the intermediate class being styled ortho-cephalic, or sub-dolicho-cephalic, or sub-brachy-cephalic according as it approaches one or the other of these types. Now from the examination of the different skulls found in the Neolithic beds it has been ascertained that Europe in those early days was inhabited by four different races, and that the existing European types are directly descended from them. Of these four races two were dolicho-cephalic, one tall and one short ; and two brachy-cephalic similarly divided. But the Aryan languages are,

---

1 See Geikie's Fragments of Earth Lore, p. 252.

at present, spoken in Europe by races exhibiting the characteristics of all these types. It is, however, evident that one alone of these four ancient races can be the real representative of the Aryan race, though there is a strong difference of opinion as to which of them represented the primitive Aryans. German writers, like Posche and Penka, claim that the tall dolicho-cephalic race, the ancestors of the present Germans, were the true representatives of the primitive Aryans; while French writers, like Chavee and M. de Mortillet, maintain that the primitive Aryans were brachy-cephalic and the true Aryan type is represented by the Gauls. Canon Taylor in his *Origin of the Aryans* sums up the controversy by observing that when two races come in contact, the probability is that the speech of the most cultured will prevail, and therefore "it is" he says "an easier hypothesis to suppose that the dolicho-cephalic savages of the Baltic coast acquired Aryan speech from their brachy-cephalic neighbours, the Lithuanians, than to suppose, with Penka, that they succeeded in some remote age in Aryanising the Hindus, the Romans and the Greeks."[1]

Another method of determining which of these four races represented the primitive Aryans in Europe is to compare the grades of civilisation attained by the undivided Aryans, as ascertained from linguistic palæontology, with those attained by the Neolithic races as disclosed by the remains found in their dwellings. As for the Palæolithic man his social condition appears to have been far below that of the undivided Aryans; and Dr. Schrader considers it as indubitably either non-Indo-European or pre-Indo-European in character. The Palæolithic man used stone hatchets and bone needles, and had attained some proficiency in the art of sculpture and drawing, as exhibited by outlines of various animals carved on bones &c.; but he was clearly unacquaint-

1. See Taylor's Origin of the Aryans, p. 243.

ed with the potter's art and the use of metals. It is only in the Neolithic period that we meet with pottery in the piled villages of lake-dwellers in Switzerland. But even the oldest lake-dwellers seem to have been unacquainted with the use of metals and waggons, both of which were familiar to the undivided Aryans. No trace of woollen cloth is again found in these lake-dwellings, even when sheep had become numerous in the Bronze age. But with these exceptions the culture of the Swiss lake-dwellings is considered by Dr. Schrader to be practically of the same character as the culture common to the European members of the Indo-Germanic family, and he, therefore, ventures to suggest, though cautiously, that "from this point of view there is nothing to prevent our assuming that the most ancient inhabitants of Switzerland were a branch of the European division" of the Aryan race.[1]

But though recent discoveries have brought to light these facts about the human races inhabiting Europe in prehistoric times, and though we may, in accordance with them, assume that one of the four early Neolithic races represented the primitive Aryans in Europe, the question whether the latter were autochthonous, or went there from some other place and then succeeded in Aryanising the European races by their superior culture and civilisation, cannot be regarded as settled by these discoveries. The date assigned to the Neolithic period as represented by Swiss lake-dwellers is not later than 5000 B. C., a time when Asiatic Aryans were probably settled on the Jaxartes; and it is admitted that the primitive Aryans in Europe could not have been the descendants of the Palæolithic man. It follows, therefore, that if we discover them in Europe in the early Neolithic times they must have gone there from some other part of the

1. Dr. Schrader's Prehistoric Antiquities of the Aryan Peoples, translated by Jevons, Part IV. Ch. XI. p. 368.

globe. The only other alternative is to assume that one of the four Neolithic races in Europe developed a civilisation quite independently of their neighbours, an assumption, which is improbable on its face. Although, therefore, we may, in the light of recent scientific discoveries, give up the theory of successive migrations into Europe from a common home of the Aryan race in Central Asia in early times, yet the question of the primeval home of the Aryan race, a question with which we are mainly concerned in this book, still remains unsolved. When and where the primitive Aryan tongue was developed is again another difficult question which is not satisfactorily answered. Canon Taylor, after comparing the Aryan and Ural-Altaic languages, hazards a conjecture that at the close of the reindeer, or the last period of the Palæolithic age, a Finnic people appeared in Western Europe, whose speech remaining stationary is represented by the agglutinative Basque, and that much later, at the beginning of the pastoral age, when the ox had been tamed, a taller and more powerful Finno-Ugric people developed in Central Europe the inflexive Aryan speech.[1] But this is merely a conjecture, and it does not answer the question how the Indo-Iranians with their civilisation are found settled in Asia at a time when Europe was in the Neolithic age. The Finnic language again discloses a number of culture words borrowed from the Aryans, and it is unlikely that the language of the latter could have got its inflection from the Finnic language. A mere similarity of inflectional structure is no evidence whatsoever for deciding who borrowed from whom, and it is surprising that the above suggestion should come from scholars, who have assailed the theory of successive Aryan migrations from a common Asiatic home, a theory which, amongst others, was based on linguistic grounds. Why did the Finns twice migrate from their home is also

1. The Origin of the Aryans, p. 296.

left unexplained. For reasons like these it seems to me more probable that the Finns might have borrowed the culture words from the Aryans when they came in contact with them, and that the Aryans were autochthonous neither in Europe nor in Central Asia, but had their original home somewhere near the North Pole in the Palæolithic times, and that they migrated from this place southwards in Asia and Europe, not by any 'irresistible impulse,' but by unwelcome changes in the climatic conditions of their original home. The Avesta preserves traditions which fully support this view. But these have been treated as valueless by scholars, who worked up their theories at a time when man was regarded as post-glacial, and the Avestic traditions were, it was believed, not supported by any Vedic authority. But with the time-telescope of a wider range supplied to us by recent scientific discoveries it has become possible to demonstrate that the Avestic traditions represent a real historical fact and that they are fully supported by the testimony of the Vedas. The North Pole is already considered by several eminent scientific men as the most likely place where plant and animal life first originated; and I believe it can be satisfactorily shown that there is enough positive evidence in the most ancient books of the Aryan race, the Vedas and the Avesta, to prove that the oldest home of the Aryan people was somewhere in regions round about the North Pole. I shall take up this evidence after examining the climatic conditions of the Pleistocene or the Glacial period and the astronomical characteristics of the Arctic regions in the next two chapters.

CHAPTER II.

THE GLACIAL PERIOD.

Geological climate —Uniform and gentle in early ages —Due to different distribution of land and water —Climatic changes in the Quarternary era —The Glacial epoch —Its existence undoubtedly proved —Extent of glaciation —At least two Glacial periods —Accompanied by elevation and depression of land —Mild and genial inter-glacial climate even in the Arctic regions —Various theories regarding the cause of the Ice Age stated —Lyell's theory of geographical changes —Showing long duration of the Glacial period —Croll's theory —Effect of the precession of the equinoxes on the duration and intensity of seasons —The cycle of 21,000 years —The effect enhanced by the eccentricity of the earth's orbit —Maximum difference of 33 days between the duration of summer and winter —Sir Robert Ball's calculations regarding the average heat received by each hemisphere in summer and winter —Short and warm summers and long and cold winters, giving rise to a Glacial epoch —Dr. Croll's extraordinary estimate regarding the duration of the Glacial epoch —Based on the maximum value of the eccentricity of the earth's orbit —Questioned by astronomers and geologists —Sir Robert Ball's and Newcomb's view —Croll's estimates inconsistent with geological evidence —Opinions of Prof. Geikie and Mr. Hudleston —Long duration of the Glacial period —Summary of results.

THE climate of our globe at the present day is characterised by a succession of seasons, spring, summer, autumn, and winter, caused by the inclination of the earth's axis to the plane of the ecliptic. When the North Pole of the earth is turned *away* from the sun in its annual course round that luminary, we have winter in the northern and summer in the southern hemisphere, and *vice versa* when the North Pole is turned *towards* the sun. The cause of the rotation of seasons in the different hemispheres is thus very simple, and from the permanence of this cause one may be led to think that in the distant geological ages the climate of our planet must have been charácterised by similar rotations of hot and cold seasons. But such a supposition is directly contradicted by geological evidence. The inclination of the earth's axis to the plane of the ecliptic, or what is technically called the obliquity of the ecliptic, is not the sole cause of climatic variations on the surface of the globe. High altitude and the existence of oceanic and aerial currents, carrying and diffusing the heat of the equatorial region to the other parts of the globe, have been found to produce different climates in countries having the same latitude. The Gulf Stream is a notable instance of such oceanic currents, and had it not been for this stream the climate in the North-West of Europe would have been quite different from what it is at present. Again if the masses of land and water be differently distributed from what they are at present, there is every reason to suppose that different climatic conditions will prevail on the surface of the globe from those which we now experience, as such a distribution would materially alter the course of oceanic and aerial currents going from the equator to the Poles. Therefore, in the early geological ages, when the Alps were low and the Himalayas not yet upheaved, and when Asia and Africa were represented only by a group of islands, we need not be surprised if, from geological evidence of fossil fauna and flora, we find that an equable and uniform climate prevailed over the whole surface of the globe as the result of these geographical conditions. In Mesozoic and Cainozoic times this state of things appears to have gradually changed. But though the climate in the Secondary and the Tertiary era was not probably as remarkably uniform as in the Primary, yet there is clear geological evidence to show that until the close of the Pliocene period in the Tertiary era the climate was not yet differentiated into zones and there were then no hot and cold extremes as at present. The close of the Pliocene and the whole of the Pleistocene period was marked by violent changes of climate bringing on what is called the Glacial and Inter-Glacial epochs. But it is now conclusively established that before the advent of this period a luxuriant forest vegetation, which can only grow and exist at present in the tropical or temperate climate, flourished in the high latitude of Spitzbergen, where the sun goes below the horizon from November till March, thus showing that a warm climate prevailed in the Arctic regions in those days.

It was in the Quarternary or the Pleistocene period that the mild climate of these regions underwent sudden alterations, producing what is called the Glacial period. The limits of this Glacial period may not so exactly coincide with those of the Pleistocene as to enable us to say that they were mathematically coextensive, but still in a rough sense we may take these two periods as coinciding with each other. It is impossible within the limits of a short chapter to give even a summary of the evidence proving the existence of one or more Glacial epochs in the Pleistocene period. We may, however, briefly indicate its nature and see what the geologists and the physicists have to say as regards the causes that brought about such extensive changes of climate in the Quarternary era. The existence of the Glacial period is no longer a matter of doubt, though scientific men are not agreed as to the causes which produced it. Ice-sheets have not totally disappeared from the surface of the earth, and we can still watch the action of ice as glaciers in the valleys of the Alps or in the lands near the Pole, like Greenland which is still covered with a sheet of ice so thick as to make it unfit for the growth of plants or the habitation of animals. Studying the effects of glacial action in these places geologists have discovered abundant traces of similar action of ice in former times over the whole of Northern Europe and America. Rounded and scratched stones, till or boulder clay, and the rounded appearance of rocks and mountains clearly point out that at one period in the history of our globe northern parts of Europe and America must have been covered for a long time with a sheet of ice several hundreds of feet in thickness. The ice which thus invaded the northern portion of America and Europe did not all radiate from the Pole. The evidence of the direction of the striæ, or scratches engraved on rocks by ice, undoubtedly proves that the ice-caps spread out from all elevated places or mountains in different directions. These ice-sheets of enormous thickness covered the whole of Scandinavia, filled up the North Sea, invaded Britain down to the Thames valley, greater portion of Germany, and Russia as far south as Moscow and almost as far east as the Urals. It is calculated that at least a million of square miles in Europe and more in North America were covered by the *debris* of rocks ground down by these glaciers and ice-caps, and it is from this *debris* that geologists now infer the existence of an Ice Age in early times. The examination of this *debris* shows that there are at least two series of boulder clay indicating two periods of glaciation. The *debris* of the second period has disturbed the first layer in many places, but enough remains to show that there were two distinct beds of boulder clay and drifts, belonging to two different periods. Prof. Geikie mentions four such Glacial periods, with corresponding Inter-Glacial periods, as having occurred in succession in Europe during the Pleistocene period. But though this opinion is not accepted by other geologists, yet the existence of two Glacial epochs, with an intervening Inter-Glacial period, is now considered as conclusively established.

A succession of cold and warm climates must have characterised these Glacial and Inter-Glacial periods, which were also accompanied by extensive movements of depression and elevation of land, the depression taking place after the land was weighed down with the enormous mass of ice. Thus a period of glaciation was marked by elevation, extreme cold and the invasion of the ice-caps over regions of the present Temperate zone; while an inter-glacial period was accompanied by depression of land and milder and congenial climate which made even the Arctic regions habitable. The remains of the Palæolithic man have been found often imbedded between the two boulder clays of two different Glacial periods, a fact which conclusively establishes the existence of man in the Inter-Glacial period in the Quarternary era. Prof. Geikie speaking of the changes of climate in the Glacial and Inter-Glacial period remarks that "during the Inter-Glacial period the climate was characterised by clement winters and cool summers so that the tropical plants and animals, like elephants, rhinoceroses and hippopotamuses, ranged over the whole of the Arctic region, and in spite of numerous fierce carnivora, the Palæolithic man had no unpleasant habitation there."[1] It will thus be seen that in point of climate the Pleistocene period, or the early Quarternary era, was intermediate between the early geological ages when uniform genial climate prevailed over the globe, and the modern period when it is differentiated into zones. It was, so to speak, a transitional period marked by violent changes in the climate, that was mild and genial in the Inter-Glacial, and severe and inclement during the Glacial period. It was at the beginning of the Post-Glacial or the Recent period that modern climatic conditions were established. Prof. Geikie is, however, of opinion that even the beginning of the Post-Glacial period was marked, at least in North-Western Europe, by two alternations of genial and rainy-cold climate before the present climatic conditions became established.[2]

But though the fact of the Ice Age and the existence of a milder climate within the Arctic regions in the Inter-Glacial

1. Fragments of Earth Lore, p. 266. 2. Prehistoric Europe, p. 530.

time is indubitably proved, yet scientific men have not been as yet able to trace satisfactorily the causes of this great catastrophe. Such immense mass of ice as covered the whole of Northern Europe and America during this period could not, like anything else, come out of nothing. There must be heat enough in certain parts of the globe to create by evaporation sufficient vapour, and aerial currents are required to transfer it to the colder regions of the globe, there to be precipitated in the form of ice. Any theory regarding the cause of the Ice Age which fails to take this fact into account is not only inadequate but worthless. A succession of Glacial periods, or, at any rate, the occurrence of two Glacial periods, must again be accounted for by the theory that may be proposed to explain these changes; and if we test the different theories advanced in this way, many of them will be at once found to be untenable. It was, for instance, once urged that the Gulf Stream, which, at present, imparts warmth to the countries in the North-West of Europe might have been turned away from its course in the Pleistocene period by the submergence of the Isthmus of Panama, thus converting the countries on the North-Western coast of Europe into lands covered by ice. There is, however, no geological evidence to show that the Isthmus of Panama was submerged in the Pleistocene period, and we must, therefore, give up this hypothesis. Another theory started to account for the catastrophe was that the earth must have passed through cold and hot regions of space thus giving rise to Glacial and Inter-Glacial periods respectively. But this too is unsupported by any evidence. A third suggestion advanced was that the supply of solar heat on earth must have varied in such a way as to give rise to warm and cold climates; but this was shown to be a mere conjecture. A change in the position of the earth's axis might indeed cause such sudden changes in the climate; but a change in the axis means a change in the equator, and as the earth owing to its diurnal rotation causes the equatorial regions to bulge out, a change in the axis would give rise to a second equatorial protuberance, which, however, is not observable, and the theory cannot, therefore, be accepted. A gradual cooling of the earth would make the Polar regions habitable before the other parts of the globe; but a succession of Glacial epochs cannot be accounted for on this theory.

Thus out of the various theories advanced to account for the vicissitudes of climate in the Pleistocene period only two have now remained in the field, the first that of Lyell which explains the changes by assuming different distribution of land and water combined with sudden elevation and submergence of large landed areas, and the second that of Croll which traces the glaciation to the precession of the equinoxes combined with the high value of the eccentricity of the earth's orbit. Lyell's theory has been worked out by Wallace who shows that such geographical changes are by themselves sufficient to produce heat and cold required to bring on the Glacial and Inter-Glacial periods. We have seen that in earlier geological ages a pleasant and equable climate prevailed over the whole surface of the globe owing mainly to different distribution of land and water, and the theory advanced by Lyell to account for the Glacial epoch is practically the same. Great elevation and depression of extensive areas can be effected only in thousands of years, and those who support Lyell's theory are of opinion that the duration of the Glacial epoch must be taken to be about 200,000 years in order to account for all the geographical and geological changes, which, according to them, were the principal causes of the Glacial period. But there are other geologists, of the same school, who hold that the Glacial period may not have lasted longer than about 20 to 25 thousand years. The difference between the two estimates is enormous; but in the present state of geological evidence it is difficult to decide in favour of any one of these views. All that we can safely say is that the duration of the Pleistocene period, which included at least two Glacial and one Inter-Glacial epoch, must have been very much longer than the period of time which has elapsed since the commencement of the Post-Glacial period.

According to Sir Robert Ball the whole difficulty of finding out the causes of the Glacial period vanishes when the solution of the problem is sought for in astronomy rather than in geography. Changes which seem to be so gigantic on the globe are, it is said, but daily wrought by cosmical forces with which we are familiar in astronomy, and one of the chief merits of Croll's theory is supposed to consist in the fact that it satisfactorily accounts for a succession of Glacial and Inter-Glacial epochs during the Pleistocene period. Dr. Croll in his *Climate and Time* and *Climate and Cosmology* has tried to explain and establish his theory by elaborate calculations, showing that the changes in the values of the variable elements in the motion of the earth round the sun can adequately account for the climatic changes in the Pleistocene period. We shall first briefly state Dr. Croll's theory, and then give the opinions of experts as regards its probability.

Let $PQ'AQ$ represent the orbit of the earth round the sun. This orbit is an ellipse, and the sun, instead of being in the centre C, is in one of the focii S or s. Let the sun be at S. Then the distance of the sun from the earth when the latter is at P would be the shortest, while when the earth is at A it will be the longest. These points P and A are respectively called perihelion and aphelion. The seasons are caused, as stated above, by the axis of the earth being inclined to the plane of its orbit. Thus when the earth is at P and the axis turned away from the sun, it will produce winter in the northern hemisphere; while when the earth is at *A*, the axis, retaining its direction, will be now turned towards the sun, and there will be summer in the northern hemisphere. If the axis of the earth had no motion of its own, the seasons will always occur at the same points in the orbit of the earth, as, for instance, the winter in the northern hemisphere at *P* and the summer at *A*. But this axis describes a small circle round the pole of the ecliptic in a cycle of 25,868 years, giving rise to what is called the precession of the equinoxes,

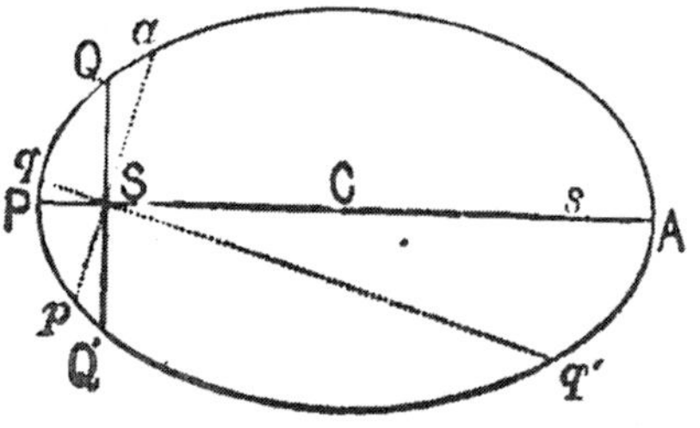

and consequently the inclination of the earth's axis to the plane of its orbit is not always the same at any given point in its orbit during this period. This causes the seasons to occur at different points in the earth's orbit during this great cycle. Thus if the winter in the northern hemisphere occurred when the earth was at *P* at one time, some time after it will occur at *p* and the succeeding points in the orbit until the end of the cycle, when it will again occur at *P*. The same will be the case in regard to summer at the point *A* and equinoxes at *Q* and *Q'*. In the diagram the dotted lines *qq'* and *pa* represent the new positions which the line *QQ'* and *PA* will assume if they revolve in the way stated above. It must also be noted that though the winter in the northern hemisphere may occur when the earth is at *p* instead of at *P*, owing to the aforesaid motion of its axis, yet the orbit of the earth and the points of perihelion and aphelion are relatively fixed and unchangeable. Therefore, if the winter in the northern hemisphere occurs at *p*, the earth's distance from the sun at the point will be greater than when the earth was at *P*. Similarly, in the course of the cycle above mentioned, the winter in the northern hemisphere will once occur at *A*, and the distance of the earth from the sun will then be the longest. Now there is a vast difference between a winter occurring when the earth is at *P* and a winter occurring when it is at *A*. In the first case, the point *P* being nearest to the sun, the severity of the winter will be greatly modified by the nearness of the sun. But at *A* the sun is farthest removed from the earth, and the winter, when the earth is at *A*, will be naturally very severe ; and during the cycle the winter must once occur at *A*. The length of the cycle is 25,868 years, and ordinarily speaking half of this period must elapse before the occurrence of winter is transferred from the earth's position at *P* to its position at *A*. But it is found that the points *P* and *A* have a small motion of their own in the direction opposite to that in which the line of equinoxes *QQ'* or the winter point *p* moves along the orbit. The above cycle of 25,868 years is, therefore, reduced to 20,984, or, in round number, 21,000 years. Thus if the winter in one hemisphere occurs when the earth is at *P*, the point nearest to the sun in the orbit, it will occur in the same hemisphere at *A* after a lapse of 10,500 years. It may be here mentioned that in about 1,250 A. D., the winter in the northern hemisphere occurred when the earth in its orbit was at *P*, and that in about 11,750 A. D. the earth will be again at *A*, that is, at its longest distance from the sun at the winter time, giving rise to a severe winter. Calculating backwards it may be seen that the last severe winter at *A* must have occurred in the year 9,250 B. C.[1] It need not be mentioned that the winter in one hemisphere corresponds with the summer in the other, and that what is said about winter in the northern hemisphere applies *mutatis mutandis* to seasonal changes in the southern hemisphere.

1. See Herschel's Outlines of Astronomy, Ed. 1883, Arts. 368, 369.

There is another consideration which we must take into account in estimating the severity of winter or the mildness of summer in any hemisphere. If the summer be defined to be the period of time required by the earth to travel from one equinoctial point Q' to another equinoctial point Q, this interval cannot always be constant for we have seen that the winter and summer points (P and A), and with them the equinoctial points (Q and Q') are not stationary, but revolve along the orbit once in 21,000 years. Had the orbit been a circle, the lines qq' and pa will have always divided it in equal parts. But the orbit being an ellipse these two sections are unequal. For instance suppose that the winter occurs when the earth is at P, then the duration of the summer will be represented by $Q'AQ$, but when the winter occurs at A the summer time will be represented by QPQ', a segment of the ellipse necessarily smaller than $Q'AQ$. This inequality is due to the ellipticity of the orbit, and the more elongated or elliptic the orbit is, the greater will be the difference between the durations of summer and winter in a hemisphere. Now the ellipticity of the orbit is measured by the difference between the mean and the greatest distance of the earth from the sun, and is called in astronomy the eccentricity of the earth's orbit. This eccentricity of the earth's orbit is not a constant quantity, but varies, though slowly, in course of time, making the orbit more and more elliptical, until it reaches a maximum value, when it again begins to reduce until the original value is reached. The duration of summer and winter in a hemisphere, therefore, varies as the value of the eccentricity of the earth's orbit at that time; and it has been stated above that the difference between the duration of summer and winter also depends on the position of the equinoctial line, or of the points in the earth's orbit at which the winter and the summer in a hemisphere occur. As the joint result of these two variations, the difference between the durations of summer and winter would be the longest, when the eccentricity of the earth is at its maximum and according as the winter and summer occur at the points of perihelion or aphelion. It has been found that this difference is equal to 33 days at the highest, and that at the present day it is about 7½ days. Thus if the winter in the northern hemisphere occurs when the earth is at *P* in its orbit and the eccentricity is at its maximum, the winter will be shorter by 33 days than the summer of the time. But this position will be altered after 10,500 years when the winter, occurring at *A*, will, in its turn, be longer than the corresponding summer by the same length of time, *viz.*, 33 days.

Now since the earth describes equal areas in equal times in its orbit, Herschel supposed that in spite of the difference between the duration of summer and winter noticed above, the whole earth received equal amount of heat while passing from one equinox to another, the "inequality in the intensities of solar radiation in the two intervals being precisely compensated by the opposite inequality in the duration of the intervals themselves." Accepting this statement Dr. Croll understated his case to a certain extent. But Sir Robert Ball, formerly the Astronomer Royal of Ireland, in his recent work *On the Cause of an Ice Age* has demonstrated, by mathematical calculation, that the above supposition is erroneous, and that the total amount of heat received from the sun by each hemisphere in summer and winter varies as the obliquity of the earth or the inclination of its axis to the ecliptic, but is practically independent of the eccentricity of the earth's orbit. Taking the total sun-heat received in a year by each hemisphere to be 365 units, or on an average one unit a day, and taking the obliquity to be 23° 27′, Sir Robert Ball has calculated that each hemisphere would receive 229 of these heat-units during summer and only 136 during winter, whatever the eccentricity of the earth may be. But though these figures are not affected by the eccentricity of the orbit, yet we have seen that the duration of the summer or winter does vary as the eccentricity. Supposing, therefore, that we have the longest winter in the northern hemisphere, we shall have to distribute 229 heat units over 166 days of a short summer, and 136 heat units over 199 days of a long winter of the same period. In other words, the difference between the daily average heat in summer and winter will, in such a case, be the greatest, producing shorter but warmer summers and longer and colder winters ; and ice and snow accumulated in the long winter will not be melted or removed by the heat of the sun in the short summer, giving rise thereby to what is known as the Glacial period in the northern hemisphere. From what has been stated above, it may be seen that the southern hemisphere during this period will have long and cool summers and short and warm winters, a condition precisely reverse to that in the northern hemisphere. In short the Glacial and Inter-Glacial periods in the two hemispheres will alternate with each other every 10,500 years, if the eccentricity of the earth be sufficiently great to make a perceptibly large difference between the winters and the summers in each hemisphere.

If Dr. Croll had gone only so far, his position would have been unassailable, for the cause, enumerated above, is sufficiently potent to produce the climatic changes attributed to it. At any rate, if this was not the sole cause of a succession of Glacial and Inter-Glacial periods, there could be no doubt that it must have been an important contributory cause in bringing about these changes. But taking the value of the eccentricity of the earth's orbit from the tables of Leverrier, Dr. Croll calculated that during the last three million years there were three periods of maximum eccentricity ; the first of 170,000, the second of 260,000, and the third of 160,000 years; and that 80,000 years have elapsed since the close of the third or the last period. According to Dr. Croll the Glacial epoch in the Pleistocene period must, therefore, have begun 240,000 years ago, and ended, followed by the Post-Glacial period, about 80,000 years ago. During this long period of 160,000 years, there must have been several alternations of mild and severe climates, according as the winter in a hemisphere occurred when the earth was at perihelion or aphelion in its orbit, which happened every 10,500 years during the period. But as the cold epoch can be at its maximum only during the early part of each period, according to Dr. Croll's theory, the last epoch of maximum glaciation must be placed 200,000 years ago, or about 40,000 years after the commencement of the last period of maximum eccentricity.

The reliability of these elaborate calculations has, however, been questioned by astronomers and geologists alike. Sir Robert Ball, who supports Croll in every other respect, has himself refrained from making any astronomical calculations regarding the maximum value of the eccentricity of the earth's orbit, or the time when the last Glacial epoch should have occurred, or when the next would take place. "I cannot say," he observes, "when the last (Glacial epoch) took place, nor when the next may be expected. No one who is competent to deal with mathematical formulæ would venture on such predictions in the present state of our knowledge."[1] Prof. Newcomb of New York, another astronomer of repute, in his review of Dr. Croll's *Climate and Time*, has also pointed out how in the present state of astronomical knowledge it is impossible to place any reliance on the values of eccentricity computed for epochs, distant by millions of years, as the value of this eccentricity depends upon elements, many of which are un-

1. On the Cause of an Ice Age, p. 152.

certain, and this is especially the case when one has to deal with long geological eras. The only reply made by Dr Croll to this criticism is that his figures were correctly worked up from the values of the eccentricity according to the latest correction of Mr. Stockwell.[1] This, however, is hardly a satisfactory reply, inasmuch as Prof. Newcomb's objection refers not to the correctness of the mathematical work, but to the impossibility of correctly ascertaining the very data from which the values of the eccentricity were obtained.

It was once supposed that the duration of each of Dr. Croll's different periods admirably fitted in with the geological evidence, and fully corroborated the estimates of time supposed to be required for the extensive geographical changes which accompanied the Glacial and Inter-Glacial periods. But geologists have now begun to take a more sober view of these extravagant figures and calculations. According to Croll's calculation there were three periods of maximum eccentricity during the last three million years, and there should, therefore, be three periods of glaciation corresponding to these, each including several Glacial and Inter-Glacial epochs. But there is no geological evidence of the existence of such Glacial epochs in early geological eras, except perhaps in the Permian and Carboniferous periods of the Palæozoic or the Primary age. An attempt is made to meet this objection by replying that though the eccentricity was greatest at one period in the early geological eras, yet as the geographical distribution of land and water was then essentially different from what it was in the Quarternary era, the high value of the eccentricity did not then produce the climatic changes it did in the Pleistocene period. This reply practically concedes that the high eccentricity of the earth's orbit, combined with the occurrence of winter when the earth is at aphelion, is not by itself sufficient to bring

1. Climate and Cosmology, p. 39.

about a Glacial period; and it may, therefore, be well urged that a Glacial epoch may occur even when the eccentricity is not at its maximum. Another point in which Dr. Croll's theory conflicts with the geological evidence is the date of the close of the last Glacial epoch, as ascertained, by the American geologists, from estimates based on the erosion of valleys since the close of the last Glacial period. It is pointed out in the last chapter that these estimates do not carry the beginning of the Post-Glacial period much further than about 10,000 years ago at the best; while Dr. Croll's calculation would carry it back to 80 or 100 thousand years. This is a serious difference, and even Prof. Geikie, who does not entirely accept the American view, is obliged to admit that though Dr. Croll's theory is the only theory that accounts for the succession of Glacial epochs, and, therefore, the only correct theory, yet the formula employed by him to calculate the values of the eccentricity of the earth's orbit may be incorrect, and that we may thus account for the wide discrepancy between his inference and the conclusions based upon hard geological facts, which cannot be lightly set aside.[1] The judgment recently pronounced by Mr. Hudleston is still more severe. In his opening address, as President of the geological section of the meeting of the British Association in 1898, he is reported to have remarked, "There is probably nothing more extraordinary in the history of modern investigation than the extent to which geologists of an earlier date permitted themselves to be led away by the fascinating theories of Croll. The astronomical explanation of that 'Will-o'-the-wisp,' the cause of the great Ice Age, is at present greatly discredited, and we begin to estimate at their true value those elaborate calculations which were made to account for events, which, in all probability, never occurred. Extravagance begets extravagance, and the un-

1. Fragments of Earth Lore, p. 287.

reasonable speculations of men like Belt and Croll have caused some of our recent students to suffer from the nightmare."[1] This criticism appears to be rather severe; for though Dr. Croll's elaborate calculations may be extravagant, yet we must give him the credit for not merely suggesting, but working out, the effect of a cosmical cause which under certain circumstances is powerful enough to produce extensive changes in the climate of the globe.

But in spite of these remarks, it cannot be doubted that the duration of the Glacial period, comprising at least two Glacial and one Inter-Glacial epoch, must have been very much longer than that of the Post-Glacial period. For independently of the eccentricity of the earth's orbit, the occurrence of winter at aphelion is by itself sure to contribute to the production of the Ice Age, if other causes and circumstances, either those suggested by Lyell or others, are favourable, and 21,000 years must elapse between two successive occurrences of winter at aphelion. For two Glacial epochs with an intervening Inter-Glacial period, we must, therefore, allow a period longer than 21,000 years, even if the question of the eccentricity of the earth's orbit be kept aside; while if, with Prof. Geikie, we suppose that there were five Glacial (four in the Pleistocene and one at the close of the Pliocene period) and four Inter-Glacial epochs the duration must be extended to something like 80,000 years.

It is unnecessary to go further into these scientific and geological discussions. I have already stated before that my object is to trace from positive evidence contained in the Vedic literature the home of the Vedic, and, therefore, also of the other Aryan races, long before they settled in Europe, or on the banks of the Oxus, the Jaxartes, or the Indus; and so far as this purpose is concerned, the results of the latest

1. See The *Nature*, Sept. 15, 1898.

scientific researches, discussed in this and the previous chapter, may now be summed up as follows :—

(1) In the very beginning of the Neolithic age Europe is found to be inhabited by races, from whom the present races of Europe speaking Aryan languages are descended.

(2) But though the existence of an Aryan race in Europe in early Neolithic times is thus established, and, therefore, the theory of migrations from an Asiatic home in Post-Glacial times is untenable, it does not prove that the Aryan race was autochthonous in Europe, and the question of its original home cannot, therefore, be regarded as finally settled.

(3) There are good reasons for supposing that the metal age was introduced into Europe by foreign people.

(4) The different ages of Stone, Bronze and Iron were not synchronous in different countries, and the high state of civilisation in Egypt is not, therefore, inconsistent with the Neolithic stage of European civilisation at the time.

(5) According to the latest geological evidence, which cannot be lightly set aside, the last Glacial period must have closed and the Post-Glacial commenced at about 10,000 years ago, or 8,000 B. C. at the best, and the freshness of the Siberian fossil-deposits favours this view.

(6) Man is not merely Post-Glacial as he was believed to be some years ago, and there is conclusive geological evidence to prove his wide-spread existence in the Quarternary, if not also in the Tertiary, era.

(7) There were at least two Glacial and one Inter-Glacial period, and the geographical distribution of land and water on the earth during the Inter-Glacial period was quite different from what it is at present.

(8) There were great vicissitudes of climate in the Pleistocene period, it being cold and inclement during the Glacial, and mild and temperate in the Inter-Glacial period, even as far as the Polar regions.

(9) There is enough evidence to show that the Arctic regions, both in Asia and Europe, were characterised in the Inter-Glacial period by cool summers and warm winters,—a sort of, what Herschel calls, a *perpetual spring*; and that places like Spitzbergen, where the sun goes below the horizon from November till March, were once the seat of luxuriant vegetation, that grows, at present, only in the temperate or the tropical climate.

(10) It was the coming on of the Glacial age that destroyed this genial climate, and rendered the regions unsuited for the habitation of tropical plants and animals.

(11) There are various estimates regarding the duration of the Glacial period, but in the present state of our knowledge it is safer to rely on geology than on astronomy in this respect, though as regards the causes of the Ice Age the astronomical explanation appears to be more probable.

(12) According to Prof. Geikie there is evidence to hold that there were, in all, five Glacial and four Inter-Glacial epochs, and that even the beginning of the Post-Glacial period was marked by two successions of cold and genial climate, at least in the North-West of Europe.

(13) Several eminent scientific men have already advanced the theory that the cradle of the human race must be sought for in the Arctic regions and that the plant and animal life also originated in the same place.

It will thus be seen that if the Vedic evidence points to an Arctic home, where the ancestors of the Vedic Rishis lived in ancient times, there is at any rate nothing in the latest scientific discoveries which would warrant us in considering this result as *a priori* improbable. On the contrary there is much in these researches that suggests such a hypothesis, and, as a matter of fact, several scientific men have now been led to think that we must look for the cradle of the human race in the Arctic regions.

CHAPTER III.

THE ARCTIC REGIONS.

Existence of a Circum-polar continent in early times —Probable also in the Inter-Glacial period —Milder climate at the time —Necessity of examining Vedic Myths —Difference between Polar and circumpolar characteristics —The precession of the equinoxes used as chronometer in Vedic chronology —Characteristics of the North Pole —The horizontal motion of the celestial hemisphere —Spinning round of the stars without rising or setting —The Sun rising in the South —A day and a night of six months each —Aurora Borealis —Continuous fortnightly moonlight, and long morning and evening twilights —Dawn lasting from 45 to 60 days —The Polar year —The darkness of the Polar night reduced only to two, or two and a half, months —Dr. Warren's description of the Polar dawn with its revolving splendours —Characteristics of regions to the South of the North Pole —Stars moving obliquely and a few rising and setting as in the tropical zone —The Southernly direction of the Sun —A long day and a long night, but of less than six months' duration —Supplemented by the alternations of ordinary days and nights for some time during the year —Long dawn, but of shorter duration than at the Pole —Comparison with the features of the year in the tropics —Summary of Polar and Circum-Polar characteristics.

We have seen that in the Pleistocene period there was great elevation and submergence of land accompanied by violent changes in the climate, over the whole surface of the globe. Naturally enough the severity of the Glacial period must have been very intense within the Arctic circle, and we shall be perfectly justified in supposing that geographical changes like the elevation and depression of land occurred on a far more extensive scale in regions round about the Pole than anywhere else. This leads us to infer that the distribution of land and water about the Pole during the Inter-Glacial period must have been different from what it is at present. Dr. Warren, in his *Paradise Found*, quotes a number of authorities to show that within a comparatively recent geological period a wide stretch of Arctic land, of which Novaia Zemlia and Spitzbergen formed a part, had been submerged; and one of the conclusions he draws from these authorities is that the present islands of the Arctic ocean, such as the two mentioned above, are simply mountain-tops still remaining above the surface of the sea which has come in and covered up the primeval continent to which they belonged. That an extensive circumpolar continent existed in Miocene times seems to have been conceded by all geologists, and though we cannot predicate its existence in its entirety during the Pleistocene period, yet there are good reasons to hold that a different configuration of land and water prevailed about the North Pole during the Inter-Glacial period, and that, as observed by Prof. Geikie, the Palæolithic man, along with other Quarternary animals, freely ranged over the whole of the Arctic regions in those times. Even now there is a considerable tract of land to the north of the Arctic circle, in the old world, especially in Siberia, and there is evidence to show that it once enjoyed a mild and temperate climate. The depth of the Arctic ocean to the north of Siberia is, at present, less than a hundred fathoms, and if great geographical changes took place in the Pleistocene period, it is not unlikely that this tract of land, which is now submerged, may have been once above the level of the sea. In other words, there are sufficient indications of the existence of a continent round about the North Pole before the last Glacial period.

As regards climate, we have seen that during the Inter-Glacial period there were cool summers and warm winters even within the Arctic circle. Sir Robert Ball gives us a good idea of the genial character of this climate by reducing to figures the distribution of heat-units over summers and winters. A longer summer, with 229 heat-units spread over it, and a shorter winter of 136 heat-units, would naturally produce a climate, which, according to Hershel, would be 'an approach to perpetual spring.' If the Palæolithic man, therefore, lived in these regions during the Inter-Glacial period, he must have found it very pleasant, in spite of the fact that the sun went below his horizon for a number of days in a year according to the latitude of the place. The present inclement climate of the Arctic regions dates from the Post-Glacial period, and we must leave it out of consideration in dealing with earlier ages.

But supposing that an Arctic continent, with an equable and pleasant climate, existed during the Inter-Glacial period, and that the Palæolithic man ranged freely over it, it does not follow that the ancestors of the Aryan race lived in the Arctic regions during those days, though it may render such a hypothesis highly probable. For that purpose, we must either wait until the existence of the Aryan race, within the Arctic regions in inter-glacial times, is proved by new archæological discoveries; or failing them, try to examine the ancient traditions and beliefs of the race, incorporated in such admittedly oldest Aryan books, as the Vedas and the Avesta, and see if they justify us in predicating the inter-glacial existence of the Aryan people. It is admitted that many of the present explanations of these traditions and legends are unsatisfactory, and as our knowledge of the ancient man is increased, or becomes more definite, by new discoveries in archæology, geology, or anthropology, these explanations will have to be revised from time to time, and any defects in them, due to our imperfect understanding of the sentiments, the habits and even the surroundings of the ancient man, corrected. That human races have preserved their ancient traditions is undoubted, though some or many of them may have become distorted in course of time; and it is for us to see if they do or do not accord with what we know of the ancient man from latest scientific researches. In the case of the Vedic traditions, myths and beliefs, we have the further advantage that they were collected thousands of years ago, and handed down unchanged from that remote time. It is, therefore, not unlikely that we may find traces of the primeval Polar home in these oldest books, if the Aryan man did live within the Arctic circle in early times, especially as a portion of the Ṛig-Veda is still admittedly unintelligible on any of the existing methods of interpretation, although the words and expressions are plain and simple in many places. Dr. Warren has quoted some Vedic traditions, along with those of other nations, in support of his theory that the Arctic regions were the birth-place of the human race. But the attempt, so far as the Vedic texts are concerned, is desultory, as it was bound to be, inasmuch as these Vedic legends and texts have, as yet, never been examined by any Vedic scholar from the new standpoint furnished by the latest scientific researches, and as Dr. Warren had to depend entirely on the existing translations. It is proposed, therefore, to examine the Vedas from this new point of view; but before doing so it is necessary to ascertain such peculiar characteristics, or what in logic are called *differentiæ*, of the Polar or the Arctic regions, as are not found elsewhere on the surface of the globe, so that if we meet with them in the Vedic traditions, the Polar origin of the latter would be indubitably established. We have seen that the inclemency of climate, which now characterises the Polar regions, was not a feature of the Polar climate in early times; and we must, therefore, turn to astronomy to find out the characteristics required for our purpose.

It has been a fashion to speak of the Polar regions as characterised by light and darkness of 6 months each, for it is well-known that the sun shines at the North Pole continuously for 6 months, and then sinks down below the horizon, producing a night of 6 months' duration. But a closer examination of the subject will show that the statement is only roughly true, and requires to be modified in several particulars before it can be accepted as scientifically accurate. In the first place we must distinguish between the Pole and the Polar regions. The Pole is merely a point, and all the inhabitants of the original ancient home, if there was one near the North Pole, could not have lived precisely at this single point. The Polar or the Arctic regions, on the other hand, mean the tracts of land included between the North Pole and the Arctic circle. But the duration of day and night, as well as the seasons, at different places within the Arctic regions cannot be, and are not, the same as at the point called the North Pole. The characteristics of the circum-polar regions may indeed be derived from the strictly Polar characteristics; but still they are so unlike each other that it is absolutely necessary to bear this distinction in mind in collecting evidence of a circum-polar Aryan home in ancient times. Men living round about the Pole, or, more accurately speaking, in regions between the North Pole and the Arctic circle, when these regions were habitable, were sure to know of a day and night of 6 months, but living a little southward from the Pole, their own calendar must have been different from the strictly Polar calendar; and it is, therefore, necessary to examine the Polar and the circum-polar characteristics separately, in order that the distinction may be clearly understood.

The terrestrial Poles are the termini of the axis of the earth, and we have seen that there is no evidence to show that this axis ever changed its position, relatively to the earth, even in the earliest geological eras.. The terrestrial poles and the circum-polar regions were, therefore, the same in early ages as they are at present, though the past and present climatic conditions of these places may be totally different. But the axis of the earth has a small motion round the pole of the ecliptic, giving rise to what is known as the precession of the equinoxes, and causing a change only in the celestial, and not in the terrestrial, poles. Thus the polar star 7000 years ago was different from what it is at present, but the terrestrial pole has always remained the same. This motion of the earth's axis, producing the precession of the equinoxes, is important from an antiquarian point of view, inasmuch as it causes a change in the times when different seasons of the year begin; and it was mainly by utilising this chronometer that I showed in my *Orion* or *Researches in the Antiquity of the Vedas* that the vernal equinox was in Orion when some of the Ṛig-Vedic traditions were formed, and that the Vedic literature contained enough clear evidence of the successive changes of the position of the vernal equinox upto the present time. Thus the vernal equinox was in the Kṛittikâs in the time of the Taittirîya Saṁhitâ and Brâhmaṇa, and the express text stating that "The Kṛittikâs never swerve from the *due* east; all other Nakṣhatras do." (Shat. Brâ. II. 1, 2, 3.), recently published by the late Mr. S. B. Dixit, serves to remove whatever doubts there might be regarding the interpretation of other passages.[1] This record of the early position of the Kṛittikâs, or the Pleiades, is as important for the determination of the Vedic chronology as the orientation of pyramids and temples has been shown to be in the case of the Egyptian, by Sir Norman Lockyer in his *Dawn of Ancient Astronomy*. But the chronometer, which I now mean to employ, is a different one. The North Pole and the Arctic regions

1. See The Indian Antiquary, Vol. XXIV, (August, 1895), p. 245. The text is :—एता (कृत्तिकाः) ह वै प्राच्यै दिशो न च्यवंते सर्वाणि ह वा अन्यानि नक्षत्राणि प्राच्यै दिशश्च्यवंते । शत. ब्रा. ।

possess certain astronomical characteristics which are peculiar to them, and if a reference to these can be discovered in the Vedas, it follows, in the light of modern researches, that the ancestors of the Vedic Ṛishis must have become acquainted with these characteristics, when they lived in those regions, which was possible only in the inter-glacial times. We shall, therefore, now examine these characteristics, dividing them in the two-fold way stated above.

If an observer is stationed at the North Pole, the first thing that will strike him is the motion of the celestial sphere above his head. Living in the temperate and tropical zones, we see all heavenly objects rise in the east and set in the west, some passing over our head, others travelling obliquely. But to the man at the Pole, the heavenly dome above will seem to revolve round him, from left to right, somewhat like the motion of a hat or umbrella turned over one's head. The stars will not rise and set, but will move round and round, in horizontal planes, turning like a potter's wheel, and starting on a second round when the first is finished, and so on, during the long night of six months. The sun, when he is above the horizon for 6 months, would also appear to revolve in the same way. The centre of the celestial dome over the head of the observer will be the celestial North Pole, and naturally enough his north will be over-head, while the invisible regions below the horizon would be in the south. As regards the eastern and western points of the compass, the daily rotation of the earth round its axis will make them revolve round the observer from right to left, thereby causing the celestial objects in the east to daily revolve round and round along the horizon from left to right, and not rise in the east, pass over-head, and set every day in the west, as with us, in the temperate or the tropical zone. In fact to an observer stationed at the

North Pole, the northern celestial hemisphere will alone be visible spinning round and round over his head, and the southern half, with all the stars in it, will always remain invisible, while the celestial equator, dividing the two, will be his celestial horizon. To such a man the sun going into the northern hemisphere in his annual course will appear as coming up from the south, and he will express the idea by saying that "the sun has risen in the south," howsoever strange the expression may seem to us. After the sun has risen in this way in the south,—and the sun will rise there only once a year,—he will be constantly visible for 6 months, during which time he will attain a height of about 23½° above the horizon, and then begin to lower down until he drops into the south below the horizon. It will be a long and continuous sunshine of 6 months, but, as the celestial dome over the head of the observer will complete one revolution in 24 hours, the sun also will make one horizontal circuit round the observer in every 24 hours; and to the observer at the North Pole the completion of one such circuit, whether of the sun or of the stars, will serve as a measure of ordinary days, or periods of 24 hours, during the long sunshine or night of six months. When about 180 such rounds, (the exact number will depend upon the difference in the durations of summer and winter noticed in the last chapter), are completed, the sun will again go down below the horizon, and the stars in the northern hemisphere, which had disappeared in his light, will become visible all at once, and not rise one after the other as with us. The light of the sun had, so to say, eclipsed them, though they were over the head of the observer; but as soon as this obstruction is removed the whole northern starry hemisphere will again appear to spin round the observer for the remaining period of six months. The horizontal motion of the celestial hemisphere, only one long continuous morning and evening in the year, and one day and one night of six months each, are thus the chief special features of the calendar at the North Pole.

We have stated that to an observer at the North Pole, there will be a night of 6 months, and one is likely to infer therefrom that there will be total darkness at the Pole for one half the portion of the year. Indeed one is likely to contemplate, with horror, the perils and difficulties of a long night of six months, during which not only the light but the warmth of the sun has to be artificially supplied. As a matter of fact, such a supposition is found to be erroneous. First of all, there will be the electric discharges, known as Aurora Borealis, filling the polar night with their charming glories, and relieving its darkness to a great extent. Then we have the moon, which, in her monthly revolution, will be above the polar horizon for a continuous fortnight, displaying her changing phases, without intermission, to the polar observer. But the chief cause, which alleviates the darkness of the polar night, is the twilight before the rising and after the setting of the sun. With us in the tropical or the temperate zone, this twilight, whether of morning or evening, lasts only for an hour or two; but at the Pole this state of things is completely altered, and the twilight of the annual morning and evening is each visible for several days. The exact duration of this morning or evening twilight is, however, still a matter of uncertainty. Some authorities fix the period at 45 days, while others make it last for full two months. In the tropical zone, we see the first beams of the dawn, when the sun is about 16° below the horizon. But it is said that in higher latitudes the light of the sun is discernible when he is from 18° to 20° below the horizon. Probably this latter limit may prove to be the correct one for the North Pole, and in that case the dawn there will last continuously for two months. Captain Pim, quoted by Dr. Warren, thus describes the Polar year :—

"On the 16th of March the sun rises, preceded by a long dawn of forty-seven days, namely, from the 29th January, when the first glimmer of light appears. On the 25th of September the sun sets, and after a twilight of forty-eight days, namely, on the 13th November, darkness reigns supreme, so far as the sun is concerned, for seventy-six days, followed by one long period of light, the sun remaining above the horizon one hundred and ninety-four days. The year, therefore, is thus divided at the Pole :— 194 days sun ; 76 darkness ; 47 days dawn ; 48 twilight."[1]

But other authorities assign a longer duration to the morning and evening twilight, and reduce the period of total darkness from 76 to 60 days, or only to two months. Which of these calculations is correct can be settled only by actual observation at the North Pole. It has been ascertained that this duration depends upon the powers of refraction and reflection of the atmosphere, and these are found to vary according to the temperature and other circumstances of the place. The Polar climate is at present extremely cold ; but in the inter-glacial epoch it was different, and this, by itself, would alter the duration of the Polar dawn in inter-glacial times. But whatever the cause may be, so much is beyond doubt that at the Pole the twilight of the yearly morning and evening lingers on for several days. For even taking the lowest limit of 16°, the sun, in his course through the ecliptic, would take more than a month to reach the horizon from this point ; and during all this time a perpetual twilight will prevail at the Pole. Long dawn and long evening twilight are, therefore, the principal factors in shortening the darkness of the Polar night, and if we

1. See Paradise Found, 10th Ed., p. 64.

deduct these days from the duration of the night, the period of darkness is reduced from six to two, or at the most, to two-and-half months. It is, therefore, erroneous to suppose that the half yearly Polar night is such a continuous period of darkness as will make the Polar regions uncomfortable. On the contrary, it will be the peculiar privilege of the Polar man to witness the splendid spectacle of a long continuous dawn with its charming lights, revolving, like the stars at the place, every day in horizontal planes, round and round him, as long as the dawn may last.

The dawn in the tropical or the temperate zone is but brief and evanescent, and it recurs after every 24 hours. But still it has formed the subject of poetical descriptions in different countries. If so, how much more the spectacle of a splendid long dawn, after a darkness of two months, would delight the heart of a Polar observer, and how he will yearn for the first appearance of the light on the horizon, can be better imagined than described. I quote the following description of this long Polar dawn from Dr. Warren's *Paradise Found*, and invite special attention to it, inasmuch as it forms one of the principal characteristics of the North Pole. Premising that the splendours of the Polar dawn are indescribable, Dr. Warren proceeds :—

"First of all appears low in the horizon of the night-sky a scarcely visible flush of light. At first it only makes a few stars' light seem a trifle fainter, but after a little it is seen to be increasing, and to be moving laterally along the yet dark horizon. Twenty-four hours later it has made a complete circuit around the observer, and is causing a larger number of stars to pale. Soon the widening light glows with the lustre of 'Orient pearl.' Onward it moves in its stately rounds, until the pearly whiteness burns into ruddy rose-light, fringed with purple and gold. Day after day, as we measure days, this splendid panorama circles on, and, according as atmospheric conditions and clouds present more or less favourable conditions of reflection, kindles and fades, kindles and fades,—fades only to kindle next time yet more brightly as the still hidden sun comes nearer and nearer his point of emergence. At length, when for two long months such prophetic displays have been filling the whole heavens with these increscent and revolving splendours, the sun begins to emerge from his long retirement, and to display himself once more to human vision. After one or two circuits, during which his dazzling upper limb grows to a full-orbed disk, he clears all hill-tops of the distant horizon, and for six full months circles around and around the world's great axis in full view, suffering no night to fall upon his favoured home-land at the Pole. Even when at last he sinks again from view he covers his retreat with a repetition of the deepening and fading splendours which filled his long dawning, as if in these pulses of more and more distant light he were signalling back to the forsaken world the promises and prophecies of an early return."[1]

A phenomenon like this cannot fail to be permanently impressed on the memory of a Polar observer, and it will be found later on that the oldest traditions of the Aryan race have preserved the recollection of a period, when its ancestors witnessed such wonderful phenomenon,—a long and continuous dawn of several days, with its lights laterally revolving on the horizon, in their original home.

Such are the distinguishing characteristics of the North Pole, that is, the point where the axis of the earth terminates in the north. But as a Polar home means

1. See Paradise Found, 10th Ed., p. 69.

practically a home in the regions round about the North Pole, and not merely the Polar point, we must now see what modifications are necessary to be made in the above characteristics owing to the observer being stationed a little to the south of the North Pole. We have seen that at the Pole the northern hemisphere is seen spinning round the observer, and all the stars move with it in horizontal planes without rising or setting; while the other celestial hemisphere is always invisible. But when the observer is shifted downwards, his zenith will no longer correspond with the Pole Star, nor his horizon with the celestial equator. For instance let *Z*, in the annexed figure, be the zenith of the observer, and *P* the celestial North Pole. When the observer was stationed at the terrestrial North Pole, his zenith coincided with *P*, and his horizon with the celestial equator, with the result that all the stars in the dome *Q'PQ* revolved round him in horizontal planes. But when the zenith is shifted to *Z*, this state of things is at once altered, as the heavens will revolve, as before, round the line *POP'*, and not round the zenith-line *ZOZ'*. When the observer was stationed at the North Pole these two lines coincided, and hence the circles of revolution described by the stars round the celestial Pole were also described round the zenith-line.

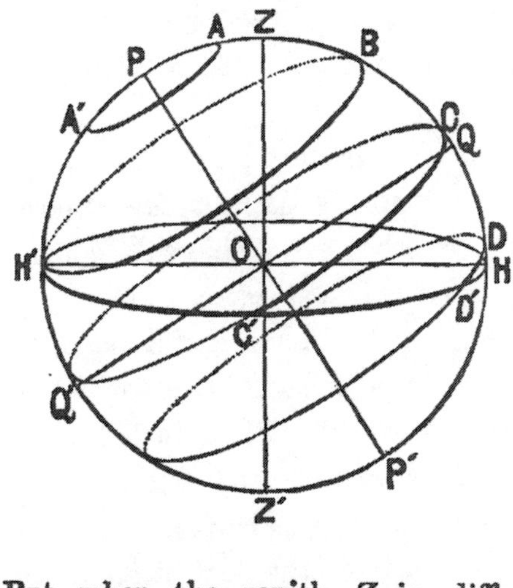

But when the zenith *Z* is different from *P*, as in the figure, the celestial horizon of the observer will be *H'H*, and the stars will now appear to move in circles inclined to his horizon, as shown in the figure by the black lines *AA'*, *BH'* and *CC'*. Some of the stars, *viz.*, those that are situated in the part of the celestial dome represented by *H'PB*, will be visible throughout the night, as their circles of revolution will be above the horizon *H'C'D'H*. But all the stars, whose Polar distance is greater than *PB* or *PH'*, will, in their daily revolution, be partly above and partly below the horizon. For instance, the stars at *C* and *D* will describe circles, some portions of which will be below the horizon *H'H*. In other words, the appearance of the visible celestial hemisphere to a person, whose zenith is at *Z*, will be different from the appearance presented by the heavens to an observer at the North Pole. The stars will not now revolve in horizontal planes, but obliquely. A great number of them would be circumpolar and visible during the whole night, but the remaining will rise and set as with us in the tropics, moving in oblique circles. When *Z* is very near *P*, only a few stars will rise and set in this way, and the difference will not be a marked one ; but as *Z* is removed further south, the change will become more and more apparent.

Similar modifications will be introduced in the duration of day and night, when the observer's position is shifted to the south of the terrestrial North Pole. This will be clear by a reference to the figure on the next page. Let *P* be the celestial North Pole, and *Q'Q* the celestial equator. Then since the sun moves in the ecliptic *E'E*, which is inclined at an angle of about $23\frac{1}{2}°$ (23° 28′) to the equator, the circles *T'E* and *E'T* will correspond with the terrestrial circles of latitude, called the *Tropics*, and the circle *AC* with the *Arctic Circle* on the terrestrial globe. Now as the sun moves in the ecliptic *E'E*, in his annual course he will always be twice over-head for an observer stationed at a place within the terrestrial tropical zone, once in his course from E' to E, and again in his return, from E to E'. The sun will also appear for some time to the north of the observer's zenith, and for the rest of the year to the south. But as the altitude of the sun above the equator is never greater than $23\frac{1}{2}°$ or EQ, an observer whose zenith lies to the north of the circle $T'E$, will always see the sun to the south of his zenith, and the zenith distance of the sun will be greater and greater as the observer advances towards the North Pole. But still the sun will be above the horizon every day, for some hours at least, to an observer whose zenith lies between $T'E$ and AC.

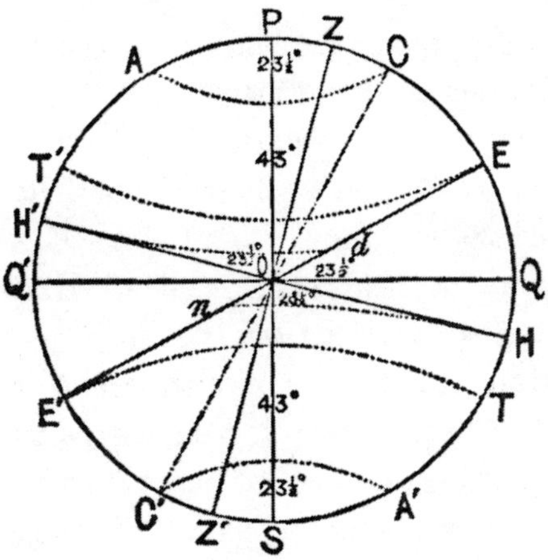

To take a concrete instance, let the observer be so stationed that his zenith will be at C, that is, on the extreme northern latitude of the temperate zone. Then his celestial horizon will extend 90° on each side, and will be represented by $T'CT$, and the sun moving along the ecliptic $E'E$ will be above his horizon, at least for some portion of day, during the whole year. But as the observer passes into the Frigid zone, the sun during his annual course will be altogether below the horizon for some days, and the maximum limit is reached at the North Pole, where the sun is below the horizon for six months. We may, therefore, state that the duration of the night, which is six months at the Pole, is gradually diminished as we come down from the Pole, until, in the temperate zone, the sun is above the horizon, at least, for some time out of twenty-four hours every day. In the foregoing figure let *Z* represent the zenith of an observer within the Arctic regions, then *H'H* will represent his horizon, and the sun in his annual course will, for some time, be altogether below this horizon. For instance, suppose the sun to be at *n*. Then his diurnal circle of rotation will be represented by *nH*, the whole of which is below the horizon *H'H* of the observer whose zenith is *Z*. Therefore, the sun, during his annual course along the ecliptic from *E'* to *n*, and back from *n* to *E'*, will be invisible to an observer whose zenith is *Z*. Corresponding to this total disappearance of the sun for some time, the luminary will be perpetually above the horizon for the same period during his northern course. For instance, let the sun be at *d*, then his diurnal circle of rotation, *dH'*, will be entirely above the horizon *H'H*, and so it will continue to be for all the time that the sun moves from *d* to *E*. and back again from *E* to *d*, in his annual course. During this time the sun will neither rise nor set, but will move, like the circumpolar stars, in oblique circles, round and round the observer like a wheel. For all positions between *n* and *d*, and the corresponding portion of the ecliptic on the other side, the sun, in his diurnal course of twenty-four hours, would be partially above and partially below the horizon, producing ordinary days and nights, as with us, the day being longer than the night when the sun is in the northern, and the night longer than the day when the sun is in the southern hemisphere. Instead of a single day and a single night of six months, the year, to a person living in the Arctic regions, but not exactly at the North Pole, will, therefore, be divided into three parts, one of which will be a long night, one a long day, and one made up of a succession of days and nights, a single day and night of which will together never exceed twenty-four hours. The long night will always be shorter than six months and longer than 24 hours, and the same will be the case with the long day. The long night and the long day will mark the two opposite extremities of the year, the middle of the long day occurring when the sun is at the summer solstice, and the middle of the long night when he is at the winter solstice. This triple division of the year is very important for our purpose, and I shall, therefore, illustrate it by a concrete example. Suppose, for instance, that the observer is so far below the North Pole that instead of a night of six months, he has a night of 2 months, or, in other words, the sun goes below his horizon only for two months. As the winter solstice will fall in the middle of this long continuous night, we may say that the night will extend a month before and a month after December 21, when the sun is at the winter solstice. Corresponding to this long night, there will be a continuous day of two months, a month before and a month after June 21, when the sun is at the summer solstice. If these four months are deducted from the year, there will remain eight months, and during all these months there will be days and nights, as in the temperate zone, a nycthemeron, or a day and a night together, never exceeding, as with us, the ordinary period of twenty-four hours. This alternation of ordinary days and nights will commence after the close of the long night in January, and in the beginning, the night will be longer than the day; but as the sun passes from the southern into the northern hemisphere, the day will gain over the night, and eventually, after four months, terminate into a continuous day for two months. At the close of this long day in July, the alternation of ordinary days and nights will again commence, the day in the beginning being longer than the night, but a nycthemeron never exceeding, as in the previous case, a period of twenty-four hours. As the sun passes from the northern into the southern hemisphere, the night will begin to gain over the day, until, after four months of such succession of ordinary days and nights, it terminates into the continuous night of two months mentioned above. The same description applies, *mutatis mutandis,* where the long night may last for 3, 4 or 5 months, until we reach the Polar condition of a day and a night of six months each, when the intermediate succession of ordinary days and nights will vanish.[1]

We have seen that a long dawn of two months is a special and important characteristic of the North Pole. As we descend southward, the splendour and the duration of the dawn will be witnessed on a less and less magnificent scale. But the dawn, occurring at the end of the long night of two, three or more months, will still be unusually long,

---

1. Cf. Bhâskarâchârya's Siddhânta Shiromaṇi, Golâdhyâya, Chapter VII., verses 6-7, which are as follows :—

षट्षष्टिभागाभ्यधिकाः पलांशाः । यत्राथ तत्रास्त्यपरो विशेषः ॥
लंबाधिका क्रांतिरुदक् च यावत् । तावद्दिनं संततमेव तत्र ।
याम्या च याम्या सततं तमिस्रा । तत्रश्च मेरौ सततं समार्धम् ॥

"There is a peculiarity at the place, where the latitude is greater than 66° N. Whenever the northern declination of the sun exceeds the complement of the latitude, there will be perpetual day, for such time as that excess continues. Similarly, when the southern (declination exceeds), there will be perpetual night. On Meru, therefore, there is equal half-yearly perpetual day and night." Thus if the latitude of a place be 70°, its complement will be 90 — 70 = 20°; and as the sun's height above the celestial equator (that is, his declination) is never greater than 23° 28′, there will be a continuous day at the place, so long as the declination is greater than 20° and less than 23° 28′, and there will be a similar continuous night when the sun is in the southern hemisphere. Paul Du Chaillu mentions that at Nordkyn or North Cape (N. lat. 71° 6′ 50″), the northernmost place on the continent of Europe, the long night commences on 18th November, and ends on 24th January, lasting, in all, for 67 days of twenty-four hours each.

often of several days' duration. As stated above, at first only a pale flush of light will appear, and it will continue visible on the horizon, revolving round and round, if the observer is sufficiently near the Pole, for some days, when at last the orb of the sun will emerge, and start the alternation of day and night described above, to be eventually terminated into a long day. The splendours of the Aurora Borealis would also be less marked and conspicuous in the southern latitudes than at the North Pole.

But if the characteristics of the Arctic regions are different from those of the North Pole, they are no less different from the features of the year with which we are familiar in the temperate or the tropical zone. With us the sun is above the horizon, at least for some time every day, during all the twelve months of the year; but to persons within the Arctic circle, he is below the horizon, and, therefore, continuously invisible for a number of days. If this period of continuous night be excluded from our reckoning, we might say that within the Arctic regions the year, or the period marked by sunshine, only lasts from six to eleven months. Again the dawn in the temperate and the tropical zone is necessarily short-lived, for a day and a night together do not exceed twenty-four hours, and the dawn which comes between them can last only for a few hours; but the annual dawn at the Pole, and the dawn at the end of the long night in the Arctic regions will each be a dawn of several days' duration. As for the seasons, we have our winters and summers; but the winter in the Arctic regions will be marked by the long continuous night, while the summer will make the night longer than the day, but within the limit of twenty-four hours, until the day is developed into a long continuous sunshine of several days. The climate of the Polar regions is now extremely cold and severe, but, as previously stated, different climatic conditions prevailed in early times, and we cannot, therefore, include climate amongst the points of contrast under consideration.

It will be seen from the foregoing discussion that we have two distinct sets of characteristics, or *differentiæ*; one for an observer stationed *exactly* at the terrestrial North Pole, and the other for an observer located in the Circum-Polar regions, or tracts of land between the North Pole and the Arctic circle. For brevity's sake, we shall designate these two sets of *differentiæ* as *Polar* and *Circum-Polar*, and sum them up as follows :—

I. The Polar Characteristics.

(1) The sun rises in the south.

(2) The stars do not rise and set; but *revolve*, or spin round and round, *in horizontal planes*, completing one round in 24 hours. The northern celestial hemisphere is alone over-head and visible during the whole year; and the southern or the lower celestial world is always invisible.

(3) The year consists only of *one long day* and *one long night of six months each.*

(4) There is only *one morning* and *one evening*, or the sun rises and sets only once a year. But the *twilight*, whether of the morning or of the evening, *lasts continuously* for about *two months*, or 60 periods of 24 hours each. The ruddy light of the morn, or the evening twilight, is not again confined to a particular part of the horizon (eastern or western) as with us; but *moves*, like the stars at the place, *round and round along the horizon*, like a potter's wheel, completing one round in every 24 hours. These rounds of the morning light continue to take place, until the orb of the sun comes above the horizon; and then the sun follows the same course for six months, that is, moves, without setting, round and round the observer, completing one round every 24 hours.

II. The Circum-Polar Characteristics.

(1) The sun will *always be to the south* of the zenith of the observer; but as this happens even in the case of an observer stationed in the temperate zone, it cannot be regarded as a special characteristic.

(2) A large number of stars are *circum-polar*, that is, they are above the horizon during the entire period of their revolution and hence always visible. The remaining stars rise and set, as in the temperate zone, but revolve in more oblique circles.

(3) The *year* is made up of *three parts* :—(i) *one long continuous night,* occurring at the time of the winter solstice, and lasting for a period, greater than 24 hours and less than six months, according to the latitude of the place; (ii) *one long continuous day* to match, occurring at the time of the summer solstice; and (iii) *a succession of ordinary days and nights* during the rest of the year, a nycthemeron, or a day and a night together, never exceeding a period of 24 hours. The day, after the long continuous night, is at first shorter than the night, but it goes on increasing until it developes into the long continuous day. At the end of the long day, the night is, at first, shorter than the day, but, in its turn, it begins to gain over the day, until the commencement of the long continuous night, with which the year ends.

(4) The dawn, at the close of the long continuous night, lasts for several days, but its duration and magnificence is proportionally less than at the North Pole, according to the latitude of the place. For places, within a few degrees of the North Pole, the phenomenon of revolving morning light will still be observable during the greater part of the duration of the dawn. The other dawns, *viz.*, those between ordinary days and nights, will, like the dawns in the temperate zone, only last for a few hours. The sun, when he is above the horizon during the continuous day,

will be seen revolving, without setting, round the observer, as at the Pole, but in oblique, and not horizontal circles, and during the long night he will be entirely below the horizon; while during the rest of the year he will rise and set, remaining above the horizon for a part of 24 hours, varying according to the position of the sun in the ecliptic.

Here we have two distinct sets of *differentiæ*, or special characteristics, of the Polar and Circum-Polar regions, —characteristics which are not found anywhere else on the surface of the globe. Again as the Poles of the earth are the same to-day as they were millions of years ago, the above astronomical characteristics will hold good for all times, though the Polar climate may have undergone violent changes in the Pleistocene period. In short, we can take these *differentiæ* as our unerring guides in the examination of the Vedic evidence bearing on the point at issue. If a Vedic description or tradition discloses any of the characteristics mentioned above, we may safely infer that the tradition is Polar or Circum-Polar in origin, and the phenomenon, if not actually witnessed by the poet, was at least known to him by tradition faithfully handed down from generation to generation. Fortunately there are many such passages or references in the Vedic literature, and, for convenience, these may be divided into two parts: the *first* comprising those passages which directly describe or refer to the long night, or the long dawn; and the *second* consisting of myths and legends which corroborate and indirectly support the first. The evidence in the first part being direct, is, of course, more convincing; and we shall, therefore, begin with it in the next chapter, reserving the consideration of the Vedic myths and legends to the latter part of the book.

CHAPTER IV.

THE NIGHT OF THE GODS.

Vedic sacrifices, regulated by the luni-solar calendar —A year of six seasons and twelve months, with an intercalary month in the Taittirîya Samhitâ —The same in the Rig-Veda —Present results of the Vedic mythology —All presuppose a home in the temperate or the tropical zone—But further research still necessary —The special character of the Rig-Veda explained —Polar tests found in the Rig-Veda —Indra supporting the heavens with a pole, and moving them like a wheel —A day and a night of six months, in the form of the half-yearly day and night of the Gods —Found in the Sûrya Sidhânta and older astronomical Samhitâs —Bhâskarâchârya's error explained —Gods' day and night mentioned by Manu and referred to by Yâska —The description of Meru or the North Pole in the Mahâbhârata —In the Taittirîya Aranyaka —The passage in the Taittirîya Brâhmana about the year-long day of the Gods —Improbability of explaining it except as founded on the observation of nature —Parallel passage in the Vendidad—Its Polar character clearly established by the context —The Vara of Yima in the Airyana Vaejo —The sun rising and setting there only once a year —The Devayâna and the Pitriyâna in the Rig-Veda —Probably represent the oldest division of the year, like the day and the night of the Gods —The path of Mazda in the Parsi scriptures —Death during Pitriyâna regarded inauspicious—Bâdarâyana's view —Probable explanation suggested —Death during winter or Pitriyâna in the Parsi scriptures —Probably indicates a period of total darkness —Similar Greek traditions —Norse Twilight of the Gods —The idea of half-yearly day and night of the Gods thus proved to be not only Indo-Iranian, but Indo-Germanic —A sure indication of an original Polar home.

At the threshold of the Vedic literature, we meet with an elaborately organised sacrificial system so well regulated by the luni-solar calendar as to show that the

Vedic bards had, by that time, attained considerable proficiency in practical astronomy. There were daily, fortnightly, monthly, quarterly, half-yearly and yearly sacrifices, which, as I have elsewhere shown, also served as chronometers in those days.[1] The Taittirîya Saṁhitâ and the Brâhmaṇas distinctly mention a lunar month of thirty days and a year of twelve such months, to which an intercalary month was now and then added, to make the lunar and the solar year correspond with each other. The ecliptic, or the belt of the zodiac, was divided into 27 or 28 divisions, called the Nakshatras, which were used as mile-stones to mark the annual passage of the sun, or the monthly revolution of the moon round the earth. The two solstitial and the two equinoctial points, as well as the passage of the sun into the northern and the southern hemisphere, were clearly distinguished, and the year was divided into six seasons, the festivals in each month or the year being accurately fixed and ascertained. The stars rising and setting with the sun were also systematically observed and the eastern and western points of the compass determined as accurately as the astronomical observations of the day could permit. In my *Orion or the Antiquity of the Vedas*, I have shown how the changes in the position of the equinoxes were also marked in these days, and how they enable us to classify the periods of Vedic antiquity. According to this classification the Taittirîya Saṁhitâ comes under the Kṛittikâ period (2500 B. C.), and some may, therefore, think that the details of the Vedic calendar given above are peculiar only to the later Vedic literature. A cursory study of the Ṛig-Veda will, however, show that such is not the case. A year of 360 days, with an intercalary month occasionally added, or a year of twelve lunar months,

1. See The Orion or the Antiquity of the Vedas, Chap. II.

with twelve intercalary days inserted at the end of each year, was familiar to the poets of the Ṛig-Veda and is often mentioned in the hymns.[1] The northern and the southern passage of the sun from equinox to equinox, the Devayâna and the Pitṛiyâna, together with the yearly *sattras*, have also been referred to in several places, clearly showing that the Ṛig-Vedic calendar differed, if at all, very little from the one in use at the time of the Taittirîya Saṁhitâ or the Brâhmaṇas. A calendar of twelve months and six seasons is peculiar only to the temperate or the tropical zone, and if we were to judge only from the facts stated above, it follows that the people who used such a calendar, must have lived in places where the sun was above the horizon during all the days of the year. The science of Vedic mythology, so far as it is developed at present, also supports the same view. Vṛitra is said to be a demon of drought or darkness, and several myths are explained on the theory that they represent a daily struggle between the powers of light and the powers of darkness, or of eventual triumph of summer over winter, or of day over night, or of Indra over water-tight clouds. Mr. Nârâyaṇa Âiyangâr of Bangalore has attempted to explain some of these myths on the astral theory, showing that the myths point out to the position of the vernal equinox in Orion, in the oldest period of Vedic civilisation. But all these theories or methods of interpretation *assume* that the Vedic people have always been the inhabitants of the temperate or the tropical zone, and all these myths and traditions were formed or developed in such a home.

---

1. See Ṛig. I, 25, 8,—वेद मासो धृतव्रतो द्वादश प्रजावतः । वेदा य उपजायते । Also Ṛig. IV, 33, 7,—द्वादश द्यून्यदगोह्यस्यातिथ्ये रणन्नृभवः ससंतः । See Orion, page 167 *f.* In Ṛig. I, 164, 11, 360 days and 360 nights of the year are expressly mentioned.

Such are the results of the latest researches in Vedic philology, mythology or calendar, regarding the ancient home of the Vedic people, and the origin and the antiquity of their mythology. But to a man who is working in the same field, the question whether we have reached the utmost limit of our researches naturally occurs. It is a mistake to suppose that all the traditions and myths, and even the deities, mentioned in the Ṛig-Veda were the creation of one period. To adopt a geological phrase, the Ṛig-Veda, or we might even say the whole Vedic literature, is not arranged into different strata according to their chronological order, so that we can go on from one stratum to another and examine each separately. The Ṛig-Veda is a book in which old things of different periods are so mixed up that we have to work long and patiently before we are able to separate and classify its contents in chronological order. I have stated before how owing to our imperfect knowledge of the ancient man and his surroundings this task is rendered difficult, or even impossible in some cases. But, as observed by Prof. Max Muller, it is the duty of each generation of Vedic scholars to reduce as much as possible the unintelligible portion of the Ṛig-Veda, so that with the advance of scientific knowledge each succeeding generation may, in this matter, naturally be in a better position than its predecessors. The Vedic calendar, so far as we know, or the Vedic mythology may not have, as yet, disclosed any indication of an Arctic home, but underneath the materials that have been examined, or even by their side, we may still find facts, which, though hitherto neglected, may, in the new light of scientific discoveries, lead to important conclusions. The mention of the luni-solar calendar in the Ṛig-Veda ought not, therefore, to detain us from further pursuing our investigation by examining the texts and legends which have not yet been satisfactorily explained, and ascertaining how far such texts and legends indicate the existence of a Polar or Circum-Polar home in early times. The distinguishing characteristics of these regions have been already discussed and stated in the previous chapter, and all that we have now to do is to apply these tests, and decide if they are satisfied or fulfilled by the texts and legends under consideration.

The spinning round of the heavenly dome over the head is one of the special characteristics of the North Pole, and the phenomenon is so peculiar that one may expect to find traces of it in the early traditions of a people, if they, or their ancestors ever lived near the North Pole. Applying this test to the Vedic literature, we do find passages which compare the motion of the heavens to that of a wheel, and state that the celestial vault is supported as if on an axis. Thus in Ṛig. X, 89, 4, Indra is said "to separately uphold by his power heaven and earth as the two wheels of a chariot are held by the axle."[1] Prof. Ludwig thinks that this refers to the axis of the earth, and the explanation is very probable. The same idea occurs in other places, and sometimes the sky is described as being supported even without a pole, testifying thereby to the great power or might of Indra (II, 15, 2; IV, 56, 3).[2] In X, 89, 2, Indra is identified with Sûrya and he is described as "turning the widest expanse like the wheels of a chariot."[3] The word for 'expanse' is *varâṁsi*, which Sâyaṇa understands to mean 'lights', or 'stars.' But whichever meaning we adopt, it is clear that the verse in question refers to the revolution of the sky,

1. Ṛig. X, 89, 4,—यो अक्षेणेव चक्रिया शचीभिर्विष्वक्तस्तंभ पृथिवीमुत द्यां ।

2. Ṛig. II, 15, 2,—अवंशे द्यामस्तभायत् । IV, 56, 3,—स इमे द्यावापृथिवी जजान उर्वी गभीरे रजसी सुमेके अवंशे धीरः शच्या समैरत् ।

3. Ṛig. X, 89, 2,—स सूर्यः पर्युरू वरांस्येन्द्रो ववृत्याद्रथ्येव चक्रा ।

and compares it to the motion of a chariot wheel. Now the heavens in the temperate and the tropical regions may be described as moving like a wheel from east to west and then back again to the east, though the latter half of this circuit is not visible to the observer. But we can not certainly speak of the tropical sky as being supported on a pole, for the simple reason that the North Pole, which must be the point of support in such a case, will not be sufficiently near the zenith in the tropical or the temperate zone. If we, therefore, combine the two statements, that the heavens are supported as on a pole, and that they move like a wheel, we may safely infer that the motion referred to is such a motion of the celestial hemisphere as can be witnessed only by an observer at the North Pole. In the Ṛig-Veda I, 24, 10, the constellation of Ursa Major (*Ṛikṣhaḥ*) is described as being placed 'high' (*uchhâḥ*), and, as this can refer only to the altitude of the constellation, it follows that it must then have been over the head of the observer, which is possible only in the Circum-Polar regions. Unfortunately there are few other passages in the Ṛig-Veda which describe the motion of the celestial hemisphere or of the stars therein, and we must, therefore, take up another characteristic of the Polar regions, namely, 'a day and a night of six months each,' and see if the Vedic literature contains any references to this singular feature of the Polar regions.

The idea that the day and the night of the Gods are each of six months' duration is so widespread in

---

1. Ṛig. I, 24, 10,—अमी य ऋक्षा निहितास उच्चा नक्तं ददृश्रे कुहचिद्दिवेयुः । It may also be remarked, in this connection, that the passage speaks of the appearance (not rising) of the Seven Bears at night, and their disappearance (not setting) during the day, showing that the constellation was circum-polar at the place of the observer.

the Indian literature, that we must examine it here at some length, and, for that purpose, commence with the Post-Vedic literature and trace it back to the most ancient books. It is found not only in the Purâṇas, but also in astronomical works, and as the latter state it in a more definite form we shall begin with the later Siddhântas. Mount Meru is the terrestrial North Pole of our astronomers, and the Sûrya-Siddhânta, XII, 67, says :— "At Meru Gods behold the sun after but a *single rising* during the half of his revolution beginning with Aries." Now according to Purâṇas Meru is the home or seat of all the Gods, and the statement about their half-year-long night and day is thus easily and naturally explained; and all astronomers and divines have accepted the accuracy of the explanation. The day of the Gods corresponds with the passage of the sun from the vernal to the autumnal equinox, when the sun is visible at the North Pole, or the Meru; and the night with the southern passage of sun, from the autumnal back to the vernal equinox. But Bhâskarâchârya, not properly understanding the passage which states that the "Uttarâyaṇa is a day of Gods," has raised the question how Uttarâyaṇa, which in his day meant the passage of the sun from the winter to the summer solstice, could be the day of the Gods stationed at the North Pole; for an observer at the Pole can only see the sun in his passage from the vernal to the autumnal equinox. But, as shown by me elsewhere,[1] Bhâskarâchârya has here fallen into an error by attributing to the word *Uttarâyaṇa*, a sense which it did not bear in old times, or at least in the passages embodying this tradition. The old meaning of *Uttarâyaṇa*, literally, the northern passage of the sun, was the period of time required by the sun to travel from the vernal to

1. See Orion, p. 29.

the autumnal equinox, or the portion of the ecliptic in the northern hemisphere; and if we understand the word in this sense, the statement that the Uttarâyaṇa is a day of the Devas is at once plain and intelligible. Bhâskarâchârya's reference to older astronomical Saṁhitâs clearly shows that the tradition was handed down from the oldest times. It is suggested that in these passages Gods may mean the apotheosized ancestors of the human race. But I do not think that we need any such explanation. If the ancestors of the human race ever lived at the North Pole, so must have their Gods; and I shall shew in a subsequent chapter that the Vedic deities are, as a matter of fact, clothed with attributes, which are distinctly Polar in origin. It makes, therefore, no difference for our purpose, if a striking feature of the primitive home is traditionally preserved and remembered as a characteristic of the Gods, or of the apotheosized ancestors of the race. We are concerned with the tradition itself, and our object is gained if its existence is clearly established.

The next authority for the statement is Manu I, 67. While describing the divisions of time it says, "A year (human) is a day and a night of the Gods; thus are the two divided, the northern passage of the sun is the day and the southern the night."[1] The day and the night of the Gods are then taken as a unit for measuring longer periods of time as the *Kalpas* and so on, and Yâska's Nirukta, XIV, 4, probably contains the same reference. Muir, in the first Volume of his *Original Sanskrit Texts*, gives some of these passages so far as they bear on the *yuga*-system found in the Purâṇas. But we are not concerned with the later development of the idea that the day and the night of the Gods each lasted for

1. Manu, I, 67,—दैवे रात्र्यहनी वर्षं प्रविभागस्तयोः पुनः । अहस्तत्रोदगयनं रात्रिः स्याद्दक्षिणायनम् ॥

six months. What is important, from our point of view, is the persistent prevalence of this tradition in the Vedic and the Post-Vedic literature, which can only be explained on the hypothesis that originally it must have been the result of actual observation. We shall, therefore, next quote the Mahâbhârata, which gives such a clear description of Mount Meru, the lord of the mountains, as to leave no doubt about its being the North Pole, or possessing the Polar characteristics. In chapters 163 and 164 of the Vanaparvan, Arjuna's visit to the Mount is described in detail, and we are therein told, "At Meru the sun and the moon go round from left to right (*pradakṣhinam*) every day, and so do all the stars." Later on the writer informs us:—"The mountain, by its lustre, so overcomes the darkness of night, that the night can hardly be distinguished from the day." A few verses further, and we find, "The day and the night are together equal to a year to the residents of the place."[1] These quotations are quite sufficient to convince any one that at the time when the great epic was composed Indian writers had a tolerably accurate knowledge of the meteorological and astronomical characteristics of the North Pole, and this knowledge cannot be supposed to have been acquired by mere mathematical calculations. The reference to the *lustre of the mountain* is specially interesting, inasmuch as, in all probability, it is a description of the splen-

1. The verses (Calcutta Ed.) are as follows,—

एवं त्वहरहर्मेरुं सूर्याचंद्रमसौ ध्रुवं । प्रदक्षिणमुपावृत्य कुरुतः कुरुनंदन ॥
ज्योतींषि चाप्यशेषेण सर्वाण्यनघ सर्वतः । परियांति महाराज गिरिराजं प्रदक्षिणं ॥

Vana-parvan, Chap. 163, vv. 37, 38.

स्वतेजसा तस्य नगोत्तमस्य महौषधीनां च तथा प्रभावात् ।
विभक्तभावो न बभूव कश्चिदहोनिशानां पुरुषप्रवीर ॥
बभूव रात्रिर्दिवसश्च तेषां संवत्सरेणैव समानरूपः ॥

Ibid, Chap. 164, vv. 11, 13.

dours of the Aurora Borealis visible at the North Pole. So far as the Post-Vedic literature is concerned we, have, therefore, not only the tradition of the half-year-long night and day of the Gods persistently mentioned, but the Mount Meru, or the North Pole, is described with such accuracy as to lead us to believe that it is an ancient tradition, whose origin must be traced to a time when these phenomena were daily observed by the people; and this is confirmed by the fact that the tradition is not confined only to the Post-Vedic literature.

Passing on, therefore, to the Vedic literature, we find Mount Meru described as the seat of seven Âdityas in the Taittirîya Âraṇyaka I, 7, 1, while the eighth Âditya, called Kashyapa, is said never to leave the great Meru or Mahâmeru. Kashyapa is further described as communicating light to the seven Âdityas, and himself perpetually illumining the great mountain. It is, however, in the Taittirîya Brâhmaṇa, (III, 9, 22, 1), That we meet with a passage which clearly says, "That which is a year is but a single day of the Gods." The statement is so clear that there can be no doubt whatever about its meaning. A year of the mortals is said to be but a day of the Gods; but, at one time, I considered it extremely hazardous[1] to base any theory even upon such a clear statement, inasmuch as it then appeared to me to be but solitary in the Vedic literature. I could not then find anything to match it in the Saṁhitâs, and especially in the Ṛig-Veda, and I was inclined to hold that Uttarâyaṇa and Dakshiṇâyana were, in all probability, described in this way as 'day' and 'night' with a qualifying word to mark their special nature. Later researches have however *forced* on me the conclusion that the tradition, represented by

1. Taitt. Br. III, 9, 22, 1,—एकं वा एतद्देवानामहः यत्संवत्सरः। See Orion, p. 29, note.

this passage, indicates the existence of a Polar home in old days, and I have set forth in the sequel the evidence on which I have come to the above conclusion. There are several theories on which the above statement in the Taittirîya Brâhmaṇa can be explained. We may regard it as the outcome of pure imagination, or of a metaphor expressing in figurative language a fact quite different from the one denoted by the words used, or it may be the result of actual observation by the writer himself or by persons from whom he traditionally derived his information. It may also be considered as based on astronomical calculations made in later days, what was originally an astronomical inference being subsequently converted into a real observed fact. The last of these suppositions would have appeared probable, if the tradition had been confined only to the Post-Vedic literature, or merely to the astronomical works. But we can not suppose that during the times of the Brâhmaṇas the astronomical knowledge was so far advanced as to make it possible to fabricate a fact by mathematical calculation, even supposing that the Vedic poets were capable of making such a fabrication. Even in the days of Herodotus the statement that 'there existed a people who slept for six months' was regarded 'incredible' (IV, 24); and we must, therefore, give up the idea, that several centuries before Herodotus, a statement regarding the day or the night of the Gods could have been fabricated in the way stated above. But all doubts on the point are set at rest by the occurrence of an almost identical statement in the sacred books of the Parsis. In the Vendidad, Fargard II, para 40, (or, according to Spiegel, para 133), we find the sentence, *Tae cha ayara mainyaente yat yare*, meaning "They regard, as a day, what is a year." This is but a paraphrase of the statement, in the Taittirîya Brâhmaṇa, and the context in the Parsi scriptures removes all possible doubts regarding the Polar character of the statement. The latter part of the second Fargard, wherein this passage occurs, contains a discourse between Ahura Mazda and Yima.[1] Ahura Mazda warns Yima, the first king of men, of the approach of a dire winter, which is to destroy every living creature by covering the land with a thick sheet of ice, and advises Yima to build a Vara, or an enclosure, to preserve the seeds of every kind of animals and plants. The meeting is said to have taken place in the Airyana Vaejo, or the Paradise of the Iranians. The Vara, or the enclosure, advised by Ahura Mazda, is accordingly prepared, and Yima asked Ahura Mazda, "O Maker of the material world, thou Holy One! What lights are there to give light in the Vara which Yima made?" Ahura Mazda answered, "There are uncreated lights and created lights. There the stars, the moon and the sun are only *once (a year) seen to rise and set*, and *a year seems only as a day.*" I have taken Darmesteter's rendering, but Spiegel's is substantially the same. This passage is important from various standpoints. First of all it tells us, that the Airyana Vaejo, or the original home of the Iranians, was a place which was rendered uninhabitable by glaciation; and secondly that in this original home the sun rose and set only *once in the year*, and that the *year was like a day* to the inhabitants of the place. The bearing of the passage in regard to glaciation will be discussed later on. For the present, it is enough to point out how completely it corroborates and ellucidates the statement in the Taittirīya Brâhmaṇa stated and discussed above. The yearly rising and setting of the sun is possible only at the North Pole, and the mention of this characteristic leaves no room for doubting that the Vara

1. See Sacred Books of the East Series, Vol. IV, pp. 15-31.

and the Airyana Vaejo were both located in the Arctic or Circum-Polar regions, and that the passage in the Taittirîya Brâhmaṇa also refers to the Polar year. The fact that the statement is found both in the Iranian and the Indian literature further negatives the probability of its being a fabrication from mathematical calculation. Nor can we suppose that both the branches of the Aryan race became acquainted with this fact simply by an effort of unassisted imagination, or that it was a mere metaphor. The only remaining alternative is to hold, as Sir Charles Lyell[1] has remarked, that the tradition was "founded on the observation of Nature."

It is true, that the statement, or anything similar to it, is not found in the Ṛig-Veda; but it will be shewn later on that there are many other passages in the Ṛig-Veda which go to corroborate this statement in a remarkable way by referring to other Polar characteristics. I may, however, mention here the fact that the oldest Vedic year appears to have been divided only into two portions, the Devayâna and the Pitṛiyâna, which originally corresponded with the Uttarâyaṇa and the Dakṣhiṇâyana, or the day and the night of the Gods. The word *Devayâna* occurs several times in the Ṛig-Veda Saṁhitâ, and denotes 'the path of the Gods.' Thus in the Ṛig-Veda, I, 72, 7 Agni is said to be cognizant of the *Devayâna* road, and in Ṛig. I, 183, 6, and 184, 6, the poet says, "We have, O Ashvins! reached the *end of darkness*; now come to us by the *Devayâna* road."[2] In VII, 76, 2, we again read, "The *Devayâna* path has become visible to me ... The banner of the Dawn has appeared in the east." Passages like

1. See Elements of Geology, 11th Ed., Vol. I, p. 8.

2. Ṛig. I. 183, 6,—अतरिष्म तमसस्पारमस्य प्रति वां स्तोमो अश्विनावधायि । एह यातं पथिभिर्देवयानैः ॥ Ṛig. VII, 76, 2,—प्र मे पंथा देवयाना अदृश्रन्......अभूदु केतुरुषसः पुरस्तात् ।

these clearly indicate that the road of the Devayâna commenced at the rise of the Dawn, or after the end of darkness; and that it was the road by which Agni, Ashvins, Ushas, Sûrya and other matutinal deities travelled during their heavenly course. The path of the Pitṛis, or the Pitṛiyâna, is, on the other hand, described in X, 18, 1, as the "reverse of Devayâna, or the path of Death." In the Ṛig-Veda, X, 88, 15, the poet says that he has "heard" only of "two roads, one of the Devas and the other of the Pitṛis." If the Devayâna, therefore, commenced with the Dawn, we must suppose that the Pitṛiyâna commenced with the advent of darkness. Sâyaṇa is, therefore, correct in interpreting V, 77, 2, as stating that "the evening is not for the Gods (*devayâḥ*)." Now if the Devayâna and the Pitṛiyâna were only synonymous with ordinary day and night, there was obviously no propriety in stating that these were the only two paths or roads known to the ancient Ṛishis, and they could not have been described as consisting of three seasons each, beginning with the spring, (Shat. Brâ. II, 1, 3, 1-3).[1] It seems, therefore, very probable that the Devayâna and the Pitṛiyâna originally represented a two-fold division of the year, one of continuous light and the other of continuous darkness as at the North Pole; and that though it was not suited to the later home of the Vedic people it was retained, because it was an established and recognised fact in the language, like the seven suns, or the seven horses of a single sun. The evidence in support of this view will be stated in subsequent chapters. It is sufficient to observe in this place, that if we interpret the two-fold division of the Devayâna and the Pitṛiyâna in this way, it fully corroborates the statement in the Taittirîya Brâhmaṇa that a year was but a day of the Gods. We may also note in this connection that the expression 'path

1. For a full discussion of the subject see Orion, pp. 24-30.

of the Gods' occurs even in the Parsi scriptures. Thus in the Farvardîn Yasht, paras 56, 57, the Fravashis, which correspond with the Pitṛis in the Vedic literature, are said to have shown to the sun and the moon "the path made by Mazda, the way made by the Gods," along which the Fravashis themselves are described as growing. The sun and the moon are, again, said to have "stood for a long time in the same place, without moving forwards through the oppression of the Daevas (Vedic *Asuras*, or the demons of darkness)," before the Fravashis showed 'the path of Mazda,' to these two luminaries.[1] This shows that 'the path of Mazda' commenced, like the Devayâna road, when the sun was set free from the clutches of the demons of darkness. In other words, it represented the period of the year when the sun was above the horizon at the place where the ancestors of the Indo-Iranian lived in ancient days. We have seen that the Devayâna, or the path of the Gods, is the way along which Sûrya, Agni and other matutinal deities are said to travel in the Ṛig-Veda; and the Parsi scriptures supplement this information by telling us that the sun stood still before the Fravashis showed to him 'the path of Mazda', evidently meaning that the Devayâna, or 'the path of Mazda,' was the portion of the year when the sun was above the horizon after being confined for some time by the powers of darkness.

But the correspondence between the Indian and the Parsi scriptures does not stop here. There is a strong prejudice, connected with the Pitṛiyâna, found in the later Indian literature, and even this has its parallel in the Parsi scriptures. The Hindus consider it inauspicious for a man to die during the Pitṛiyâna, and the great Mahâbhârata warrior, Bhîṣhma, is said to have waited on his death-bed until the sun passed through the winter solstice, as the

1. See Sacred Books of the East Series, Vol. XXIII, pp. 193-194.

Dakṣhiṇâyana, which is synonymous with the Pitṛiyâna, was then understood to mean the time required by the sun to travel from the summer to the winter solstice.[1] A number of passages scattered over the whole Upanishad literature support the same view, by describing the course of the soul of a man according as he dies during the Devayâna or the Pitṛiyâna, and exhibiting a marked preference for the fate of the soul of a man dying during the path of the Gods, or the Devayâna. All these passages will be found collected in Shankarâchârya's Bhâshya on Brahma-Sûtras, IV, 2, 18-21, wherein Bâdarâyaṇa,[2] anxious to reconcile all these passages with the practical difficulty sure to be experienced if death during the night of the Gods were held to be absolutely unmeritorious from a religious point of view, has recorded his opinion that we must *not* interpret these texts as predicating an uncomfortable future life for every man dying during the Dakṣhiṇâyana or the night of the Gods. As an alternative Bâdarâyaṇa, therefore, adds that these passages may be taken to refer to the Yogins who desire to attain to a particular kind of heaven after death. Whatever we may think of this view, we can, in this attempt of Bâdarâyaṇa, clearly see a distinct consciousness of the existence of a tradition, which, if it did not put an absolute ban on death during the night of the Gods, did, at any rate, clearly disapprove of such occurrences from a religious point of view. If the Pitṛiyâna originally represented, as stated above, a period of continuous darkness the tradition can be easily and rationally explained; for as the Pitṛiyâna then meant an uninterrupted night, the funeral ceremonies of any one dying during the period

1. For the text and discussion thereon, see Orion, p. 39.

2. The Sûtras are,—रश्म्यनुसारी ।१८। निशि नेति चेन्न, संबंधस्य यावद्देहभावित्वाद्दर्शयति च ।१९। अतश्चायनेऽपि दक्षिणे ।२०। योगिनः प्रति च स्मर्यते स्मार्ते चैते ।२०। See also Orion, pp. 23-25.

were deferred till the break of the dawn at the end of the Pitṛiyâna, or the commencement of the Devayâna. Even now death during night is considered inauspicious, and the funeral generally takes place after daybreak.

The Parsi scriptures are still more explicit. In the Vendidad, Fargards V, 10, and VIII, 4, a question is raised how the worshipper of Mazda should act, when a death takes place in a house when the summer has passed and the winter has come; and Ahura Mazda answers, "In such case a *Kata* (ditch) should be made in every house and there the lifeless body should be allowed to lie for two nights, or for three nights, or for a month long, until the birds begin to fly, the plants to grow, the floods to flow, and the wind to dry up the water from off the earth." Considering the fact, that the dead body of a worshipper of Mazda is required to be exposed to the sun before it is consigned to birds, the only reason for keeping the dead body in the house for one month seems to be that it was a month of darkness. The description of birds beginning to fly, and the floods to flow, &c., reminds one of the description of the dawn in the Ṛig-Veda, and it is quite probable that the expressions here denote the same phenomenon as in the Ṛig-Veda. In fact they indicate a winter of total darkness during which the corpse is directed to be kept in the house, to be exposed to the sun on the first breaking of the dawn after the long night.[1] It will, however, be more convenient to discuss these passages, after examining the whole of the Vedic evidence in favour of the Arctic home. I have referred to them here to show the complete correspondence between the Hindu and the Parsi scriptures regarding the day and the night of the Gods, and their unmistakable Polar characteristics indicating the existence of an early home within the Arctic circle.

---

1. See *infra* Chapter IX.

The same traditions are also found in the literature of many other branches of the Aryan race, besides the Hindus and the Parsis. For instance, Dr. Warren quotes Greek traditions similar to those we have discussed above. Regarding the primitive revolution of the sky, Anaximenes, we are told, likened the motions of the heaven in early days to "the rotating of a man's hat on his head".[1] Another Greek writer is quoted to show that "at first the Pole-star always appeared in the zenith." It is also stated, on the authority of Anton Krichenbauer, that in the Iliad and Odyssey two kinds of days are continually referred to, one of a year's duration, especially when describing the life and exploits of the Gods, and the other of twenty-four hours. The night of the Gods has its parallel also in the Norse mythology, which mentions "the Twilight of the Gods," denoting by that phrase the time when the reign of Odin and the Æsir, or Gods, would come to an end, not forever, but to be again revived; for we are told that "from the dead sun springs a daughter more beautiful than her sire, and mankind starts afresh from the Life-raiser and his bride Life."[2] If these traditions and statements are correct, they show that the idea of half-yearly night and day of the Gods is not only Indo-Iranian, but Indo-Germanic, and that it must, therefore, have originated in the original home of the Aryans. Comparative mythology, it will be shown in a subsequent chapter, fully supports the view of an original Arctic home of the Aryan races, and there is nothing surprising if the traditions about a day and a night of six months are found not only in the Vedic and the Iranian, but also in the Greek and the Norse literature. It seems to have been an

1. See Paradise Found, 10th Ed., pp. 192 and 200.

2. See Cox's Mythology of the Aryan Nations, p. 41, quoting Brown's Religion and Mythology of the Aryans of the North of Europe, Arts. 15-17.

idea traditionally inherited by all the branches of the Aryan race, and, as it is distinctly Polar in character, it is alone enough to establish the existence of an Arctic home. But fortunately for us our edifice need not be erected on this solitary pillar, as there is ample evidence in the Vedic literature which supports the Arctic theory by satisfying almost all the Polar and Circum-Polar tests laid down in the last chapter. The long revolving dawn is another peculiar characteristic of the North Pole, and we shall see in the next chapter that the Ṛig-Vedic account of the dawn is intelligible only if we take it as referring to the Polar dawn.

CHAPTER V.

THE VEDIC DAWNS.

Dawn-hymns the most beautiful in the Rig-Veda —The Deity fully described, unobscured by personification —First hints about the long duration of dawn —Recitation of a thousand verses, or even the whole Rig-Veda, while the dawn lasts —Three or five-fold division of the dawn —Both imply a long dawn —The same inferred from the two words *Ushas* and *Vyushti* —Three Rig-Vedic passages about long dawns, hitherto misunderstood, discussed —Long interval of several days between the first appearance of light and sunrise —Expressly mentioned in the Rig-Veda, VII, 76, 3 —Sâyana's explanation artificial and unsatisfactory —Existence of many dawns before sunrise —Reason why dawn is addressed in the plural in the Rig-Veda —The plural address not honorific —Nor denotes dawns of consecutive days —Proves a team of continuous dawns —The last view confirmed by the Taittirîya Samhitâ, IV, 3, 11 —Dawns as 30 sisters —Direct authority from the Taittirîya Brâhmana for holding that they were continuous or unseparated —Sâyana's explanation of 30 dawns examined —Thirty dawns described as thirty steps of a single dawn—Rotatory motion of the dawn, like a wheel, directly mentioned in the Rig-Veda —Their reaching the same appointed place day by day —All indicate a team of thirty closely-gathered dawns —Results summed up —Establish the Polar character of the Vedic dawns —Possible variation in the duration of the Vedic dawn —The legend of Indra shattering the Dawn's car explained —Direct passages showing that the dawns so described were the events of a former age —The Vedic Dawns Polar in character.

The Ṛig-Veda, we have seen, does not contain distinct references to a day and a night of six months' duration, though the deficiency is more than made up by parallel passages from the Iranian scriptures. But in the case of the dawn, the long continuous dawn with its revolving splendours, which is the special characteristic of the North

Pole, there is fortunately no such difficulty. Ushas, or the Goddess of Dawn, is an important and favourite Vedic deity, and is celebrated in about twenty hymns of the Ṛig-Veda, and mentioned more than three hundred times, sometimes in the singular and sometimes in the plural. These hymns, according to Muir, are amongst the most beautiful,—if not the most beautiful,—in the entire collection ; and the deity, to which they are addressed, is considered by Macdonell to be the most graceful creation of Vedic poetry, there being no more charming figure in the descriptive religious lyrics of any other literature.[1] In short, Ushas, or the Goddess of Dawn, is described in the Ṛig-Veda hymns with more than usual fulness, and what is still more important for our purpose is that the physical character of the deity is not, in the least, obscured by the description or the personification in the hymns. Here, therefore, we have a fine opportunity of proving the validity of our theory, by showing, if possible, that the oldest description of the dawn is really Polar in character. *A priori* it does not look probable that the Vedic poets could have gone into such raptures over the short-lived dawn of the tropical or the temperate zone, or that so much anxiety about the coming dawn should have been evinced, simply because the Vedic bards had no electric light or candles to use during the short night of less than 24 hours. But the dawn-hymns have not, as yet, been examined from this stand-point. It seems to have been tacitly assumed by all interpreters of the Vedas, Eastern and Western, that the Ushas of the Ṛig-Veda can be no other than the dawn with which we are familiar in the tropical or the temperate zone. That Yâska and Sâyaṇa thought so is natural enough, but even the Western scholars have taken the same view, probably

1. See Muir's Original Sanskrit Texts, Vol. V, p. 181 ; and Macdonell's Vedic Mythology, p. 46.

under the influence of the theory that the plateau of Central Asia was the original home of the Aryan race. Therefore several expressions in the dawn-hymns, which would have otherwise suggested the inquiry regarding the physical or the astronomical character of the Vedic dawn, have been either ignored, or some-how explained away, by scholars, who could certainly have thrown more light on the subject, had they not been under the influence of the assumption mentioned above. It is with passages like these that we are here chiefly concerned, and we shall presently see that if these are interpreted in a natural way, they fully establish the Polar nature of the Vedic dawn.

The first hint, regarding the long duration of the Vedic dawn, is obtained from the Aitareya Brâhmaṇa, IV, 7. Before commencing the *Gavâm-ayana* sacrifice, there is a long recitation of not less than a thousand verses, to be recited by the Hotṛi priest. This *Ashvina-shastra*, as it is called, is addressed to Agni, Uṣhas and Ashvins, which deities rule at the end of the night and the commencement of the day. It is the longest recitation to be recited by the Hotṛi, and the time for reciting it is after midnight, when "the darkness of the night is about to be relieved by the light of the dawn," (Nir. XII, 1; Ashv. Shr. Sûtra, VI, 5, 8).[1] The same period of time is referred to also in the Ṛig-Veda, VII, 67, 2 and 3. The *shastra* is so long, that the Hotṛi, who has to recite it, is directed to refresh himself by drinking beforehand melted butter after sacrificing thrice a little of it, (Ait. Br. IV, 7; Ashv. Shr. Sutra, VI, 5, 3). "He ought to eat gheė," observes the Aitareya Brâhmaṇa, "before he commences repeating. Just as in this world a cart or a carriage goes well if smeared (with oil),[2] thus his repeating proceeds well if he be smear-

1. Nir. XII, 1,—तयोः काल ऊर्ध्वमर्धरात्रात्प्रकाशीभावस्यानुविष्टंभम् ।
2. See Haug's Translation of Ait. Br., p. 270.

ed with ghee (by eating it)." It is evident that if such a recitation has to be finished before the rising of the sun, either the Hotṛi must commence his task soon after midnight when it is dark, or the duration of the dawn must then have been sufficiently long to enable the priest to finish the recitation in time, after commencing to recite it on the first appearance of light on the horizon as directed. The first supposition is out of question, as it is expressly laid down that the *shastra* is not to be recited until the darkness of the night is relieved by light. So between the first appearance of light and the rise of the sun, there must have been, in those days, time enough to recite the long laudatory song of not less than a thousand verses. Nay, in the Taittirîya Saṁhitâ (II, 1, 10, 3) we are told that sometimes the recitation of the *shastra*, though commenced at the proper time, ended long before sunrise, and in that case, the Saṁhitâ requires that a certain animal sacrifice should be performed. Ashvalâyana directs that in such a case the recitation should be continued upto sunrise by reciting other hymns (Ashv. S. S. VI, 5, 8); while Âpastamba, (S. S. XIV, 1 and 2), after mentioning the sacrifice referred to in the Taittirîya Saṁhitâ, adds that all the ten Maṇḍalas of the Ṛig-Veda may be recited, if necessary, in such a case.[1] It is evident from this that the actual rising of the sun above the horizon was a phenomenon often delayed beyond expectation, in those days; and in several places in the Taittirîya Saṁhitâ, (II, 1, 2, 4),[2] we are told that

---

1. The Sûtras referred to are as follows:—Ashv. S. S. VI, 5, 8, प्रातरनुवाकन्यायेन तस्यैव समाम्नायस्य सहस्रावममोदेतोः शंसेत् । Âpastamba XIV, 1 & 2—यस्याश्विने शस्यमाने सूर्यो नाविर्भवति सौर्यं बहुरूपमालभेत ॥ १ ॥ सर्वा अपि दाशतयीरनुब्रूयात् ॥ २ ॥ The first of these two Sûtras is the reproduction of T. S. II, 1, 10, 3.

2. T. S. II, 1, 2, 4,—असावादित्यो न व्यरोचत तस्मै देवाः प्रायश्चित्तिमैच्छन् । Cf. also T. S. II, 1, 4, 1.

the Devas had to perform a *prâyaschitta* because the sun did not shine as expected.

Another indication of the long duration of the dawn is furnished by the Taittirîya Saṁhitâ, VII, 2, 20.[1] Seven oblations are here mentioned, one to *Ushas*, one to *Vyushṭi*, one to *Udeshyat*, one to *Udyat*, one to *Uditâ*, one to *Suvarga* and one to *Loka*. Five of these are evidently intended for the dawn in its five forms. The Taittirîya Brâhmaṇa (III, 8, 16, 4) explains the first two, *viz.*, to *Ushas* and *Vyushṭi*, as referring to dawn and sunrise, or rather to night and day, for according to the Brâhmaṇa, "*Ushas* is night, and *Vyushṭi* is day."[2] But even though we may accept this as correct, and take *Ushas* and *Vyushṭi* to be the representatives of night and day, because the former signalises the end of the night and the latter the beginning of the day, still we have to account for three oblations, *viz.*, one to the dawn about to rise (*Udeshyat*), one to the rising dawn (*Udyat*), and one to the dawn that has risen (*Uditâ*), the first two of which are, according to the Taittirîya Brâhmaṇa, to be offered before the rising of the sun. Now the dawn in the tropical zone is so short that the three-fold distinction between the dawn that is about to rise, the dawn that is rising, and one that has risen or that is full-blown (*vi-ushṭi*), is a distinction without a difference. We must, therefore, hold that the dawn, which admitted such manifold division for the practical purpose of sacrifice, was a long dawn.

---

1. T. S. VII, 2, 20,—उषसे स्वाहा व्युष्ट्यै स्वाहोदेष्यते स्वाहोद्यते स्वाहोदिताय स्वाहा सुवर्गाय स्वाहा लोकाय स्वाहा ।

2. Tait. Br. III, 8, 16, 4, explains the above passage as follows .—उषसे स्वाहा व्युष्ट्यै स्वाहेत्याह । रात्रिर्वा उषाः । अहर्व्युष्टिः । अहोरात्रे एवावरुन्धे । अथो अहोरात्रयोरेव प्रतितिष्ठति । स यद्युभयीर्दिवा वा नक्तं वा जुहुयात् अहोरात्रे मोहयेत् । उषसे स्वाहा व्युष्ट्यै स्वाहोदेष्यते स्वाहोद्यते स्वाहेत्यनुदिते जुहोति । उदिताय स्वाहा सुवर्गाय स्वाहा लोकाय स्वाहेत्युदिते जुहोति ।

The three-fold division of the dawn does not seem to be unknown to the poets of the Ṛig-Veda. For, in VIII, 41, 3, Varuṇa's "dear ones are said to have prospered the three dawns for him,"[1] and by the phrase *tisraḥ dânuchitrâḥ* in I, 174, 7, 'three due-lighted' dawns appear to be referred to. There are other passages in the Ṛig-Veda[2] where the dawn is asked not to delay, or tarry long, lest it might be scorched like a thief by the sun (V, 79, 9); and in II, 15, 6, the steeds of the dawn are said to be 'slow' (*ajavasaḥ*), showing that the people were sometimes tired to see the dawn lingering long on the horizon. But a still more remarkable statement is found in I, 113, 13, where the poet distinctly asserts,[3] "the Goddess Uṣhas dawned continually or perpetually (*shasvat*) in former days (*purâ*);" and the adjective *shashvat-tamâ* (the most lasting) is applied to the dawn in I, 118, 11. Again the very existence and use of two such words as *uṣhas* and *vi-uṣhṭi* is, by itself, a proof of the long duration of the dawn; for, if the dawn was brief, there was no practical necessity of speaking of the full-blown state (*vi + uṣhṭi*) of the dawn as has been done several times in the Ṛig-Veda. The expression, *uṣhasaḥ vi-uṣhṭau*, occurs very often in the Ṛig-Veda, and it has been translated by the phrase, "on the flashing forth of the dawn." But no one seems to have raised the question why two separate words, one of which is derived from the other simply by prefixing the preposition *vi*, should be used in this connection. Words are made to denote ideas, and if *uṣhas* and *vi-uṣhṭi* were not required to denote two distinct phenomena, no one, espe-

1. Ṛig. VIII, 41, 3,—स क्षपः परि षस्वजे...तस्य वेनीरनु व्रतमुषस्तिस्रो अवर्धयन् ।

2. Ṛig. V, 79, 9,—व्युच्छा दुहितर्दिवो मा चिरं तनुथा अपः । नेत्त्वा स्तेनं यथा रिपुं तपाति सूरो अर्चिषा ।

3. Ṛig. I, 113, 13,—शश्वत्पुरोषा व्युवास देवी ।

cially in those early days, would have cared to use a phrase, which, for all ordinary purposes, was superfluously cumbrous. But these facts, howsoever suggestive, may not be regarded as conclusive, and we shall, therefore, now turn to the more explicit passages in the hymns regarding the duration of the Vedic dawn.

The first verse I would quote in this connection is Ṛig-Veda I, 113, 10:—[1]

Kiyâti â yat samayâ bhavâti
yâ vyûṣhur yâsh cha nûnaṁ vyuchhân ।
Anu pûrvâḥ kṛipate vâvashânâ
pradîdhyânâ joṣham anyâbhir eti ॥

The first quarter of the verse is rather difficult. The words are *kiyâti â yat samayâ bhavâti*, and Sâyaṇa, whom Wilson follows, understands *samayâ* to mean 'near.' Prof. Max Muller translates *samayâ* (Gr. *Omos*, Lat. *Simul*,) by 'together,' 'at once'; while Roth, Grassmann and Aufrecht take *samayâ bhavâti* as one expression meaning 'that which intervenes between the two.'[2] This has given rise to three different translations of the verse :—

WILSON, (following Sâyaṇa) :—For how long a period is it that the dawns have arisen? For how long a period will they rise? Still desirous to bring us light, Uṣhas pursues the functions of those that have gone before, and, shining brightly, proceeds with the others (that are to follow).

GRIFFITH, (following Max Muller):—How long a time, and they shall be together,—Dawns that have shone and Dawns to shine hereafter? She yearns for former Dawns with eager longing, and goes forth gladly shining with the others.

---

1. Ṛig. I, 113, 10,—कियात्या यत्समया भवाति या व्यूषुर्याश्च नूनं व्युच्छान् । अनु पूर्वाः कृपते वावशाना प्रदीध्याना जोषमन्याभिरेति ॥

2. See Petersberg Lexicon, and Grassmann's Worterbuch, s. v. *Samayâ*; and Muir's O. S. Texts, Vol. V., p. 189.

MUIR, (following Aufrecht) :—How great is the interval that lies between the Dawns which have arisen, and those which are yet to rise? Uṣhas yearns longingly after the former Dawns, and gladly goes on shining with the others (that are to come).

But in spite of these different renderings, the meaning of the verse, so far as the question before us is concerned, can be easily gathered. There are two sets of dawns, one of those that have past, and the other of those that are yet to shine. If we adopt Wilson's and Griffith's translations, the meaning is that these two classes of dawns, taken together, occupy such a long period of time as to raise the question,—How long they will be together? In other words, the two classes of dawns, taken together, were of such a long duration that men began to question as to when they would teminate, or pass away. If, on the other hand, we adopt Aufrecht's translation, a long period appears to have intervened between the past and the coming dawns; or, in other words, there was a long break or hiatus in the regular sequence of these dawns. In the first case, the description is only possible if we suppose that the duration of the dawns was very long, much longer than what we see in the temperate or the tropical zone; while in the second, a long interval between the past and the present dawns must be taken to refer to a long pause, or night, occurring immediately before the second set of dawns commenced their new course,—a phenomenon which is possible only in the Arctic regions. Thus whichever interpretation we adopt—a long dawn, or a long night between the two sets of dawns,—the description is intelligible, only if we take it to refer to the Polar conditions previously mentioned. The Vedic passages, discussed hereafter, seem, however, to support Sâyaṇa's or Max Muller's view. A number of dawns is spoken of, some past and some yet to come; and the two groups are said to occupy a very long interval. That seems to be the real meaning of the verse. But without laying much stress on any particular meaning for the present, it is enough for our purpose to show that, even adopting Aufrecht's rendering, we cannot escape from the necessity of making the description refer to the Polar conditions. The verse in question is the tenth in the hymn, and it may be noticed that in the 13th verse of the same hymn we are told that "in former days, perpetually (*shashvat*) did the Goddess Uṣhas shine," clearly indicating that the Dawn, in early days, lasted for a long time.

The following verse is, however, still more explicit, and decisive on the point. The seventh Maṇḍala of the Ṛig-Veda contains a number of dawn-hymns. In one of these (VII, 76), the poet, after stating in the first two verses that the Dawns have raised their banner on the horizon with their usual splendour, expressly tells us, (verse 3), that a period of *several days* elapsed between the first appearance of the dawn on the horizon and the actual rising of the sun that followed it. As the verse[1] is very important for our purpose, I give below the *Pada* text with an interlineal word for word translation :—

Tâni	*it*	*ahâni*	*bahulâni*	*âsan*
Those	verily	days	many	were
yâ	*prâchînam*	*ud-itâ*	*sûryasya* ।	
which	aforetime	on the uprising	of the sun	
Yataḥ	*pari*	*jâre-iva*	*â-charantî*	
from which	after	towards a lover, like	moving on	
Uṣhaḥ	*dadṛikṣhe*	*na*	*punaḥ*	*yatî-iva* ॥
O Dawn!	wast seen	not	again	forsaking (woman), like

I have followed Sâyaṇa in splitting *jâra-iva* of the *Saṁhitâ* text into *jâre+iva*, and not *jâraḥ+iva* as Shâkala

1. Ṛig. VII, 76, 3,—तानीदहानि बहुलान्यासन् या प्राचीनमुदिता सूर्यस्य। यतः परि जार इवाचरंत्युषो ददृक्षे न पुनर्यतीव ॥

has done in the *Pada* text; for *jâre+iva* makes the simile more appropriate than if we were to compare *ushas* with *jârah*. Literally rendered the verse, therefore, means, "Verily, many were those *days*, which were aforetime at the uprising of the sun, and about which, O Dawn! thou wast seen moving on, as towards a lover, and not like one (woman) who forsakes." I take *pari* with *yatah*, meaning that the dawn goes *after* the days. *Yatah pari*, thus construed, means 'after which,' or 'about which.' Sâyaṇa takes *pari* with *dadṛikshe*, and Griffith renders *yatah* by 'since.' But these constructions do not materially alter the meaning of the second half of the verse, though taking *pari* with *yatah* enables us to take the second line as an adjectival clause, rendering the meaning more plain. In IV, 52, 1, the Dawn is said to shine after her sister (*svasuh pari*), and *pari*, with an ablative, does not necessarily denote 'from' in every case, but is used in various senses, as, for instance, in III, 5, 10, where the phrase *Bhṛigubhyah pari* occurs, and is rendered by Grassmann as equivalent to 'for the sake of Bhṛigus,' while Sâyaṇa paraphrases *pari* by *paritah* 'round about.' In the verse under consideration we can, therefore, take *pari* with *yatah*, and understand the expression as meaning 'after, about or around which (days).' It must also be borne in mind that there must be an expression to correspond with *jâre* in the simile, and this we get only if we construe *yatah pari* in the way proposed above. If we now analyse the verse it will be found to be made up of three clauses, one principal and two adjectival. The principal statement asserts that those days were many. The demonstrative 'those' (*tâni*) is then followed by two relative clauses, *yâ prâchînam* &c., and *yatah pari* &c. The first of these states that the days referred to in the principal clause were those that '*preceded* the rising of the sun.' But if the days preceded the rising of the sun, one might think that they were pervaded with darkness. The poet, therefore, further adds, in the second relative clause, that though these days were anterior to the rising of the sun, yet they were such that 'the Dawn was seen to move after or about them as after a lover, and not like a woman who forsakes.' In short, the verse states in unmistakable terms (1) that *many days* (*bahulâni ahâni*) passed between the appearance of the first morning beams and sunrise, and (2) that these days were faithfully attended by the Dawn, meaning that the whole period was one of *continuous* Dawn which never vanished during the time. The words as they stand convey no other meaning but this, and we have now to see how far it is intelligible to us.

To the commentators the verse is a perfect puzzle. Thus Sâyaṇa does not understand how the word 'days' (*ahâni*) can be applied to a period of time anterior to sunrise; for, says he, "The word day (*ahaḥ*) is used only to denote such a period of time as is invested with the light of the Dawn."[1] Then, again, he is obviously at a loss to understand how a number of days can be said to have elapsed between the first beams of the dawn and sunrise. These were serious difficulties for Sâyaṇa, and the only way to get over them was to force an unnatural sense upon the words, and make them yield some intelligible meaning. This was no difficult task for Sâyaṇa. The word *ahâni*, which means 'days,' was the only stumbling block in his way, and instead of taking it in the sense in which it is ordinarily used, without exception, everywhere in the Ṛig-Veda, he went back to its root-meaning, and interpreted it as equivalent to 'light' or 'splendour.' *Ahan* is derived from the root *ah* (or philologically *dah*), 'to burn,' or 'shine,' and *Ahanâ* meaning 'dawn' is derived from the same root. Ety-

1. उषःप्रकाशयुक्तस्यैव कालस्याहःशब्दव्यवहारात् ।

mologically *ahâni* may, therefore, mean splendours; but the question is whether it is so used anywhere, and why we should here give up the ordinary meaning of the word. Sâyaṇa's answer is given above. It is because the word 'day' (*ahan*) can, according to him, be applied only to a period after sunrise and before sunset. But this reasoning is not sound, because in the Ṛig-Veda, VI, 9, 1, *ahaḥ* is applied to the dark as well as to the bright period of time, for the verse says, "There is a dark day (*ahaḥ*)' and a bright day (*ahaḥ*)." This shows that the Vedic poets were in the habit of using the word *ahaḥ* (day) to denote a period of time devoid of the light of the sun.[1] Sâyaṇa knew this, and in his commentary on I, 185, 4, he expressly says that the word *ahaḥ* may include night. His real difficulty was different, *viz*., the impossibility of supposing that a period of several days could have elapsed between the first appearance of light and sunrise, and this difficulty seems to have been experienced even by Western scholars. Thus Prof. Ludwig materially adopts Sâyaṇa's view and interprets the verse to mean that the splendours of the dawn were numerous, and that they appear either before sunrise, or, if *prâchînam* be differently interpreted, 'in the east' at the rising of the sun. Roth and Grassmann seem to interpret *prâchînam* in the same way. Griffith translates *ahâni* by 'mornings' and *prâchînam* by 'aforetime.' His rendering of the verse runs thus:—"Great is, in truth, the number of the mornings, which were aforetime at the sun's uprising; since thou, O Dawn, hast been beheld repairing as to thy love, as one no more to leave him." But Griffith does not ex-

1. Ṛig. VI. 9, 1,—अहश्च कृष्णमहरर्जुनं च वि वर्तेते रजसी वेद्याभिः। Also cf. T. S. III, 3, 4, 1,—एतद्वा अह्नो रूपं यद्रात्रिः। Similarly in T. S. VI, 3, 9, 1, the phrase द्यमहोभ्याम् (I, 3, 9, 1) is thus explained :—द्यमहोभ्यामिति दिनवत्स्वहोरात्राभ्यामेव।

plain what he understands by the expression, "a number of mornings which were aforetime at the sun's uprising."

The case is, therefore, reduced to this. The word *ahan*, of which *ahâni* (days) is a plural form, can be ordinarily interpreted to mean (1) a period of time between sunrise and sunset; (2) a nycthemeron, as when we speak of 360 days of the year; or (3) a measure of time to mark a period of 24 hours, irrespective of the fact whether the sun is above or below the horizon, as when we speak of the long Arctic night of 30 days. Are we then to abandon all these meanings, and understand *ahâni* to mean 'splendours' in the verse under consideration? The only difficulty is to account for the interval of many days between the appearance of the banner of the Dawn on the horizon and the emergence of the sun's orb over it; and this difficulty vanishes if the description be taken to refer to the dawn in the Polar or Circum-Polar regions. That is the real key to the meaning of this and similar other passages, which will be noted hereafter; and in its absence a number of artificial devices have been made use of to make these passages somehow intelligible to us. But now nothing of the kind is necessary. As regards the word 'days,' it has been observed that we often speak 'a night of several days,' or 'a night of several months' when describing the Polar phenomena. In expressions like these the word 'day' or 'month' simply denotes a measure of time, equivalent to 'twenty-four hours,' or 'thirty days;' and there is nothing unusual in the exclamation of the Ṛig-Vedic poet that "many were the days between the first beams of the dawn and actual sunrise." We have also seen that, at the Pole, it is quite possible to mark the periods of twenty-four hours by the rotations of the celestial sphere or the circum-polar stars, and these could be or rather must have been termed 'days' by the inhabitants of the place. In the first chapter of the Old Testament we are told that God created the heaven and the earth and also light "on the first day;" while the sun was created on the fourth "to divide the day from the night and to rule the day." Here the word 'day' is used to denote a period of time even before the sun was created; and, *a fortiori*, there can be no impropriety in using it to denote a period of time before sunrise. We need not, therefore, affect a hypercritical spirit in examining the Vedic expression in question. If Sâyaṇa did it, it was because he did not know as much about the Polar regions as we now do. We have no such excuse, and must, therefore, accept the meaning which follows from the natural construction and reading of the sentence.

It is therefore clear that the verse in question (VII, 76, 3) expressly describes a dawn continuously lasting for many days, which is possible only in the Arctic regions. I have discussed the passage at so much length because the history of its interpretation clearly shows how certain passages in the Ṛig-Veda, which are unintelligible to us in spite of their simple diction, have been treated by commentators, who know not what to make of them if read in a natural way. But to proceed with the subject in hand, we have seen that the Polar dawn could be divided into periods of 24 hours owing to the circuits it makes round the horizon. In such a case we can very well speak of these divisions as so many day-long dawns of 24 hours each, and state that so many of them are past and so many are yet to come, as has been done in the verse (I, 113, 10) discussed above. We may also say that so many day-long dawns have passed, and yet the sun has not risen, as in II, 28, 9, a verse addressed to Varuṇa, wherein the poet asks for the following boon from the deity :—

Para ṛiṇâ sâvir adha mat-kṛitâni
mâ aham râjan anya-kṛitena bhojam ।
Avyushṭâ in nu bhûyasîr ushâsa
â no jivân Varuṇa tâsu shâdhi ॥

Literally translated this means "Remove far the debts (sins) incurred by me. May I not, O King! be affected by others' doings. Verily, many dawns (have) not fully (*vi*) flashed forth. O Varuṇa! direct that we may be alive during them."[1] The first part of this verse contains a prayer usually addressed to Gods, and we have nothing to say with respect to it, so far as the subject in hand is concerned. The only expression necessary to be discussed is *bhûyasîh ushâsaḥ avyushṭâḥ* in the third quarter of the verse. The first two words present no difficulty. They mean 'many dawns.' Now *avyushṭa* is a negative participle from *vyushṭa*, which again is derived from *ushṭa* with *vi* prefixed. I have referred to the distinction between *ushas* and *vyushṭi* suggested by the three-fold or the five-fold division of the dawn. *Vyushṭi*, according to the Taittirîya Brâhmaṇa, means 'day,' or rather 'the flashing forth of the dawn into sunrise'; and the word *a + vi + ushṭa*, therefore, means "not-fully-flashed-forth into sunrise." But Sâyaṇa and others do not seem to have kept in view this distinction between the meanings of *ushas* and *vyushṭi*; or if they did, they did not know or had not in their mind the phenomenon of the long continuous dawn in the Arctic regions, a dawn, that lasted for several day-long periods of time before the sun's orb appeared on the horizon. The expression, *bhûyasîh ushâsaḥ avyushṭâḥ*, which literally means "many dawns have not dawned, or fully flashed forth," was, therefore, a riddle to these commentators. Every dawn, they saw, was followed by sunrise; and

1. Ṛig. II, 28, 9,—पर ऋणा सावीरध मत्कृतानि माहं राजन्नन्यकृतेन भोजम्। अव्युष्टा इन्नु भूयसीरुषास आ नो जीवान्वरुण तासु शाधि ॥

they could not, therefore, understand how 'many dawns' could be described as "not-fully-flashed-forth." An explanation was thus felt to be a necessity, and this was obtained by converting, in sense, the past passive participle *avyushṭa* into a future participle; and the expression in question was translated as meaning, "during the dawns (or days) that have not *yet* dawned," or, in other words, "in days to come." But the interpretation is on the face of it strained and artificial. If future days were intended, the idea could have been more easily and briefly expressed. The poet is evidently speaking of things present, and, taking *vi-ushṭa* to denote what it literally signifies, we can easily and naturally interpret the expression to mean that though *many* dawns, meaning *many* day-long portions of time during which the dawn lasted, have passed, yet it is not *vyushṭa*, that is, the sun's orb has not yet emerged from below the horizon, and that Varuṇa should protect the worshipper under the circumstances.

There are many other expressions in the Ṛig-Veda which further strengthen the same view. Thus corresponding to *bhûyasîḥ* in the above passage, we have the adjective *pûrvîḥ* (many) used in IV, 19, 8 and VI, 28, 1, to denote the number of the dawns, evidently shewing that numerically more than one dawn is intended. The dawns are again not unfrequently addressed in the plural number in the Ṛig-Veda, and the fact is well-known to all Vedic scholars. Thus in I, 92, which is a dawn-hymn, the bard opens his song with the characteristically emphatic exclamation, "these (*etâḥ*) are those (*tyâḥ*) dawns (*ushasaḥ*), which have made their appearance on the horizon," and the same expression again occurs in VII, 78, 3. Yâska explains the plural number *ushasaḥ* by considering it to be used only honorifically (Nirukta XII, 7); while Sâyaṇa interprets it as referring to the number of divinities that preside over the morn. The Western scholars have not made any improvement on these explanations; and Prof. Max Muller is simply content with observing that the Vedic bards, when speaking of the dawn, did sometimes use the plural just as we would use the singular number! But a little reflection will show that neither of these explanations is satisfactory. If the plural is honorific why is it changed into singular only a few lines after in the same hymn? Surely the poet does not mean to address the Dawn respectfully only at the outset, and then change his manner of address and assume a familiar tone. This is not, however, the only objection to Yâska's explanation. Various similes are used by the Vedic poets to describe the appearance of the Dawns on the horizon, and an examination of these similes will convince any one that the plural number, used in reference to the Dawn, cannot be merely honorific. Thus in the second line of I, 92, 1, the Dawns are compared to a number of 'warriors' (*dhṛishṇavaḥ*), and in the third verse of the same hymn they are likened to 'women (*nârîḥ*) active in their occupations.' They are said to appear on the horizon like 'waves of waters' (*apâm na urmayaḥ*) in VI, 64, 1; or like 'pillars planted at a sacrifice' (*adhvareṣhu svaravaḥ*) in IV, 51, 2. We are again told that they work like 'men arrayed' (*visho na yuktâḥ*), or advance like 'troops of cattle' (*gavâm na sargâḥ*), in VII, 79, 2, and IV, 51, 8, respectively. They are described as all 'alike' (*sadṛishîḥ*); and are said to be of 'one mind' (*sañjânante*), or 'acting harmoniously' in IV, 51, 6, and VII, 76, 5. In the last verse the poet again informs us that they 'do not strive against each other' (*mithah na yatante*), though they live jointly in the 'same enclosure' (*samâne urve*). Finally in X, 88, 18, the poet distinctly asks the question, "How many fires, how many suns and how many dawns (*ushâsaḥ*) are there?" If the Dawn were addressed in plural simply out of respect for the deity, where was the necessity of informing us that they do not quarrel though collected in the same place? The expressions 'waves of waters,' or 'men arrayed' &c., are again too definite to be explained away as honorific. Sâyaṇa seems to have perceived this difficulty, and has, probably for the same reason, proposed an explanation slightly different from that of Yâska. But, unfortunately, Sâyaṇa's explanation does not solve the difficulty, as the question still remains, why the deities presiding over the dawn should be more than one in number. The only other explanation put forward, so far as I know, is that the plural number refers to the dawns on successive days during the year, as we perceive them in the temperate or the tropical zone. On this theory there would be 360 dawns in a year, each followed by the rising of the sun every day. This explanation may appear plausible at the first sight. But on a closer examination it will be found that the expressions used in the hymns cannot be made to reconcile with this theory. For, if 360 dawns, all separated by intervals of 24 hours, were intended by the plural number used in the Vedic verses, no poet, with any propriety, would speak of them, as he does in I, 92, 1, by using the double pronoun *etâḥ* and *tyâḥ*, as if he was pointing out to a physical phenomenon before him; nor can we understand how 360 dawns, spread over the whole year, can be described as advancing like 'men arrayed' for battle. It is again absurd to describe the 360 dawns of the year as being collected in the 'same enclosure' and 'not striving against or quarrelling with each other.' We are thus forced to the conclusion that the Ṛig-Veda speaks of a team, or a group of dawns, unbroken or uninterrupted by sunlight, so that, if we be so minded, we can regard them as constituting a single long continuous dawn. This is in perfect accord with the statement discussed above, *viz.*, that many days passed between the first appearance of light on the horizon and the uprising of the sun (VII, 76, 3). We cannot, therefore, accept the explanation of consecutive dawns, nor that of Yâska, nor of Sâyaṇa regarding the use of the plural number in this case. The fact is that the Vedic dawn represents one long physical phenomenon which can be spoken of in plural by supposing it to be split up into smaller day-long portions. It is thus that we find Ushas addressed sometimes in the plural, and sometimes in the singular number. There is no other explanation on which we can account for and explain the various descriptions of the dawn found in the different hymns.

But to clinch the matter, the Taittirîya Saṁhitâ, IV, 3, 11, expressly states that the dawns are thirty sisters, or, in other words, they are thirty in number, and that they go round and round in five groups, reaching the same appointed place and having the same banner for all. The whole of this *Anuvâka* may be said to be practically a dawn-hymn of 15 verses, which are used as Mantras for the laying down of certain emblematical bricks called the 'dawn-bricks' on the sacrificial altar. There are sixteen such bricks to be placed on the altar, and the *Anuvâka* in question gives 15 Mantras, or verses, to be used on the occasion, the 16th being recorded elsewhere. These 15 verses, together with their *Brâhmaṇa* (T. S., V, 3, 4, 7), are so important for our purpose that I have appended to this chapter the original passages, with their translation, comparing the version in the Taittirîya Saṁhitâ with that of the Atharva-Veda, in the case of those verses which are found in the latter. The first verse of the section or the *Anuvâka*, is used for laying down the first dawn-brick, and it speaks only of a single dawn first appearing on the horizon. In the second verse we have, however, a couple of dawns mentioned as 'dwelling in the same abode.' A third dawn is spoken in the third verse, followed by the fourth and the fifth dawn. The five dawns are then said to have five sisters each, exclusive of themselves, thus raising the total number of dawns to thirty. These 'thirty sisters' (*triṁshat svasârah*) are then described as 'going round' (*parî yanti*) in groups of six each, keeping up to the same goal (*nishkṛitam*). Two verses later on, the worshipper asks that he and his followers should be blessed with the same concord as is observed amongst these dawns. We are then told that one of these five principal dawns is the child of *Ṛita*, the second upholds the greatness of Waters, the third moves in the region of Sûrya, the fourth in that of Fire or Gharma, and the fifth is ruled by Savitṛi, evidently showing that the dawns are not the dawns of consecutive days. The last verse of the *Anuvâka* sums up the description by stating that the dawn, though it shines forth in various forms, is but *one* in reality. Throughout the whole *Anuvâka* there is no mention of the rising of the sun or the appearance of sun-light, and the *Brâhmaṇa* makes the point clear by stating "There was a time, when all this was neither day nor night, being in an undistinguishable state. It was *then* that the Gods perceived these dawns and laid them down, *then* there was light; therefore, it brightens to him and destroys his darkness for whom these (dawn-bricks) are placed." The object of this passage is to explain how and why the dawn-bricks came to be laid down with these Mantras, and it gives the ancient story of thirty dawns being perceived by the Gods, not on consecutive days, but during the period of time when it was neither night nor day. This, joined with the express statement at the end of the *Anuvâka* that in reality it is but one dawn, is sufficient to prove that the thirty dawns mentioned in the *Anuvâka* were continuous and not consecutive. But, if a still more explicit authority be needed it will be found in the Taittirîya Brâhmaṇa, II, 5, 6, 5. This is an old Mantra, and not a portion of the explanatory *Brâhmaṇa*, and is, therefore, as good an authority as any of the verses quoted above. It is addressed to the Dawns and means "These very Dawns are those that first shone forth, the Goddesses make five forms; eternal (*shashvatiḥ*), (they) are not separated (*na avapṛijyanti*), nor do (they) terminate (*na gamanti antam*)."[1] The 'five forms' here referred to correspond with the division of 30 dawns into 5 groups of 6 each, made in the Taittirîya Saṁhitâ, after the manner of sacrificial *shaḷ-ahas*, or groups of six days; and we are expressly told that the dawns, which make these 5 forms, are continuous, unseparated, or uninterrupted. In the Ṛig-Veda I, 152, 4, the garment of the lover of the dawns (*lit.* the maidens, *kanînâm jâram*) is described as 'inseparable' and 'wide' (*an-avapṛigṇa* and *vitata*), and reading this in the light of the aforesaid Mantra from the Taittirîya Brâhmaṇa we are led to conclude that in the Ṛig-Veda itself the dawny garment of the sun, or the garment, which the dawns, as mothers, weave for him (cf. V, 47, 6), is considered as 'wide' and 'continuous.' Translated into common language this means that the dawn described in the Ṛig-Veda was a long and continuous phenomenon. In the Atharva-Veda (VII, 22, 2) the dawns are described as *sachetasaḥ* and *samichiḥ*, which means that they are 'harmonious' and 'walk together' and not separately. The first expression is found in the Ṛig-Veda, but not the second, though it could be easily inferred, from the fact that the dawns are there described as "collected in the same enclosure." Griffith renders *samichiḥ* by 'a closely gathered band' and translates the verse thus:—"The Bright one hath

1. Taitt. Br. II, 5, 6, 5,—इमा एव ता उषसो या प्रथमा व्यौच्छन्। ता देव्यः कुर्वते पंच रूपा। शश्वतीर्नावपृज्यंति न गमन्त्यन्तम्॥

sent forth the Dawns, a closely gathered band, immaculate, unanimous, brightly refulgent in their homes."[1] Here all the adjectives of the dawns clearly indicate a group of undivided dawns acting harmoniously; and yet, strange to say, Griffith, who translates correctly, misses the spirit altogether. We have thus sufficient direct authority for holding that it is a 'team,' or, in Griffith's words, 'a closely gathered band' of thirty continuous dawns that is described in the Vedic hymns, and not the evanescent dawn of the temperate or the tropical zone, either single or as a series of consecutive dawns.

It is interesting to examine how Sâyaṇa explains the existence of as many as thirty dawns, before we proceed to other authorities. In his commentary on the Taittirîya Saṁhitâ IV, 3, 11, he tells us that the first dawn spoken of in the first verse in the *Anuvâka*, is the dawn at the beginning of the creation, when every thing was undistinguishable according to the *Brâhmaṇa*. The second dawn in the second verse is said to be the ordinary dawn that we see every day. So far it was all right; but the number of dawns soon outgrew the number of the kinds of dawn known to Sâyaṇa. The third, fourth and fifth verses of the *Anuvâka* describe three more dawns, and Sâyaṇa was at last forced to explain that though the dawn was one yet by its Yogic or occult powers it assumed these various shapes! But the five dawns multiplied into thirty sisters in the next verse, and Sâyaṇa finally adopted the explanation that thirty separate dawns represented the thirty consecutive dawns of one month. But, why only thirty dawns of one month out of 360 dawns of a year should thus be selected in these Mantras is nowhere explained. The explanations, besides being mutually incon-

1. Ath. Veda, VII, 22, 2,—अभ्रः समीचीरुषसः समैरयन् । अरेपसः सचेतसः स्वसरे मन्युमत्तमाश्चिते गोः ॥

sistent, again conflict with the last verse in the *Anuvâka*, with the *Brâhmaṇa* or the explanation given in the Saṁhitâ itself, and with the passage from the Taittirîya Brâhmaṇa quoted above. But Sâyaṇa was writing under a firm belief that the Vedic dawn was the same as he and other Vedic scholars like Yâska perceived it in the tropical zone; and the wonder is, not that he has given us so many contradictory explanations, but that he has been able to suggest so many apparently plausible explanations as the exigencies of the different Mantras required. In the light of advancing knowledge about the nature of the dawn at the North Pole, and the existence of man on earth before the last Glacial epoch, we should, therefore, have no hesitation in accepting more intelligible and rationalistic view of the different passages descriptive of the dawns in the Vedic literature. We are sure Sâyaṇa himself would have welcomed a theory more comprehensive and reasonable than any advanced by him, if the same could have been suggested to him in his own day. Jyotiṣh or astronomy has always been considered to be the 'eye of the Veda,'[1] and as with the aid of the telescope this eye now commands a wider range than previously it will be our own fault if we fail to utilise the knowledge so gained to elucidate those portions of our sacred books which are still unintelligible.

But to proceed with the subject, it may be urged that it is only the Taittirîya Saṁhitâ that gives us the number of the dawns, and that it would not be proper to mix up these statements with the statements contained in the hymns of the Ṛig-Veda, and draw a conclusion from both taken together. The Taittirîya Saṁhitâ treats of sacrificial

1. Cf. Shikṣhâ, 41-42,—छंदः पादौ तु वेदस्य हस्तौ कल्पोऽथ पठ्यते। ज्योतिषामयनं चक्षुर्निरुक्तं श्रोत्रमुच्यते॥ शिक्षा घ्राणं तु वेदस्य मुखं व्याकरणं स्मृतम्। तस्मात् सांगमधीत्यैव ब्रह्मलोके महीयते॥

rites, and the Mantras relating to the dawn-bricks may not be regarded as being originally connected. The fact that only some of these are found in the Atharva-Veda Saṁhitâ, might lend some support to this view. But a critical study of the *Anuvâka*, will remove all these doubts. The 'thirty sisters' are not mentioned one by one, leaving it to the hearer, or the reader, to make up the total, and ascertain the final number for himself. The sixth verse in the *Anuvâka* expressly mentions 'the thirty sisters', and is, by itself, sufficient to prove that in ancient days the number of dawns was considered to be thirty. But if an authority from the Ṛig-Veda be still needed, we have it in VI, 59, 6, where Dawn is described as having traversed 'thirty steps' (*triṁshat padâni akramit*).[1] This statement has, as yet, remained unexplained. 'A single dawn traversing thirty steps' is but a paraphrase of the statement that 'dawns are thirty sisters, keeping to the same goal in their circuits.' Another verse which has not yet been satisfactorily explained is the Ṛig-Veda, I, 123, 8. It says "The dawns, alike to-day and alike to-morrow, dwell long in the abode of Varuṇa. Blameless, they forthwith go round (*pari yanti*) thirty *yojanas*; each its destined course (*kratum*)."[2] The first half of the verse presents no difficulty. In the second we are told that the dawns go round thirty *yojanas*, each following its own 'plan,' which is the meaning of *kratu*, according to the Petersberg Lexicon. But the phrase 'thirty *yojanas*' has not been as yet satisfactorily explained. Griffith following M. Bergaigne understands it to mean thirty regions or spaces,

1. Ṛig. VI, 59, 6,—इंद्राग्नी अपादियं पूर्वागात्पद्वतीभ्यः। हित्वी शिरो जिह्वया वावदच्चरत्त्रिंशत्पदान्यक्रमीत् ॥ Ṛig. X, 189, 3, which speaks of thirty realms (*triṁshat dhâma*), refers very probably to the same fact.

2. Ṛig. I, 123, 8,—सदृशीरद्य सदृशीरिदु श्वो दीर्घं सचंते वरुणस्य धाम । अनवद्यास्त्रिंशतं योजनान्येकैका क्रतुं परि यंति सद्यः ॥

indicating the whole universe; but there is no authority for this meaning. Sâyaṇa, whom Wilson follows, gives an elaborate astronomical explanation. He says that the sun's rays precede his rising and are visible when the sun is below the horizon by thirty *yojanas*, or, in other words, the dawn is in advance of the sun by that distance. When dawns are, therefore, said to traverse thirty *yojanas*, Sâyaṇa understands by it the astronomical phenomenon of the dawn illumining a space of thirty *yojanas* in advance of the sun, and, that when the dawn, at one place, is over, it is to be found in another place, occupying a space of thirty *yojanas* in that place. The explanation is very ingenious; and Sâyaṇa also adds that the dawns are spoken of in the plural number in the verse under consideration, because the dawns at different places on the surface of the earth, brought on by the daily motion of the sun, are intended. But unfortunately the explanation cannot stand scientific scrutiny. Sâyaṇa says that the sun travels 5,059 *yojanas* round the Meru in 24 hours; and as Meru means the earth and the circumference of the earth is now known to be about 24,877 miles, a *yojana* would be about 4·9, or in round number, about 5 miles. Thirty such *yojanas* will, therefore, be 150 miles; while the first beams of the dawn greet us on the horizon when the sun is not less than 16° below the horizon. Taking one degree equal to 60 miles, 16° would mean 960 miles, a distance far in excess of the thirty *yojanas* of Sâyaṇa. Another objection to Sâyaṇa's explanation is that the Vedic bard is evidently speaking of a phenomenon present before him, and not mentally following the astronomical dawns at different places produced by the daily rotation of the earth on its axis. The explanation is again inapplicable to 'thirty steps (*padâni*)' of the dawn expressly mentioned in VI, 59, 6. Therefore, the only alternative left is to take the phrases 'thirty *yojanas*,' 'thirty sisters,' and 'thirty steps' as different versions of one and the same fact, *viz*., the circuits of the dawn along the Polar horizon. The phrase 'each its destined course' also becomes intelligible in this case, for though thirty dawns complete thirty rounds, each may well be described as following its own definite course. The words *pari yanti* in the text literally apply to a circular (*pari*) motion, (cf. the words *pari-ukṣhaṇam*, *pari-staraṇam*, &c.); and the same term is used in the Taittirîya Saṁhitâ with reference to 'thirty sisters'. The word *yojana* primarily means 'a chariot' (VIII, 72, 6), and then it came to denote 'a distance to be accomplished without unharnessing the horses', or what we, in the vernacular, call a '*ṭappâ*.' Now this *ṭappâ*, or 'the journey to be accomplished without unharnessing the horses', may be a day's journey, and Prof. Max Muller has in one place interpreted the word *yojana* in this way.[1] In V, 54, 5, the Maruts are said "to have extended their greatness as far as the sun extends his daily course," and the word in the original for 'daily course' is *yojanum*. Accepting this meaning, we can interpret the expression 'the dawns forthwith go round (*pari yanti*) thirty *yojanas*' to mean that the dawns complete thirty *daily* rounds as at the North Pole. That circular motion is here intended is further evident from III, 61, 3, which says, in distinct terms, "Wending towards the same goal (*samânam artham*), O Newly-born (Dawn)! turn on like a wheel (*chakram iva â vavṛitsva*)."[2] Although the word *navyasi* (newly-born) is here in the vocative case, yet the meaning is that the dawn, ever anew or becoming new every day, revolves like a wheel. Now a wheel may either move in

1. See S. B. E. Series, Vol. XXXII, pp. 177 and 325.

2. Ṛig. III, 61, 3,—उषः प्रतीची भुवनानि विश्वोर्ध्वा तिष्ठस्यमृतस्य केतुः। समानमर्थं चरणीयमाना चक्रमिव नव्यस्या ववृत्स्व ॥

a perpendicular plane, like the wheel of a chariot, or in a horizontal plane like the potter's wheel. But the first of these two motions can not be predicated of the dawn anywhere on the surface of the earth. The light of the morning is, everywhere, confined to the horizon, as described in the Ṛig-Veda, VII, 80, 1, which speaks of the dawn as "unrolling the two *rajasî*, which border on each other (*samante*), and revealing all things."[1] No dawn, whether in the frigid, the temperate, or the tropical zone can, therefore, be seen travelling, like the sun, from east to west, over the head of the observer in a perpendicular plane. The only possible wheel-like motion is, therefore, along the horizon, and this can be witnessed only in regions near the Pole. A dawn in the temperate or the tropical zone is visible only for a short time on the eastern horizon, and is swallowed up, in the same place, by the rays of the rising sun. It is only in the Polar regions that we see the morning lights revolving along the horizon for some day-long periods of time, and if the wheel-like motion of the dawn, mentioned in III, 61, 2, has any meaning at all, we must take it to refer to the revolving splendours of the dawn in the Arctic regions previously described. The expressions "reaching the appointed place (*nish-kṛitam*) day by day" (I, 123, 9), and "wending ever and ever to the same goal" (III, 61, 3) are also ill-suited to describe the dawn in latitudes below the Arctic circle; but if we take these expressions to refer to the Polar dawn they become not only intelligible, but peculiarly appropriate, as such a dawn in its daily circuits must come to the point from which it started every twenty-four hours. All these passages taken together, therefore, point out only to one conclusion, and that is that both the Ṛig-Veda and the

1. Ṛig. VII, 80, 1,—विवर्तयंती रजसी समंते आविष्कृण्वती भुवनानि विश्वा। See Wallis' Cosmology of the Ṛig-Veda, p. 116.

Taittirîya Saṁhitâ describe a long and continuous dawn divided into thirty dawn-days, or periods of twenty-four hours each, a characteristic found only in the Polar dawn.

There are a number of other passages where the dawn is spoken of in the plural, especially in the case of matutinal deities, who are said to follow or come after not a single dawn, but dawns in the plural, (I, 6, 3; I, 180, 1; V, 76, 1; VII, 9, 1; VII, 63, 3). These passages have been hitherto understood as describing the appearance of these deities after the consecutive dawns of the year. But now a new light is thrown upon them by the conclusion established above from the examination of the different passages about the dawn in the Ṛig-Veda, the Taittirîya and the Atharva-Veda Saṁhitâ. It may, however, be mentioned that I do not mean to say that in the whole of the Ṛig-Veda not a single reference can be found to the dawn of the tropical or the temperate zone. The Veda which mentions a year of 360 days is sure to mention the evanescent dawn which accompanies these days in regions to the south of the Arctic circle. A greater part of the description of the dawn is again of such a character that we can apply it either to the long Polar dawn, or to the short-lived dawn of the tropics. Thus both may be said to awaken every living being (I, 92, 9), or disclose the treasures concealed by darkness (I, 123, 4). Similarly when dawns of different days are said to depart and come, a new sister succeeding each day to the sister previously vanished (I, 124, 9), we may either suppose that the consecutive dawns of different days are intended, or that a number of day-long dawns, which succeed one another after every 24 hours at the Pole, were in the mind of the poet. These passages do not, therefore, in any way affect the conclusion we have arrived at above, by the consideration of the *special* characteristics of the dawns mentioned in the hymns. What we mean to prove is that Ushas, or the Goddess of Dawn, the first appearance of which was so eagerly and anxiously looked to, and which formed the subject of so many beautiful hymns in the Vedic literature, is not the evanescent dawn of the tropics, but the long, continuous and revolving dawn at the Pole; and if we have succeeded in proving this from the passages discussed above, it matters little if a passage or more are found elsewhere in the Ṛig-Veda, describing the ordinary tropical dawn. The Vedic Ṛishis, who sang the present hymns, must have been familiar with the tropical dawn, if they now and then added a 13th month to secure the correspondence of the lunar and the solar year. But the deity of the Dawn was an ancient deity, the attributes of which had become known to the Ṛishis by orally preserved traditions, about the primeval home; and the dawn-hymns, as we now possess them, faithfully describe these characteristics. How these old characteristics of the Goddess of Dawn were preserved for centuries is a question to which I shall revert after examining the whole of the Vedic evidence bearing on the Polar theory. For the present we may assume that these reminiscences of the old home were preserved much in the same way as we have preserved the hymns, accent for accent and letter for letter, for the last three or four thousand years.

It will be seen from the foregoing discussion that if the dawn-hymns in the Ṛig-Veda be read and studied in the light of modern scientific discoveries and with the aid of passages in the Atharva-Veda and the Taittirîya Saṁhitâ and Brâhmaṇa, they clearly establish the following results :—

(1) The Ṛig-Vedic dawn was so long that *several days* elapsed between the first appearance of light on the horizon and the sunrise which followed it, (VII, 76, 3); or,

as described in II, 28, 9, many dawns appeared one after another before they ripened into sunrise.

(2) The Dawn was addressed in the plural number not honorifically, nor as representing the consecutive dawns of the year, but because it was made up of *thirty parts* (I, 123, 8; VI, 59, 6; T. S. IV, 3, 11, 6).

(3) Many dawns *lived in the same place, acted harmoniously* and *never quarrelled* with each other, (IV, 51, 7-9; VII, 76, 5; A. V. VII, 22, 2).

(4) The *thirty parts* of the dawn were *continuous* and *inseparable*, forming 'a closely gathered band,' or 'a group of dawns,' (I, 152, 4; T. Br. II, 5, 6, 5; A. V. VII, 22, 2).

(5) These thirty dawns, or thirty parts of one dawn *revolved round and round like a wheel*, reaching the same goal every day, each dawn or part following its own destined course, (I, 123, 8, 9; III, 61, 3; T. S. IV, 3, 11, 6).

These characteristics it is needless to say are possessed only by the dawn at or near the Pole. The last or the fifth especially is to be found only in lands very near the North Pole and not everywhere in the Arctic regions. We may, therefore, safely conclude that the Vedic Goddess of Dawn is Polar in origin. But it may be urged that while the Polar dawn lasts from 45 to 60 days, the Vedic dawn is described only as made up of thirty day-long parts, and that the discrepancy must be accounted for before we accept the conclusion that the Vedic dawn is Polar in character. The discrepancy is not, however, a serious one. We have seen that the duration of the dawn depends upon the powers of refraction and reflection of the atmosphere; and that these again vary according to the temperature of the place, or other meteorological conditions. It is, therefore, not unlikely that the duration of the dawn at the Pole, when the climate there was mild and genial, might be somewhat shorter than what we may expect it to be at present when the climate is severely cold. It is more probable, however, that the dawn described in the Ṛig-Veda is not exactly such a dawn as may be seen by an observer stationed precisely at the North Pole. As observed previously, the North Pole is a point, and if men lived near the Pole in early days, they must have lived somewhat to the south of this point. Within this tract it is quite possible to have 30 day-long dawns revolving like a wheel, after the long Arctic night of four or five months; and, so far as astronomy is concerned, there is, therefore, nothing improbable in the description of the dawn found in the Vedic literature. We must also bear in mind that the Vedic Dawn often tarried longer on the horizon, and the worshippers asked her not to delay lest the sun might scorch her like an enemy (V, 79, 9). This shows that though 30 days was the usual duration of the Dawn it was sometimes exceeded, and people grew impatient to see the light of the sun. It was in cases like these, that Indra, the God who created the dawns and was their friend, was obliged to break the car of the Dawn and bring the sun above the horizon (II, 15, 6; X, 73, 6).[1] There are other places in which the same legend is referred to (IV, 30, 8), and the obscuration of the Dawn by a thunderstorm is, at present, supposed to be the basis of this myth. But the explanation, like others of its kind, is on the face of it unsatisfactory. That a thunderstorm should occur just at the time of the dawn would be a mere accident, and it is improbable that it could have been made the basis of a legend. Again, it is not the obscuration, but the delaying of the Dawn,

1. Ṛig. II, 15, 6,—वज्रेणान उषसः सं पिपेष। Ṛig. IV, 30, 8,—एतद् घेदुत वीर्यमिन्द्र चकर्थ पौंस्यम् । स्त्रियं यद्दुर्हणायुवं वधीर्दुहितरं दिवः ॥

or its tarrying longer on the horizon than usual, that is referred to in the legend, and we can better account for it on the Polar theory, because the duration of dawn, though usually of 30 days, might have varied at different places according to latitude and climatic conditions, and Indra's bolt was thus needed to check these freaks of the Dawn and make way for the rising sun. There are other legends connected with the Dawn and the matutinal deities on which the Polar theory throws quite a new light; but these will be taken up in the chapter on Vedic myths, after the whole direct evidence in support of the theory is examined.

But if the Vedic dawn is Polar in origin, the ancestors of the Vedic bards must have witnessed it, not in the Post-Glacial, but in the Pre-Glacial era; and it may be finally asked why a reference to this early age is not found in the hymns before us? Fortunately the hymns do preserve a few indications of the time when these long dawns appeared. Thus, in I, 113, 13, we are told that the Goddess Dawn shone perpetually in *former* days (*purâ*), and here the word *purâ* does not mean the foregone days of this *kalpa*, but rather refers to a by-gone age, or *purâ kalpa*, as in the passage from the Taittirîya Saṁhitâ (I, 5, 7, 5), quoted and discussed in the next chapter. The word *prathamâ*, in the Taittirîya Saṁhitâ, IV, 3, 11, 1, and the Taittirîya Brâhmaṇa, II, 5, 6, 5, does not again mean simply 'first in order,' but refers to 'ancient times,' as when Indra's 'first' or 'oldest' exploits are mentioned in I, 32, 1, or when certain practices are said to be 'first' or 'old' in X, 90, 16. It is probable that it was this import of the word *prathamâ* that led Sâyaṇa to propose that the first dawn, mentioned in the Taittirîya Saṁhitâ, IV, 3, 11, represented the dawn at the beginning of the creation. The Vedic poets could not but have been conscious that the Mantras they used to lay down the dawn-bricks were inapplicable to the dawn as they saw it, and the Taittirîya Saṁhitâ (V, 3, 4, 7), which explains the Mantras, clearly states that this story or the description of the dawns is a tradition of old times when the Gods perceived the thirty dawns. It is not, therefore, correct to say that there are no references in the Vedic hymns to the time when these long dawns were visible. We shall revert to the point later on, when further evidence on the subject will be noticed and discussed. The object of the present chapter was to examine the *duration* of the Vedic Dawn, the Goddess of the morning, the subject of so many beautiful hymns in the Ṛig-Veda, and to show that the deity is invested with Polar characteristics. The evidence in support of this view has been fully discussed; and we shall, therefore, now take up the other Polar and Circum-Polar tests previously mentioned, and see whether we can find out further evidence from the Ṛig-Veda to strengthen our conclusions.

THE VEDIO DAWNS.

The sun is abont 16° below the horizon; and the morning lights will go round and round the horizon (one round being completed in 24 hours) in the direction of the arrow-heads, until the sun appears above the horizontal plane.

Appendix to Chapter V.

THE THIRTY DAWNS.

The following are the passages from the Taittirîya Samhitâ referred to on page 98 :—

TAITTIRÎYA SAMHITÂ, KÂNḌA IV, PRAPÂṬHAKA 3, ANUVÂKA, 11.

इयमेव सा या प्रथमा व्यौच्छदन्तरस्यां चरति प्रविष्टा ।
वधूर्जजान नवगज्जनित्री त्रय एनां महिमानः सचन्ते ॥ १ ॥
छन्दस्वती उषसा पेपिशाने समानं योनिमनु सञ्चरन्ती ।
सूर्यपत्नी वि चरतः प्रजानती केतुं कृण्वाने अजरे भूरि-रेतसा ॥ २ ॥
ऋतस्य पन्थामनु तिस्र आगुस्त्रयो घर्मासो अनु ज्योतिषाऽऽगुः ।
प्रजामेका रक्षत्यूर्जमेका व्रतमेका रक्षति देवयूनाम् ॥ ३ ॥
चतुष्टोमो अभवद्या तुरीया यज्ञस्य पक्षावृषयो भवन्ती ।
गायत्रीं त्रिष्टुभं जगतीमनुष्टुभं बृहदर्कं युञ्जानाः सुवराभरन्निदम् ॥ ४ ॥
पञ्चभिर्धाता विदधाविदं यत्तासां स्वसॄरजनयत् पञ्चपञ्च ।
तासामु यन्ति प्रयवेण पञ्च नाना रूपाणि क्रतवो वसानाः ॥ ५ ॥

VERSE 1,—This verse, with slight modifications, occurs twice in the Atharva-Veda Samhitâ (III, 10, 4 ; VIII, 9, 11). It runs thus :—

इयमेव सा या प्रथमा व्यौच्छदास्वितरासु चरति प्रविष्टा ।
महान्तो अस्यां महिमानो अन्तर्वधूर्जिगाय नवगज्जनित्री ॥

VERSES 2, 3, and 4,—The Atharva-Veda reading (VIII, 9, 12—14) is slightly different :—

छन्दःपक्षे उषसा पेपिशाने समानं योनिमनु सं चरेते ।
सूर्यपत्नी सं चरतः प्रजानती केतुमती अजरे भूरि-रेतसा ॥
ऋतस्य पन्थामनु तिस्र आगुस्त्रयो घर्मा अनु रेत आगुः ।
प्रजामेका जिन्वत्यूर्जमेका राष्ट्रमेका रक्षति देवयूनाम् ॥
अग्नीषोमावदधुर्या तुरीयासीद्यज्ञस्य पक्षावृषयः कल्पयन्तः ।
गायत्रीं त्रिष्टुभं जगतीमनुष्टुभं बृहदर्कीं यजमानाय स्वराभरन्तीम् ॥

त्रिंशत्स्वसार उप यन्ति निष्कृतं समानं केतुं प्रतिमुञ्चमानाः ।
ऋतूंस्तन्वते कवयः प्रजानतीर्मध्येछन्दसः परि यन्ति भास्वतीः ॥ ६ ॥

ज्योतिष्मती प्रति मुञ्चते नभो रात्री देवी सूर्यस्य व्रतानि ।
वि पश्यन्ति पशवो जायमाना नानारूपा मातुरस्या उपस्थे ॥ ७ ॥

एकाष्टका तपसा तप्यमाना जजान गर्भं महिमानमिन्द्रम् ।
तेन दस्यून् व्यसहन्त देवा हन्ताऽसुराणामभवच्छचीभिः ॥ ८ ॥

अनानुजामनुजां मामकर्त सत्यं वदन्त्यन्विच्छ एतत् ।
भूयासमस्य सुमतौ यथा यूयमन्या वो अन्यामति मा प्र युक्त ॥ ९ ॥

अभून्मम सुमतौ विश्ववेदा आष्ट प्रतिष्ठामविदद्धि गाधम् ।
भूयासमस्य सुमतौ यथा यूयमन्या वो अन्यामति मा प्र युक्त ॥ १० ॥

पञ्च व्युष्टीरनु पञ्च दोहा गां पञ्चनाम्नीमृतवोऽनु पञ्च ।
पञ्च दिशः पञ्चदशेन क्लृप्ताः समानमूर्ध्नीरभि लोकमेकम् ॥ ११ ॥

ऋतस्य गर्भः प्रथमा व्यूषुष्यपामेका महिमानं बिभर्ति ।
सूर्यस्यैका चरति निष्कृतेषु घर्मस्यैका सवितैकां नि यच्छति ॥ १२ ॥

या प्रथमा व्यौच्छत् सा धेनुरभवद्यमे ।
सा नः पयस्वती धुक्ष्वोत्तरामुत्तराꣳ समाम् ॥ १३ ॥

शुक्रर्षभा नभसा ज्योतिषाऽऽगाद् विश्वरूपा शबलीरग्निकेतुः ।
समानमर्थꣳ स्वपस्यमाना बिभ्रती जरामजर उष आगाः ॥ १४ ॥

VERSE 8,—This verse is also found in the Atharva-Veda (III, 10, 12); but the reading of the second half is as follows :—

तेन देवा व्यषहन्त शत्रून् हन्ता दस्यूनामभवच्छचीपतिः ।

VERSE 11,—Compare A. V. VIII. 9, 15. For समानमूर्ध्नीः A. V. reads सा एकमूर्ध्नीः । The rest is the same in both.

VERSE 13,—Compare A. V. III, 10, 1. For या प्रथमा व्यौच्छत् A. V. reads प्रथमा ह व्युवास । And for धुक्ष्व A. V. has दुहाम् । Compare also Ṛig. IV, 57, 7, where the second line is found as in A. V.

ऋतूनां पत्नी प्रथमेयमागादह्नां नेत्री जनित्री प्रजानाम् ।
एका सती बहुधोषो व्युच्छस्यजीर्णा त्वं जरयसि सर्वमन्यत् ॥ १५ ॥

TAITTIRÎYA SAMHITÂ, KÂṆḌA V, PRAPÂṬHAKA 3,
ANUVÂKA 4, SECTION 7.

न वा इदं दिवा न नक्तमासीदव्यावृत्तं ते देवा एता व्युष्टीरपश्यन् ता उपादधत ततो वा इदं व्यौच्छद्यस्यैता उपधीयन्ते व्येवास्मा उच्छत्यथो तम एवापहते ।

TRANSLATION AND NOTES.

Taitt. Samhitâ IV. 3, 11.

1. This, verily, is *She* that dawned first; (she) moves entered into her (*i.e.* above the horizon). The bride, the new-come mother, is born. The three great ones follow her.

---

1. *She that dawned first:* evidently meaning the first of a series of thirty dawns, mentioned in the following verses. In verse 13 we are told that it is the dawn which commences the year. The thirty dawns are, therefore, the dawns at the beginning of the year, and the first of them is mentioned in the first verse. Sâyaṇa, however, says—आदिसृष्टिकाले प्रथमो यः प्रभातकालस्तद्रूपेयम्, meaning that the dawn at the beginning of the creation is here intended. But the explanation does not suit the context, and Sâyaṇa has himself given different explanations afterwards.

Entered into her: according to Sâyaṇa *asyâm* (into her) means "into the earth;" compare Ṛig. III, 61, 7, where the sun, the speeder of the dawns, is said to have 'entered into the mighty earth and heaven.' According to A. V. reading the meaning would be "entered into the other (dawns)," shewing that the first dawn is a member of a larger group.

The three great ones: Sûrya, Vâyu and Agni according to Sâyaṇa. The three typical deities or Devatâs mentioned by Yâska (VII, 5) are Agni, Vâyu or Indra, and Sûrya. In Ṛig. VII, 33, 7, the three Gharmas (fires) are said to attend the dawn, (*trayo Gharmâsa ushasam sachante*); and in VII, 78, 3, the Dawns are said to have created Sûrya, Yajña (Sacrifice) and Agni. Also compare A. V. IX, 1, 8, and Bloomfield's note thereon in S. B. E. Series, Vol. XLII, p. 590. Though the three may be variously named, the reference is evidently to the rise of the sun and the commencement of sacrifices or the kindling of sacrificial fires after the first dawn, (Cf. Ṛig. I, 113, 9).

2. Possessed of songs, decorating (themselves), and moving together in a common abode, the Two Dawns, the (two) wives of the sun, unwasting, rich in seed, move about displaying their banner and knowing well (their way).

3. The Three Maidens have come along the path of Ṛita; the three fires (*Gharmas*), with light, have followed. One (of these Maidens) protects the progeny, one the vigour, and one the ordinance of the pious.

4. That, which (was) the Fourth, acting as Ṛishis, the

---

2. *Possessed of songs:* Sâyaṇa thus interprets *chchandas-vatî*; but the Pet. Lex. translates the word by 'lovely.' I have followed Sâyaṇa because the A. V. reading *chchandas-pakshe*, 'having *chchandas* for the two wings,' supports Sâyaṇa's meaning. That the morning atmosphere resounded with the recitation of hymns and songs may be seen, amongst others, from Ṛig. III, 61, 1 and 6. The phrase *madye-chchandasaḥ*, in verse 6 below, denotes the same idea. But the word *chchandas* may perhaps be understood to mean 'shine' in all these places; Cf. Ṛig. VIII, 7, 36, where the phrase, *chchando na sûro archishâ* is translated by Max Muller to mean "like the shine by the splendour of the sun," (See S. B. E. Series, Vol. XXXII, pp. 393, 399.)

Decorating, moving together in the same place, wives of the sun, un-wasting &c: These and others are the usual epithets of the Dawn found in the Ṛig-Veda, Cf. Ṛig I, 92, 4; VII, 76, 5; IV, 5, 13; I, 113, 13.

The Two Dawns: Ushasâ does not here mean *Ushâsâ-naktâ* or 'Day and Night,' as supposed by Mr. Griffith, but denotes two dawns, as such, the third, the fourth &c. being mentioned in the following verses. Sâyaṇa says द्वे उषसौ, एका सृष्टिकालीना 'प्रथमा' इतिपूर्वमंत्रोक्ता, अपरा प्रतिदिनसंचारिणी, meaning that the first dawn is the dawn which appeared at the beginning of the creation and the second the diurnal one, as we see it. But Sâyaṇa had to abandon this explanation later on. The couple of Dawns obviously includes the first Dawn mentioned in the first verse, which, with its successor, now forms a couple. Since *groups* of two, three, five or thirty dawns are mentioned as *moving together*, they cannot be the dawns of consecutive days, that is, separated by sunlight, as with us in the tropical or the temperate zone.

3. *The Three Maidens:* the number of Dawns is now increased to three; but Sâyaṇa gives no explanation of the number.

4. *The Fourth:* Sâyaṇa now says यद्यप्येकैव उषा तथापि जगद्रक्षणाय योगैश्वर्यादनेकशरीरस्वीकारे सति बहव उषसो भवन्ति, meaning that the single Deity of Dawn appears as many different dawns through yogic powers!

two wings of the sacrifice, has become the four-fold Stoma (*Chatu-shṭoma*). Using Gâyatrî, Trishṭup, Jagatî, Anushṭup the great song, they brought this light.

5. The creator did it with the Five, that he created five-and-five sisters to them (each). Their five courses (*kratavaḥ*), assuming various forms, move on in combination (*prayaveṇa*).

6. The Thirty Sisters, bearing the same banner, move on to the appointed place (*nish-kṛitam*). They, the wise, create the seasons. Refulgent, knowing (their way), they go round (*pari yanti*) amidst-songs (*madye-chchandasaḥ*).

Acting as Rishis ... four-fold Stoma: The group of four Dawns appears to be here compared to the *Chatu-shṭoma* or the four-fold song. (For a description of the four-fold Stoma see Ait. Br. III, 42, Haug's Trans. p. 237). *Gâyatrî &c.* are the metres used. The light brought on by the Dawns is the reward of this Stoma. Sâyaṇa interprets *suvas* to mean 'heaven,' but compare Ṛig. III, 61, 4, where the adjective, *svar janantî*, 'creating light,' is applied to the Dawn.

5. *Did it with the Five:* after the number of Dawns was increased to five, the creation proceeded by fives; compare verse 11 below.

Their five courses: I construe *tâsâm pañcha kratavaḥ prayaveṇa yanti.* Sâyaṇa understands *kratavaḥ* to mean sacrificial rites performed on the appearance of the dawn; but compare Ṛig. I, 123, 8, which says "The blameless Dawns (plu.) go round thirty *yojanas*, each her own *kratu* (destined course)," (*supra* p. 103). *Kratavaḥ* in the present verse must be similarly interpreted.

In combination: We have thirty Dawns divided into five groups of six each; compare Taitt. Br. II, 5, 6, 5, quoted above (p. 100), which says *tâ devyaḥ kurvate pañcha rûpâ*, "the Goddesses (Dawns) make five forms." Five groups of thirty Dawns, each group having its own destined course, are here described; but as each group is made of six Dawns, the five courses are again said to assume different forms, meaning that the members of each group have again their own courses within the larger course chalked out for the group.

6. *Thirty Sisters:* Sâyaṇa, in his commentary on the preceding verse says पञ्चसंख्याका ज्येष्ठा उषसः तासां स्वसारः पञ्चविंशतिसंख्याका इत्येकस्मिन् मासि प्रतिपदादिरूपास्त्रिंशदुषसः संपद्यन्ते, meaning that the thirty Dawns mentioned are the thirty dawns of a month. But Sâyaṇa does not explain why one month out of twelve, or only 30 out of 360 dawns should be thus selected. The explanation is again unsuited to the context, (See *supra* p. 101, and

7. Through the sky, the illumined Goddess of Night accepts the ordinances of the sun. The cattle, of various forms, (begin to) look up as they rise on the lap of the mother.

8. The Ekâshṭakâ, glowing with holy fervour (*tapas*), gave birth to a child, the great Indra. Through him the

---

T. S. V, 3, 4, 7, quoted below.) The Dawns are called sisters also in the Ṛigveda, (Cf. I, 124, 8 and 9).

Appointed place : nish-kritam, (Nir. XII, 7), used in reference to the course of the Dawns also in Ṛig. I, 123, 9. It is appropriate only if the Dawns returned to the same point in their daily rounds, (See *supra* p. 106).

Go round amidst-songs : pari yanti, 'go round' is also the phrase used in Ṛig. I, 123, 8. *Madye-chchandasaḥ* is interpreted by Sâyaṇa to mean "about the sun, which is always surrounded by songs." But we need not go so far, for *madye-chchandasaḥ* may be more simply taken to mean 'amidst-songs,' that are usually sung at the dawn, (Ṛig. VII, 80, 1).

7. *Through the sky :* I take *nabhas* as an accusative of space. Sâyaṇa appears to take it as an adjective equivalent to *nabhasthasya* and qualifying *sûryasya*. In either case the meaning is the same, *viz.*, that the night was grâdually changing into day-light.

The cattle : morning rays or splendours usually spoken of as cows. In Ṛig. I, 92, 12, the Dawn is described as spreading cattle (*pashûn*) before her; and in I, 124, 5, we are told that she fills the lap of both parents, heaven and earth. I construe, with Sâyaṇa, *nânâ-rûpa pashavaḥ vi pashyanti*, taking *vi pashyanti* intransitively, and *nânâ-rûpa* as an adjective. The same phrase is found used in reference to a woman's children in the Atharva-Veda, XIV, 2, 25. For the intransitive use of *vi pashyanti*, see Ṛig. X, 125, 4.

8. *The Ekâshṭakâ :* The birth of Indra is evidently the birth of the sun after the expiry of thirty dawns. Sâyaṇa, quoting Âpastamba Gṛihya Sûtra (VIII, 21, 10), interpretes Ekâshṭakâ to mean the 8th day of the dark half of the month of Mâgha (January-February); and in the Taittirîya Samhitâ, VII, 4, 8, quoted and explained by me in Chapter III of *Orion*, it seems to have same meaning, (See *Orion* p. 44 ff.). Ekâshṭakâ was the first day, or the consort, of the Year, when the sun turned towards the north from the winter solstice; and the commencement of all annual *sattras* is, therefore, directed to be made on the Ekâshṭakâ day. This meaning was, however, settled when the vernal equinox had receded from the asterism of Mriga (Orion) to that of the Krittikâs (Pleiades). But in earlier days Ekâshṭakâ seems to have meant the last of the dawns which preceded the rise of the sun after the long darkness, and thus com-

Gods have subdued their enemies; by his powers (he) has become the slayer of the Asuras.

9. You have made a companion (*lit.* the after-born) for me, who was (before) without a companion. Truth-teller (as thou art), I desire this, that I may have his good will, just as you do not transgress each the other.

10. The All-knowing has my good will, has got a hold (on it), has secured a place (therein). May I have his good will, just as you do not transgress each the other.

11. Five milkings answer to the five dawns; the five seasons to the five-named cow. The five sky-regions, made by

---

menced the year, which began with the period of sunshine. The word *eka* in Ekâshṭakâ perhaps denotes the *first* month, the last dawn probably falling on the 8th day of the first lunar month of the year.

9. *A companion for me:* that is, Indra or the sun, whose birth is mentioned in the previous verse; and the poet now prays that his new friend, the after-born follower or companion, should be favourable to him. It should be noted that the birth of the sun is described after the lapse of thirty dawns, during which the poet had no companion.

Truth-teller: Sâyaṇa seems to take *satyam vadantî* as a vocative plural; but it is not in strict accordance with grammar. In the *pada* text, it is evidently a feminine form of nom. sing., and I have translated accordingly, though not without some difficulty. In Ṛig. III, 61, 2, the Dawn is called *sûnṛitâ îrayantî* which expresses the same idea.

Just as you do not trangress each the other: compare the Ṛig-Veda, VII, 76, 5, where we are told that the Dawns, though collected in the same place, do not strive against or quarrel with each other.

10. *The All-knowing:* Sâyaṇa takes *vishva-vedâḥ* to mean the Dawn; but it obviously refers to the companion (*anujâm*) mentioned in the preceding verse. The worshipper asks for a reciprocity of good will. The All-knowing (Indra) has his good will; let him, he prays, have now the All-knowing's good will. The adjective *vishva-vedâḥ* is applied in the Ṛig-veda to Indra or Agni several times, Cf. Ṛig. VI, 47, 12; I, 147, 3.

11. *Five milkings:* Sâyaṇa refers to Taitt. Brâh. II, 2, 9, 6-9, where darkness, light, the two twilights, and day are said to be the five milkings (*dohâḥ*) of Prajâpati. The idea seems to be that all the five-fold groups in the creation proceeded from the five-fold dawn-groups.

Five-named Cow: the earth, according to Sâyaṇa, who says that the earth has five different names in the five seasons, *e.g.*, *pushpa-*

the fifteen, have a common head, directed to one world.

12. The first dawn (is) the child of Ṛita, one upholds the greatness of Waters, one moves in the regions of Sûrya, one (in those) of Gharma (fire), and Savitṛi rules one.

13. That, which dawned first, has become a cow in Yama's realm. Rich in milk, may she milk for us each succeeding year.

14. The chief of the bright, the omniform, the brindled, the fire-bannered has come, with light, in the sky. Working well towards a common goal, bearing (signs of) old age, (yet) O un-wasting! O Dawn! thou hast come.

15. The wife of the seasons, this first has come, the leader of days, the mother of children. Though one, O Dawn! thou shinest manifoldly; though un-wasting, thou causest all the rest to grow old (decay).

---

vatî (blossomy) in Vasanta (Spring), *tápa-vatî* (heated) in Grîṣhma (Summer), *vṛiṣhṭi-vatî* (showery) in Varṣhâ (Rains), *jala-prasâda-vatî* (clear-watered) in Sharad (Autumn), and *shaitya-vatî* (cold) in Hemanta-Shishira (Winter). The seasons are taken as five by combining Hemanta and Shishira into one.

The fifteen: The fifteen-fold Stoma, called *pañcha-dasha*, (See Haug's Trans. Ait. Br. p. 238).

13. *Each succeeding year:* This shows. that the Dawn here described is the first dawn of the year. In Ṛig. I, 33, 10, light (cows) is said to be milked from darkness.

14. *Working well towards a common goal:* compare Ṛig. III, 61, 3, where, the Dawn "wending to one and the same goal" is asked to "turn on like a wheel."

Bearing (signs of) old age: I construe *jarâm bibhratî* and yet *ajare*. Sâyaṇa takes *svapasya-mânâ* (working well) as an independent adjective; and connects *bibhratî* with *artham*, and *jarâm* with *âgâḥ*. The meaning would then be "Working well, having a common end, O unwasting Dawn! thou hast reached old age." But it does not make any appreciable change in the general sense of the verse.

15. *Though one . . shinest manifoldly:* shews that only one continuous dawn, though made up of many parts, is described in this hymn.

Leader of days, mother of children.—the epithets *ahnâm netrî* and *gavâm mâtâ* are also found used in the Ṛig-Veda, VII, 77, 2.

Taitt. Saṁhitâ V, 3, 4, 7.

It was *un*-distinguished,[1] neither day nor night. The Gods perceived these dawn-bricks (for the laying of which the 15 verses given above are to be used). They laid them. *Then* it shone forth.[2] Therefore for whom these are laid, it shines forth to him, destroys (his) darkness.

REMARKS.

It has been previously mentioned that the fifteen verses, quoted above, are used or recited as Mantras at the time of laying down certain emblematical bricks, called *Vyushṭî-ishṭakâs*, or dawn-bricks, on the sacrificial altar. But as the Mantras, or verses, used for sacrificial purposes are often taken from different Vedic hymns, these verses are likely to be regarded as unconnected with each other. The account of the thirty dawns, contained therein, however, shews that these verses must have originally formed an entire or one homogeneous hymn. Again if the Mantras had been selected from different hymns, one for each dawn-brick, there would naturally be 16 verses in all, as 16 dawn-bricks are to be laid on the altar. The very fact, that the *Anuvâka* contains only 15 verses (leaving the sacrificer to select the 16th from elsewhere), therefore, further supports the same view. It is true that some of these verses are found in the Atharva-Veda, either detached or in connection with other subjects. But that does not prevent us from treating the passage in the Taittirîya Saṁ-

1. *It was undistinguished:* This paragraph, which is found later on in the Saṁhitâ, explains how the dawn-bricks came to be laid with the fifteen verses given above. The portions of the Taittirîya Saṁhitâ, which contain such explanations are called *Brâhmaṇa.*

2. *Then it shone forth:* This shews that *all* the thirty Dawns were understood to have preceded the rise of the sun. I have already quoted (*supra* p. 100) a passage from Taitt. Brâh. (II, 5, 6, 5), which says that these dawns were continuous and unseparated.

hitâ, as containing a connected account of thirty dawns divided into five groups of six each. The question is not, however, very material, inasmuch as verses 5 and 6, whether they formed part of an entire hymn or not, are by themselves sufficient to prove the point at issue, *viz.*, that the Vedic Goddess of Dawn constituted a group of thirty sisters. The Ṛig-Veda speaks of "thirty steps" traversed by the Dawn, (VI, 59, 6), or of Dawns going round "thirty *yojanas*" (I, 123, 8); but both these statements have, as yet, remained totally unexplained, or have been but imperfectly explained by Indian and Western scholars alike. But now that we know that the Vedic Dawns were thirty in number, both the aforesaid statements become at once easily comprehensible. The only other point necessary to be decided, so far as the subject in hand is concerned, is whether these thirty dawns were the dawns of thirty consecutive days, or whether they formed a 'closely-gathered band' of thirty continuous dawns; and on reading the two aforesaid passages from the Taittirîya Saṁhitâ, the one from the Taittirîya Brâhmaṇa, II, 5, 6, 5, and other authorities cited in the foregoing chapter, I do not think, there can be any doubt that the Goddess of Dawn, worshipped by the Vedic bards, was originally a group of thirty continuous dawns. It is not contended that the ancestors of the Vedic bards were unacquainted with ordinary dawns, for, even in the circumpolar regions there are, during certain parts of the year, successions of ordinary days and nights and with them of ordinary dawns. But so far as the Vedic Goddess of morning is concerned, there is enough evidence to shew that it was no other than the continuous and revolving Dawn at the end of the long night in those regions, the Dawn that lasted for thirty periods of 24 hours each, which is possible only within a few degrees roundabout the North Pole.

CHAPTER VI.

LONG DAY AND LONG NIGHT.

Independent evidence about the long night —Vritra living in long darkness —Expressions denoting long darkness or long night —Anxiety to reach the end of darkness —Prayers to reach safely the other end of night —A night, the other boundary of which was not known according to the Atharva Veda—The Taittirîya Samhitâ explains that these prayers were due to fears entertained by the ancient priests that the night would not dawn —Not caused by long winter nights as supposed by Sâyana —Description of days and nights in the Rig-Veda —Divided into two typical pairs —One described as bright, dark and *virûpe* —*Virûpe* means 'of varying lengths' and not 'of various colours' —Second pair, *Ahanî*, different from the first —Durations of days and nights on the globe examined —*Ahanî* can only be a couple of the long Arctic day and night —Described as forming the right and left, or opposite, sides of the Year in the Taittirîya A'ranyaka —The sun is described in the Rig-Veda as unyoking his car in the midst of the sky —And thereby retaliating *Dâsa's* mischief —Represents the long day and the long night —Summary of evidence regarding long day and long night —Ushas and Sûrya as *Dakshinâ* and *Dakshinâ's* son —Probably imply the southerly course of both.

When a long continuous dawn of thirty days, or a closely-gathered band of thirty dawns, is shown to have been expressly referred to in the Vedic literature, the long night preceding such a dawn follows as a matter of course; and where a long night prevails, it must have a long day to match it during the year. The remaining portion of the year, after deducting the period of the long night, the long day and the long morning and evening twilights, would also be characterised by a succession of ordinary days and nights, a day and night together never exceeding twenty-four hours, though, within that limit, the day may gradually gain over the night at one time and the night over the day at another, producing a variety of ordinary days and nights of different lengths. All these phenomena are so connected astronomically that if one of them is established, the others follow as a matter of scientific inference. Therefore, if the long duration of the Vedic dawn is once demonstrated, it is, astronomically speaking, unnecessary to search for further evidence regarding the existence of long days and nights in the Ṛig-Veda. But as we are dealing with a state of things which existed several thousand years ago, and with evidence, which, though traditionally handed down, has not yet been interpreted in the way we have done, it is safer to treat, in practice, the aforesaid astronomical phenomena as disconnected facts, and separately collect evidence bearing on each, keeping the astronomical connection in reserve till we come to consider the cumulative effect of the whole evidence in support of the several facts mentioned above. I do not mean to imply that there is any uncertainty in the relation of sequence between the above astronomical facts. On the contrary, nothing can be more certain than such a sequence. But in collecting and examining the evidence bearing on facts like those under consideration, it is always advisable in practice to collect as much evidence and from as many different points of view as possible. In this and the following two chapters, we, therefore, propose to examine separately the evidence that can be found in the Vedic literature about the long day, the long night, the number of months of sunshine and of darkness, and the character of the year, and see if it discloses characteristics found only at, or around, the North Pole.

And first regarding the long night,—a night of several days' duration, such as makes the northern latitudes too cold or uncomfortable for human habitation at present, but which, in inter-glacial times, appeared to have caused no further inconvenience than what might result from darkness, long and continuous darkness for a number of days, though, by itself, it was not a desirable state of things, and the end of which must have been eagerly looked for by men who had to undergo such experience. There are many passages in the Ṛig-Veda that speak of long and ghastly darkness, in one form or another, which sheltered the enemies of Indra, and to destroy which Indra had to fight with the demons or the *Dâsas*, whose strongholds are all said to be concealed in this darkness. Thus in I, 32, 10, Vṛitra, the traditional enemy of Indra, is said to be engulfed in long darkness (*dîrgham tamaḥ âshayad Indra-shatruḥ*), and in V, 32, 5, Indra is described as having placed Shushṇa, who was anxious to fight, in 'the darkness of the pit' (*tamasi harmye*), while the next verse speaks of *asûrye tamasi* (*lit.* sunless darkness), which Max Muller renders by 'ghastly darkness.'[1] In spite of these passages the fight between Vṛitra and Indra is considered to be a daily and not a yearly struggle, a theory the validity of which will be examined when we come to the discussion of Vedic myths. For the present it is sufficient to note that the above expressions lose all their propriety, if the darkness, in which the various enemies of Indra are said to have flourished, be taken to be the ordinary darkness of twelve, or, at best, of twenty-four hours' duration. It was, in reality, a *long* and a *ghastly* or sunless darkness, which taxed all the powers of Indra and his associate Gods to overcome.

But apart from this legendary struggle, there are other verses in the Ṛig-Veda which plainly indicate the existence of a night longer than the longest cis-Arctic night. In the first place the Vedic bards are seen frequently in-

1. See S. B. E. series, Vol. XXXII, p. 218.

voking their deities to release them from darkness. Thus in II, 27, 14, the poet says "Aditi, Mitra and also Varuṇa, forgive if we have committed any sin against you! May I obtain the wide fearless light, O Indra! May not the long darkness come over us." The expression in the original for 'long darkness' is *dîrghâh tamisrâh*, and means rather an 'uninterrupted succession of dark nights (*tamisrâḥ*)' than simply 'long darkness.' But even adopting Max Muller's rendering given above,[1] the anxiety here manifested for the disappearance of the long darkness is unmeaning, if the darkness never lasted for more than twenty-four hours. In I, 46, 6, the Ashvins are asked "to vouchsafe such strength to the worshipper as may carry him through darkness"; and in VII, 67, 2 the poet exclaims:—"The fire has commenced to burn, the ends of darkness have been seen, and the banner of the Dawn has appeared in the east!"[2] The expression 'ends of darkness' (*tamasaḥ antâḥ*) is very peculiar, and it would be a violation of idiom to take this and other expressions indicating 'long darkness' to mean nothing more than long winter nights, as we have them in the temperate or the tropical zone. As stated previously the longest winter night in these zones must be, at best, a little short of twenty-four hours, and even then these long nights prevail only for a fortnight or so. It is, therefore, very unlikely that Vedic bards perpetuated the memory of these long nights by making it a grievance of such importance as to require the aid of their deities to relieve them from

---

1. Hibbert Lectures, p. 231. The verse is:—अदिते मित्र वरुणोत मृळ यद्वो वयं चकृमा कच्चिदागः। उर्वश्यामभयं ज्योतिरिन्द्र मा नो दीर्घा अभि नशन्तमिस्राः॥

2. Ṛig. I, 46, 6,—या नः पीपरदश्विना ज्योतिष्मती तमस्तिरः। तामस्मे रासाथामिषम्॥ Ṛig. VII, 67, 2,—अशोच्यग्निः समिधानो अस्मे उपो अदृश्रन्तमसश्चिदन्ताः।

it. There are other passages where the same longing for the end of darkness or for the appearance of light is expressed, and these cannot be accounted for on the theory that to the old Vedic bards night was as death, since they had no means, which a civilised person in the twentieth century possesses, of dispelling the darkness of night by artificial illumination. Even the modern savages are not reported to be in the habit of exhibiting such impatience for the morning light as we find in the utterances of the Vedic bards; and yet the latter were so much advanced in civilisation as to know the use of metals and carriages. Again not only men, but Gods, are said to have lived in long darkness. Thus, in X, 124, 1, Agni is told that he has stayed "*too long* in the *long* darkness," the phrase used being *jyog eva dîrgham tama âshayishṭâḥ*. This double phrase *jyog* (long) and *dîrgham* is still more inappropriate, if the duration of darkness never exceeded that of the longest winter-night. In II, 2, 2, the same deity, Agni, is said to shine during "continuous nights," which, according to Max Muller, is the meaning of the word *kshapaḥ* in the original.[1] The translation is no doubt correct, but Prof. Max Muller does not explain to us what he means by the phrase "continuous nights." Does it signify a succession of nights uninterrupted by sunlight? or, is it only an elegant rendering, meaning nothing more than a number of nights? The learned translator seems to have narrowly missed the true import of the phrase employed by him.

But we need not depend on stray passages like the above to prove that the long night was known in early days. In the tenth Maṇḍala of the Ṛig-Veda we have a hymn (127) addressed to the Goddess of Night, and in the 6th verse of this hymn Night is invoked to "become

1. See S. B. E. Series, Vol. XLVI, p. 195.

easily fordable" to the worshipper (*nah sutarâ bhava*). In the Parishishṭa, which follows this hymn in the Ṛig-Veda, and which is known as *Râtri-sûkta* or *Durgâ-stava*, the worshipper asks the Night to be favourable to him, exclaiming "May we reach the other side in safety! May we reach the other side in safety!"[1] In the Atharva-Veda, XIX, 47, which is a reproduction, with some variations, of the above Parishishṭa, the second verse runs thus: "Each moving thing finds rest in her (Night), *whose yonder boundary is not seen, nor that which keeps her separate.* O spacious, darksome Night! May we, uninjured, reach the end of thee, reach, O thou blessed one, thine end!" And in the third verse of the 50th hymn of the same book the worshippers ask that they may pass uninjured in their body, "through each succeeding night, (*râtrim râtrim*)." Now a question is naturally raised why should every one be so anxious about safely reaching the other end of the night? And why should the poet exclaim that "its yonder boundary is not seen, nor what keeps it separate?" Was it because it was an ordinary winter night, or, was it because it was the long Arctic night? Fortunately, the Taittirîya Saṁhitâ preserves for us the oldest traditional reply to these questions, and we need not, therefore, depend upon the speculations of modern commentators. In the Taittirîya Saṁhitâ I, 5, 5, 4,[2] we

---

1. The 4th verse in the Râtri-Sûkta is:—प्रपद्योऽहं शिवां रात्रीं भद्रे पारमशीमहि भद्रे पारमशीमहि। The Atharva-Veda, XIX, 47, 2,—न यस्याः पारं ददृशे न योयुवद्विश्वमस्यां नि विशते यदेजति । अरिष्टासस्त उर्वि तमस्वति रात्रि पारमशीमहि भद्रे पारमशीमहि ॥ Ibid, XIX, 50, 3,—रात्रिं रात्रिमरिष्यन्तस्तरेम तन्वा वयम् ।

2. Taitt. Sam. I, 5, 5, 4,—चित्रावसो स्वस्ति ते पारमशीय ॥ Taitt. Sam. I, 5, 7, 5,—चित्रावसो स्वस्ति ते पारमशीयेत्याह । रात्रिर्वै चित्रावसुरव्युष्ट्यै वा एतस्यै पुरा ब्राह्मणा अभैषुः ॥ Sâyaṇa thus explains the passage हेमंततौ रात्रेर्दीर्घत्वेन प्रभातं न भविष्यत्येवेति कदाचिद् ब्राह्मणा भीता अतः पारमशीयेति प्रार्थनया प्रभातं लभते ।

have a similar Mantra or prayer addressed to Night in these words :—" O Chitrâvasu ! let me safely reach thy end." A little further, (I, 5, 7, 5), the Saṁhitâ itself explains this Mantra, or prayer thus :—" Chitrâvasu is (means) the night; in old times (*purâ*), the Brâhmans (priests) were afraid that it (night) would not dawn." Here we have an express Vedic statement, that, in old times, the priests or the people, felt apprehensions regarding the time when the night would end. What does it signify? If the night was not unusually long, where was the necessity for entertaining any misgivings about the coming dawn? Sâyaṇa, in commenting on the above passage, has again put forward his usual explanation, that nights in the winter were long and they made the priests apprehensive in regard to the coming dawn. But here we can quote Sâyaṇa against himself, and show that he has dealt with this important passage in an off-hand manner. It is well known that the Taittirîya Saṁhitâ often explains the Mantras, and this portion of the Saṁhitâ is called Brâhmaṇa, the whole of the Taittirîya Saṁhitâ being made up in this way of Mantras and the Brâhmaṇa, or prayers and their explanations or commentary mixed up together. The statement regarding the apprehensions of the priests about the coming dawn, therefore, falls under the Brâhmaṇa portion of the Saṁhitâ. Now the contents of the Brâhmaṇas are usually classified by Indian divines under the ten following heads[1]:—(1) *Hetu* or reason; (2) *Nirvachana*, or etymological explanation; (3) *Nindâ*, or censure; (4) *Prashaṁsâ*, or praise; (5) *Saṁshaya*, or doubt; (6) *Vidhi*, or the rule; (7) *Parakriyâ*, or others' doings; (8) *Purâ-kalpa*, or ancient rite or tradition; (9) *Vyavadhâraṇa-kalpanâ*, or determining the

---

1. These are enumerated in the following verses :—

हेतुर्निर्वचनं निंदा प्रशंसा संशयोविधिः । परक्रिया पुराकल्पो व्यवधारणकल्पना ॥
उपमानं दशैवैते विधयो ब्राह्मणस्य तु । एतद्वै सर्ववेदेषु नियतं विधिलक्षणम् ॥

limitations; (10) *Upamâna*, an apt comparison or simile. Sâyaṇa in his introduction to the commentary on the Ṛig-Veda mentions the first nine of these, and as an illustration of the eighth, *Purâ-kalpa*, quotes the explanatory passage from the Taittirîya Saṁhitâ, I, 5, 7, 5, referred to above. According to Sâyaṇa the statement, "In former times the priests were afraid that it would not dawn," therefore, comes under *Purâ-kalpa*, or ancient traditional history found in the Brâhmaṇas. It is no *Arthavâda*, that is, speculation or explanation put forth by the Brâhmaṇa itself. This is evident from the word *purâ* which occurs in the Saṁhitâ text, and which shows that some piece of ancient traditional information is here recorded. Now if this view is correct, a question naturally arises why should ordinary long winter nights have caused such apprehensions in the minds of the priests only 'in former times,' and why should the long darkness cease to inspire the same fears in the minds of the present generation. The long winter nights in the tropical and the temperate zone are as long to-day as they were thousands of years ago, and yet none of us, not even the most ignorant, feels any misgiving about the dawn which puts an end to the darkness of these long nights. It may, perhaps, be urged that in ancient times the bards had not acquired the knowledge necessary to predict the certain appearance of the dawn after a lapse of some hours in such cases. But the lameness of this excuse becomes at once evident when we see that the Vedic calendar was, at this time, so much advanced that even the question of the equation of the solar and the lunar year was solved with sufficient accuracy. Sâyaṇa's explanation of winter nights causing misgivings about the coming dawn must, therefore, be rejected as unsatisfactory. It was not the long winter-night that the Vedic bards were afraid of in former ages. It was something else, something very long, so long that, though you knew it would not last permanently, yet, by its very length, it tired your patience and made you long for, eagerly long for, the coming dawn. In short, it was the long night of the Arctic region, and the word *purâ* shows that it was a story of former ages, which the Vedic bards knew by tradition. I have shown elsewhere that the Taittirîya Saṁhitâ must be assigned to the Kṛittikâ period. We may, therefore, safely conclude that at about 2500 B. C., there was a tradition current amongst the Vedic people to the effect that in former times, or rather in the former age, the priests grew so impatient of the length of the night, the yonder boundary of which was not known, that they fervently prayed to their deities to guide them safely to the other end of that tiresome darkness. This description of the night is inappropriate unless we take it to refer to the long and continuous Arctic night.

Let us now see if the Ṛig-Veda contains any direct reference to the long day, the long night, or to the Circum-polar calendar, besides the expressions about long darkness or the difficulty of reaching the other boundary of the endless night noticed above. We have seen before that the Ṛig-Vedic calendar is a calendar of 360 days, with an intercalary month, which can neither be Polar nor Circum-polar. But side by side with it the Ṛig-Veda preserves the descriptions of days and nights, which are not applicable to the cis-Arctic days, unless we put an artificial construction upon the passages containing these descriptions. Day and Night is spoken of as a couple in the Vedic literature, and is denoted by a compound word in the dual number. Thus we have *Ushâsâ-naktâ* (I, 122, 2), Dawn and Night; *Naktoshâsâ* (I, 142, 7), Night and Dawn; or simply *Ushâsau* (I, 188,6), the two Dawns; all meaning a couple of Day and Night. The word *Aho-râtre* also means Day and Night; but it does not occur in the Ṛig-Veda, though Aitareya Brâhmaṇa (II, 4) treats it as synonymous with *Ushâsâ-naktâ*. Sometimes this pair of Day and Night is spoken of as two sisters or twins; but whatever the form in which they are addressed, the reference is usually unambiguous. Now one of the verses which describes this couple of Day and Night is III, 55, 11.[1] The deity of the verse is *Aho-râtre*, and it is admitted on all hands that it contains a description of Day and Night. It runs thus :—

Nânâ chakrâte yamyâ vapûṁṣhi
tayor anyad rochate kṛishṇam anyat ।
Shyâvî cha yad arushî cha svasârau
mahad devânâm asuratvam ekam ॥

The first three quarters or feet of this verse contain the principal statements, while the fourth is the refrain of the song or the hymn. Literally translated it means :— "The twin pair (females) make many forms; of the two one shines, the other (is) dark: two sisters (are) they, the dark (*shyâvî*), and the bright (*arushî*). The great divinity of the Gods is *one* (unique)." The verse looks simple enough at the first sight, and simple it is, so far as the words are concerned. But it has been misunderstood in two important points. We shall take the first half of the verse first. It says "the twin pair make many forms; of the two one shines and the other is dark." The twin pair are Day and Night, and one of them is bright and the other dark. So far, therefore, there is no difficulty. But the phrase 'make many forms' does not seem to have been properly examined or interpreted. The words used in the original verse are *nânâ chakrâte vapûṁṣhi*,

---

1. Ṛig. III, 55, 11,—नाना चक्राते यम्या वपूंषि तयोरन्यद्रोचते कृष्णमन्यत्। श्यावी च यदरुषी च स्वसारौ महद्देवानामसुरत्वमेकम् ॥

and they literally mean 'make many bodies or forms.'' We have thus a two-fold description of the couple; it is called the shining and the dark, and also described as possessed of many forms. In I, 123, 7, the couple of Day and Night is said to be *vishurûpe*; while in other places the adjective *virûpe* is used in the same sense. It is evident, therefore, that the 'bodies' or 'forms' intended to be denoted by these words must be different from the two-fold character of the couple as shining and dark; and if so, the phrases *vishurûpe*, *virûpe*, or *nânâ vapûṁṣhi* used in connection with the couple of Day and Night must be taken to mean something different from 'bright and dark', if these expressions are not to be considered as superfluous or tautological. Sâyaṇa interprets these phrases as referring to different colours (*rûpa*), like black, white. &c., and some of the Western scholars seem to have adopted this interpretation. But I cannot see the propriety of assigning different colours to Day and Night. Are we to suppose that we may have sometimes green, violet, yellow or blue days and nights? Again though the word *rûpa* lends itself to this construction, yet *vapûṁṣhi* cannot ordinarily be so understood. The question does not, however, seem to have attracted the serious attention of the commentators; so that even Griffith translates *vishurûpe* by 'unlike in hue' in I, 123, 7. The *Naktoshâsâ* are described as *virûpe* also in I, 113, 3, but there too Sâyaṇa gives the same explanation. It does not appear to have occurred to any one that the point requires any further thought. Happily, in the case of Ṛig. I, 113, 3, we have, however, the advantage of consulting a commentator older than Sâyaṇa. The verse occurs in the *Uttarârchika* of Sâma-Veda (19, 4, 2, 3), and Mâdhava in his *Vivaraṇa*, a commentary on the Sâma-Veda, explains *virûpe* thus:—"In the *Dakshiṇâyana* during the year there is the increase of night, and in the *Uttarâyaṇa* of day."[1] Mâdhava's *Vivaraṇa* is a scarce book, and I take the above quotation from an extract from his commentary given in a footnote to the Calcutta edition of the Sâma-Veda Saṁhitâ, with Sâyaṇa's commentary, published by Satya-vrata Sâmashramî, a learned Vedic scholar of Calcutta. It is not known who this Mâdhava is, but Pandit Satyavrata states that he is referred to by Durga, the commentator of Yâska. We may, therefore, take Mâdhava to be an old commentator, and it is satisfactory to find that he indicates to us the way out of the difficulty of interpreting the phrases *vishurûpe* and *virûpe*, occurring so many times in the Ṛig-Veda, in connection with the couple of Day and Night. The word 'form' (*rûpa*) or body (*vapus*) can be used to denote the extent, duration, or length of days and nights, and *virûpe* would naturally denote the varying *lengths* of days and nights, *in addition* to their colour, which can be only two-fold, dark or bright. Taking our cue from Mâdhava, we may, therefore, interpret the first half of the verse as meaning "The twin pair assume various (*nânâ*) lengths (*vapûṁṣhi*); of the two one shines and the other is dark."

But though the first half may be thus interpreted, another difficulty arises, as soon as we take up the third quarter of the verse. It says, "Two sisters are they, the dark (*shyâvî*) and the bright (*arushî*)." Now the question is whether the two sisters (*svasârau*) here mentioned are the same as, or different from, the twin pair (*yamyâ*) mentioned in the first half of the verse. If we take them as

1. See Sâma-Veda, Cal. Ed., Utta. 19, 4, 2, 3. The verse in the Veda is,—समानो अध्वा स्वस्रोरनन्तस्तमन्यान्या चरतो देवशिष्टे। न मेथेते न तस्थतुः सुमेके नक्तोषासा समनसा विरूपे॥ Mâdhava's Vivaraṇa says, "सुमेके—संवत्सरे, दक्षिणायने रात्रेर्वृद्धिः, उत्तरायणे अह्नः, नक्तं रात्रिः, उषाकालमनुस्वहः।"

identical, the third *pâda* or quarter of the verse becomes at once superfluous. If we take them as different, we must explain how and where the two pairs differ. The commentators have not been able to solve the difficulty, and they have, therefore, adopted the course of regarding the twins (*yamyâ*) and the sisters (*svasârau*) as identical, even at the risk of tautology. It will surely be admitted that this is not a satisfactory course, and that we ought to find a better explanation, if we can. This is not again the only place where two distinct couples of Day and Night are mentioned. There is another word in the Ṛig-Veda which denotes a pair of Day and Night. It is *Ahanî*, which does not mean 'two days,' but Day and Night, for, in VI, 9, 1, we are expressly told that "there is a dark *ahaḥ* (day) and a bright *ahaḥ* (day)." *Ahanî*, therefore, means a couple of Day and Night, and we have seen that *Uṣhâsâ-naktâ* also means a couple of Day and Night. Are the two couples same or different? If *Ahanî* be regarded as synonymous with *Uṣhâsâ-naktâ* or *Aho-râtre*, then the two couples would be identical; otherwise different. Fortunately, Ṛig. IV, 55, 3, furnishes us with the means of solving this difficulty. There *Uṣhâsâ-naktâ* and *Ahanî* are separately invoked to grant protection to the worshipper, and the *separate* invocation clearly proves that the two couples are two separate dual deities, though each of them represents a couple of Day and Night.[1] Prof. Max Muller has noticed this difference between *Uṣhâsâ-naktâ* and *Ahanî* or the two *Ahans*; but he does not seem to have pushed it to its logical conclusion. If all the 360 days and nights of the year were of the same class as with us, there was no necessity of dividing them into two representative couples as *Uṣhâsâ-naktâ*

1. Ṛig. IV, 55, 3,—उभे यथा नो अहनी निपात उषासानक्ता करतामदब्धे। See Max Muller's Lectures on the Science of Language, Vol. II, p. 534.

and *Ahani*. The general description "dark, bright and of various lengths" would have been quite sufficient to denote all the days and nights of the year. Therefore, if the distinction between *Uṣhâsâ-naktâ* and *Ahani*, made in IV, 55, 3, is not to be ignored, we must find out an explanation of this distinction; and looking to the character of days and nights at different places on the surface of the earth from the Pole to the Equator, the only possible explanation that can be suggested is that the year spoken of in these passages was a circum-Polar year, made up of one long day and one long night, forming one pair, and a number of ordinary days and nights of various lengths, which, taking a single day and night as the type, can be described as the second couple, "bright, dark and of varying lengths." There is no other place on the surface of the earth where the description holds good. At the Equator, we have only equal days and nights throughout the year, and they can be represented by a single couple "dark and bright, but always of the same length." In fact, instead of *virûpe* the pair would be *sarûpe*. Between the Equator and the Arctic Circle, a day and night together never exceed twenty-four hours, though there may be a day of 23 hours, and a night of one hour and *vice versa*, as we approach the Arctic Circle. In this case, the days of the year will have to be represented by a typical couple, "dark and bright, but of various lengths, *virûpe*." But as soon as we cross the Arctic Circle and go into "The Land of the Long Night," the above description requires to be amended by adding to the first couple, another couple of the long day and the long night, the lengths of which would vary according to latitude. This second couple of the long day and the long night, which match each other, will have also to be designated as *virûpe*, with this difference, however, that while the length of days and nights in the temperate zone would vary at the same place, the length of the long night and the long day would not vary at one and the same place, but only at different latitudes. Taking a couple of Day and Night, as representing the days and nights of the year, we shall have, therefore, to divide the different kinds of diurnal changes over the globe into three classes :—

(i) At the Equator,—*A single* couple; dark and bright, but always of the *same* form, or length (*sarûpe*).

(ii) Between the Equator and the Arctic Circle,—A *single* couple ; dark and bright, but of *various* forms, or lengths, (*virûpe*).

(iii) Between the Arctic Circle and the Pole,—*Two* couples ; each dark and bright, but of *various* forms, or lengths, (*virûpe*).

At the Pole, there is only one day and one night of six months each. Now if we have an express passage in the Ṛig-Veda (IV, 55, 3) indicating two different couples of Day and Night, *Ushâsâ-naktâ* and *Ahanî*, it is evident that the *aho-râtre* represented by them are the days and nights of the Circum-Polar regions, and of those alone. In the light of IV, 55, 3, we must, therefore, interpret III, 55, 11, quoted above, as describing two couples, one of the twin pair and the other of two sisters. The verse must, therefore, be translated :—"The twin pair (the first couple) make many forms (lengths); of the two one shines and the other is dark. Two sisters are they, the *shyâvî* or the dark and *arushî* or the bright, (the second couple)." No part of the verse is thus rendered superfluous, and the whole becomes far more comprehensible than otherwise.

We have seen that days and nights are represented by two distinct typical couples in the Ṛig-Veda *Ushâsâ-naktâ* and *Ahanî* ; and that if the distinction is not unmeaning we must take this to be the description of the days and nights within the Arctic Circle. Whether *Ahanî* means a couple of Day and Night distinct from *Ushâsâ-naktâ* in every place where the word occurs, it is difficult to say. But that in some places, at least, it denotes a peculiar couple of the Day and Night, not included in, and different from, *Ushâsâ-naktâ* is evident from IV, 55, 3. Now if *Ahanî* really means the couple of the long day and the long night, as distinguished from the ordinary days and nights, there is another way in which these two couples can be differentiated from each other. The ordinary days and nights follow each other closely, the day is succeeded by the night and the night by the day; and the two members of the couple, representing these days and nights, can not be described as separated from each other. But the long night and the long day, though of equal duration, do not follow each other in close succession. The long night occurs about the time when the sun is at the winter solstice, and the long day when he is at the summer solstice; and these two solstitial points are separated by 180°, being opposite to each other in the ecliptic. This character of *Ahanî* seems to have been traditionally known in the time of the *Araṇyakas*. Thus the Taittirîya Âraṇyaka, I, 2, 3, in discussing the personified Year,[1] first says that the Year has one head, and two different mouths, and then remarks that all this is 'season-characteristic', which the commentator explains by stating that the Year-God is said to have two mouths because it has two *Ayanas*, the northern and the southern, which include the seasons. But the statement important for our purpose is the one which follows next. The Âraṇyaka continues "To the right and the left side of the Year-God (are) the bright and the dark (days); and the following verse refers to it:—'Thy one (form) is bright, thy another sacrificial (dark), two

1. Taitt. Âran. I, 2, 3,—एक हि शिरो । नाना मुखे । कृत्स्नं तदृतुलक्षणम् ।

Ahans of different forms, thou art like *Dyau*. Thou, O Self-dependent! protectest all magic powers, O Pûṣhan! let thy bounty be here auspicious."[1] The verse, or the Mantra, here referred to is Ṛig. VI, 58, 1. Pûṣhan is there compared to Dyau and is said to have two forms, dark and bright, like the *Ahanî*. These dark and bright forms of *Ahanî* are said to constitute the right and the left side of the Year-God, that is, the two opposite parts of the body of the personified year. In other words the passage clearly states that the dark and the bright part of *Ahanî*, do not follow each other closely, but are situated on the diametrically opposite sides of the year. This can only be the case if the couple of Day and Night, represented by *Ahanî*, be taken to denote the long night and the long day in the Arctic regions. There the long night is matched by the long day, and while the one occurs when the sun is at the winter-solstice, the other occurs when he is at the summer-solstice. The two parts of *Ahanî* are, therefore, very correctly represented as forming the right and the left side of the Year-God in the *Âraṇyaka*, and the passage thus materially supports the view about the nature of *Ahanî* mentioned above.

Lastly, we have express passages in the Ṛig-Veda where a long day is described. In V, 54, 5, an extended daily course (*dîrgham yojanam*) of the sun is mentioned and the Maruts are said to have extended their strength and greatness in a similar way.[2] But the most explicit statement about the long day is found in X, 138, 3. This

1. Taitt. Âraṇyaka, I, 2, 4,— शुक्लकृष्णे संवत्सरस्य। दक्षिणवामयोः पार्श्वयोः। तस्यैषा भवति। शुक्रं ते अन्यद्यजतं ते अन्यद्विषुरूपे अहनी द्यौरिवासि। विश्वा हि माया अवसि स्वधावो भद्रा ते पूषन्निह रातिरस्तु। नास्य भुवनं। न पूषा न पशवः। नादित्यः। संवत्सर एव प्रत्यक्षेण प्रियतमं विद्यात्।

2. Ṛig. V, 54, 5—तद्वीर्यं वो मरुतो महित्वनं दीर्घं ततान सूर्यो न योजनम्।

hymn celebrates the exploits of Indra, all of which are performed in aerial or heavenly regions. In the first verse the killing of Vṛitra, and the releasing of the dawns and the waters are mentioned; and in the second the sun is said to have been made to shine by the same process. The third verse[1] is as follows:—

Vi sûryo madhye amuchad rathan divo
vidad dâsâya pratimânam âryaḥ ।
Dṛiḍhâni Pipror asurasya mâyinaḥ
Indro vyâsyach chakṛivâṁ Ṛijishvanâ ॥

The fourth, fifth and the sixth verses all refer to the destruction of Vṛitra's forts, the chastisement of Ushas and the placing of the moons in the heaven. But the third verse quoted above is alone important for our purpose. The words are simple and easy, and the verse may be thus translated, "The sun unyoked his car in the midst of heaven; the Ârya found a counter-measure (*pratimânam*) for the Dâsa. Indra, acting with Ṛijishvan, overthrew the solid forts of Pipru, the conjuring Asura." It is the first half of the verse that is relevant to our purpose. The sun is said to have unyoked his car, not at sunset, or on the horizon, but in the midst of heaven, there to rest for some time. There is no uncertainty about it, for the words are so clear; and the commentators have found it difficult to explain this extraordinary conduct of the sun in the midway of the heavens. Mr. Griffith says that it is, perhaps, an allusion to an eclipse, or to the detention of the sun to enable the Aryans to complete the overthrow of their enemies. Both of these suggestions are, however, not satisfactory. During an eclipse the sun is covered with the dark shadow of the earth, and is not besides stationary. The description that the sun unyoked his car in the mid-heaven

1. Ṛig. X, 138, 3— वि सूर्यो मध्ये अमुचद्रथं दिवो विददासाय प्रतिमानमार्यः । दृळ्हानि पिप्रोरसुरस्य मायिन इंद्रो व्यास्यच्चकृवाँ ऋजिश्वना ॥

cannot, therefore, apply to the eclipsed sun. As regards the other suggestion, *viz.*, that the sun remained stationary for a while to allow his favourite race, the Aryans, to overthrow their enemies, it seems to have had its origin in the Biblical passage (Joshua, X, 12, 13), where the sun is said to have stood still, at the word of Joshua, until the people had avenged themselves upon their enemies. But there is no authority for importing this Biblical idea into the Ṛig-Veda. Indra's exploits are described in a number of hymns in the Ṛig-Veda, but in no other hymn he is said to have made the sun stand still for the Aryans. We must, therefore, reject both the explanations suggested by Griffith. Sâyaṇa gets over the difficulty by interpreting the phrase, *ratham vi amuchat madhye divaḥ*, as meaning that "the sun loosened (*vi amuchat*) his carriage, that is, set it free to travel, towards the middle (*madhye*) of heaven, (*ratham prasthânâya vi-muktavân*)." Sâyaṇa's meaning, therefore, is that when Indra obtained compensation from Vṛitra, he let loose the chariot of the sun to travel towards the midst of the sky. But the construction is evidently a strained one. The verb *vi much* is used in about a dozen places in the Ṛig-Veda in relation to horses, and everywhere it means to 'unharness,' 'unyoke,' or '*separate* the horses *from* the carriage for rest;' and even Sâyaṇa has interpreted it in the same way. Thus *vi-muchya* is explained by him as *rathât vishlishya* in I, 104, 1, and *rathât vi-muchya* in III, 32, 1, and *rathât visṛijya* in X, 160, 1, (also compare I, 171, 1; I, 177, 4; VI, 40, 1). The most natural meaning of the present verse would, therefore, be that the 'sun unyoked his carriage.' But even supposing that *vi much* can be interpreted to mean 'to loosen for travel,' the expression would be appropriate only when there is an antecedent stoppage or slow motion of the sun. The question why the sun stopped or slackened his motion in the midst of the sky would, therefore, still remain unsolved. The phrase *divaḥ madhye* naturally means '*in* the midst of the sky,' and cannot be interpreted to mean '*towards* the mid-heaven.' Of course if the sun was below the horizon, we may describe him as having loosened his horses for travel as in V, 62, 1; but even there the meaning seems to be that the horses rested at the place. In the present case the sun is already in the midst of heaven, and we cannot take him below the horizon without a palpable distortion of meaning. Nor can we properly explain the action of retaliation (*pratimânam*), if we accept Sâyaṇa's interpretation. We must, therefore, interpret the first half of the verse to mean that "the sun unyoked his carriage in the midst of heaven." There is another passage in the Ṛig-Veda which speaks of the sun halting in the midst of heaven. In VII, 87, 5, the king Varuṇa is said to have made "the golden (sun) rock like a swing in the heaven" (*chakre divi preṅkhâm hiraṇmayam*), clearly meaning that the sun swayed backwards and forwards in the heaven being visible all the time, (cf. also VII, 88, 3). The idea expressed in the present verse is exactly the same, for even within the Arctic regions the sun will appear as swinging only during the long continuous day, when he does not go below the horizon once every twenty-four hours. There is, therefore, nothing strange or uncommon in the present verse which says that "the sun unyoked his carriage for some time in the midst of the sky;" and we need not be impatient to escape from the natural meaning of the verse. A long halt of the sun in the midst of the heaven is here clearly described, and we must take it to refer to the long day in the Arctic region. The statement in the second line further supports the same view. European scholars appear to have been misled, in this instance, by the words *Ârya* and *Dâsa*, which they are accustomed to interpret as meaning the Aryan and the non-Aryan race. But though the words may be interpreted in this way in some passages, such is not the case everywhere. The word *Dâsa* is applied to Indra's enemies in a number of places. Thus Shambara is called a *Dâsa* (IV, 30, 14), and the same adjective is applied to Pipru in VIII, 32, 2, and to Namuchi in V, 30, 7. Indra is said to inspire fear into the *Dâsa* in X, 120, 2, and, in II, 11, 2, he is described as having rent the *Dâsa*, who considered himself immortal. In the verse under consideration Indra's victory over Pipru is celebrated, and we know that Pipru is elsewhere called a *Dâsa*. It is, therefore, quite natural to suppose that the words *Arya* and *Dâsa*, in the above verse, refer to Indra and Pipru, and not to the Aryan and the non-Aryan race. The exploits described are all heavenly, and it jars with the context to take a single sentence in the whole hymn as referring to the victory of the Aryan over the non-Aryan race. There is again the word *pratimâna* (*lit.* counter-measure), which denotes that what has been done is by way of retaliation, a sort of counter-poise or counter-blast, with a view to avenge the mischief done by *Dâsa*. A battle between the Aryans and the non-Aryans cannot be so described unless a previous defeat of the Aryans is first alluded to. The plain meaning of the verse, therefore, is that the sun was made to halt in the midst of the sky, producing a long day, and Indra thus found a counter-poise for *Dâsa*, his enemy. For we know that darkness is brought on by the *Dâsa*, and it is he who brings on the long night; but if the Dâsa made the night long, Indra retaliated or counter-acted by making the day as long as the night of the Dâsa. The long night of the Arctic regions is, we have seen, *matched* by the long day in those regions, and the present verse expresses the same idea of matching the one by the other. There is no reference to the victory of the Aryan race over the non-Aryans, or anything of that kind as supposed by Western scholars. Sâyaṇa, who had no historic theories to mislead him, has rightly interpreted *Ârya* and *Dâsa* in this verse as referring to Indra and his enemy; but he, in his turn, has misinterpreted, as shewn above, the first half of the verse in regard to the sun's long halt in the midst of the sky. The misinterpretation of the second hemistich comes from Western scholars, like Muir, who interprets *Arya*, as meaning the Aryans and *Dâsa*, the non-Aryans. This shows how in the absence of the true key to the meaning of a passage, we may be led away by current theories, even where the words are plain and simple in themselves.

We thus see that the Ṛig-Veda speaks of *two* different couples of Day and Night, one alone of which represents the ordinary days and nights in the year, and the second, the *Ahanî*, is a distinct couple by itself, forming, according to the Taittirîya Âraṇyaka, the right and the left hand side of the Year, indicating the long Arctic day and night. The Taittirîya Saṁhitâ again gives us in clear terms a tradition that in the former age the night was so long that men were afraid it would not dawn. We have also a number of expressions in the Ṛig-Veda denoting 'long nights' or 'long and ghastly darkness,' and also the 'long journey' of the sun. Prayers are also offered to Vedic deities to enable the worshipper to reach safely the end of the night, the 'other boundary of which is not known.' Finally we have an express text declaring that the sun halted in the midst of the sky and thereby retaliated the mischief brought on by Dâsa's causing the long night. Thus we have not only the long day and the long night mentioned in the Ṛig-Veda, but the idea that the two match each other is also found therein, while the Taittirîya Âraṇyaka tells us that they form the opposite sides of the Year-God. Besides the passages proving the long duration of the dawn, we have, therefore, sufficient independent evidence to hold that the long night in the Arctic regions and its counterpart the long day were both known to the poets of the Ṛig-Veda, and the Taittirîya Saṁhitâ distinctly informs us that it was a phenomenon of the former (*purâ*) age.

I shall close this chapter with a short discussion of another Circum-Polar characteristic, I mean the southern course of the sun. It is previously stated, that the sun can never appear over-head at any station in the temperate or the frigid zone, and that an observer stationed within these zones in the northern hemisphere will see the sun to his right hand or towards the south, while at the North Pole the sun will seem to rise from the south. Now the word *dakṣhiṇa* in Vedic Sanskrit denotes both the 'right hand' and the 'south,' as it does in other Aryan languages; for, as observed by Prof. Sayce, these people had to face the rising sun with their right hands to the south, in addressing their gods, and hence "Sanskrit *dakṣhiṇa*, Welsh *dehau* and Old Irish *des* all mean at once 'right hand' and 'south'."[1] With this explanation before us, we can now understand how in a number of passages in the Ṛig-Veda Western scholars translate *dakṣhiṇa* by 'right side,' where Indian scholars take the word to mean 'the southern direction.' There is a third meaning of *dakṣhiṇâ*, *viz.*, 'largess' or 'guerdon,' and in some places the claims of rich largesses seem to have been pushed too far. Thus when the suns are said to be only for *dakṣhiṇâvats* in I, 125, 6, it looks very probable that originally the expression had some reference to the southern direction rather than to the gifts given at sacrifices. In III, 58, 1, Sûrya is called the son of *Dakṣhiṇâ*, and even if *Dakṣhiṇâ* be here taken to mean the Dawn, yet the question why the Dawn was called

1. See Sayce's Introduction to the Science of Language, Vol. II, p. 130.

Dakshiṇâ remains, and the only explanation at present suggested is that *Dakshiṇâ* means 'skilful' or 'expert.' A better way to explain these phrases is to make them refer to the southerly direction; and after what has been said above such an explanation will seem to be highly probable. It is, of course, necessary to be critical in the interpretation of the Vedic hymns, but I think that we shall be carrying our critical spirit too far, if we say that in no passage in the Ṛig-Veda *dakshiṇâ* or its derivatives are used to denote the southerly direction (I, 95, 6; II, 42, 3). Herodotus informs us (IV, 42) that certain Phœnician mariners were commanded by Pharoah Neco, king of Egypt, to sail round Lybia (Africa) and return by the Pillars of Hercules (Straits of Gibralter). The mariners accomplished the voyage and returned in the third year. But Herodotus disbelieves them, because, on their return, they told such (to him incredible) stories, that in rounding Lybia they saw the sun to their right. Herodotus could not believe that the sun would ever appear in the north; but he little thought that what was incredible to him would itself be regarded as indisputable evidence of the authenticity of the account in later days. Let us take a lesson from this story, and not interpret *dakshiṇâ*, either by 'right-hand side' or by 'largess,' in every passage in the Ṛig-Veda. There may not be distinct passages to show that the sun, or the dawn, came from the south. But the very fact that Ushas is called *Dakshiṇâ* (I, 123, 1; X, 107, 1), and the sun, the son of *Dakshiṇâ* (III, 58, 1), is itself very suggestive, and possibly we have here phrases which the Vedic bards employed because in their days these were old and recognised expressions in the language. Words, like fossils, very often preserve the oldest ideas or facts in a language; and though Vedic poets may have forgotten the original meaning of these phrases, that is no reason why we should refuse to draw from the history of these words such conclusions as may legitimately follow from it. The fact that the north is designated by the word *ut-tara*, meaning 'upper,' and the south by *adha-ra*, meaning 'lower,' also points to the same conclusion; for the north cannot be over-head or 'upper' except to an observer at or near the North Pole. In later literature, we find a tradition that the path of the sun lies through regions which are lower (*adhaḥ*) than the abode of the Seven Ṛishis, or the constellation of Ursa Major.[1] That the ecliptic lies to the south of the constellation is plain enough, but it cannot be said to be *below* the constellation, unless the zenith of the observer is in the constellation, or between it and the North Pole, a position, possible only in the case of an observer in the Arctic region. I have already quoted a passage from the Ṛig-Veda, which speaks of the Seven Bears (*Ṛikshâḥ*), as being placed on high in the heavens (*uchchâḥ*). But I have not been able to find out any Vedic authority for the tradition that the sun's path lies below the constellation of the Seven Bears. It has also been stated previously that mere southerly direction of the sun, even if completely established, is not a sure indication of the observer being within the circum-polar region, as the sun will appear to move always to the south of the observer even in the temperate zone. It is, therefore, not necessary to pursue this point further. It has been shown that the Ṛig-Veda mentions the long night and the long day, and we shall see in the next chapter that the months and the seasons mentioned in this Old Book fully accord with the theory we have formed from the evidence hitherto discussed.

---

1. See Kâlidâsa's Kumârasambhava, VI, 7,—अधःप्रस्थापिताश्वेन समावर्जितकेतुना । सहस्ररश्मिना साक्षात्सप्रणाममुदीक्षिताः । Also I, 16,—सप्तर्षिहस्तावचितावशेषानधो विवस्वान् परिवर्तमानः । See also Mallinâtha's commentary on these verses.

CHAPTER VII.

MONTHS AND SEASONS.

Evidence of rejected calendar generally preserved in sacrificial rites by conservative priests —Varying number of the months of sunshine in the Arctic region —Its effect on sacrificial sessions considered —Seven-fold character of the sun in the Vedas —The legend of Aditi —She presents her seven sons to the gods and casts away the eighth —Various explanations of the legend in the Brâhmanas and the Taittiriya A'ranyaka —Twelve suns understood to be the twelve month-gods in later literature —By analogy seven suns must have once indicated seven months of sunshine —Different suns were believed to be necessary to produce different seasons —Aditi's legend belongs to the former age, or *pûrvyam yugam* —Evidence from sacrificial literature —The families of sacrificers in primeval times — Called 'our ancient fathers' in the Rig-Veda —Atharvan and Angiras traced to Indo-European period —Navagvas and Dashagvas, the principal species of the Angirases —Helped Indra in his fight with Vala —They finished their sacrificial session in ten months —The sun dwelling in darkness —Ten months' sacrifices indicate only ten months of sunshine, followed by the long night —Etymology of Navagva and Dashagva —According to Sâyana the words denote persons sacrificing for nine or ten months —Prof. Lignana's explanation improbable —The adjective *Virûpas* applied to the Angirases —Indicates other varieties of these sacrificers —Saptagu, or seven Hotris or Vipras —Legend of Dîrghatamas —As narrated in the Mahâbhârata —A protege of Ashvins in the Rig-Veda —Growing old in the tenth *yuga* —Meaning of *yuga* discussed —*Mânushâ yugâ* means 'human ages,' and not always 'human tribes' in the Rig-Veda —Two passages in proof thereof —Interpretations of Western scholars examined and rejected —*Mânushâ yugâ* denoted months after the long dawn and before the long night —Dîrghatamas represents the sun setting in the tenth month —*Mânushâ yugâ* and continuous nights —The *five* seasons in ancient times —A Rig-Veda passage bearing on it discussed —The year of five seasons described as residing in waters

—Indicates darkness of the long night —Not made up by combining any two consecutive seasons out of six —The explanation in the Brâhmanas improbable —Summary.

STARTING with the tradition about the half-yearly night of the gods found everywhere in Sanskrit literature, and also in the Avesta, we have found direct references in the Ṛig-Veda to a long continuous dawn of thirty days, the long day and the long night, when the sun remained above the horizon or went below it for a number of 24 hours; and we have also seen that the Ṛig-Vedic texts describe these things as events of a bye-gone age. The next question, therefore, is—Do we meet in the Vedas with similar traces of the Arctic conditions of seasons, months or years? It is stated previously that the calendar current at the time of the Vedic Saṁhitâs was different from the Arctic calendar. But if the ancestors of the Vedic people ever lived near the North Pole, "we may," as observed by Sir Norman Lockyer with reference to the older Egyptian calendar, "always reckon upon the conservatism of the priests of the temples retaining the tradition of the old rejected year in every case." Sir Norman Lockyer first points out how the ancient Egyptian year of 360 days was afterwards replaced by a year of 365 days; and then gives two instances of the traditional practice by which the memory of the old year was preserved. "Thus even at Philæ in later times," says he, "in the temple of Osiris, there were 360 bowls for sacrifice, which were filled daily with milk by a specified rotation of priests. At Acanthus there was a perforated cask into which one of the 360 priests poured water from the Nile daily."[1] And what took place in Egypt, we may expect to have taken place in Vedic times. The characteristics of an Arctic year are so unlike those of a year in the temperate zone, that if the ancestors of the Vedic

1. See Lockyer's Dawn of Astronomy, p. 248.

people ever lived within the Arctic regions, and imigrated southwards owing to glaciation, an adaptation of the calendar to the altered geographical and astronomical conditions of the new home was a necessity, and must have been effected at the time. But in making this change, we may, as remarked by Sir Norman Lockyer, certainly expect the conservative priests to retain as much of the old calendar as possible, or at least preserve the traditions of the older year in one form or another especially in their sacrificial rites. Indo-European etymological equations have established the fact that sacrifices, or rather the system of making offerings to the gods for various purposes, existed from the primeval period;[1] and if so, the system must have undergone great modifications as the Aryan races moved from the Arctic to the temperate zone. I have shown elsewhere that calendar and sacrifice, especially the annual *sattras*, are closely connected, and that in the case of the annual *sattras*, or the sacrificial sessions which lasted for one year, the priests had in view, as observed by Dr. Haug,[2] the yearly course of the sun. It was the duty of these priests to keep up the sacrificial fire, as the Parsi priests now do, and to see that the yearly rounds of sacrifices were performed at proper times (*ṛitus*). The sacrificial calendar in the Arctic home must, however, have been different from what it came to be afterwards; and happily many traces of this calendar are still discoverable in the sacrificial literature of Vedic times, proving that the ancient worshippers or sacrificers of our race must have lived in circum-polar regions. But before discussing this evidence, it is necessary to briefly describe the points wherein we might expect the an-

1. See Schrader's Prehistoric Antiquities of the Aryan Peoples, Part IV, Chap. XIII, translated by Jevons, p. 421. Cf. Sans. *yaj*; Zend *yaz*; Greek *azomai*, *agios*. See *Orion*, Chap. II.

2. See Dr. Haug's Aitareya Brâh. Vol. I, Introduction, p. 46.

cient or the oldest sacrificial system to differ from the one current in Vedic times.

In the Saṁhitâs and Brâhmaṇas, the annual *sattras*, or yearly sacrificial sessions, are said to extend over twelve months. But this was impossible within the Arctic region, where the sun goes below the horizon for a number of days or months during the year, thereby producing the long night. The oldest duration of the annual *sattras*, if such *sattras* were ever performed within the Polar regions, would, therefore, be shorter than twelve months. In other words, an annual *sattra* of *less* than twelve months would be the chief distinguishing mark of the older sacrificial system, as contrasted with the later annual *sattra* of twelve months. It must also be borne in mind that the number of the months of sunshine and darkness cannot be the same everywhere in the Circum-Polar regions. At the Pole the sun is alternately above and below the horizon for six months each. But as all people cannot be expected to be stationed precisely at the Pole, practically the months of sunshine will vary from seven to eleven for the inhabitants of the Arctic region, those nearest to the North Pole having seven month's sunshine, while those living farther south from the Pole having the sun above their horizon for eight, nine or ten months according to latitude. These periods of sunshine would be made up of the long Arctic day at the place and a succession of ordinary days and nights closely following each other; and sacrificial sessions would be held, or principal business transacted, and important religious and social ceremonies performed only during this period. It would, so to say, be a period of action, as contrasted with the long night, by which it was followed. The long dawn following the long night, would mark the beginning of this period of activity; and the Arctic sacrificial year would, practically, be made up, only of these months of sunshine. Therefore, the varying number of the months of sunshine would be the chief peculiarity of the Arctic sacrificial calendar, and we must bear it in mind in examining the traces of the oldest calendar in the Ṛig-Veda, or other Saṁhitâs.

A dawn of thirty days, as we measure days, implies a position so near the North Pole, that the period of sunshine at the place could not have been longer than about seven months, comprising, of course, a long day of four or five months, and a succession of regular days and nights during the remaining period; and we find that the Ṛig-Veda does preserve for us the memory of such months of sunshine. We refer first to the legend of Aditi, or the seven Âdityas (suns), which is obviously based on some natural phenomenon. This legend expressly tells us that the oldest number of Âdityas or suns was seven, and the same idea is independently found in many other places in the Ṛig-Veda. Thus in IX, 114, 3, *seven* Âdityas and *seven* priests are mentioned together, though the names of the different suns are not given therein. In II, 27, 1, Mitra, Aryaman, Bhaga, Varuṇa, Dakṣha and Aṁsha are mentioned by name as so many different Âdityas, but the seventh is not named. This omission does not, however, mean much, as the septenary character of the sun is quite patent from the fact that he is called *saptâshva* (seven-horsed) in V, 45, 9, and his 'seven-wheeled' chariot is said to be drawn by 'seven bay steeds' (I, 50, 8), or by a single horse 'with seven names' in I, 164, 2. The Atharva Veda also speaks of "the seven bright rays of the sun" (VII, 107, 1); and the epithet *Âditya*, as applied to the sun in the Ṛig-Veda, is rendered more clearly by *Aditeḥ putraḥ* (Aditi's son) in A. V. XIII, 2, 9. Sâyaṇa, following Yâska, derives this seven-fold character of the sun from his seven rays; but why solar rays were taken to be seven still remains unexplained, unless we hold that the Vedic bards had anticipated the discovery of seven prismatic rays or colours, which were unknown even to Yâska or Sâyaṇa. Again though the existence of seven suns may be explained on this hypothesis, yet it fails to account for the death of the eighth sun; for the legend of Aditi (Ṛig. X, 72, 2-3) tells us, "Of the eight sons of Aditi, who were born from her body, she approached the gods with seven, and cast out Mârtâṇḍa. With seven sons Aditi approached (the gods) in the former age (*pûrvyam yugam*); she brought thither Mârtâṇḍa again for birth and death."[1] The story is discussed in various places in the Vedic literature, and many other attempts, unfortunately all unsatisfactory, have been made to explain it in a rational and intelligent way. Thus in the Taittirîya Saṁhitâ, VI, 5, 6, 1*f*., the story of Aditi cooking a *Brahmaudana* oblation for the gods, the Sâdhyas, is narrated. The remnant of the oblation was given to her by the gods, and four Âdityas were born to her from it. She then cooked a second oblation, and ate it herself first; but the Âditya born from it was an imperfect egg. She cooked a third time and the Âditya Vivasvat, the progenitor of man, was born. But the Saṁhitâ does not give the number and names of the eight Âdityas, and this omission is supplied by the Taittirîya Brâhmaṇa (I, 1, 9, 1*f*.). The Brâhmaṇa tells us that Aditi cooked the oblation four times, and each time the gods gave her the remnant of the oblation. Four pairs of sons were thus born to her; the first pair was Dhâtṛi and Aryaman, the second Mitra and Varuṇa, the third Aṁsha and Bhaga and the fourth Indra and Vivasvat. But the Brâhmaṇa does not explain why the eighth son was called Mârtâṇḍa, and cast away. The Taittirîya Âraṇyaka, I, 13, 2-3, (cited by Sâyaṇa in his gloss on Ṛig. II, 27, 1, and X, 72, 8), first quotes the two verses

1. Ṛig. X, 72, 8 & 9:—अष्टौ पुत्रासो अदितेर्ये जातास्तन्वस्परि । देवाँ उप प्रैत्सप्तभिः परा मार्ताण्डमास्यत् ॥ सप्तभिः पुत्रैरदितिरुप प्रैत्पूर्व्यं युगं । प्रजायै मृत्यवे त्वत्पुनर्मार्ताण्डमाभरत् ॥ For त्वत्पुनः in the second verse the Taittirîya Âraṇyaka, I, 13, 3, reads तत्परा, see *infra*.

from the Ṛig-Veda (X, 72, 8 and 9), which give the legend of Aditi but with a slightly different reading for the second line of the second verse. Thus, instead of *tvat punaḥ Mârtâṇḍam â abharat* (she *brought again* Mârtâṇḍa thither for birth and death), the Âraṇyaka reads *tat parâ Mârtâṇḍam â abharat* (she *set aside* Mârtâṇḍa for birth and death). The Âraṇyaka then proceeds to give the names of the eight sons, as Mitra, Varuṇa, Dhâtṛi, Aryaman, Aṁsha, Bhaga, Indra and Vivasvat. But no further explanation is added, nor are we told which of these eight sons represented Mârtâṇḍa. There is, however, another passage in the Âraṇyaka (I, 7, 1—6) which throws some light on the nature of these Âdityas.[1] The names of the suns here given are different. They are :— Âroga, Bhrâja, Paṭara, Pataṅga, Svarṇara, Jyotishîmat, Vibhâsa and Kashyapa; the last of which is said to remain constantly at the great mount Meru, permanently illumining that region. The other seven suns are said to derive their light from Kashyapa and to be alone visible to man. We are then told that these seven suns are considered by some Âchâryas to be the seven manifestations of the *Prâṇas*, or the vital powers in man; while others are said to hold the opinion that they are the types of seven officiating priests

1. See Taittirîya Âraṇyaka, I, 7,—आरोगोभ्राजः पटरः पतंगः। स्वर्णरो ज्योतिषीमान् विभासः। ...। कश्यपोऽष्टमः। स महामेरुं न जहाति। ...। ते अस्मै सर्वे कश्यपाज्ज्योतिर्लभन्ते। ...। सप्त शीर्षण्याः प्राणाः सूर्या इत्याचार्याः। ...। सप्तर्त्विजः सूर्या इत्याचार्याः। तेषामेषाभवति। "सप्त दिशो नानासूर्याः सप्त होतार ऋत्विजः। देवा आदित्या ये सप्त तेभिः सोमाभि रक्ष न" इति (Ṛig. IX, 114, 3)। तदप्याम्नायः। दिग्भ्राज ऋतून् करोति। एतयैवावृता सहस्रसूर्यताया इति वैशंपायनः। ......। नानालिंगत्वादृतूनां नानासूर्यत्वं। अष्टौ तु व्यवसिता इति।

Upon this Sâyaṇa says :—'दिग्भ्राजः' तान् तान् दिशं प्राप्यावस्थिताः सूर्याः 'ऋतून्' वसंतादिसूचितानृतुधर्मान्, 'करोति' तस्यां तस्यां दिशि कुर्वंति। न हि ऋतुनिष्पादकसूर्यव्यतिरेकेण तत्तदृतुधर्माः संभवंति। तस्मात्संत्येव दिक्षु विभिन्नाः सूर्याः। And again नानालिंगत्वादिति। यद्येक एव सूर्यः स्यात् तदानीं वसंताद्यृतूनां नानालिंगत्वं न स्यात्। न हि कारणभेदमन्तरेण कार्यभेदः संभवति। तस्मादृतुधर्मवैलक्षण्यसिद्ध्ये बहुसूर्यत्वमभ्युपेयम्। .....। 'अष्टौ तु व्यवसिता' इति। यद्यपि, संत्येव तत्तल्लिंगकल्पा अनन्ताः सूर्याः। किन्तु तत्रास्ति कश्चिद्विशेषः। 'व्यवसिताः' निश्चिताः।

(*ritvijaḥ*). A third explanation is then put forward, *viz.*, that the distinction of seven suns is probably based on the different effects of sun's rays in different months or seasons, and in support of it a Mantra, or Vedic verse, *Dig-bhrâja ritûn karoti*, (resorting to, or shining in, different regions (they) make the seasons), is quoted. I have not been able to find the Mantra in the existing Saṁhitâs, nor does Sâyaṇa give us any clue to it, but simply observes "the different features of different seasons cannot be accounted for, except by supposing them to have been caused by different suns; therefore, different suns must exist in different regions".[1] But this' explanation is open to the objection (actually raised by Vaishampâyana), that we shall have, on this theory, to assume the existence of thousands of suns as the characteristics of the seasons are so numerous. The Âraṇyaka admits, to a certain extent, the force of this objection, but says—*ashṭau tu vyavasitâḥ*, meaning that the number eight is settled by the text of the scripture, and there is no further arguing about it. The Shatapatha Brâhmaṇa, III, 1, 3, 3, explains the legend of Aditi somewhat on the same lines. It says that seven alone of Aditi's sons are styled *Devâḥ Âdityâḥ* (the gods Âdityas) by men, and that the eighth Mârtâṇḍa was born undeveloped, whereupon the Âditya gods created man and other animals out of him. In two other passages of the Shatapatha Brâhmaṇa, VI, 1, 2, 8, and XI, 6, 3, 8, the number of Âdityas is, however, given as twelve. In the first (VI, 1, 2, 8) they are said to have sprung from twelve drops generated by Prajâpati and then placed in different regions (*dikshu*); while in the second (XI, 6, 3, 8)[2] these

1. See Sâyaṇa's explanation quoted on tha last page.

2. Shatapatha Brâhmaṇa, VI, 1, 2, 8,—स मनसैव वाचं मिथुनं समभवत्। स द्वादश द्रप्सान् गर्भ्यभवत्। ते द्वादशादित्या असृज्यंत तान्दिक्षूपादधात्। Again XI, 6, 3, 8— कतम आदित्या इति। द्वादश मासाः संवत्सरस्यैत आदित्याः।

twelve Âdityas are identified with the twelve months of the year. The number of Âdityas is also given as twelve in the Upanishads; while in the post-Vedic literature they are everywhere said to be twelve, answering to the twelve months of the year. Muir, in his *Original Sanskrit Texts*, Volumes IV and V, gives most of these passages, but offers no explanation as to the legend of Aditi, except such as is to be found in the passages quoted. There are many different speculations or theories of Western Scholars regarding the nature and character of Aditi, but as far as the number of Âdityas is concerned, I know of no satisfactory explanation as yet suggested by them. On the contrary the tendency is, as observed by Prof. Max Muller, to regard the number, seven or eight, as unconnected with any solar movements. A suggestion is made that the eight Âdityas may be taken to represent the eight cardinal points of the compass, but the death or casting away of the eighth Âditya seals the fate of this explanation, which thus seems to have been put forward only to be rejected like Mârtâṇḍa, the eighth Âditya.

We have here referred to, or quoted, the texts and passages bearing on Aditi's legend, or the number of Âdityas, at some length, in order to show how we are apt to run into wild speculations about the meaning of a simple legend when the key to it is lost. That the twelve Âdityas are understood to represent the twelve month-gods in later Vedic literature is evident from the passage in the Shatapatha Brâhmaṇa (XI, 6, 3, 8=Bṛih. Âṛṇ. Up. III, 9, 5), which says "There are twelve months of the year; these are the Âdityas." With this explanation before us, and the belief that different seasonal changes could be explained only by assuming the existence of different suns, it required no very great stretch of imagination to infer that if twelve Âdityas now represent the twelve months of the year, the seven Âdityas must have once (*pûrvyam yugam*) represented the seven months of the year. But this explanation, reasonable though it was, did not commend itself, or we might even say, occur to Vedic scholars, who believed that the home of the Aryans lay somewhere in Central Asia. It is, therefore, satisfactory to find that the idea of different suns producing different months is recognised so expressly in the Taittirîya Âraṇyaka, which quotes a Vedic text, not now available, in support thereof, and finally pronounces in favour of the theory, which regards the seven suns as presiding over seven different heavenly regions and thereby producing different seasons, in spite of the objection that it would lead to the assumption of thousands of suns—an objection, which the Âraṇyaka disposes of summarily by observing that eight is a settled number, and that we have no right to change it. That this explanation is the most probable of all is further evident from Ṛig. IX, 114, 3, which says "There are seven sky-regions (*sapta dishaḥ*), with their different suns (*nânâ-sûryâḥ*), there are seven Hotṛis as priests, those who are the seven gods, the Âdityas,—with them, O Soma! protect us." Here *nânâ-sûryâḥ* is an adjective which qualifies *dishaḥ* (*sapta*), and the co-relation between seven regions and seven suns is thus expressly recognised. Therefore, the simplest explanation of Aditi's legend is that she presented to the gods, that is, brought forth into heavens, her seven sons, the Âdityas, to form the seven months of sunshine in the place. She had an eighth son, but he was born in an undeveloped state, or, was, what we may call, still-born; evidently meaning that the eighth month was not a month of sunshine, or that the period of darkness at the place commenced with the eighth month. All this occurred not in this age, but in the previous age, and the words *pûrvyam yugam* in X, 72, 9, are very important from this point of view. The word *yuga* is evidently used to denote a period of time in the first and second verses of the hymn, which refer to the former age of the gods (*de-*

vânâm pûrvye yuge) and also of the later age (*uttare yuge*). Western scholars are accustomed to interpret *yuga* to mean 'a generation of men' almost in every place where the phrase is met with; and we shall have to consider the correctness of this interpretation later on. For the purpose of this legend it is enough to state that the phrase *pûrvyam yugam* occurs twice in the hymn, and that where it first occurs (in verse 2), it clearly denotes 'an early age' or 'some division of time.' Naturally enough we must, therefore, interpret it in the same way where it occurs again in the same hymn, *viz.*, in the verse describing the legend of Aditi's seven sons. The sun having seven rays, or seven horses, also implies the same idea differently expressed. The seven months of sunshine, with their different temperatures, are represented by seven suns producing these different results by being differently located, or as having different kinds of rays, or as having different chariots, or horses, or different wheels to the same chariot. It is one and the same idea in different forms, or as the Ṛig-Veda puts it, "one horse with seven names," (I, 164, 2). A long dawn of thirty days indicates a period of sunshine for seven months; and we now see that the legend of Aditi is intelligible only if we interpret it as a relic of a time when there were seven flourishing month-gods, and the eighth was either still-born, or cast away. *Mârtâṇḍa* is etymologically derived from *mârta* meaning 'dead or undeveloped', (being connected with *mṛita*, the past participle of *mṛi*, to die) and *âṇḍa*, an egg or a bird; and it denotes a dead sun, or a sun that has sunk below the horizon, for in Ṛig. X, 55, 5, we find the word *mamâra* (died) used to denote the setting of the daily sun. The sun is also represented as a bird in many places in the Ṛig-Veda (V, 47, 3; X, 55, 6; X, 177, 1; X, 119, 3). A cast away bird (*Mârtâṇḍa*) is, therefore, the sun that has set or sunk below the horizon, and the whole legend is obviously a reminiscence of the place where the sun shone above the horizon for seven months, and went below it in the beginning of the eighth. If this nature of the sun-god is once impressed on the memory, it can not be easily forgotten by any people simply by their being obliged to change their residence; and thus the seven-fold character of the sun-god must have been handed down as an old tradition, though the Vedic people lived later on in places presided over by the twelve Âdityas. That is how ancient traditions are preserved everywhere, as, for instance, those relating to the older year in the Egyptian literature, previously referred to.

We have seen above that the peculiar characteristic of the Arctic region is the *varying* number of the months of sunshine in that place. It is not, therefore, enough to say that traces of a period of seven months' sunshine are alone found in the Ṛig-Veda. If our theory is correct, we ought to find references to periods of eight, nine or ten months' sunshine along with that of seven months either in the shape of traditions, or in some other form; and fortunately there are such references in the Ṛig-Veda, only if we know where to look for them. We have seen that the sun's chariot is said to be drawn by seven horses, and that this seven-fold character of the sun has reference to the seven suns, conceived as seven different month-gods. There are many other legends based on this seven-fold division, but as they do not refer to the subject under discussion, we must reserve their consideration for another occasion. The only fact necessary to be mentioned in this place is that the number of the sun's horses is said to be not only *seven* (I, 50, 8), but also *ten* in IX, 63, 9; and if the first be taken to represent seven months, the other must be understood to stand for ten months as well. We need not, however, depend upon such extension of the legend of seven Âdityas to prove that the existence of nine or ten months of sunshine was known to the poets of the Ṛig-Veda. The evidence, which I am now going to cite comes from another source I mean, the sacrificial literature, which is quite independent of the legend of the seven Âdityas. The Ṛig-Veda mentions a number of *ancient* sacrificers styled 'our fathers' (II, 33, 13; VI, 22, 2), who instituted the sacrifice *in ancient times*, and laid down, for the guidance of man, the path which he should, in future, follow. Thus the sacrifice offered by Manu, is taken as the type, and other sacrifices are compared with it in I, 76, 5. But Manu was not alone to offer this ancient sacrifice to the gods. In X, 63, 7, he is said to have made the first offerings to the gods along with the seven Hotṛis ; while Aṅgiras and Yayâti are mentioned with him as ancient sacrificers in I, 31, 17, Bhṛigu and Aṅgiras in VIII, 43, 13, Atharvan and Dadhyañch in I, 80, 16, and Dadhyañch, Aṅgiras, Atri and Kaṇva in I, 139, 9. Atharvan by his sacrifices is elsewhere described, as having first extended the paths, whereupon the sun was born (I, 83, 5), and the Atharvans, in the plural, are styled 'our fathers' (*naḥ pitaraḥ*) along with Angirases, Navagvas and Bhṛigus in X, 14, 6. In II, 34, 12, the Dashagvas are said to have been the first to offer a sacrifice ; while in X, 92, 10 Atharvan is spoken of, as having established order by sacrifices, when the Bhṛigus showed themselves as gods by their skill. Philologically the name of Atharvan appears as Athravan, meaning a fire-priest, in the Avesta, and the word Aṅgiras is said to be etymologically connected with the Greek *Aggilos*, a 'messenger' and the Persian *Angara* 'a mounted courier.' In the Aitareya Brâhmaṇa (III, 34) Aṅgirases are said to be the same as *Aṅgârâḥ*, 'burning coals or fire' (Cf. Ṛig. X. 62, 5). Whether we accept these etymologies as absolutely correct or not, the resemblance between the different words sufficiently warrants the assumption that Atharvan and Aṅgiras must have been the anci ent sacrificers of the whole Aryan race and not merely of the Vedic people. Therefore, even though Manu, Atharvan, Aṅgiras be not the names of particular individuals, still there can be little doubt that they represented families of priests who conducted, if not originated, the sacrifices in primeval times, that is, before the Aryan separation, and who, for this reason, seem to have attained almost divine character in the eyes of the poets of the Ṛig-Veda. They have all been described as more or less connected with Yama in X, 14, 3-6 ; but it does not follow therefrom that they were all Yama's agents or beings without any human origin. For, as stated above, there are a number of passages in which they are described as being the *first* and the *most ancient* sacrificers of the race ; and if after their death they are said to have gone to Yama and become his friends and companions, that does not, in any way, detract from their human character. It is, therefore, very important in the history of the sacrificial literature to determine if any traditions are preserved in the Ṛig-Veda regarding the duration of the sacrifices performed by these ancient ancestors of the Vedic people (*naḥ pûrve pitaraḥ*, VI, 22, 2), in times before the separation of the Aryan people, and see if they lend any support to the theory of an early Circum-Polar home.

Now so far as my researches go, I have not been able to find any Vedic evidence regarding the duration of the sacrifices performed by Manu, Atharvan, Bhṛigu or any other ancient sacrificers, except the Aṅgirases. There is an annual *sattra* described in the Shrauta Sûtras, which is called the *Aṅgirasâm-ayanam*, and is said to be a modification of the *Gavâm-ayanam*, the type of all yearly *sattras*. But we do not find therein any mention of the duration of the *sattra* of the Aṅgirases. The duration of the *Gavâm-ayanam* is, however, given in the Taittirîya Saṁhitâ, and will be discussed in the next chapter. For the present, we confine ourselves to the *sattra* of the Aṅgirases, and have to see if we can find out other means for determining its duration. Such a means is, fortunately, furnished by the Ṛig-Veda itself. There are two *chief* species of the Aṅgirases (*Aṅgiras-tama*), called the Navagvas and the Dashagvas, mentioned in the Ṛig-Veda (X, 62, 5 and 6). These two classes of ancient sacrificers are generally mentioned together, and the facts attributed to the Aṅgirases are also attributed to them. Thus the Navagvas are spoken of as 'our ancient fathers,' in VI, 22, 2, and as 'our fathers' along with Aṅgirases and Bhṛigu in X, 14, 6. Like the Aṅgirases, the Navagvas are also connected with the myth of Indra overthrowing Vala, and of Saramâ and Paṇis (I, 62, 3 and 4; V, 29, 12; V,45, 7; X, 108, 8). In one of these Indra is described as having taken their assistance when he rent the rock and Vala (I, 62, 4); and in V, 29, 12, the Navagvas are said to have praised Indra with songs and broken open the firmly closed stall of the cows. But there are only two verses in which the duration of their sacrificial session is mentioned. Thus V, 45, 7 says, "Here, urged by hands, hath loudly rung the press-stone, with which the Navagvas sang (sacrificed) for *ten months*"; and in the eleventh verse of the same hymn the poet says, "I place upon (offer to) the waters your light-winning prayers wherewith the Navagvas completed their *ten months*."[1] In II, 34, 12, we again read, "They, the Dashagvas, brought out (offered) sacrifice first of all. May they favour us at the flashing forth of the dawn": while in IV, 51, 4,[2] the Dawns are said "to have dawned richly on the Navagva Aṅgira,

1. Ṛig. V, 45, 7,—अनूनोदत्र हस्तयतो अद्रिरार्चन् येन दश मासो नवग्वाः । V, 45, 11,—धियं वो अप्सु दधिषे स्वर्षां ययातरन् दश मासो नवग्वाः ।

2. Ṛig. IV, 51, 4,—कुविदस्स देवीः सनयो नवो वा यामो बभूयादुषसो वो अद्य । येना नवग्वे अंगिरे दशग्वे सप्तास्ये रेवती रेवदूष ॥

and on the seven-mouthed Dashagva," evidently showing that their sacrifice was connected with the break of the dawn and lasted only for *ten months.* What the Navagvas or the Dashagvas accomplished by means of their sacrifices is further described in V, 29, 12, which says, "The Navagvas and the Dashagvas, who had offered libations of Soma, praised Indra with songs; labouring (at it) the men laid open the stall of kine though firmly closed;" while in III, 39, 5, we read, "Where the friend (Indra), with the friendly energetic Navagvas, followed up the cows on his knees, there verily with ten Dashagvas did Indra find the sun dwelling in darkness (*tamasi kṣhiyantam*)."[1] In X, 62, 2 and 3, the Aṅgirases, of whom the Dashagvas and the Navagvas were the principal species (*Aṅgiras-tama*, X, 62, 6), are, however, said to have themselves performed the feat of vanquising Vala, rescuing the cows and bringing out the sun, at the end of the year (*pari vatsare Valam abhindan*); but it obviously means that they helped Indra in achieving it at the end of the year. Combining all these statements we can easily deduce (1) that the Navagvas and the Dashagvas completed their sacrifices in *ten months*: (2) that these sacrifices were connected with the early flush of the Dawn; (3) that the sacrificers helped Indra in the rescue of the cows from Vala at the *end of the year*; and (4) that at the place where Indra went in search for the cows, he discovered the sun "dwelling in darkness."

Now we must examine a little more closely the meaning of these four important statements regarding the Navagvas and the Dashagvas. The first question that arises in this connection is—What is meant by their sacrifices being completed in ten months, and why did they not continue sacrificing for the whole year of twelve months? The

1. Ṛig. III, 39, 5,—सखा ह यत्र सखिभिर्नवग्वैरभिज्ञ्वा सत्वभिर्गा अनुग्मन्। सत्यं तदिन्द्रो दशभिर्दशग्वैः सूर्यं विवेद तमसि क्षियन्तम् ॥

expression for 'ten months' in the original is *dasha mâsâḥ*, and the words are so plain that there can be no doubt about their import. We have seen that the Navagvas used to help Indra in releasing the cows from the grasp of Vala, and in X, 62, 2 and 3, the Añgirases are said to have defeated Vala *at the end of the year*, and raised the sun to heaven. This exploit of Indra, the Añgirases, the Navagvas and the Dashagvas, therefore, clearly refers to the *yearly* rescue of the sun, or the cows of the morning, from the dark prison into which they are thrown by Vala; and the expression "Indra found the sun dwelling in darkness", mentioned above further supports this view. In I, 117, 5, the Ashvins are said to have rescued Vandana, like some bright buried gold, "like one asleep in the lap of Nir-ṛiti (death), like the sun dwelling in darkness (*tamasi kṣhiyantam*)". This shows that the expression 'dwelling in darkness,' as applied to the sun, means that the sun was hidden or concealed below the horizon so as not to be seen by man. We must, therefore, hold that Indra killed or defeated Vala at the end of the year, in a place of darkness, and that the Dashagvas helped Indra by their songs at the time. This might lead any one to suppose that the Soma libations, offered by the Navagvas and the Dashagvas for ten months, were offered during the time when war with Vala was waging. But the Vedic idea is entirely different. For instance the morning prayers are recited before the rise of the sun, and so the sacrifices to help Indra against Vala had to be performed *before* the war. Darkness or a dark period, of ten months is again astronomically impossible anywhere on the globe, and as there cannot be ten months of darkness the only other alternative admissible is that the Dashagvas and the Navagvas carried on their ten months' sacrifice during the period of sunshine. Now if this period of sunshine had extended to twelve months, there was no reason for the Dashagvas to curtail their sacrifices and complete them in ten months. Consequently the only inference we can draw from the story of the Navagvas and the Dashagvas is that they carried on their sacrifices during ten months of sunshine and after that period, the sun went to dwell in darkness or sank below the horizon, and Indra, invigorated by the Soma libations of the Dashagvas, then entered into the cave of Vala, rent it open, released the cows of the morning and brought out the sun at the end of the old and the beginning of the new year, when the Dashagvas again commenced their sacrifices after the long dawn or dawns. In short, the Dashagvas and the Navagvas, and with them all the ancient sacrificers of the race, lived in a region where the sun was above the horizon for ten months, and then went down, producing a long yearly night of two months' duration. These ten months, therefore, formed the *annual* sacrificial session, or the calendar year, of the oldest sacrificers of the Aryan race, and we shall see in the next chapter that independently of the legend of the Dashagvas this view is fully supported by direct references to such a session in the Vedic sacrificial literature.

The etymology of the words Navagva and Dashagva leads us to the same conclusion. The words are formed by prefixing *nava* and *dasha* to *gva*. So far there is no difference of opinion. But Yâska (XI, 19) takes *nava* in *navagva* to mean either 'new' or 'charming', interpreting the word to mean 'those, who have charming or new career (*gva*, from *gam* to go).' This explanation of Yâska is, however, unsatisfactory, inasmuch as the Navagvas and the Dashagvas are usually mentioned together in the Ṛig-Veda, and this close and frequent association of their names makes it necessary for us to find out such an etymological explanation of the words as would make Navagva bear the same relation to *nava* as Dashagva may have to *dasha*. But *dasha* or rather *dashan*, is a numeral signifying 'ten,' and cannot be taken in any other sense; therefore, as observed by Prof. Lignana,[1] *nava* or rather *navan* must be taken to mean 'nine'. The meaning of *gva* (*gu*+*a*) is, however, yet to be ascertained. Some derive it from *go*, a cow, and others from *gam*, to go. In the first case the meaning would be 'of nine cows' or 'of ten cows'; while in the second case the words would signify 'going in nine' or 'going in ten,' and the fact, that the Dashagvas are said to be *ten* in III, 39, 5, lends support to the latter view. But the use of the words Navagva and Dashagva, sometimes even in the singular number as an adjective qualifying a singular noun, shows that a group or a company of nine or ten men, is not, at any rate, always intended. Thus in VI, 6, 3, the rays of Agni are said to be *navagvas*, while Adhrigu is said to be *dashagva* in VIII, 12, 2, and Dadhyañch *navagva* in IX, 108, 4. We must, therefore, assign to these epithets some other meaning, and the only other possible explanation of the numerals 'nine' and 'ten' is that given by Sâyaṇa, who says (Comm. on Ṛig. I, 62, 4), "The Aṅgirases are of two kinds, the Navagvas or those who rose after completing the *sattra* in nine months, and the Dashagvas, or those who rose after finishing the *sattra* in ten months."[2] We have seen that in the Ṛig-Veda V, 45, 7 and 11, the Dashagvas and

---

1. See his Essay on "The Navagvas and the Dashagvas of the Ṛig-Veda" in the Proceedings of the 7th International Congress of Orientalists, 1886, pp. 59-68. The essay is in Italian, and I am indebted to the kindness of Mr. Shrinivâs Iyengar, B. A., B. L., High Court Pleader, Madras, for a translation of the same.

2. Sâyaṇa, in his gloss. on Ṛig. I, 62, 4, says:—अंगिरसो द्विविधाः । सत्रयागमनुतिष्ठन्तो ये नवभिर्मासैः समाप्य गतास्ते नवग्वाः । ... 'नवग्वा नवनीतगतय' इति यास्को व्याचख्यौ । ये तु दशभिर्मासैः समाप्य जग्मुस्ते दशग्वाः । Again in his gloss. on X, 62, 6, he states:—सत्रमासीनानामंगिरसां मध्ये केचन नवसु मासेषु कर्म कृत्वोदतिष्ठन् केचन दशसु मासेष्वति । एवमंगिरसामयनमुक्तम् । तेषामभिर्नवग्वश्च दशग्वश्चोक्तः ।

the Navagvas are said to have completed their sacrifices in ten months. Sâyaṇa's explanation is, therefore, fully warranted by these texts, and very probably it is based on some traditional information about the Dashagvas. Prof. Lignana of Rome,[1] suggests that the numerals *navan* and *dashan* in these names should be taken as referring to the period of gestation, as the words *nava-mâhya* and *dasha-mâhya* occur in the Vendidad, V, 45, (136), in the same sense. Thus interpreted Navagva would mean 'born of nine months,' and Dashagva 'born of ten months.' But this explanation is highly improbable, inasmuch as we cannot first suppose that a number of persons were born prematurely in early times, and secondly that it was specially such persons that attained almost divine honours. The usual period of gestation is 280 days or ten lunar months (V, 78, 9), and those that were born a month earlier cannot be ordinarily expected to live long or to perform feats which would secure them divine honours. The reference to the Vendidad proves nothing, for there the case of a still-born child after a gestation of 1, 2, 3, 4, 5, 6, 7, 8, 9 or 10 months is under consideration, and Ahura Mazda enjoins that the house where such a still-born child is brought forth should be cleaned and sanctified in a special way. Prof. Lignana's explanation again conflicts with the Vedic texts which say that the Dashagvas were ten in number (III, 39, 5), or that the Navagvas sacrificed only for ten months (V, 4, 7). Sâyaṇa's explanation is, therefore, the only one entitled to our acceptance. I may here mention that the Ṛig-Veda (V, 47, 7 and 11) speaks of ten months' sacrifice only in connection with the Navagvas, and does not mention any sacrifice of *nine* months. But the etymology of the names now helps us in assigning the ten months' sacrifice to the Dashagvas and

1. See his Essay in the Proceedings of the 7th International Congress of the Orientalists, pp. 59-68.

the nine months' to the Navagvas. For *navan* in Navagva is only a numerical variation for *dashan* in Dashagva, and it follows, therefore, that what the Dashagvas did by tens, the Nanagvas did by nines.

There is another circumstance connected with the Aṅgirases which further strengthens our conclusion, and which must, therefore, be stated in this place. The Aṅgirases are sometimes styled the *Virûpas.* Thus in III, 53, 7, the Aṅgirases are described as "*Virûpas*, and sons of heaven"; and the name Virûpa once occurs by itself as that of a single being, who sings the praises of Agni, in a stanza (VIII, 64, 6) immediately following one in which Aṅgiras is invoked, showing that Virûpa is here used as a synonym for Aṅgiras. But the most explicit of these references is X, 62, 5 and 6. The first of these verses states that the Aṅgirases are *Virûpas*, and they are the sons of Agni; while the second describes them along with the Navagva and the Dashagva in the following terms, "And which Virûpas were born from Agni and from the sky; the Navagva or the Dashagva, as the best of the Aṅgirases (*Aṅgiras-tama*), prospers in the assemblage of the gods."[1] Now *Virûpas* literally means 'of various forms,' and in the above verses it seems to have been used as an adjective qualifying Aṅgirases to denote that there are many species of them. We are further told that the Navagvas and the Dashagvas were the most important (*Aṅgiras-tamaḥ*) of these species. In the last chapter I have discussed the meaning of the adjective *Virûpa* as applied to a couple of Day and Night and have shown, on the authority of Mâdhava, that the word, as applied to days and nights, denotes their duration, or the period of time over which they extend. *Virûpas* in the present instance appears to be used precisely in the same

1. Ṛig. X, 62, 6,—ये अग्नेः परि जज्ञिरे विरूपासो दिवस्परि । नवग्वो नु दशग्वो अंगिरस्तमः सचा देवेषु मंहते ॥

sense. The Navagvas and the Dashagvas were no doubt the most important of the early sacrificers, but these too were not their only species. In other words they were not merely 'nine-going,' and 'ten-going,' but 'various-going' (*virûpas*), meaning that the duration of their sacrifices was sometimes shorter than nine and sometimes longer than ten months. In fact a *Sapta-gu* (seven-going) is mentioned in X, 47, 6, along with Bṛihaspati, the son of Aṅgiras, and it seems to be used there as an adjective qualifying Bṛihaspati; for Bṛihaspati is described in another place (IV, 50, 4) as *saptâsya* (seven-mouthed), while the Atharva-Veda IV, 5, 1, describes the first Brâhmaṇa, Bṛihaspati, as *dashâsya* or ten-mouthed. We have also seen that in IV, 51, 4, the Dashagva is also called 'seven-mouthed.' All these expressions can be satisfactorily explained only by supposing that the Aṅgirases were not merely 'nine-going' or 'ten-going', but *virûpas* or 'various-going', and that they completed their sacrifices within the number of months for which the sun was above the horizon at the place where these sacrifices were performed. It follows, therefore, that in ancient times the sacrificial session lasted from seven to ten months; and the number of sacrificers (*Hotṛis*) corresponded with the number of the months, each doing his duty by rotation somewhat after the manner of the Egyptian priests previously referred to. These sacrifices were over when the long night commenced, during which Indra fought with Vala and vanquished him by the end of the year (*parivatsare*, X, 62, 2). The word *parivatsare* (at the end of the year) is very suggestive and shows that the year closed with the long night.

Another reference to a period of ten months' sun-shine is found in the legend of Dîrghatamas whom the Ashvins are said to have saved or rescued from a pit, into which he was thrown, after being made blind and infirm. I have devoted a separate chapter later on to the discussion of

Vedic legends. But I take up here the legend of Dîrghatamas because we have therein an express statement as to the life of Dîrghatamas, which remarkably corroborates the conclusion we have arrived at from the consideration of the story of the Dashagvas. The story of Dîrghatamas is narrated in the Mahâbhârata, Âdiparvan, Chap. 104. He is said to be the son of Mamatâ by Utathya, and born blind through the curse of Bṛihaspati his uncle. He was, however, married and had several sons by Pradveshî. The wife and the sons eventually became tired of feeding the blind Dîrghatamas (so called because he was born blind), and the sons abandoned him afloat on a worn-out raft in the Ganges. He drifted on the waters for a long time and distance, when at last the king Bali picked him up. Dîrghatamas then had several sons born to him from a *dâsi* or a female slave, and also from the wife of Bali, the sons of Bali's wife becoming kings of different provinces. In the Ṛig-Veda Dîrghatamas is one of the proteges of the Ashvins, and about 25 hymns in the first Maṇḍala are ascribed to him. He is called Mâmateya, or the son of Mamatâ in I, 152, 6, and Uchathya's offspring in I, 158, 4. In the latter hymn he invokes the Ashvins for the purpose of rescuing him from the ordeals of fire and water to which he was subjected by the Dâsa Traitana. In I, 147, 3 and IV, 4,13, Agni is, however, said to have restored to Dîrghatamas his eyesight. But the statement need not surprise us as the achievements of one deity are very often ascribed to another in the Ṛig-Veda. Dîrghatamas does not stand alone in being thus rescued by the Ashvins. Chyavâna is spoken of as another protege of the Ashvins, and they are said to have restored him to youth. Vandana and a host of others are similarly mentioned as being saved, rescued, cured, protected or rejuvenated by the Ashvins. All these achievements are now understood as referring to the exploit of restoring to the sun his decayed power in the winter. But with the expression "like the sun dwelling in darkness" before us, in the legend of Vandana (I, 117, 5), we must make these legends refer not merely to the decayed power of the sun in winter, but to his actual sinking below the horizon for some time. Bearing this in mind, let us try to see what inference we can deduce, so far as the subject in hand is concerned, from the legend of Dîrghatamas.

The statement in the myth or legend, which is most important for our purpose, is contained in I, 158, 6. The verse may be literally translated as follows:—"Dîrghatamas, the son of Mamatâ, having grown decrepit in the tenth *yuga*, becomes a Brahman charioteer of the waters wending to their goal."[1] The only expressions which require elucidation in this verse are "in the tenth *yuga*" and "waters wending to their goal." Otherwise the story is plain enough. Dîrghatamas grows old in the tenth *yuga*, and riding on waters, as the Mahâbhârata story has it, goes along with them to the place which is the goal of these waters. But scholars are not agreed as to what *yuga* means. Some take it to mean a cycle of years, presumably five as in the Vedâṅga-Jyotiṣha, and invest Dîrghatamas with infirmity at the age of fifty. The Petersburg Lexicon would interpret *yuga*, wherever it occurs in the Ṛig-Veda, to mean not 'a period of time,' but 'a generation,' or 'the relation of descent from a common stock'; and it is followed by Grassmann in this respect. According to these scholars the phrase "in the tenth *yuga*" in the above verse would, therefore, signify "in the tenth generation" whatever that may mean. Indeed, there seems to be a kind of prejudice against interpreting *yuga* as meaning 'a period of time' in the Ṛig-Veda, and it is, therefore, necessary to examine the

(1) Rig. I, 158, 6—दीर्घतमा मामतेयो जुजुर्वान् दशमे युगे । अपामर्थं यतीनां ब्रह्मा भवति सारथिः ॥

point at some length in this place. That the word *yuga* by itself means 'a period of time,' or that, at any rate, it is one of its meanings goes without saying. Even the Petersburg Lexicon assigns this meaning to *yuga* in the Atharva Veda VIII, 2, 21; but so far as the Ṛig-Veda is concerned *yuga*, according to it, must mean 'descent,' or 'generation,' or something like it, but never 'a period of time.' This is especially the case with the phrase *Mânushâ yugâ*, or *Mânushyâ yugâni*, which occurs several times in the Ṛig-Veda. Western scholars would everywhere translate it to mean 'generations of men,' while native scholars, like Sâyaṇa and Mahîdhara, take it to refer to 'mortal ages' in a majority of places. In some cases (I, 124, 2; I, 144, 4) Sayâṇa, however, suggests, as an alternative, that the phrase may be understood to mean 'conjunction' or 'couples (*yuga*) of men'; and this has probably given rise to the interpretation put upon the phrase by Western scholars. Etymologically the word *yuga* may mean 'conjunction' or 'a couple,' denoting either (1) 'a couple of day and night,' or (2) 'a couple of months,' *i. e.* 'a season,' or (3) 'a couple of fortnights,' or 'the time of the conjunction of the moon and the sun,' *i. e.* 'a month.' Thus at the beginning of the Kali-Yuga the planets and the sun were, it is supposed, in conjunction and hence it is said to be called a *yuga*. It is also possible that the word may mean 'a conjunction, or a couple, or even a generation of men.' Etymology, therefore, does not help us in determining which of these meanings should be assigned to the word *yuga*, or the phrase *Mânushâ yugâ* in the Ṛig-Veda, and we must find out some other means for determining it. The prejudice we have referred to above, appears to be mainly due to the disinclination of the Western scholars to import the later Yuga theory into the Ṛig-Veda. But it seems to me that the caution has been carried too far, so far as almost to amount to a sort of prejudice.

Turning to the hymns of the Ṛig-Veda, we find as remarked by Muir, the phrase *yuge yuge* used at least in half a dozen places (III, 26, 3 ; VI, 15, 8; X, 94, 12, &c.), and it is interpreted by Sâyaṇa to mean a period of time. In III, 33, 8, and X, 10, 10, we have *uttara yugâni* 'later ages,' and in X, 72, 1, we read *uttare yuge* 'in a later age'; whilst in the next two verses we have the phrases *Devânâm pûrvye yuge* and *Devânâm prathame yuge* clearly referring to the later and earlier ages of the gods. The word *Devânâm* is in the plural and *yuga* is in the singular, and it is not therefore possible to take the phrase to mean 'generations of gods.' The context again clearly shows that a reference to time is intended, for the hymn speaks of the creation and the birth of the gods in early primeval times. Now if we interpret *Devânâm yugam* to mean 'an age of gods,' why should *manuṣhyâ yugâni* or *mânuṣhâ yugâ* be not interpreted to mean 'human ages,' is more than I can understand. There are again express passages in the Ṛig-Veda where *mânuṣhâ yugâ* cannot be taken to mean 'generations of men.' Thus in V, 52, 4, which is a hymn to Maruts, we read *Vishve ye mânuṣhâ yugâ pânti martyam riṣhaḥ.* Here the verb is *pânti* (protect), the nominative *vishve ye* (all those), and the object is *martyam* (the mortal man), while *riṣhaḥ* (from injury), in the ablative, denotes the object against which the protection is sought. So far the sentence, therefore, means "All those who protect man from injury"; and now the question, is what does *mânuṣhâ yugâ* mean? If we take it to mean "generations of men" in the objective case it becomes superfluous, for *martyam* (man) is already the object of *pânti* (protect). It is, therefore, necessary to assign to *mânuṣhâ yugâ* the only other meaning we know of, *viz.*, 'human ages' and take the phrase as an accusative of time. Thus interpreted the whole sentence means "All those, who protect man from injury during human ages." No other construction is more natural or reasonable than this; but still Prof. Max Muller translates the verse to mean "All those who protect the generations of men, who protect the mortal from injury,"[1] in spite of the fact that this is tautological and that there is no conjunctive particle in the text (like *cha*) to join what according to him are the two objects of the verb 'protect.' Mr. Griffith seems to have perceived this difficulty, and has translated, "Who all, through ages of mankind, guard mortal man from injury." Another passage which is equally decisive on this point, is X, 140, 6. The verse[2] is addressed to Agni, and people are said to have put him in front to secure his blessings. It is as follows:—

Ṛitâvânam mahishaṁ vishva-darshatam
agniṁ sumnâya dadhire puro janâḥ ।
Shrut-karṇaṁ saprathas-taman
tvâ girâ daivyam mânushâ yugâ ॥

Here *ṛitâvânam* (righteous), *mahisham* (strong), *vishva-darshatam* (visible to all), *agnim* (Agni, fire), *shrut-karṇam* (attentive-eared), *saprathas-tamam* (most widely-reaching), *tvâ* (thee) and *daivyam* (divine) are all in the accusative case governed by *dadhire* (placed), and describe the qualities of Agni. *Janâḥ* (people) is the nominative and *dadhire* (placed) is the only verb in the text. *Sumnâya* (for the welfare) denotes the purpose for which the people placed Agni in front (*puro*); and *girâ* (by praises) is the means by which the favour of Agni is to be secured. If we, therefore, leave out the various adjectives of Agni, the verse means, "The people have placed Agni (as described) in front for their welfare, with praises." The only expression that remains is *mânushâ yugâ*, and it can go in with other words in a natural way only as an accusative of time. The verse would then mean

1. See S. B. E. Series, Vol. XXXII, p. 312.

2. Ṛig. X, 140, 6,—ऋतावानं महिषं विश्वदर्शतमग्निं सुम्नाय दधिरे पुरो जनाः । श्रुत्कर्णं सप्रथस्तमं त्वा गिरा दैव्यं मानुषा युगा ॥

"The people have placed Agni (as described) in front for their welfare, with praises, during human ages." But Griffith takes *yugâ* to mean 'generations,' and supplying a verb of his own, translates the last part of the verse thus: "Men's generations magnify (Agni) with praise-songs (*girâ*)." This shows what straits we are reduced to if we once make up our mind not to interpret *mânushâ yugâ* to mean 'a period of time'; for the word 'magnify' does not exist in the original. This verse also occurs in the Vâjasaneyî Saṁhitâ (XII, 111) and Mahîdhara there explains *mânushâ yugâ* to mean 'human ages' or 'periods of time' such as fortnights. We have, therefore, at least two passages, where *mânushâ yugâ*, must, according to the recognised rules of interpretation, be taken to mean 'periods of time,' and not 'generations of men,' unless we are prepared to give up the natural construction of the sentence. There are no more passages in the Ṛig-Veda where *mânushâ yugâ* occurs in juxtapposition with words like *janâḥ* or *martyam*, so as to leave no option as regards the meaning to be assigned to *yuga*. But if the meaning of a phrase is once definitely determined even from a single passage, we can safely understand the phrase in the same sense in other passages, provided the meaning does not conflict there with the context. That is how the meaning of many a Vedic word has been determined by scholars like Yâska, and we are not venturing on a new path in adopting the same process of reasoning in the present case.

But if *mânushâ yugâ* means 'human ages' and not 'human generations,' we have still to determine the exact duration of these ages. In the Atharva-Veda VIII, 2, 21, which says, "We allot to thee, a hundred, ten thousand years, two, three or four *yugas*," the word *yuga* obviously stands for a period of time, not shorter than ten thousand years. But there are grounds to hold that in the early days of the Ṛig-Veda *yuga* must have denoted a shorter period of time, or, at least, that was one of its meanings in early days. The Ṛig-Veda often speaks of 'the first' (*prathamâ*) dawn, or 'the first of the coming' (*âyatînâm prathamâ*) dawns, (Ṛig. I, 113, 8; 123, 2; VII, 76, 6; X, 35, 4); while 'the last' (*avamâ*) dawn is mentioned in VII, 71, 3, and the dawn is said to have 'the knowledge of the *first* day' in I, 123, 9. Now, independently of what I have said before about the Vedic dawns, the ordinal numeral 'first' as applied to the dawn is intelligible only if we suppose it to refer to the first dawn of the year, or the dawn on the first day of the year, somewhat like the phrase 'first night' (*prathamâ râtriḥ*) used in the Brâhmaṇas (see *Orion*, p. 67). The 'first' (*prathamâ*) and the 'last' (*avamâ*) dawn must, therefore, be taken to signify the beginning and the end of the year in those days; and in the light of what has been said about the nature of the Vedic dawns in the fifth chapter, we may safely conclude that the 'first' of the dawns was no other than the first of a set or group of dawns that appeared at the close of the long night and commenced the year. Now this 'first dawn' is described as "wearing out human ages" (*praminati manushyâ yugâni*) in I, 124, 2, and I, 92, 11; while in I, 115, 2, we are told that "the pious or godly men extend the *yugas*" on the appearance of the dawn (*yatrâ naro devayanto yugâni vitanvate*). European scholars interpret *yuga* in the above passages to mean 'generations of men.' But apart from the fact that the phrase *mânushâ yugâ* must be understood to mean 'human ages' in at least two passages discussed above, the context in I, 124, 2 and I, 92, 11 is obviously in favour of interpreting the word *yuga*, occurring therein, as equivalent to a period of time. The dawn is here described as commencing a new course of heavenly ordinances, or holy sacrifices (*daivyani vratâni*), and setting in motion the *manushyâ yugâni*, obviously implying that with the first dawn came the sacrifices, as well as the cycle of time known as 'human ages,' or that 'the human ages' were reckoned from the first dawn. This association of *mânushâ yugâ*, or 'human ages,' with the 'first dawn' at once enables us to definitely determine the length or duration of 'human ages'; for if these ages (*yugas*) commenced with the first dawn of the year they must have ended on the last (*avamâ*) dawn of the year. In other words *mânushâ yugâ* collectively denoted the whole period of time between the first and the last dawn of the year, while a single *yuga* denoted a shorter division of this period.

Apart from the legend of Dîrghatamas, we have, therefore, sufficient evidence in the Ṛig-Veda to hold that the word *yuga* was used to denote a period of time, shorter than one year, and that the phrase *mânushâ yugâ* meant 'human ages,' or 'the period of time between the first and the last dawn of year,' and not 'human generations.' The statement that "Dîrghatamas grew old in the *tenth yuga*" is now not only easy to understand, but it enables us to determine, still more definitely, the meaning of *yuga* in the days of the Ṛig-Veda. For, if *yuga* was a part of *mânushâ yugâ*, that is, of the period between the first and the last dawn of the year, and the legend of Dîrghatamas a solar legend, the statement that "Dîrghatamas grew old in the tenth *yuga*" can only mean that 'the sun grew old in the tenth *month*.' In other words, ten *yugas* were supposed to intervene between the first and the last dawn, or the two termini, of the year; and as ten days or ten fortnights would be too short, and ten seasons too long a period of time to lie between these limits, the word *yuga*, in the phrase *dashame yuge*, must be interpreted to mean 'a month' and nothing else. In short, Dîrghatamas was the sun that grew old in the tenth month, and riding on the aerial waters was borne by them to their goal, that is, to the ocean (VII, 49, 2) below the horizon. The waters here referred to are, in fact, the same over which the king Varuṇa is said to rule, or which flow by his commands, or for which he is said to have dug out a channel (VII, 49, 1-4; II, 28, 4; VII, 87, 1) and so cut out a path for Sûrya, and which being released by Indra from the grasp of Vṛitra, bring on the sun (I, 51, 4). Prof. Max Muller, in his *Contributions to the Science of Mythology* (Vol. II, pp. 583-598), has shown that most of the achievements of the Ashvins can be rationally explained by taking them as referring to the decaying sun. The legend of Dîrghatamas is thus only a mythical representation of the Arctic sun, who ascends above the 'bright ocean' (VII, 60, 4), becomes visible for *mânushâ yugâ*, or ten months, and then drops again into the nether waters. What these waters are and how their nature has been long misunderstood will be further explained in a subsequent chapter, when we come to the discussion of Vedic myths. Suffice it to say for the present that the legend of Dîrghatamas, interpreted as above, is in full accord with the legend of the Dashagvas, who are described as holding their sacrificial session only for ten months.

I have discussed here the meaning of *yuga* and *mânushâ yugâ* at some length, because the phrases have been much misunderstood, in spite of clear passages shewing that 'a period of time' was intended to be denoted by them. These passages (V, 52, 4; X, 140, 6) establish the fact that *mânushâ yugâ* denoted 'human ages,' and the association of these ages with the 'first dawn' (I, 124, 2; I, 115, 2) further shews that the length of a *yuga* was regarded to be shorter than a year. The mention of the tenth *yuga* finally settles the meaning of *yuga* as 'one month.' That is how I have arrived at the meaning of these phrases, and I am glad to find that I have been anticipated in my conclusions by Prof. Raṅgâchârya, of Madras, on different grounds. In his essay on the *yugas*,* he discusses the root meaning of *yuga*, and,

* The *Yugas*, or a Question of Hindu Chronology and History, p. 19.

taking it to denote 'a conjunction,' observes as follows, "The phases of the moon being so readily observable, it is probable that, as suggested by Professor Weber, the idea of a period of time known as a *yuga* and depending upon a conjunction of certain heavenly bodies, was originally derived from a knowledge of these phases. The Professor (Weber) further strengthens his supposition by referring to a passage cited in the Ṣhaḍviṁsha Brâhmaṇa (IV, 6)[1] wherein the four *yugas* are still designated by their more ancient names, and are connected with the four lunar phases to which they evidently owe their origin." Mr. Rangâchârya then refers to *darsha*, the ancient name for the conjunction of the sun and the moon, and concludes, "There is also old mythological or other evidence which leads us to conclude that our forefathers observed many other kinds of interesting celestial conjunctions; and in all probability the earliest conception of a *yuga* meant the period from new moon to new moon," that is, one lunar month. The passage stating that it was the first dawn that set the cycle of *mânuṣhâ yugâ* in motion is already quoted above; and if we compare this statement with Ṛig. X, 139, 6, where Indra, after killing Vṛitra and producing the dawn and the sun, is said "to have set the ordering of the months in the sky," it will be further evident that the cycle of time which began with the first dawn was a cycle of months. We may, therefore, safely conclude that *mânuṣhâ yugâ* represented, in early days, a cycle of months during which the sun was above the horizon, or rather that period of sunshine and action when the ancestors of the Aryan race held their sacrificial sessions or performed other religious and social ceremonies.

There are many other passages in the Ṛig-Veda which support the same view. But *mânuṣhâ yugâ* being everywhere

1. पुष्ये (कलौ) चानुमतिर्ज्ञेया सिनीवालीति द्वापरे। खार्वायां (त्रेतायां) तु भवेद्राका कृतपर्वे कुहूर्भवेत् ॥

interpreted by Western scholars to mean 'human generations or tribes,' the real meaning of these passages has become obscure and unintelligible. Thus in VIII, 46, 12, we have "All (sacrificers), with ladles lifted, invoke that mighty Indra for *mânushâ yugâ*"; and the meaning evidently is that Soma libations were offered to Indra during the period of human ages. But taking *mânushâ yugâ* to denote 'human tribes,' Griffith translates "All races of mankind invoke &c," a rendering, which, though intelligible, does not convey the spirit of the original. Similarly, Agni is said to shine during 'human ages' in VII, 9, 4. But there too the meaning 'human tribes' is unnecessarily foisted upon the phrase. The most striking illustration of the impropriety of interpreting *yuga* to mean 'a generation' is, however, furnished by Ṛig. II, 2, 2. Here Agni is said to shine for *mânushâ yugâ* and *kshapaḥ*. Now *kshapaḥ* means 'nights' and the most natural interpretation would be to take *mânushâ yugâ* and *kshapaḥ* as allied expressions denoting a period of time. The verse will then mean:—"O Agni! thou shinest during human ages and nights." It is necessary to mention 'nights,' because though *mânushâ yugâ* is a period of sunshine, including a long day and a succession of ordinary days and nights, yet the long or the continuous night which followed *mânushâ yugâ* could not have been included in the latter phrase. Therefore, when the whole period of the solar year was intended, a compound expression like "*mânushâ yugâ* and the continuous nights," was necessary, and that is the meaning of the phrase in II, 2, 2. But Prof. Oldenberg,[1] following Max Muller, translates as follows, "O Agni! thou shinest on human tribes, on continuous nights." Here, in the first place, it is difficult to understand what 'shining on human tribes' means; and secondly if *kshapaḥ* means 'continu-

1 See S. B. E. Series, Vol. XLVI, pp. 193, 195.

ous nights,' it could mean nothing except 'the long continuous night,' and if so, why not take *mânushâ yugâ* to represent the period of the solar year, which remains after the long night is excluded from it? As observed by me before, Prof. Max Muller has correctly translated *kshapaḥ* by 'continuous nights,' but has missed the true meaning of the expression *mânushâ yugâ* in this place. A similar mistake has been committed with respect to IV, 16, 19, where the expression is *kshapaḥ madema sharadas cha pûrvîh*. Here, in spite of the accent, Max Muller takes *kshapaḥ* as accusative and so does Sâyaṇa. But Sâyaṇa correctly interprets the expression as "May we rejoice for many autumns (seasons) and nights." 'Seasons and nights' is a compound phrase, and the particle *cha* becomes unmeaning if we split it up and take nights (*kshapaḥ*) with one verb, and seasons (*sharadaḥ*) with another. Of course so long as the Arctic theory was unknown the phrase 'seasons and nights' or '*mânushâ yugâ* and nights' was unintelligible, inasmuch as nights were included in the seasons or the *yugas*. But Prof. Max Muller has himself suggested the solution of the difficulty by interpreting *kshapaḥ* as 'continuous nights' in II, 2, 2; and adopting this rendering, we can, with greater propriety, take seasons and nights together, as indicated by the particle *cha*, and understand the expression to mean a complete solar year including the long night. The addition of *kshapaḥ* to *mânushâ yugâ*, therefore, further supports the conclusion that the phrase indicated a period of sunshine as stated above. There are many other passages in translating which unnecessary confusion or obscurity has been caused by taking *mânushâ yugâ* to mean human tribes; but a discussion of these is not relevant to the subject in hand.

An independent corroboration of the conclusion we have drawn from the legends of the Dashagvas and Dîrghatamas is furnished by the number of seasons mentioned in certain Vedic texts. A period of sunshine of ten months followed by a long night of two months can well be described as five seasons of two months each, followed by the sinking of the sun into the waters below the horizon; and as a matter of fact we find the year so described in I, 164,12, a verse, which occurs also in the Atharva Veda (IX, 9, 12) with a slight variation and in the Prashnopanishad, I, 11. It may be literally translated as follows:— "The five-footed (*pañcha-pâdam*) Father of twelve forms, they say, is full of watery vapours (*purîshiṇam*) in the farther half (*pare ardhe*) of the heaven. These others again say (that) He the far-seeing (*vichakshaṇam*) is placed on the six-spoked (*shaḍ-are*) and seven-wheeled (car), in the nearer (*upare*, scil. *ardhe*) half of the heaven."[1] The adjective 'far-seeing' is made to qualify 'seven-wheeled' instead of 'He' in the Atharva Veda, *vichakshaṇe* being in the locative case; while Shankarâchârya in his commentary on the Prashnopanishad splits *upare* into two words *u* and *pare*, taking *u* as an expletive. But these readings do not materially alter the meaning of the verse. The context everywhere clearly indicates that the year-god of twelve months (*âkṛiti*, X, 85, 5) is here described. The previous verse in the hymn (Rig. I, 164) mentions "The twelve-spoked wheel, in which 720 sons of Agni are established," a clear reference to a year of twelve months with 720 days and nights. There is, therefore,

(1) Rig. I., 164, 12,—पञ्चपादं पितरं द्वादशाकृतिं दिव आहुः परे अर्धे पुरीषिणम् । अथेमे अन्य उपरे विचक्षणं सप्तचक्रे षळर आहुरर्पितम् ॥ For विचक्षणम् A. V. (IX, 9, 12) reads विचक्षणे; while Shankarâchârya in his gloss on Prashnopanishad takes उ and परे as two different words. Shankarâchârya's explanation of परे अर्धे is also noteworthy. He translates it by तृतीयस्यां दिवि, 'in the third heaven,' the seat of the third step of Vishṇu, meaning that the five-footed year-god is then hidden in the remotest part of the heaven.

no doubt that the passage contains the description of the year, and the two halves of the verse, which are introduced by the phrases 'they say' and 'others say,' give us two opinions about the nature of the year-god of twelve forms. Let us now see what these opinions are. Some say that the year-god is five-footed (*pañcha-pâdam*), that is, divided into five seasons; and the others say that he has a six-spoked car, or six seasons. It is clear from this that the number of seasons was held to be five by some and six by others in early days. Why should there be this difference of opinion? The Aitareya Brâhmaṇa I, 1, (and the Taittirîya Saṁhitâ I, 6, 2, 3) explains that the two seasons of *Hemanta* and *Shishira* together made a joint season, thereby reducing the number of seasons from six to five. But this explanation seems to be an afterthought, for in the Shatapatha Brâhmaṇa, XIII, 6, 1, 10, *Varṣhâ* and *Sharad* are compounded for this purpose instead of *Hemanta* and *Shishira*. This shews that in the days of the Taittirîya Saṁhitâ and the Brâhmaṇas it was not definitely known or settled which two seasons out of six should be compounded to reduce the number to five; but as five seasons were sometimes mentioned in the Vedas, some explanation was felt to be necessary to account for the smaller number, and such explanation was devised by taking together any two consecutive seasons out of six and regarding them as one joint season of four months. But the explanation is too vague to be true; and we cannot believe that the system of compounding *any two* seasons according to one's choice was ever followed in practice. We must, therefore, give up the explanation as unsatisfactory, and see if the verse from the Ṛig-Veda, quoted above, enables us to find out a better explanation of the fact that the seasons were once held to be five. Now the first half of this verse describes the five-footed father as full of watery vapours in the farther part of heaven, while the year of six-spoked car is said to be far-seeing. In short, *purîshiṇam* (full of, or dwelling in, waters) in the first line appears to be a counterpart of *vichakshaṇam* (far-seeing) in the second line. This is made clear by the verses which follow. Thus the 13th verse in the hymn speaks of "the five-spoked wheel" as remaining entire and unbroken though ancient; and the next or the 14th verse says that "the unwasting wheel with its felly revolves; the ten draw (it) yoked over the expanse. The sun's eye goes covered with *rajas* (aerial vapour); all worlds are dependent on him."[1] Comparing this with the 11th verse first quoted, it may be easily seen that *purîshiṇam* (full of watery vapours) and *rajasâ âvṛitam* (covered with *rajas*) are almost synonymous phrases, and the only inference we can draw from them is that the five-footed year-god or the sun went to dwell in watery vapours *i. e.* became invisible, or covered with darkness (*rajas*), for some time in the farther part of the heaven. The expression that "The ten, yoked, draw his carriage," (also cf. Ṛig. IX, 63, 9) further shows that the five seasons were not made by combining any two consecutive seasons out of six as explained in the Brâhmaṇas (for in that case the number of horses could not be called ten), but that a real year of five seasons or ten months was here intended. When the number of seasons became increased to six, the year-god ceased to be *purîshin* (full of waters), and became *vichakshaṇam* or far-seeing. We have seen that the sun, as represented by Dîrghatamas, grew old in the tenth month, and riding on aerial waters went into the ocean. The same idea is expressed in the present verse which describes two different views about the nature of the year, one of five, and the other of six seasons, and contrasts their leading features with each other.

(1) Rig. I, 164, 13 & 14,—पंचारे चक्रे परिवर्तमाने तस्मिन्ना तस्थुर्भुवनानि विश्वा । तस्य नाक्षस्तप्यते भूरिभारः सनादेव न शीर्यते सनाभिः ॥ सनेमि चक्रमजरं वि वावृत उत्तानायां दश युक्ता वहंति । सूर्यस्य चक्षू रजसैत्यावृतं तस्मिन्नार्पिता भुवनानि विश्वा ॥

Thus *pare ardhe* is constrasted with *upare ardhe* in the second line, *pañcha-pâdam* (compare *pañchâre* in the next verse, *i. e.*, Ṛig-Veda I, 164, 13) with *shaḍ-are*, and *purishiṇam* with *vichakshṇam*. In short, the verse under consideration describes the year either (1) as five-footed, and lying in waters in the farther part of heaven, or (2) as mounted on a six-spoked car and far-seeing in the nearer part of the heaven. These two descriptions cannot evidently apply to seasons in one and the same place, and the artifice of combining two consecutive seasons cannot be accepted as a solution of the question. Five seasons and ten months, followed by the watery residence of the sun or dark nights, is what is precisely described in the first half of this passage (I, 164, 12), and, from what has been said hitherto, it will be easily seen that it is the Arctic year of ten months that is here described. The verse, and especially the contrast between *purishiṇam* and *vichakshaṇam*, does not appear to have attracted the attention it deserves. But in the light of the Arctic theory the description is now as intelligible as any. The Vedic bards have here preserved for us the memory of a year of five seasons or ten months, although their year had long been changed into one of twelve months. The explanation given in the Brâhmaṇas are all so many *post facto* devices to account for the mention of five seasons in the Ṛig-Veda, and I do not think we are bound to accept them when the fact of five seasons can be better accounted for. I have remarked before that in searching for evidence of ancient traditions we must expect to find later traditions associated with them, and Ṛig. I, 164, 12, discussed above, is a good illustration of this remark. The first line of the verse, though it speaks of five seasons, describes the year as twelve-formed; while the second line, which deals with a year of six seasons or twelve months, speaks of it as 'seven-wheeled,' that is, made up of seven months or seven suns, or seven rays of the sun. This may appear rather inconsistent at the first sight; but the history of words in any language will show that old expressions are preserved in the language long after they have ceased to denote the ideas primarily expressed by them. Thus we now use coins for exchange, yet the word 'pecuniary,' which is derived from *pecus* = cattle, is still retained in the language; and similarly, we still speak of the rising of the sun, though we now know that it is not the luminary that rises, but the earth, by rotating round its axis, makes the sun visible to us. Very much in the same way and by the same process, expressions like *saptâshva* (seven-horsed) or *sapta-chakra* (seven-wheeled), as applied to the year or the sun, must have become recognised and established as current phrases in the language before the hymns assumed their present form, and the Vedic bards could not have discarded them even when they knew that they were not applicable to the state of things before them. On the contrary, as we find in the Brâhmaṇas, every artifice, that ingenuity could suggest, was tried to make these old phrases harmonise with the state of things then in vogue, and from the religious or the sacrificial point of view it was quite necessary to do so. But when we have to examine the question from a historical stand-point, it is our duty to separate the relics of the older period from facts or incidents of the later period with which the former are sometimes inevitably mixed up; and if we analyse the verse in question (I, 164, 12) in this way we shall clearly see in it the traces of a year of ten months and five seasons. The same principle is also applicable in other cases, as, for instance, when we find the Navagvas mentioned together with the seven *vipras* in VI, 22, 2. The bards, who gave us the present version of the hymns, knew of the older or primeval state of things only by traditions, and it is no wonder if these traditions are occasionally mixed up with later events.

On the contrary the preservation of so many traditions of the primeval home is itself a wonder, and it is this fact, which invests the oldest Veda with such peculiar importance from the religious as well as the historical point of view.

To sum up: there are clear traditions preserved in the Ṛig-Veda, which show that the year once consisted of seven months or seven suns, as in the legend of Aditi's sons, or that there were ten months of the year as in the legend of the Dashagvas or Dîrghatamas; and these cannot be accounted for except on the Arctic theory. These ten months formed the sacrificial session of the primeval sacrificers of the Aryan race; and the period was denominated as *mânushâ yugâ*, or human ages, an expression much misunderstood by Western scholars. The sun went below the horizon in the tenth of these *yugas*, and Indra fought with Vala in the period of darkness which followed, and, at the end of the year, again brought back the sun "dwelling in darkness" during the period. The whole year of twelve months was thus made up of "*mânushâ yugâ* and continuous nights," and, in spite of the fact that the Vedic bards lived later on in places where the sun was above the horizon for twelve months, the expression "*mânushâ yugâ* and *kshapaḥ* (nights)" is still found in the Ṛig-Veda. It is true that the evidence discussed in this chapter is mostly legendary; but that does not lessen its importance in any way, for it will be seen later on that some of these traditions are Indo-European in character. The tradition that the year was regarded by some to have been made up only of five seasons, or that only *ten* horses were yoked to the chariot of the sun, is again in full accord with the meaning of these legends; and it will be shown in the next chapter that in the Vedic literature there are express statements about a sacrificial session of ten months, which are quite independent of these traditions, and which, therefore, independently prove and strengthen the conclusions deduced from the legends discussed in this chapter.

CHAPTER VIII.

THE COWS' WALK.

The Pravargya ceremony —Symbolises the revival of the yearly sacrifice —Milk representing seed heated in *Gharma* or *Mahâvîra* —Mantras used on the occasion of pouring milk into it —The two creating the five, and the ten of Vivasvat —Indicate the death of the year after five seasons or ten months —The tradition about the sun falling beyond the sky —Annual *Sattras* —Their type, the *Gavâm-ayanam* or the Cows' walk —Lasted for 10 or 12 months according to the Aitareya Brâhmana —Two passages from the Taittirîya Samhitâ describing the *Gavâm-ayanam* —Mention 10 months' duration of the *Sattra*, but give no reason except that it was an ancient practice —Plainly indicates an ancient sacrificial year of ten months —Comparison with the old Roman year of ten months or 304 days —How the rest of 360 days were disposed of by the Romans not yet known —They represented a long period of darkness according to the legend of the Dashagvas —Thus leading to the Arctic theory —Prof. Max Muller on the threefold nature of cows in the Vedas —Cows as animals, rain and dawns or days in the Rig-Veda—Ten months' Cows' walk thus means the ten months' duration of ordinary days and nights —350 oxen of Helios—Implies a night of ten days —The stealing of Apollon's oxen by Hermes —Cows stolen by Vritra in the Vedas —Represent the stealing of day-cows thereby causing the long night —Further sacrificial evidence from the Vedas —Classification of the Soma-sacrifices —Difference between *Ekâha* and *Ahîna* —A hundred nightly sacrifices —Annual *Sattras* like the *Gavâm-ayanam* —Model out-line or scheme of ceremonies therein —Other modifications of the same —All at present based upon a civil year —But lasted for ten months in ancient times —Night-sacrifices now included amongst day-sacrifices —The reason why the former extend only over 100 nights is yet unexplained —Appropriately accounted for on the Arctic theory —Soma juice extracted at night in the *Atirâtra*, or the trans-nocturnal sacrifice even now —The analogy applied to other night-sacrifices—*Râtri Sattras* were the sacrifices of the long night in ancient times —Their object —Soma libations exclusively offered to Indra to help him in his fight against

Vala —*Shata-râtra* represented the maximum duration of the long night —Corroborated by Aditi's legend of seven months' sunshine —Explains why Indra was called *Shata-kratu* in the Purânas —The epithet misunderstood by Western scholars —Similarity between Soma and Ashvamedha sacrifices —The epithet *Shata-kratu*, unlike other epithets, never paraphrased in the Vedas —Implies that it was peculiar or proper to Indra —Dr. Haug's view that *kratu* means a sacrifice in the Vedas —Hundred forts or *puraḥ* (cities) of Vritra —Explained as hundred seats of darkness or nights —Legend of Tishtrya's fight with Apaosha in the Avesta —Only a reproduction of Indra's fight with Vritra —Tishtrya's fight described as lasting from one to a hundred nights in the Avesta —Forms an independent corroboration of hundred nightly Soma sacrifices —The phrase *sato-karahe* found in the Avesta —The meaning and nature of *Ati-râtra* discussed —Means a trans-nocturnal Soma sacrifice at either end of the long night —Production of the cycle of day and night therefrom —Hence a fitting introduction to the annual *Sattras* —Marked the close of the long night and the beginning of the period of sunshine —*Sattra*, *Ati-râtra*, night-sacrifices and *Ati-râtra* again thus formed the yearly round of sacrifices in ancient times —Clearly indicate the existence of a long darkness of 100 nights in the ancient year —Ancient sacrificial system thus corresponded with the ancient year —Adaptation of both to the new home effected by the Brâhmanas, like Numa's reform in the old Roman Calender —The importance of the results of sacrificial evidence.

THE legend of the Dashagvas, who completed their sacrifices during ten months, is not the only relic of the ancient year preserved in the sacrificial literature. The Pravargya ceremony, which is described in the Aitareya Brâhmaṇa, (I, 18-22), furnishes us with another instance, where a reference to the old year seems to be clearly indicated. Dr. Haug, in his translation of the Aitareya Brâhmaṇa, has fully described this ceremony in a note to I, 18. It lasts for three days and precedes the animal and the Soma sacrifice, as no one is allowed to take part in the Soma feast without having undergone this ceremony. The whole ceremony symbolises the revival of the sun or the sacrificial ceremony (*yajña*), which, for the time being, is preserved as seed in order that it may grow again in due time (Ait. Br. I, 18). Thus one of the chief implements used in the ceremony is a peculiar earthen pot called *Gharma* or *Mahâvîra*. Placing it on the Vedic altar the Adhvaryu makes a circle of clay called *khara*, because it is made of earth brought on the back of a donkey to the sacrificial ground. He places the pot on the circle and heats it so as to make it quite hot (*gharma*). It is then lifted by means of two *shaphas* (two wooden pieces), and then milking a cow, the milk is poured into the heated pot and mixed with the milk of a goat whose kid is dead. After this has been done, the contents of the *Mahâvîra* are thrown into the Âhavanîya fire. But all the contents of the pot are not thus thrown away, for the Hotṛi is described as eating the remainder of the contents of the *Gharma*, which are said to be full of honey, full of sap, full of food and quite hot. The Aitareya Brâhmaṇa (I, 22) gives us a rational of this ceremony as follows, "The milk in the vessel is the seed. This seed (in the shape of milk) is poured in Agni (fire) as the womb of the gods for production, for Agni is the womb of the gods." This explanation proves the symbolic nature of the ceremony, and shows that the sun, the sacrifice or the year is thus preserved as seed for some time, and then revived at the proper season. The Mantra or the verse, which is recited on the occasion of pouring the milk into the *Mahâvîra*, is taken from the Ṛig-Veda VIII, 72 (61), 8, and it is very likely that the verse was selected not simply on account of mere verbal correspondence. The hymn, where this verse occurs, is rather obscure. But the verse itself, as well as the two preceding verses (VIII, 72 (61), 6-7-8), present no verbal difficulty and may be translated as follows :—

"6. And now that mighty and great chariot of his, with horses, (as well as) the line of his chariot, is seen."

"7. The seven milk the one, and the two create the five, on the ocean's loud-sounding bank."

"8. With the ten of Vivasvat, Indra, by his three-fold hammer, caused the heaven's bucket to drop down." [1]

Here, first of all, we are told that his (sun's) chariot, the great chariot with horses, has become visible, evidently meaning that the dawn has made its appearance on the horizon. Then the seven, probably the seven *Hotṛis*, or seven rivers, are said to milk this dawn and produce the two. This milking is a familiar process in the Ṛig-Veda, and in one place the cows of the morning are said to be milked from darkness (I, 33, 10). The two evidently mean day and night, and as soon as they are milked, they give rise to the five seasons. The day and the night are said to be the two mothers of Sûrya in III, 55, 6, and here they are the mothers of the five seasons. What becomes after the expiry of the seasons is described in the eighth verse. It says that with the ten of Vivasvat, or with the lapse of ten months, Indra with his three-fold hammer shook down the heavenly jar. This means that the three storing places of the aerial waters (VII, 101, 4) were all emptied into the ocean at this time, and along with it the sun also went to the lower world, for sunlight is described to be three-fold in VII, 101, 2, and Sâyaṇa there quotes the Taittirîya Saṁhitâ (II, 1, 2, 5), which says that the sun has three lights, the morning light being the *Vasanta*, the mid-day the *Grîṣhma*, and the evening the *Sharad*. The verse, therefore, obviously refers to the three-fold courses of waters in the heaven and the three-fold light of the sun; and all this is said to come to an end with the ten of Vivasvat. The sun and the sacrifice are then preserved as seed to be re-generated some time after,—a process symbolised in the Pravargya ceremony. The

1. Ṛig. VIII, 72, 6-8,—उतो न्वस्य यन्महदश्वावद्योजनं बृहत् । दामा रथस्य ददृशे ॥ दुहन्ति सप्तैकामुप द्वा पञ्च सृजतः । तीर्थे सिन्धोरधिस्वरे ॥ आ दशभिर्विवस्वत इंद्रः कोशमचुच्यवीत् । खेदया त्रिवृता दिवः ॥

idea of the sun dropping from heaven is very common in the sacrificial literature. Thus in the Aitareya Brâhmaṇa (IV, 18) we read, "The gods, being afraid of his (sun's) falling *beyond* them, being turned upside down, supported him by placing above him the highest worlds";[1] and the same idea is met with in the Tâṇḍya Brâhmaṇa (IV, 5, 9-11). The words "falling beyond" (*parâchas atipâtât*) are very important, inasmuch as they show that the sun dropped into regions that were on the yonder side. One of the Ashvin's protege is also called Chyavâna, which word Prof. Max Muller derives from *chyu* to drop. The Ashvins are said to have restored him to youth, which, being divested of its legendary form, means the rehabilitation of the sun that had dropped into the nether world. The Pravargya ceremony, which preserves the seed of the sacrifice, is, therefore, only one phase of the story of the dropping sun in the sacrificial literature, and the verses employed in this ceremony, if interpreted in the spirit of that ceremony, appear, as stated above, to indicate an older year of five seasons and ten months.

But the Mantras used in the Pravargya ceremony are not so explicit as one might expect such kind of evidence to be. Therefore, instead of attempting to give more evidence of the same kind,—and there are many such facts in the Vedic sacrificial literature,—I proceed to give the direct statements about the duration of the annual *Sattras* from the well-known Vedic works. These statements have nothing of the legendary character about them, and are, therefore, absolutely certain and reliable. It has been stated before that the institution of sacrifice is an old one, and found amongst both the Asiatic and the European branches of the Aryan race. It was, in fact, the main ritual of the religion of these people, and naturally enough every detail concerning the sacrifices was

1. Ait. Brâh. IV, 18—तस्य पराचोऽतिपातादबिभयुस्तं परमैः स्वर्गैर्लोकैः परस्तात्प्रत्यस्तभ्नुवन् । Also cf. Tâṇḍya Brâh. IV, 5, 9-11.

closely watched, or accurately determined by the priests, who had the charge of these ceremonies. It is true that in giving reasons for the prevalence of a particular practice, these priests sometimes indulged in speculation; but the details of the sacrifice were facts that were settled in strict accordance with custom and tradition, whatever explanations might be given in regard to their origin. But sometimes the facts were found to be so stubborn as to defy any explanation, and the priests had to content themselves with barely recording the practice, and adding that "such is the practice from times immemorial." It is with such evidence that we have now to deal in investigating the duration of the annual *Sattras* in ancient times.

There are many annual *Sattras* like *Âdityânâm-ayanam*, *Aṅgirasâm-ayanam*, *Gavâm-ayanam*, &c. mentioned in the Brâhmaṇas and the Shrauta Sûtras; and, as observed by Dr. Haug, they seem to have been originally established in imitation of the sun's yearly course. They are the oldest of the Vedic sacrifices, and their duraion and other details have been all very minutely and carefully noted down in the sacrificial works. All these annual *Sattras* are not, however, esentially different from each other, being so many different varieties or modifications, according to circumstances, of a common model or type, and the *Gavâm-ayanam* is said to be this type, (*vide*, com. on Âshv. S. S. 11, 7, 1). Thus in the Aitareya Brâhmaṇa (IV, 17) we are told that "They hold the *Gavâm-ayanam*, that is, the sacrificial session called 'the Cows' walk.' The cows are the Âdityas (gods of the months). By holding the session called the Cows' walk they also hold the *Adityânâm-ayanam* (the walk of the Âdityas)."[1] If we, therefore, ascertain the duration of the *Gavâm-ayanam*, the same rule would apply to all other annual *Sattras*, and we need not examine the latter separately. This *Gavâm-ayanam*, or the Cows' walk, is fully

1. See Dr. Haug's Ait. Brâh. Vol. II, p. 287. The original is as follows,—गवामयनेन यंति । गावो वा आदित्या आदित्यानामेव तदयनेन यंति

described in three places. Once in the Aitareya Brâhmaṇa and twice in the Taittirîya Saṁhitâ. We begin with the Aitareya Brâhmaṇa (IV, 17), which describes the origin and duration of the *Sattra* as follows :—

"The cows, being desirous of obtaining hoofs and horns, held (once) a sacrificial session. In the tenth month (of their sacrifice) they obtained hoofs and horns. They said, 'We have obtained fulfilment of that wish for which we underwent the initiation into the sacrificial rites. Let us rise (the sacrifice being finished).' Those, that arose, are these, who have horns. Of those, who, however, sat (continued the session) saying, 'Let us finish the year,' the horns went off on account of their distrust. It is they, who are hornless (*tûparâḥ*). They (continuing their sacrificial session) produced vigour (*ûrjam*) Thence after (having been sacrificing for twelve months and) having secured all the seasons, they rose (again) at the end. For they had produced the vigour (to reproduce horns, hoofs, &c. when decaying). Thus the cows made themselves beloved by all (the whole world), and are beautified (decorated) by all."[1]

Here it is distinctly mentioned that the cows first obtained the fulfilment of their desire in *ten months*, and a number of them left off sacrificing further. Those, that remained and sacrificed for two months more, are called 'distrustful,' and they had to suffer for their distrust by forfeiting the horns they had obtained. It is, therefore, clear, that this yearly *Sattra*, which in the Saṁhitâs and Brâhmaṇas is a *Sattra* of twelve months in imitation of the sun's yearly

1. See Dr. Haug's Ait. Brâh. Trans. Vol. II, p. 287. The passage is as follows,—गावो वै सत्रमासत । शफाँछृंगाणि सिषासन्त्यस्तासां दशमे मासि शफाः शृंगाण्यजायंत । ता अब्रुवन् यस्मै कामायादीक्षामह्यापाम तमुत्तिष्ठामेति । ता या उदतिष्ठंस्ता एता शृंगिण्योऽथ याः समापयिष्यामः संवत्सरमित्यासत तासामश्रद्धया शृंगाणि प्रावर्तंत । ता एतास्तूपरा ऊर्जं त्वसुन्वंस्तस्मादु ताः सर्वानृतून्प्राप्त्वोत्तरमुत्तिष्ठंत्यूर्जं ह्यसुन्वत सर्वस्य वै गावः प्रेमाणं सर्वस्य चारुतां गताः । सर्वस्य प्रेमाणं सर्वस्य चारुतां गच्छति य एवं वेद ।

course, was once completed in ten months. Why should it be so? Why was a *Sattra*, which is annual in its very nature and which now lasts for twelve months, once completed in ten months? How did the sacrificers obtain all the religious merit of a twelve months' sacrifice by sacrificing for ten months only? These are very important questions; but the Aitareya Brâhmaṇa neither raises them, nor gives us any clue to their solution. If we, however, go back to the Taittirîya Saṁhitâ, the oldest and most authoritative work on the sacrificial ceremonies, we find the questions distinctly raised. The Saṁhitâ expressly states that the *Gavâm-ayanam* can be completed in *ten* or *twelve* months, according to the choice of the sacrificer; but it plainly acknowleges its inability to assign any reason how a *Sattra* of twelve months could be completed in ten, except the fact that "it is an old practice sanctioned by immemorial usage." These passages are very important for our purpose, and I give below a close translation of each. The first occurs in the Taittirîya Saṁhitâ (VII, 5, 1, 1-2)[1], and may be rendered as follows:—

"The cows held this sacrificial session, desiring that 'being hornless let horns grow unto us.' Their session lasted (for) ten months. Then when the horns grew (up), they rose saying, 'We have gained.' But those, whose (horns) were not grown, they rose after completing the year, saying 'We have gained.' Those, that had their horns grown, and those that had not, both rose saying 'We have gained.' Cows' session is thus the year (year-session). Those, who know this, reach the year and prosper verily. Therefore, the hornless (cow) moves

1. Taitt. Saṁ. VII, 5, 1, 1-2,—गावो वा एतत् सत्रमासताशृंगाः सतीः शृंगाणि नो जायंता इति कामेन। तासां दश मासा निषण्णा आसन्नथ शृंगाण्यजायंत ता उदतिष्ठन्नराल्स्मेत्यथ यासां नाजायंत ताः संवत्सरमाप्त्वोदतिष्ठन्नराल्स्मेति। यासां चाजायंत यासां च न ता उभयीरुदतिष्ठन्नराल्स्मेति। गोसत्रं वै संवत्सरो य एवं विद्वांसः संवत्सरमुपयंत्यृध्नुवंत्येव तस्मात्तूपरा वार्षिकौ मासौ पर्त्वा चरति सत्राभिजितं ह्यस्यै तस्मात्संवत्सरसदो यत्किंच गृहे क्रियते तदाप्तमवरुद्धमभिजितं क्रियते।

(grazes) pleased during the two rainy months. This is what the *Sattra* has achieved for her. Therefore, whatever is done in the house of one performing the yearly *Sattra* is successfully, timely and properly done."

This account slightly differs from that given in the Aitereya Brâhmana. In the Saṁhitâ the cows, whose session lasted for twelve months, are said to be still hornless; but instead of getting vigour (*ûrjam*), they are said to have obtained as a reward for their additional sitting, the pleasure of comfortable grazing in the two rainy months, during which, as the commentator observes, the horned cows find their horns an impediment to graze freely in the field, where new grass has grown up. But the statement regarding the duration of the *Sattra*, *viz*., that it lasted for *ten* or *twelve* months, is the same both in the Saṁhitâ and in the Brâhmaṇa. The Saṁhitâ again takes up the question in the next *Anuvâka* (VII, 5, 2, 1-2)[1], and further describes the cows' session as follows :—

"The cows held this sacrificial session, being hornless (and) desiring to obtain horns. Their session lasted (for) ten months; then when the horns grew (up), they said, 'We have gained, let us rise, we have obtained the desire for which we sat (commenced the session).' Half, or as many, of them as said, 'We shall certainly sit for the two twelfth (two last) months, and rise after completing the year,' (some) of them had horns in the twelfth month by trust, (while) by distrust those that (are seen) hornless (remained so). Both, that is, those who got horns, and those who obtained vigour (*ûrjam*), thus

1. Taitt. Saṁ. VII, 5, 2, I-2,—गावो वा एतत् सत्रमासताशृंगाः सतीः शृंगाणि सिषासंतीस्तासां दश मासा निषण्णा आसन्नथ शृंगाण्यजायंत ता अब्रुवन्नराल्स्मोत्तिष्ठामाव तं काममरुत्स्महि येन कामेन न्यषदामेति तासामु त्वा अब्रुवन्नर्धा वा यावतीर्वाऽऽसामहा एवेमौ द्वादशौ मासौ संवत्सरं संपाद्योत्तिष्ठामेति तासां द्वादशे मासि शृंगाणि प्रावर्तन्त श्रद्धया वाऽश्रद्धया वा ता इमा यास्तूपरा उभय्यो वाव ता आर्ध्नुवन् याश्च शृंगाण्यसन्वन् याश्चोर्जमवारुंधतर्ध्नोति दशसु मासूत्तिष्ठन्नृध्नोति द्वादशसु य एवं वेद पदेन खलु वा एते यंति विन्दति खलु वै पदेन यन्तद्वा एतदृद्धमयनं तस्मादेतद्गोसनि।

attained their object. One, who knows this, prospers, whether rising (from the sacrifice) in the tenth month or in the twelfth. They indeed go by the path (*padena*) ; he going by the path indeed attains (the end). This is that successful *ayanam* (session). Therefore, it is *go-sani* (beneficial to the cows)."

This passage, in its first part, repeats the story given in the previous *Anuvâka* of the Saṁhitâ and in the Aitareya Brâhmaṇa with slight variations. But the latter part contains two important statements : firstly that whether we complete the sacrifice within ten months or twelve months, the religious merit or fruit obtained is the same in either case, for both are said to prosper equally; and secondly, this is said to be the case because it is the '*path*,' or Sâyaṇa explains "an immemorial custom." The Saṁhitâ is, in fact, silent as to the reason why an annual *Sattra*, which ought to and as a matter of fact does now last for twelve months, could be completed in ten months; and this reticence is very remarkable, considering how the Saṁhitâ sometimes indulges in speculations about the origin of sacrificial rites. Any how we have two facts clearly established, (1) that at the time of the Taittirîya Saṁhitâ the *Gavâm-ayanam*, the type of all annual *Sattras*, could be completed in ten months ; and (2) that no reason was known at the time, as to why a *Sattra* of twelve months could be thus finished in ten, except that it was 'an immemorial custom.' The Tâṇḍya Brâhmaṇa, IV, 1, has a similar discussion about *Gavâm-ayanam*, and clearly recognises its two-fold character so far as its duration is concerned. Sâyaṇa and Bhaṭṭa-Bhâskara, in their commentaries on the Taittirîya Saṁhitâ, cannot, therefore, be said to have invented any new theory of their own as regards the double duration of this annual *Sattra*. We shall discuss later on what is denoted by "cows" in the above passages. At present we are concerned with the duration of the *Sattra* ; and if we compare the above matter-of-fact statements in the Saṁhitâ about the double duration of the annual

Sattra with the legend of the Dashagvas sacrificing for ten months, the conclusion, that in ancient times the ancestors of the Vedic Aryas completed their *annual* sacrificial session in *ten months*, becomes irresistible. This duration of the *Sattra* must have been changed and all such *Sattras* made to last for twelve months, when the Vedic people came to live in regions where such an annual session was impossible. But conservatism in such matters is so strong that the old practice must have outlived the change in the calendar, and it *had* to be recognised as an alternative period of duration for this *Sattra* in the Saṁhitâs. The Taittirîya Saṁhitâ had thus to record the alternative period, stating that it is an ancient practice, and I think it settles the question, so far as the duration of these *Sattras* in ancient times is concerned. Whatever reasons we may assign for it, it is beyond all doubt that the oldest annual *Sattras* lasted only for *ten* months.

But the Tattirîya Saṁhitâ is not alone in being thus unable to assign any reason for this relic of the ancient calendar, or the duration of the annual *Sattra*. We still designate the twelfth month of the European solar year as *December*, which word etymologically denotes the tenth month, (Latin *decem*, Sans. *dashan*, ten; and *ber* Sans. *vâra*, time or period), and we all know that Numa added two months to the ancient Roman year and made it of twelve months. Plutarch, in his life of Numa, records another version of the story, *viz.*, that Numa, according to some, did not add the two months, but simply transferred them from the end to the beginning of the year. But the names of the months clearly show that this could not have been the case, for the enumeration of the months by words indicating their order, as the fifth or *Quintilis* (old name for July), the sixth or *Sixtilis*, (old name for August), the seventh or *September* and so on the rest in their order, cannot, after it is once begun, be regarded to have abruptly stopped at *December*, allowing only the last two months to be differently named.

Plutarch has, therefore, rightly observed that "we have a proof in the name of the last (month) that the Roman year contained, at first, ten months only, and not twelve[1]." But if there was any doubt on the point, it is now removed by the analogy of the *Gavâm-ayanam* and the legends of the Dashagvas and Dîrghatamas. Macrobius (*Saturnal. Lib.* I. *Chap.* 12) confirms the story of Numa's adding, and not simply transposing, two months to the ancient year of ten months. What the Avesta has to say on this subject we shall see later on where traditions about the ancient year amongst the other Aryan races will also be considered. Suffice it to say for the present that, according to tradition, the ancient Roman year consisted only of ten months, and like the duration of the *Gavâm-ayanam*, it was subsequently changed into a year of twelve months; and yet, so far as I know, no reason has yet been discovered, why the Roman year in ancient times was considered to be shorter by two months. On the contrary, the tendency is either to explain away the tradition some how as inconvenient, or to ignore it altogether as incredible. But so long as the word *December* is before us, and we know how it is derived, the tradition cannot be so lightly set aside. The Encyclopædia Britanica (*s. v.* calendar) records the ancient tradition that the oldest Roman year of Romulus was of ten months of 304 days, and observes "it is not known how the remaining days were disposed of." If, with all the resources of modern science at our command, we have not yet been able to ascertain why the oldest Roman year was of ten months only, and how the remaining days were disposed of, we need not be surprised if the Taittirîya Saṁhitâ refrained from speculating on the point and contented itself with stating that such was the '*path*' or the old custom or practice handed down from generation to generation from times immemorial.

---

1. See Plutarch's Lives, translated into English by the Rev. John and William Langhorne (Ward, Lock & Co.), p. 54, f.

The Arctic theory, however, now throws quite a new light on these ancient traditions, Vedic as well as Roman; and if we take the *Gavâm-ayanam* of ten months and the old Roman year of ten months as relics of the period when the ancestors of both these races lived together within the circum-polar regions, there is no difficulty of explaining how the remaining days were disposed of. It was the period of the long night,—a time when Indra fought with Vala, to regain the cows imprisoned by the latter, and Hercules killed the giant Cacus, a three-headed fire-vomiting monster, who had carried off Hercules' cows and hid them in a cave, dragging them backwards in order that the foot-marks might not be traced. When the Aryan people migrated southwards from this ancient home they had to change this calendar to suit their new home by adding two more months to the old year. But the traces of the old calendar could not be completely wiped off, and we have still sufficient evidence, traditional or sacrificial, to warrant us in holding that a year of ten months followed by a night of two months was known in the Indo-Germanic period—a conclusion, which is further confirmed by Teutonic myths and legends, as explained by Prof. Rhys, whose views will be found summarised in a subsequent chapter.

The Taittirîya Samhitâ and the Aitareya Brâhmaṇa speak of the *Gavâm-ayanam* as being really held by the cows. Was it really a session of these animals? Or was it something else? The Aitareya Brâhmaṇa, we have seen, throws out a suggestion that 'the cows are the Âdityas,' that is, the month-gods, and the Cows' session is really the session of the monthly sun-gods.[1] Comparative mythology now fully bears out the truth of this remarkable suggestion put forward by the Brâhmaṇa. Cows, such as we meet them in the mythological legends, represent days and nights of the year, not only in the Vedic

1. See Aitareya Brâh. IV, 17, quoted *supra*; गवामयनेन यंति। गावो वा आदित्या आदित्यानामेव तदयनेन यंति।

but also in the Greek mythology ; and we can, therefore, now give a better account of the origin of this sacrificial session than that it was a session of bovine animals for the purpose of obtaining horns. Speaking of cows in the Aryan mythology, Prof. Max Muller in his *Contributions to the Science of Mythology* (Vol. II. p. 761) writes as follows :—

"There were thus three kinds of cows, the real cows, the cows in the dark cloud (rain = milk), and the cows stepping forth from the dark stable of the night (the rays of the morning). These three are not always easy to distinguish in the Veda, nay, while we naturally try to distinguish between them, the poets themselves seem to delight in mixing them up. In the passage quoted above (I, 32, 11), we saw how the captive waters were compared to cows that had been stolen by Paṇi (*niruddhâḥ âpaḥ Paṇinâ iva gâvaḥ*), but what is once compared in the Veda is soon identified. As to the Dawn, she is not only compared to a cow, she is called the cow straight out. Thus when we read, R.V. I, 92, 1, 'These dawns have made a light, on the eastern half of the sky, they brighten their splendour, the bright cows approach, the mothers,' the cows, *gâvaḥ*, can only be the dawns themselves, the plural of dawn being constantly in the Veda used where we should use the singular. In R.V. I, 93, 4, we read that 'Agnîṣhomau deprived Paṇi of his cows and found light for many.' Here again the cows are the dawns kept by Paṇi in the dark stable or cave of the night, discovered by Saramâ and delivered every morning by the gods of light."

"We read in R.V. I, 62, 3, that Bṛihaspati split the rock and found the cows."

"Of Indra it is said, II, 19, 3, that he produced the sun and found the cows ; of Bṛihaspati, II, 24, 3, that he drove out the cows, that he split the cave by his word, that he hid the darkness, and lighted up the sky. What can be clearer ? The Maruts also, II, 34, 1, are said to uncover the cows, and Agni,

V, 14, 4, is praised for killing the fiends, for having overcome darkness by light, and having found the cows, water and the sun."

"In all these passages we find no *iva* or *na*, which would indicate that the word cow was used metaphorically. The dawns or days as they proceed from the dark stable, or are rescued from evil spirits, are spoken of directly as the cows. If they are spoken of in the plural, we find the same in the case of the Dawn (*ushas*) who is often conceived as many, as in II, 28, 2, *upâyane ushasâm gomatînâm*, 'at the approach of the dawns with their cows.' From that it required but a small step to speak of the one Dawn as the mother of the cows, IV, 52, 2, *mâtâ gavâm.*"

"Kuhn thought that these cows should be understood as the red clouds of the morning. But clouds are not always present at sunrise, nor can it well be said that they are carried off and kept in prison during the night by the powers of darkness."

"But what is important and settles the point is the fact that these cows or oxen of the dawn or of the rising sun occur in other mythologies also and are there clearly meant for days. They are numbered as 12×30, that is, the thirty days of the 12 lunar months. If Hêlios has 350 oxen and 350 sheep, that can only refer to the days and to the nights of the year, and would prove the knowledge of a year of 350 days before the Aryan separation."

Thus the cows in mythology are the days and nights, or dawns, that are imprisoned by Paṇi, and not real living cows with horns. Adopting this explanation and substituting these metaphorical cows for *gâvaḥ* in the *Gavâm-ayanam*, it is not difficult to see that underneath the strange story of cows holding a sacrificial session for getting horns, there lies concealed the remarkable phenomenon, that, released from the clutches of Paṇi, these cows of days and nights walked on for ten months, the oldest duration of the session known as Cows' walk. In plain language this means, if it means anything, that the oldest Aryan year was one of ten months followed by the long night, during which the cows were again carried away by the powers of darkness. We have seen that the oldest Roman year was of ten months, and the Avesta, as will be shown later on, also speaks of ten months' summer prevailing in the Airyana Vaejo before the home was invaded by the evil spirit, who brought on ice and severe winter in that place. A year of ten months with a long night of two months may thus be taken to be known before the Aryan separation, and the references to it in the Vedic literature are neither isolated nor imaginary. They are the relics of ancient history, which have been faithfully preserved in the sacrificial literature of India, and if they were hitherto misunderstood it was because the true key required for their solution was as yet unknown.

But as stated in the previous chapter, a year in the circum-polar region will always have a varying number of the months of sunshine according to latitude. Although, therefore, there is sufficient evidence to establish the existence of a year of ten months, we cannot hold that it was the only year known in ancient times. In fact we have seen that the legend of Aditi indicates the existence of the seven months of sunshine; and a band of thirty continuous dawns supports the same conclusion. But it seems that a year of ten months of sunshine was more prevalent, or was selected as the mean of the different varying years. The former view is rendered probable by the fact that of the Aṅgirases of various forms (*virûpas*) the Navagvas and the Dashagvas are said to be the principal or the most important in the Ṛig-Veda (X, 62, 6). But whichever view we adopt, the existence of a year of seven, eight, nine, ten or eleven months of sunshine follows as a matter of course, if the ancient Aryan home was within the Arctic circle. Prof. Max Muller, in the passage quoted above, points out that the old Greek year probably consisted of 350 days, the 350 oxen of

Hêlios representing the days, and 350 sheep representing the nights. He also notices that in German mythology 700 gold rings of Wieland, the smith, are spoken of, and comparing the number with 720 sons of Agni mentioned in I, 164, 11, he draws from it the conclusion that a year of 350 days is also represented in the German mythology. This year is shorter by ten days than the civil year of 360 days, or falls short of the full solar year by 15 days. It is, therefore, clear, that if a year of 350 days existed before the Aryan separation, it must have been followed by a continuous night of ten days; while, where the year was of 300 days, the long night extended over 60 days of 24 hours each. We shall thus have different kinds of long nights; and it is necessary to see if we can collect evidence to indicate the longest duration of the night known before the Aryan separation. Speaking of the cows or oxen of Hêlios, as stated in the passage quoted above, Prof. Max Muller goes on to observe :—

"The cows or oxen of Hêlios thus receive their background from the Veda, but what is told of them by Homer is by no means clear. When it is said that the companions of Odysseus consumed the oxen of Hêlios, and that they thus forfeited their return home, we can hardly take this in the modern sense of consuming or wasting their days, though it may be difficult to assign any other definite meaning to it. Equally puzzling is the fable alluded to in the Homeric hymn that Hermes stole the oxen of Apollon and killed two of them. The number of Apollon's oxen is given as fifty (others give the number as 100 cows, twelve oxen and one bull), which looks like the number of weeks in the lunar year, but why Hermes should be represented as carrying off the whole herd and then killing two, is difficult to guess, unless we refer it to the two additional months in a cycle of four years."

In the light of the Arctic theory the puzzle here referred to is solved without any difficulty. The stealing away or the carrying off of the cows need not now be taken to mean simple wasting of the days in the modern sense of the word; nor need we attribute such stories to the "fancy of ancient bards and story-tellers". The legend or the tradition of stealing, consuming, or carrying off the cows or oxen is but another form of stating that so many days were lost, being swallowed up in the long night that occurred at the end of the year and lasted, according to latitude, for varying periods of time. So long as every thing was to be explained on the theory of a daily struggle between light and darkness, these legends were unintelligible. But as soon as we adopt the Arctic theory the whole difficulty vanishes, and what was confused and puzzling before becomes at once plain and comprehensible. In the Vedic mythology cows are similarly said to be stolen by Vṛitra or Vala, but their number is nowhere given, unless we regard the story of Ṛijrâshva (the Red-horse) slaughtering 100 or 101 sheep and giving them to a she-wolf to devour (I, 116, 16; 117, 18), as a modification of the story of stealing the cows. The Vedic sacrificial literature does, however, preserve for us an important relic, besides the one above noted, of the older calendar and especially the long night. But in this case the relic is so deeply buried under the weight of later explanations, adaptations and emendations, that we must here examine at some length the history of the Soma sacrifices in order to discover the original meaning of the rites which are included under that general name. That the Soma sacrifice is an ancient institution is amply proved by parallel rites in the Parsi scriptures; and whatever doubt we may have regarding the knowledge of Soma in the Indo-European period, as the word is not found in the European languages, the system of sacrifices can be clearly traced back to the primeval age. Of this sacrificial system, the Soma sacrifice may, at any rate, be safely taken as the oldest representative, since it forms the main feature of the ritual of the Ṛig-Veda, and a whole

Maṇḍala of 114 hymns in the Ṛig-Veda is dedicated to the praise of Soma. A careful analysis of the Soma sacrifice may, therefore, be expected to disclose, at least partially, the nature of the oldest sacrificial system of the Aryan race; and we, therefore, proceed to examine the same.

The chief characteristic of the Soma sacrifice, as distinguished from other sacrifices, is, as the name indicates, the extraction of the Soma juice and the offering thereof to gods before drinking it. There are three libations of Soma in a day, one in the morning, one at mid-day, and the last in the evening, and all these are accompanied by the chanting of hymns during the sacrifice. These Soma sacrifices, if classed according to their duration, fall under three heads; (1) those that are performed in a single day, called *Ekâhas*, (2) those that are performed in more than one and less than thirteen days, called *Ahînas*, and (3) those that take thirteen or more than 13 days and may last even for one thousand years, called *Sattras*. Under the first head we have the Agnishṭoma, fully described in the Aitareya Brâhmaṇa (III, 39-44), as the key or the type of all the sacrifices that fall under this class. There are six modifications of Agnishṭoma, *viz*., Ati-agnishṭoma, Ukthya, Ṣhoḍashî, Vâjapeya, Atirâtra and Aptoryâma, which together with Agnishṭoma, form the seven parts, kinds or modifications of the Jyotishṭoma sacrifice, (Ashv. S. S. VI, 11, 1). The modication chiefly consists in the number of hymns to be recited at the libations, or the manner of recitation, or the number of the *Grahas* or Soma-cups used on the occasion. But with these we are not at present concerned. Of the second class of Soma sacrifices, the *Dvâdashâha* or twelve days' sacrifice is celebrated both as *Ahîna* and *Sattra* and is considered to be very important. It is made up of three *tryahas* (or three days' performances, called respectively *Jyotis*, *Go*, and *Ayus*), the tenth day and the two Atirâtras (Ait. Br. IV, 23-4). The nine days' performance (three *tryahas*) is called the *Nava-râtra*. Side by side with this, there are, under this head, a number of Soma sacrifices extending over two nights, three nights, four nights upto twelve nights, called *dvi-râtra*, *tri-râtra* and so on (Tait. Saṁ. VII, I, 4,–VII, 3, 2; Ashv. Shr. Sut. X and XI ; Tâṇ. Brâ. 20, 11,–24, 19). In the third class we have the annual *Sattras* and of these the *Gavâm-ayanam* is the type. Some *Sattras* which come under this class are described as extending over, 1,000 years, and a discussion is found in sacrificial works as to whether the phrase one thousand years signifies 1,000 real years, or whether it stands for 1,000 days. But we may pass it over as unnecessary for our purpose. The annual *Sattras* are the only important *Sattras* of this class, and to understand their nature we must see what a *ṣhaḷaha* means. The word literally denotes a group of six days (*ṣhaṭ+ahan*) and is used to denote six days' performance in the sacrificial literature. It is employed as a unit to measure a month in the same way as we now use a week, a month being made up of five *ṣhaḷahas*. The *ṣhaḷaha*, in its turn, consists of the daily sacrifices called, *Jyotis*, *Go*, *Ayus*, and the same three taken in the reverse order as, *Ayus*, *Go* and *Jyotis*. Every *ṣhaḷaha*, therefore, begins and ends with a Jyotiṣhṭoma (Ait. Br. IV, 15). The *ṣhaḷaha* is further distinguished into *Abhiplava* and *Pṛiṣhṭhya*, according to the arrangement of the *stomas* or songs sung at the Soma libations. An annual *Sattra* is, in the main, made up of a number of *ṣhaḷahas* joined with certain special rites at the beginning, the middle and the close of the *Sattra*. The central day of the *Sattra* is called *Viṣhuvân*, and stands by itself, dividing the *Sattra* into two equal halves like the wings of a house (Tait. Br. I, 2, 3, 1) ; and the rites in the latter half of the session or after the *Viṣhuvân* day are performed in an order which is the reverse of that followed in performing the ceremonies in the first half of the sacrifice. The model annual *Sattra* (the *Gavâm-ayanam*) thus consists of the following parts :—

	Parts.	*Days.*
1.	The introductory Atirâtra	1
2.	The Chaturviṁsha day, otherwise called the Ârambhaṇîya (Ait. Br. IV. 12), or the Prâyaṇiya (Tâṇḍ. Br. IV, 2), the real beginning of the *Sattra*	1
3.	Four Abhiplava, followed by one Prishṭhya shaḷaha each month; continued in this way for five months...	150
4.	Three Abhiplava and one Prishṭhya shaḷaha	24
5.	The Abhijit day	1
6.	The three Svara-Sâman days..................................	3
7.	The *Vishuvân* or *the Central day*, which stands by itself, *i. e.*, not counted in the total of the *Sattra* days.	
8.	The three Svara-Sâman days..................................	3
9.	The Vishvajit day	1
10.	One Prishṭhya and three Abhiplava shaḷahas..............	24
11.	One Prishṭhya and four Abhiplava shaḷahas each month; continued in this way for four months	120
12.	Three Abhiplava shaḷahas, one Go-shṭoma, one Âyushṭoma, and one Dasharâtra (the ten days of Dvâdashâha), making up one month	30
13.	The Mahâvrata day, corresponding to the Chaturviṁsha day at the beginning	1
14.	The concluding Atirâtra...	1
	Total Days.........	360.

It will be seen from the above scheme that there are really a few sacrificial rites which are absolutely fixed and unchangeable in the yearly *Sattra*. The two Atirâtras, the introductory and the concluding, the Chaturviṁsha and the Mahâvrata day, the Abhijit and the Vishvajit, the three Svara-Sâman days on either side of Vishuvân, the Vishuvân itself, and the ten days of Dvâdashâha, making up 22 days in all, exclusive of Vishuvân, are the only parts that have any speciality about them. The rest of the days are all made up by *Abhiplava* and *Prishṭhya* shaḷahas, which, therefore, constitute what may be called the elastic or the variable part of the yearly *Sattra*. Thus if we want a *Gavâm-ayanam* of ten months, we have only to strike off five *shaḷahas* from the parts marked 3 and 11 in the above scheme. The *Âdityânâm-ayanam* is another modification of the above scheme in which, amongst other changes, the *ṣhaḷahas* are all *Abhiplava*, instead of being a combination of *Abhiplava* and *Pṛiṣhṭhya*; while if all the *ṣhaḷahas* are *Pṛiṣhṭhya*, along with some other changes, it becomes the *Aṅgirasâm-ayanam*. All these modifications do not, however, touch the total number of 360 days. But there were sacrificers, who adopted the lunar year of 354 days, and therefore, omitted 6 days from the above scheme; and their *Sattra* is called the *Utsargiṇâm-ayanam* (Tait. Saṁ. VII, 5, 7, 1; Tâṇḍya Brâh. V, 10). In short, the object was to make the *Sattra* correspond with the year adopted, civil or lunar, as closely as possible. But these points are not relevant to our purpose. The Brâhmaṇas and the Shrauta Sûtras give further details about the various rites to be performed on the Viṣhuvân, the Abhijit and the Vishvajit or the Svara-sâman day. The Aitareya Âraṇyaka describes the Mahâvrata ceremony; while the Atirâtra and the Chaturviṁsha are described in the fourth book of the Aitareya Brâhmaṇa. The Chaturviṁsha is so called because the *stoma* to be chanted on that day is twenty-four-fold. It is the real beginning of the *Sattra* as the Mahâvrata is its end. The Aitareya Brâhmaṇa (IV, 14) says, "The Hotṛi pours forth the seed. Thus he makes the seed (which is poured forth) by means of the Mahâvrata day produce off-spring. For seed if effused every year is productive." This explanation shows that like the Pravargya ceremony, the Mahâvrata was intended to preserve the seed of the sacrifice in order that it might germinate or grow at the proper time. It was a sort of link between the dying and the coming year, and appropriately concluded the annual *Sattra*. It will be further seen that every annual *Sattra* had an Ati-râtra at each of its ends, and that the Dvâdashâha, or rather the ten days thereof, formed an important concluding part of the *Sattra*.

The above is only a brief description, a mere out-line, of the scheme of the annual *Sattras* mentioned in sacrificial works, but it is sufficient for our purpose. We can see from it that a civil year of 360 days formed their basis, and the position of the Vishuvân was of great importance inasmuch as the ceremonies after it were performed in the reverse order. I have shown elsewhere what important inferences can be drawn from the position of the Vishuvân regarding the calendar in use at time when the scheme was settled. But we have now to consider of times which preceded the settlement of this scheme, and for that purpose we must describe another set of Soma sacrifices included under the general class of *Sattras.* It has been stated above that side by side with the Dvâdashâha, there are *Ahina* sacrifices of two nights, three nights, etc., upto twelve nights. But these sacrifices do not stop with the twelve nights' performance. There are thirteen nights', fourteen nights', fifteen nights', and so on upto one hundred nights' sacrifice called *Trayodasha-râtra*, *Chaturdasha-râtra* and so on upto *Shata-râtra.* But since the *Ahîna* has been defined to be a sacrifice extending over not more than twelve or less than thirteen days, all the night-sacrifices extending over a period longer than twelve nights are included in the third class, *viz.*, the *Sattras.* If we, however, disregard this artificial division, it will be found that along with the *Ekâha*, the *Dvâdashâha* and the annual *Sattras*, there is a series of, what are termed, the night-sacrifices or *sattras* extending over a period of time from two to one hundred *nights*, but not further. These night-sacrifices or *Râtri-sattras* are mentioned in the Taittirîya Samhitâ, the Brâhmaṇas and the Shrauta Sûtras in clear terms, and there is no ambiguity about their nature, number, or duration. The Taittirîya Samhitâ in describing them often uses the word *Râtriḥ* (nights) in the plural, stating, that so and so was the first to institute or to perceive 'so many nights' meaning so many nights' sacrifice (*vimshatim râtriḥ*, VII, 3, 9, 1; *dvâtrimshatam râtriḥ*, VII, 4, 4. 1). According to the principle of division noted above all night-sacrifices of less than thirteen nights' duration will be called *Ahîna*, while those extending over longer time upto one hundred nights will come under *Sattras*; but this is, as remarked above, evidently an artificial division, and one, who reads carefully the description of these sacrifices, cannot fail to be struck by the fact that we have here a series of night-sacrifices from two to a hundred nights, or if we include the *Ati-râtra* in this series, we have practically a set of hundred nightly Soma sacrifices, though, according to the principle of division adopted, some may fall under the head of *Ahîna* and some under that of *Sattras*.

Now an important question in connection with these *Sattras* is why they alone should be designated '*night*-sacrifices' (*râtri-kratus*), or '*night*-sessions' (*râtri-sattras*)? and why their number should be one hundred? or, in other words, why there are no *night*-sattras of longer duration than one hundred nights? The Mîmâmsakas answer the first part of the question by asking us to believe that the word 'night' (*râtriḥ*) is really used to denote 'a day' in the denomination of these sacrifices (Shabara on Jaimini VIII, 1, 17). The word *Dvi-râtra*, according to this theory, means two days' sacrifice, and *Shata-râtra*, a hundred days' sacrifice. This explanation appears very good at the first sight, and as a matter of fact it has been accepted by all writers on the sacrificial ceremonies. In support of it, we may also cite the fact that as the moon was the measurer of time in ancient days, the night was then naturally more marked than the day, and instead of saying 'so many days' men often spoke of 'so many nights,' much in the same way as we now use the word 'fort-night.' This is no doubt good so far as it goes; but the question is why should there be no Soma sacrifices of a longer duration than one hundred nights? and why a gap, a serious gap, is left in the series of Soma sacrifices after one hundred nights' *Sattra* until we come to the annual *Sattra* of 360 days? Admitting that 'night' means 'day,' we have Soma sacrifices lasting from 1 to 100 days; and, if so, where was the harm to complete the series until the yearly *Sattra* of 360 days was reached? So far as I know, no writer on sacrificial ceremonies has attempted to answer this question satisfactorily. Of course, adopting the speculative manner of the Brâhmaṇas, we might say that there are no Soma sacrifices of longer than one hundred nights' duration, because the life of a man cannot extend beyond a hundred years, (Tait. Br. III, 8, 16, 2). But such an explanation can never be regarded as satisfactory, and the Mîmâṁsakas, who got over one difficulty by interpreting 'night' into 'day,' have practically left this latter question untouched, and, therefore, unsolved. In short, the case stands thus:— the sacrificial literature mentions a series of 99, or practically one hundred Soma sacrifices, called the 'night-sacrifices'; but these do not form a part of any annual *Sattra*, like the *Gavâm-ayanam*, nor is any reason assigned for their separate existence, nor is their duration, which never exceeds a hundred nights, accounted for. Neither the authors of the Brâhmaṇas nor those of the Shrauta Sûtras, much less Sâyaṇa and Yâska give us any clue to the solution of this question; and the Mîmâṁsakas, after explaining the word 'night,' occurring in the names of these sacrifices as equal to 'day,' have allowed these night-sacrifices to remain as an isolated group in the organised system of Soma sacrifices. Under these circumstances it would, no doubt, appear presumptious for any one to suggest an explanation, so many centuries after what may be called the age of the *Sattras*. But I feel that the Arctic theory, which, we have seen, is supported by strong independent evidence, not only explains, but appropriately accounts for the original existence of this isolated series of a hundred Soma sacrifices; and I, therefore, proceed to give my view on the point.

It seems to me that if the word *râtri* in *Ati-râtra* is still understood to mean 'night,' and that if the *Ati-râtra* sacrifice is even now performed during the night, there is no reason why we should not similarly interpret the same word in *Dvi-râtra*, *Tri-râtra* &c. upto *Shata-râtra*. The objection, that the Soma juice is not extracted during the night, is more imaginary than real; for as a matter of fact Soma libations are made in the usual way, during the *Ati-râtra* sacrifice. The *Ati-râtra* sacrifice is performed at the beginning and the end of every *Sattra*; and all the three libations of Soma are always offered during the three turns, or *paryâyas*, of the night. The Aitareya Brâhmaṇa (IV, 5), in explaining the origin of this sacrifice, tells us that the Asuras had taken shelter with the night, and the Devas, who had taken shelter with the day, wanted to expel them from the dark region. But amongst the Devas, Indra alone was found ready and willing to undertake this task; and entering into darkness, he, with the assistance of metres, turned the Asuras out of the first part of the night by the first Soma libation, while by means of the middle turn (*paryâya*) of passing the Soma-cup, the Asuras were turned out of the middle part, and by the third turn out of the third or the last part of the night. The three Soma libations, here spoken of, are all made during the night, and the Brâhmaṇa further observes that there is *no other deity save Indra and the Metres* to whom they are offered, (Cf. Âpas. Sh. Su. XIV, 3, 12). The next section of the Brâhmaṇa (IV, 6) distinctly raises the question, "How are the Pavamâna Stotras (to be chanted for the purification of the Soma juice) provided for the night, whereas such Stotras refer only to the day, but not to the night?" and answers it by stating that the Stotras are the same for the day and the night. It is clear from this that Soma juice was extracted and purified at night during the *Ati-râtra* sacrifice, and Indra was the *only* deity to whom the libations were offered in order to help him in his fight with the Asuras, who had taken shelter with the darkness of the night. That the *Ati-râtra* is an ancient sacrifice is further proved by the occurrence of a similar ceremony in the Parsi scriptures. The word *Ati-râtra* does not occur in the Avesta, but in the Vendidad, XVIII, 18 (43)–22 (48), we are told that there are three parts of the night, and that in the first of these parts (*thrishvai*), Fire, the son of Ahura Mazda, calls upon the master of the house to arise and put on his girdle and to fetch clean wood in order that he may burn bright; for, says the Fire, "Here comes Azi (Sans. *Ahi*), made by the Daêvas (Vedic *Asuras*), who is about to strive against me, and wants to put out my life." And the same request is made during the second and the third part of the night. The close resemblance between this and the three *paryâyas* of the *Ati-râtra* sacrifice does not seem to have been yet noticed; but whether noticed or not, it shows that the *Ati-râtra* is an ancient rite performed during the night for the purpose of helping Indra, or the deity that fought with the powers of darkness, and that such sacrificial acts as putting on the girdle (*kosti*) or squeezing the Soma, were performed during this period of darkness.

Now what applies to the sacrifice of a single night may well be extended to cases where sacrifices had to be performed for two, three or more continuous nights. I have already shown before that the ancient sacrificers completed their sacrificial sessions in ten months, and a long night followed the completion of these sacrifices. What did the sacrificers do during this long night? They could not have slept all the time; and as a matter of fact we know that the people in the extreme north of Europe and Asia do not, even at present, sleep during the whole of the long night which occurs in their part of the globe. Paul Du Chaillu, who has recently (1900) published an account of his travels in *The Land of the*

Long Night, informs us (p. 75) that although the sun went below the horizon for several days in the Arctic regions, yet during the period "the Lapps could tell from the stars whether it was night or day, for they were accustomed to gauge time by the stars according to their height above the horizon, just as we do at home with the sun"; and what the Lapps do now, must have been done by the oldest inhabitants of the circum-polar regions. It is, therefore, clear that the ancient sacrificers of the Aryan race could not have gone to sleep after sacrificing for ten months. Did they then sit idle with their hands folded when Indra was fighting for them with the powers of darkness? They performed their sacrifices for ten months with a view to help Indra in his war with Vala; and just at the time when Indra most needed the help of invigorating songs and Soma libations, are we to suppose that these sacrificers sat idle, gave up the sacrifices and left Indra to fight with Vala alone and single-handed as best as he could? The whole theory of sacrifices negatives such a supposition. Therefore, if the Arctic theory is true, and if the ancestor of the Vedic Ṛishis ever lived in a region where the darkness of the night lasted for several days, (a day being taken as a measure of time equal to 24 hours), we naturally expect to find a series of nightly Soma sacrifices performed during the period, to help the gods in their struggle with the demons of darkness; and, as a matter of fact, there are in the Vedic sacrificial literature, a number of sacrifices which, if we include the *Ati-râtra* in it, extend from one to a hundred nights. The Mîmâṁsakas and even the authors of the Brâhmaṇas, who knew little about the ancient Arctic home, have converted these night-sacrifices into day-sacrifices; but the explanation evidently appears to be invented at a time when the true nature of the *Râtri-kratus* or *Râtri-sattras* was forgotten, and it does not, therefore, preclude us from interpreting these facts in a different way. I have already stated above that if we accept the explanation of the Mîmâṁsakas, we cannot explain why the series of the night-sacrifices should abruptly end with the *Shata-râtra* or a hundred nights' sacrifice; but by the Arctic theory we can explain the fact satisfactorily by supposing that the duration of the long night in the ancient home varied from one night (of 24 hours) to a hundred continuous nights (of 2400 hours) according to latitude, and that the hundred nightly Soma sacrifices corresponded to the different durations of the night at different places in the ancient home. Thus where the darkness lasted only for ten nights (240 hours) a *Dasha-râtra* sacrifice was performed, while where it lasted for 100 nights (2400 hours) a *Shata-râtra* sacrifice was necessary. There are no sacrifices after the *Shata-râtra* because a hundred continuous nights marked the maximum duration of darkness experienced by the ancient sacrificers of the race. We have seen that the legend of Aditi indicates a period of seven months sunshine; join to it the Dawn and the Twilight of 30 days each, and there are left three months, (or if we take the year to consist of 365 days, then 95 days), for the duration of the long continuous night,—a result which remarkably corresponds to the longest duration of the night-sacrifices known in the Vedic literature. The Dawn marked the end of the long night, and could not, therefore, be included in the latter at least for sacrificial purposes. In fact separate sacrifices are enjoined for the Dawn in sacrificial works; and we may, therefore, safely exclude the long Dawn from the province of the nightly sacrifices, and the same may be said of the period of the long evening twilight. A hundred nights' sacrifice thus marked the maximum duration of darkness during which Indra fought with Vala and was strengthened by the Soma libations offered to him in this sacrifice. As there is no other theory to account for the existence of the night-sacrifices, and especially for their number, to wit, one hundred, these sacrifices may be safely taken to indicate the existence of an ancient year approximately divided into seven months' sunshine, one month's dawn, one month's evening twilight and three months' long continuous night.

There are other considerations which point out to the same conclusion. In the post-Vedic literature we have a peristent tradition that Indra alone of all gods is the master of a hundred sacrifices (*shata-kratu*), and that as this attribute formed, so to say, the very essence of Indraship, he always jealously watched all possible encroachments against it. But European scholars, relying upon the fact that even Sâyaṇa prefers, except in a few places (III, 51, 2), to interpret *shata-kratu*, as applied to Indra in the Ṛig-Veda, as meaning, not 'the master of a hundred sacrifices,' but 'the lord of a hundred mights or powers,' have not only put aside the Purâṇic tradition, but declined to interpret the word *kratu* in the Ṛig-Veda except in the sense of 'power, energy, skill, wisdom, or, generrally speaking, the power of body or mind.' But if the above explanation of the origin of the night-sacrifices is correct, we must retrace our steps, and acknowledge that the Purâṇic tradition or legend is, after all, not built upon a pure misunderstanding of the original meaning of the epithet *shata-kratu* as applied to Indra in the Vedic literature. I am aware of the fact that traditions in the post-Vedic literature are often found to have but a slender basis in the Vedas, but in the present case we have something more reliable and tangible to go upon. We have a group, an isolated group of a hundred nightly Soma sacrifices, and as long as it stands unexplained in the Vedic sacrificial literature it would be unreasonable to decline to connect it with the Purâṇic tradition of Indra's sole mastership of a hundred sacrifices, especially when in the light of the Arctic theory the two can be so well and intelligibly connected. The hundred sacrifices, which are regarded as constituting the essence of Indraship in the Purâṇas, are there said to be the Ashvamedha sacrifices; and it may, at the outset, be urged that the *Shata-râtra* sacrifice mentioned in the sacrificial works is not an Ashvamedha sacrifice. But the distinction is neither important, nor material. The Ashvameda sacrifice is a Soma sacrifice and is described in the sacrificial works along with the night-sacrifices. In the Taittirîya Saṁhitâ (VII, 2, 11,) a hundred offerings of food to be made in the Ashvamedha sacrifice are mentioned, and the Taittirîya Brâhmaṇa (III, 8, 15, 1) states that Prajâpati obtained these offerings "during the night," and consequently they are called *Râtri-homas.* The duration of the Ashvamedha sacrifice is again not fixed, inasmuch as it depends upon the return of the horse, and in the Ṛig-Veda (I, 163, 1) the sacrificial horse is identified with the sun moving in waters. The return of the sacrificial horse may, therefore, be taken to symbolise the return of the sun after the long night, and a close resemblance between the Ashvamedha and the night-sacrifices, which were performed to enable Indra to fight with Vala and rescue the dawn and the sun from his clutches, may thus be taken as established. At any rate, we need not be surprised if the *Shata-râtra* Soma sacrifice appears in the form of a hundred Ashvamedha sacrifices in the Purâṇas. The tradition is substantially the same in either case, and when it can be so easily and naturally explained on the Arctic theory, it would not be reasonable to set it aside, and hold that the writers of the Purâṇas created it by misinterpreting the word *shata-kratu* occurring in the Vedas.

We have seen that *shata-kratu* as applied to Indra is interpreted by Western scholars, and in many places even by Sâyaṇa himself, as meaning the lord of a hundred powers. Sâyaṇa now and then (III, 51, 2; X, 103, 7) suggests or gives an alternative explanation, and makes Indra 'the master of a hundred sacrifices'; but Western scholars have gone further and discarded all other explanations except the one noted above. It is, therefore, necessary to examine the meaning of this epithet, as used in the Ṛig-Veda, a little more closely in this place. If the word *kratu* in *shata-kratu* be interpreted to mean 'might' or 'power,' the numeral *shata*, which strictly denotes 'a hundred,' will have to be taken as equivalent to 'many' or 'numerous,' inasmuch as no definite set of a hundred powers can be pointed out as specially belonging to Indra. That the word *shata* may be so interpreted is evident from the fact that adjectives like *shata-nîtha* (I, 100, 12) and *shatam-ûti* (I, 102, 6 ; 130, 8), as applied to Indra in the Ṛig-Veda, are found in other places in the form of *sahasra-nîtha* (III, 60, 7), and *sahasram-ûti* (I, 52, 2). Again Indra's arrow is once called *shata-bradhna* and also *sahasra-parṇa* in the same verse (VIII, 77, 7); while Soma is represented as going in a hundred ways (*shata-yâman*) in IX, 86, 16, and a few hymns after it is said to be *sahasra-yâman* or going in a thousand ways (IX, 106, 5). Even the adjective *shata-manyu*, which Sâyaṇa interprets as meaning 'the master of a hundred sacrifices' in X, 103, 7, has its counterpart, if not in the Ṛig-Veda, at least in the Sâma-Veda which reads *sahasra-manyu* for *sahasra-mushka* in Ṛig-Veda VI, 46, 3. This shows that the Vedic bards considered *shata* (a hundred) and *sahasra* (a thousand) as interchangeable numerals in some places ; and if the numeral *shata* in *shata-kratu* had been of the same character, we should naturally have met with a paraphrase of the epithet as *sahasra-kratu* somewhere in the Vedic literature. But although the epithet *shata-kratu*, as applied to Indra, occurs about sixty times in the Ṛig-Veda and several times in other Vedic works, nowhere do we find it paraphrased as *sahasra-kratu*, which shews that the Vedic bards did not feel themselves at liberty to alter or paraphrase it as they liked. The adjective *amita-kratu* is applied to Indra in I, 102, 6; but as *amita* does not necessarily mean more than 'one hundred,' it does not follow that on this account we should give up the ordinary meaning of *shata* in *shata-kratu*. If the word *kratu* had nowhere been used in the Ṛig-

Veda to denote a sacrifice, we may have been justified in interpreting *shata-kratu* in the way suggested by Western scholars. But, as observed by Dr. Haug, when Vasishṭha prayed to Indra (VII, 32, 26) "Carry, O Indra ! our sacrificial performance (*kratum*) through, just as a father does to his sons, (by assisting them). Teach us, O thou, who art invoked by many, that we may, in this turn (of the night), reach alive the (sphere of) light (*jyotis*),"[1] the prayer in all probability refers to the sacrificial performance (*kratu*) held for the purpose of enabling the sacrificers to safely reach the other end of the night. In fact, it refers to the *Ati-râtra* sacrifice and the Aitareya Brâhmaṇa (IV, 10) quotes and interprets it in the same way. Sâyaṇa, in his commentary on the Aitareya Brâhmaṇa, though not in the Ṛig-Veda Bhâshya, also takes the same view ; and as the *Ati-râtra* sacrifice is referred to expressly by its name in the Ṛig-Veda (VII, 103, 7) it is not at all unlikely that a verse referring to this Soma sacrifice should occur in other hymns. Hence if there are passages where *kratu* can be taken to mean 'a sacrifice,' there is no reason why the epithet *shata-kratu* be not understood to mean "the master of a hundred sacrifices" as suggested by the Purâṇic tradition. Another fact which favours this interpretation, is that in the Ṛig-Veda Indra is described as destroying 90, 99 or 100 fortresses or cities (*puraḥ*) of his enemies (I, 130 7 ; II, 19, 6 ; VI, 31, 4; II, 14, 6). Now *deva-purâḥ*, which means 'the fortresses of the gods,' has been[2] interpreted to mean 'days' in the description of the *dasha-râtra* sacrifice in the Taittirîya Saṁhitâ VII, 2,

1. See Dr. Haug's Ait. Br. (IV, 10), Trans. Vol. II, p. 274, and the translator's note thereon. Dr. Haug thinks that the verse (Ṛig. VII, 32, 26) evidently refers to the *Ati-râtra* feast, for which occasion it was in all likelihood composed by Vasishṭha. The verse is :—इंद्र क्रतुं न आ भर पिता पुत्रेभ्यो यथा । शिक्षा णो अस्मिन् पुरुहूत यामनि जीवा ज्योतिरशीमहि ॥

2. Cf. Bhaṭṭa Bhâskara's Com. which says:—'देवपुराः' देवानाम् पुरस्थानीयानि पुरविपक्षया इतराण्यहानि 'पर्यूहन्ती' सर्वतो नयंति आत्मनो रक्षार्थम् । ... । 'ते देवाः' देवपुराख्यानि इतरात्मसंबंधीन्यहानि ।

5, 3-4; and if *deva-purâḥ* means 'days,' the *puraḥ* (cities, fortresses) of Shambara may well be taken to mean 'nights.' This view is confirmed by the statement in the Aitareya Brâhmaṇa, previously quoted, which says that the Asuras found shelter with the night, or, in other words, the darkness of the night was, so to say, their fortress. Indra's destroying a hundred forts of Shambara is, therefore, equivalent to his fighting with the enemy for a hundred continuous nights, a period during which the ancient sacrificers offered him Soma libations in order that he may be better prepared for the struggle with Vala. The destruction of 99 or 100 forts of the enemy, a group of a hundred nightly sacrifices, the nine and ninety rivers (*sravantîḥ*) which Indra is described as crossing during his fight with Ahi (I, 32, 14), and a hundred leather straps with which Kutsa is said to have bound down Indra to his sacrifice in the Tâṇḍya Brâhmaṇa IX, 2, 22, and from which he is invoked to free himself in Ṛig. X, 38, 5, are but so many different kaleidoscopic views of the same idea which makes Indra and Indra alone the lord of a hundred sacrifices; and if we take all these together they undoubtedly point out to the existence of a hundred continuous nights in the ancient home of the ancestors of the Vedic people. In V, 48, 3, '*a hundred*,' moving in the abode of Indra, are said to turn *on* and turn *off* the course of ordinary days when Indra strikes Vṛitra with his bolt;[1] and I think we have here a distinct allusion either to a hundred sacrifices performed or to a hundred continuous nights required for securing a complete victory over the powers of darkness in the nether world, and which nights (or rather one long night of hundred days) may well be described as *breaking off* and *bringing back* the succession of ordinary days and nights, inasmuch as the long night immediately follows and precedes the period of sunshine in the Arctic regions.

---

1. Ṛig. V, 48, 3,—आ ग्रावभिरहन्येभिरक्तुभिर्वरिष्ठं वज्रमा जिघर्ति मायिनि। शतं वा यस्य प्रचरन्त्स्वे दमे संवर्तयन्तो वि च वर्तयन्नहा॥

But a far more striking corroboration of the above view is furnished by certain passages in the Avesta which describe the fight of Tishtrya with the demon of draught called Apaosha or 'the burner' in the Parsi scriptures. In the Ṛig-Veda the fight of Indra with Vṛitra (*Vṛitra-tûrya*) is often represented as 'a struggle for waters' (*ap-túrya*), or as 'the striving for cows' (*go-ishṭi*), or 'the striving for day' (*div-ishṭi*), and Indra is said to have released the cows or waters, and brought on the dawn or the sun by killing Vṛitra (I, 51, 4 ; II 19, 3). Now Indra, as *Vṛitra-han*, appears as *Verethraghna* in the Avesta; but the fight for waters is therein ascribed not to Verethraghna but to Tishtrya, the star of rain. It is he, who knocks down Apaosha and liberates the waters for the benefit of man, "with the assistance of the winds, and the light that dwells in the waters." In short Tishtrya's conquest over Apaosha is an exact parallel of Indra's conquest over Vṛitra as described in the Ṛig-Veda ; and as the legends are interpreted at present, they are said to refer to the breaking up of the clouds and the bringing on of the rains on the earth, Tishtrya being supposed to be the star of rain. But this theory fails to account for the fact how the recovery of the dawn and the rising of the sun, or the bringing on of light, were included amongst the effects of Indra's victory over Vṛitra. It will be shown in the next chapter that the struggle for waters has very little to do with rain, and that the fight for waters and the fight for light are really synchronous, being two different versions of the same story. In short, both of these legends really represent the victory of the powers of light over darkness. Shushṇa or 'the scorcher' is one of the names given to Indra's enemy in the Ṛig-Veda (I, 51, 11), and the result of the conflict between Indra and Shushṇa is the release of the waters, as well as the finding of the morning cows (VIII, 96, 17), and the winning of the sun (VI, 20, 5). Apaosha is thus Shushṇa under a different garb, and the only difference between the two legends is that while Indra is the chief actor in the one, Tishtrya is the chief hero in the other. But this difference is immaterial inasmuch as the attributes of one deity are often transferred, even in Ṛig-Veda, to another. The Avestic legend of Tishtrya is, therefore, rightly understood by Zend scholars to be a reproduction of the Vedic legend of Indra and Vṛitra.[1] Now, in the Tîr Yasht, Tishtrya is represented as eventually overcoming Apaosha with the help of the Haoma sacrifice offered to Tishtrya by Ahura Mazda (Yt. VIII, 15-25). The fight is carried on in the region of the waters, the sea Vouru-Kasha, from which Tishtrya is described as rising up victorious after defeating Apaosha (Yt. VIII, 32). The Daêva Apaosha is again said to have assumed the form of a dark horse, while Tishtrya is represented as opposing him in the form of a bright horse, hoof against hoof (Yt. VIII, 28), and eventually coming up victorious from out of the sea Vouru-Kasha, like the sacrificial horse rising from the waters in the Ṛig-Veda (I, 163, 1). But the passage most important for our purpose is the one in which Tishtrya informs Ahura Mazda as to what should be done in order to enable Tishtrya to overcome his enemy and to appear before the faithful at the appointed time. "If men would worship me," says Tishtrya to Ahura Mazda, "with a sacrifice in which I were invoked by my own name, as they worship the other Yazatas with sacrifices in which they are invoked by their own names, then I should have come to the faithful at the appointed time; I should have come in the appointed time of my beautiful immortal life, should it be one night, or two nights, or fifty, or a hundred nights," (Yt. VIII, 11). As Tishtrya appears before man after his battle with Apaosha, the phrase "appoint-

---

1. See Darmesteter's Trans. of Zend-Avesta Part II, (Vol. XXIII S. B. E. Series), p. 92. He remarks that Tishtrya's legend is 'a *refacimento* of the old storm-myths.'

ed time" signifies the time during which the battle is fought and at the termination of which Tishtrya comes to the faithful; and the passage, therefore, means (1) that the "appointed time," when Tishtrya was to appear before man after fighting with Apaosha, varied from one night to a hundred nights, and (2) that Tishtrya required to be strengthened during the period by Haoma sacrifices in which he was to be invoked by his own name. We have seen above that a hundred nightly Soma sacrifices were offered to Indra by the ancient Vedic sacrificers to enable him to secure a victory over Vṛitra, and that Indra was the only deity to whom the libations were offered in these sacrifices. The legend of Tishtrya and Apaosha is, therefore, an exact reproduction of Indra's fight with Vṛitra or Vala; and with this correspondence before us, we should feel no hesitation in accepting the view stated above regarding the origin of the *Shata-râtra* sacrifice. Neither Darmesteter nor Spiegel explains why the appointed time for the appearance of Tishtrya is described as "one night, or two nights, or fifty, or a hundred nights," though both translate the original in the same way. The legend also forms the subject of chapter VII of the Bundahish, but there, too, we find no explanation as to why the appointed time is described as varying from one to a hundred nights. It is, however, suggested by some that the appointed time may refer to the season of rains. But rains cannot be said to come after "one night, two nights, or fifty, or a hundred nights," and the latter expression would, therefore, be utterly inappropriate in their case; nor, as stated above, does Tishtrya's fight with Apaosha represent only a struggle for rain, since we know that it is a struggle for light as well. We have also seen that the existence of night-sacrifices in the Vedic literature, extending over one, two, three, or ten, or a hundred nights, indicates the long darkness during which Indra fought with Vala; and the coincidence between this fact and the 'appointed time' of Tishtrya cannot be regarded as accidental. The legends are undoubtedly identical in character, and, taking the one to illustrate the other, the only conclusion deducible from them is that a hundred nights was regarded to be the maximum duration of the fight between Indra and Vala, or Tishtrya and Apaosha, so far as the ancestors of the Indo-Iranian people were concerned, and that the sea Vouru-Kasha, or the ocean 'encompassed with darkness,' as the Ṛig-Veda has it (II, 23, 18), was the scene of this battle between the powers of light and darkness. We also learn from them that the hero of the battle, whether he was Indra or Tishtrya, stood in need of help, derived from the performance of the sacrifices *specially offered* to him during the period; and that as a matter of fact such sacrifices were performed in ancient times. The word *shata-kratu* does not occur in the Avesta, but in the Ashi Yasht (Yt. XVII, 56) "a ram of hundred-fold energy (*maeshahe satokarahe*) is spoken of; and considering the fact that in the Bahram Yasht (Yt. XIV, 23) "a beautiful ram, with horns bent round" is said to be one of the incarnations of Verethraghna, and that Indra is also described as appearing in the form of a ram in the Ṛig-Veda (VIII, 2, 40), it is very probable that the phrase *sato-karahe maeshahe* refers to Verethraghna in the Ashi Yasht, and like the epithet *shata-kratu*, the adjective *sato-karahe* means not "possessed of hundred powers," but "the master of a hundred deeds or sacrifices." There is thus a very close correspondence between the Vedic and the Avestic ideas on this subject, and this strengthens the conclusion that the night sacrifices in the Vedic literature had their origin in the existence of a long continuous night of varying durations in the original home of the Vedic people. We can now also satisfactorily explain why Tishtrya is described (Yt. VIII, 36, *vide* Spiegel's Trans.) as "bringing hither the circling years of men." It is the Avestic parallel of the Vedic story of the Dawn setting in motion "the ages of men, or *mânushâ yugâ*," discussed in the last chapter, and shews that when Tishtrya's fight with Apaosha, or Indra's war with Vala, was over, the new year commenced with the long dawn, followed by the months of sunshine varying from seven to eleven in number, according to the latitude of the place.[1]

---

1. The passage about Tishtrya's connection with the year is noticed by Mr. Meherjibhai Nosherwanji Kuka, M. A., in his essay "On the order of Parsi months," published in the *Cama Memorial Volume* (p. 58), and of which he was kind enough to send me a separate copy.

The passage is in the Tir Yasht, § 36 :—'*Tishtrîm stârem raevantem kharenanghuantem yazamaide, yim yâre-charesho mashyche Ahuracha khratu-gûto aurunacha gairishâcho sizdaracha ravas-charâto uziyoirentem hisposentem huyâiryâicha danghee uzjasentem duzyâiryâicha, kata Airyâo danghâvo huyâiryâo bavâonti.*' Spiegel translates it thus, "We praise the star Tishtrya, the shining, the majestic, *who brings here the circling years of men.*" Darmesteter takes *yâre-charesho mashyche &c.*, with the words following, *viz.*, *uziyoirentem hisposentem*, and translates, "We praise Tishtrya, &c., whose rising is watched by men, who live on the fruits of the year." According to Dastur Erachji Meherjirana (see his *Yasht bâ mâeni*), the meaning of the whole paragraph, in which this passage occurs, is :— "We praise Tishtrya, &c. who maketh the year revolve in accordance with the notions of the mountaineers and the nomads. He riseth and is visible towards the regions where there is no correct calculation of the year."

But whatever the difficulties of interpretation may be, one thing seems to be quite clear from this passage, *viz.*, that Tishtrya was the star by which the year was reckoned. In the Tir Yasht § 5, springs of water are said to flow at the rising of Tishtrya, who in § 16 is described as 'mingling his shape with light,' or 'moving in light,' § 46. All these incidents can be satisfactorily explained if we suppose that, after Tishtrya's fight with Apaosha, lasting for 100 nights at the longest, the aerial waters, which communicated motion to the sun and other heavenly bodies (see Faravardîn Yasht 53-58) and which lay still or stagnant during the time, were set free to move again along the path made by Mazda, bringing on with them the light of the sun and thus commencing the new year after a long winter night in the Arctic region. The simultaneous character of the motion of waters, the commencement of the new year, and the winning of light after Tishtrya's fight with Apaosha, can be explained only in this way, and not by making the legend refer to the rainy season (*See* the discussion about 'waters' in the next chapter). The Pairika *Duz-yairya*, or the Bad Year, which Tishtrya is said to break asunder, is, on this theory, the wearisome dark Arctic night.

In the light of what has been stated above, we can now better understand the original nature and meaning of the *Ati-râtra* sacrifice. It is a nightly sacrifice, performed during the night even at present, and the Mîmâṁsakas have not succeeded in converting it into a day-sacrifice. So far it is all right; but the question is why should the sacrifice be called *Ati*-râtra? The prefix *ati* (corresponding with Latin *trans*) ordinarily denotes 'something beyond,' 'something on the other side, or at the other end,' and not 'something pervading, extending, or spreading through the whole extent of anything.' Even Sâyaṇa in his commentary on VII, 103, 7, the only place where the word *Ati-râtra* occurs in the Ṛig-Veda, explains it to mean 'that which is past or beyond the night' (*râtrim atîtya vartate iti atirâtraḥ*), and Rudradatta, in his commentary on the Âpastamba Shrauta Sûtra (XIV, 1, 1), gives the same explanation. The *Ati-râtra*, therefore, denotes a *trans-nocturnal* sacrifice, that is, performed at either end of the night. Now according to the Aitareya Brâhmaṇa (IV, 5), the *Ati-râtra* sacrifice is performed for the purpose of driving out the Asuras from the darkness of night; and the Tâṇḍya Brâhmaṇa (IV, 1, 4-5) tells us that Prajâpati, who first perceived the sacrifice, created from it the twin of day and night (*aho-râtre*). It follows from this that the *Ati-râtra* was performed at the close of such night as gave rise to the ordinary days and nights, or, in other words, the regular succession of days and nights followed its performance. This can only be the case if we suppose that the *Ati-râtra* was performed at the end of a long continuous night in regions where such night occurred. With us in the temperate or the tropical zone, ordinary days and nights regularly succeed each other throughout the year without any break, and it is meaningless, if not absurd, to speak of the cycle of day and night, as produced from a particular night in the year. Again, on the theory of a daily struggle between light and darkness the Asuras must be turned out of darkness every night, and strictly speaking the performance of the *Ati-râtra* is necessary on every one of the 360 nights of the *Sattra*. But as a matter of fact the *Ati-râtra* is performed only at the beginning and the end of the *Sattra*; and even then the regular *Sattra* is said to commence on the Chaturviṁsha and close on the Mahâvrata day, and not on the concluding Atirâtra day. It seems, therefore, that the performance of the *Ati-râtra* was not originally intended to drive away the Asuras from only the first of 360 nights over which the *Sattra* now extends. For in that case, there is no reason why the Asuras were not required to be expelled from every one of the 360 nights. It follows, therefore, that the *Ati-râtra* or the trans-nocturnal sacrifice refers to some night not included in the regular nights of the *Gavâm-ayanam*. It is true that the *Ati-râtra* is performed at the beginning and the end of every *Sattra*, and in one sense it is, therefore, a *trans-sattra* or *ati-sattra* sacrifice. But that does not account for the name *Ati-râtra*, as the *Sattra* is not held during night. We must, therefore, hold that the two *Ati-râtras* were originally performed not at the beginning and the end of a *Sattra*, but at the beginning and the end of a *night*, which occured or intervened between the last and the first day of the *Sattra*. When this night ended with an *Ati-râtra*, the usual *Sattra* began; and as the sun was above the horizon during the period producing the regular succession of days and nights, no *Ati-râtra* was needed during the *Sattra*, for, as stated in the Tâṇḍya Brâhmaṇa, the object of the *Ati-râtra* was gained. But the *Sattra* closed with the long night, and the *Ati-râtra* had, therefore, again to be performed at the end of the *Sattra* to drive the Asuras from this night. I have shown before that we have direct and reliable authority in the Taittirîya Saṁhitâ to hold that the *Gavâm-ayanam* was once completed in ten months or 300 days, and it was, therefore, appropriately closed with and introduced by an *Ati-râtra*. The word *Ati-râtra* is thus rationally explained, for the sacrifice was performed at the beginning and the close of the long night and, was therefore, adequately called a trans-nocturnal sacrifice. Between these two *Ati-râtras* came all the night-sacrifices mentioned above, offered exclusively to Indra. The old *Gavâm-ayanam* of ten or less than ten months, the *Ati-râtra* or the trans-nocturnal, the *Râtri-kratus* and *Râtri-sattras*, or nightly Soma sacrifices of two, three, &c., up to a hundred continuous nights' duration, and lastly the *Ati-râtra*, to be again followed by the *Gavâm-ayanam*, thus formed the complete yearly round of sacrifices performed by the primeval ancestors of the Vedic people ; and each of these sacrifices had originally the same place in the yearly round as is indicated by the root-meaning of its name.[1] But when the year of ten months was converted into one of twelve to suit the altered conditions of the new home, the *Gavâm-ayanam* expanded into a performance of 360 days, and the elastic nature of the greater portion of the performance, as pointed out above, permitted the change to be easily carried out. But though the annual *Sattra* expanded in this way, encroaching upon the night-sacrifices of the long night, which were no longer needed, the *Ati-râtra* was retained as an introductory sacrifice and was incorporated in the ceremonies of the *Sattra* itself. Thus the two *Ati-râtra* sacrifices, which were originally performed, as shown by the etymology, at the two termini of the long night, came to be converted into the introductory and concluding sacrifices of the annual *Sattra* ; and if the word *Ati-râtra* had not been retained, we could not have got any clue to reveal to us

---

1. The time here assigned to the *Râtri-sattras* appears to have been known to the authors of the Shrauta Sûtras, for in the Lâṭyâyana Shrauta Sûtra, VIII, 2, 16, we have, समाप्ते वा संवत्सरे रात्रिसत्त्रेषु राजानं क्रीणीयुः, meaning that " After the year (annual sacrificial session) is over, the Soma should be purchased during the *Râtri-sattras*," evidently shewing that the *Râtri-sattras* came at the end of the yearly *Sattras*.

the story of its changing fortune. But the night-sacrifices, the *Râtri-kratus* or *Râtri-sattras*, which were performed during the long night between the two *Ati-râtras*, were no longer needed and their nature came to be soon misunderstood, until at last the Mîmâṁsakas finally made room for them in the class of daily Soma sacrifices, partly under *Ahînas* and partly under *Sattras*, by means of the equation that *râtri* (night) is equal to *aho-râtre* (day and night) in the sacrificial literature. How this change was carried out is a question beyond the scope of this book ; but I may here state that, in my opinion, it was the authors of Brâhmaṇas, or the Brahmavâdins who preceded them, that had to perform the difficult task of adapting the ancient sacrificial calendar to the changed conditions of their new home, somewhat after the manner of Numa's reform of the ancient Roman calendar. The sacrifice was the main ritual of the Vedic religion, and naturally enough the priests must have tried to preserve as much of the old sacrificial system as they possibly could in adapting it to the new conditions. The task was by no means an easy one, and those that find fault with the Brâhmaṇas as full ot fanciful speculations must bear in mind the fact that an ancient and sacred system of sacrifices had to be adapted to new conditions, by assigning plausible reasons for the same, at a time when the true origin of the system was almost forgotten. The Brâhmaṇas could not have indulged in free speculations about the origin of the rites and ceremonies mentioned by them, had the latter originated in their own time, or in days so near to them that the real traditions about the origin of these ceremonies could be preserved intact. But so long as these traditions were fresh, no explanation was probably needed; and when they became dim, their place had to be supplied by plausible reasons based on such traditions as were known at the time. This throws quite a new light on the nature and composition of the Brâhmaṇas; but as the discussion is not pertinent to the subject in hand, we cannot enter into it more fully in this place.

We have now reviewed the leading features of the system of Soma sacrifices as described in the Vedic literature, so far as our purpose is concerned, and seen that by the aid of the Arctic theory, some hard facts therein, which have been hitherto incomprehensible, can be easily and naturally explained. A history of the whole sacrificial system from the point of view indicated above is a work quite outside the pale of this book; but so far as we have examined the subject and especially the question about the isolated group of a hundred nightly Soma sacrifices, I think, we have sufficient evidence therein to warrant us in holding that these sacrifices are a relic of the ancient times when the ancestors of the Vedic Ṛishis performed them with the object of helping Indra to fight with the powers of darkness. It has been already shown in the first part of this chapter that the *Gavâm-ayanam* or the 'Cows' walk, like the Roman year, once lasted only for ten months; and a series of suitable night-sacrifices is a natural supplement to such sessions. Both are relics of ancient times, and taken along with the evidence regarding the existence of a long dawn of thirty days and of the long day and night discussed in previous chapters, they conclusively establish the existence of an ancient home of the ancestors of the Vedic people in the circum-polar region. The sacrificial sessions of the Navagvas and the Dashagvas, the legend of Dîrghatamas growing old in the tenth month, the tradition about the ancient year of five seasons, or the yoking of seven or ten horses to the chariot of the sun, all go to strengthen the same view; and the Avestic passages regarding the duration of Tishtrya's fight with Apaosha, the Purâṇic tradition about Indra's being the master of a hundred sacrifices or the destroyer of a hundred cities, the existence of a series of one hundred nightly Soma sacrifices, which, though obsolete long since, could not have found place in the sacrificial works as *Râtri-sattras*, unless they were ancient sacrifices performed, as their name indicates, during night,—these and many other minor facts noticed before, further corroborate, if corroboration be needed, our theory regarding the original home of the Aryans near the north Pole. It must, however, be stated here that I do not wish to imply in any way that the numerous sacrificial details found in the later Vedic literature were in vogue or were known in these ancient times. On the contrary I am prepared to believe that in all probability these ancient sacrifices were very simple in character. The ancient priests probably went on sacrificing from day to day, and afterwards from night to night, without any idea that the system was capable of giving rise to various rigid annual *Sattras*. The sacrifice was the only ritual of their religion; and howsoever simple such sacrifices might have been in ancient times, it was almost a matter of duty, at least with the priests, to perform them every day. It was also a means, as remarked by me elsewhere, to keep up the calendar in ancient times, as the yearly round of sacrifices closely followed the course of the sun. It is from this latter point of view that the ancient sacrificial system is important for historical or antiquarian purposes, and I have examined it above in the same light. This examination, it will be seen, has resulted in the discovery of a number of facts which lead us directly to, and can be satisfactorily explained only by the theory of the original Arctic home; and when our conclusions are thus supported by the hymns of the Ṛig-Veda on the one hand, and the sacrificial literature on the other, I think, we need have no doubt about their correctness.

CHAPTER IX.

VEDIC MYTHS—THE CAPTIVE WATERS.

Direct evidence for the Arctic theory summed up —Different nature of the mythological evidence —Schools of mythological interpretation —The naturalistic or the Nairukta school —Its theories —The Dawn theory and the myths explained by it —The Storm theory, Indra and Vritra —The Vernal theory, the Ashvins' exploits —Vritra's legend usually explained by the Storm theory —Simultaneous effects of Indra's conquest over Vritra —The release of waters, the release of cows, the recovery of the dawn and the production of the sun —Vedic authorities in support of their simultaneous character —Passages relating to the place and time of the conflict —The simultaneous nature left unexplained by the Dawn or the Storm theory —Battle not fought in the atmosphere above, as implied by the Storm theory —Nor in the rainy season —Misinterpretation of words like *parvata, giri, adri,* &c. —The Storm theory inadequate in every respect —New explanation necessary —The real nature of waters explained —They are aerial or celestial waters, and not the waters of rain —Vedic bards knew of a region 'below the three earths' —The contrary view of Wallis refuted —The real meaning of *rajas, Nir-riti, ardhau* and *samudram* explained —Cosmic circulation of aerial waters —Nether world, the home of aerial waters —Avestic passages describing the circulation of waters cited and explained —Sarasvatî and Ardvi Sûra Anâhita are celestial rivers —The source of all plants and rain —The real nature of Vritra's fight —Simultaneous release of waters and light is intelligible, if both have the same source —Both stopped by Vritra's encompassing the waters in the lower world —The closing of the apertures in the mountains (*parvatas*) on the horizon —The movement of the waters and the sun co-related —Express passages from the Avesta to that effect —The sun stopping for a long time in waters —Avestic passages in support thereof —Its effect on the disposal of corpses —Darkness synchronous with the cessation of the flow of waters in winter —Its long duration —Cosmic circulation of waters in other mythologies —Express

texts showing that the fight with Vritra was annual and fought in winter —Inexplicable except on the Arctic theory —The exact date of Indra's fight with Vritra preserved in the Rig-Veda —The real meaning of *chatvârimshyâm sharadi* explained —Shambara found on the 40th day of *Sharad* —Denotes the commencement of the long night —Vedic passages shewing *Sharad* to be the last season of sunshine —Paleographical evidence for reckoning time by seasons —Similar reckoning in the Avesta —100 autumnal forts of Vritra and the killing of the watery demon with ice explained —The seven rivers released by Indra —Cannot be terrestrial, nor the rivers of the Panjaub —The interpretation of Western scholars examined and rejected —The connection between the seven rivers and the seven suns pointed out —The origin of the phrase *Hapta-hindu* in the Avesta —Probably a transference of an old mythological name to a place in the new home —Vritra's legend Arctic in origin —Captive waters represent the yearly struggle between light and the darkness in the ancient Arctic home.

We have now examined most of the Vedic passages, which directly show that the Polar or the Circum-Polar characteristics, determined in the third chapter, were known, by tradition, to the Vedic bards. We started with the tradition about the night of the gods, or a day and a night of six months each, and found that it could be traced back to the Indo-Iranian, if not to the Indo-Germanic, period. A close examination of the dawn-hymns in the Ṛig-Veda next disclosed the fact that Uṣhas, or the deity presiding over the dawn, is often addressed in the plural number in the Vedic hymns, and that this could be accounted for only on the supposition that the Vedic dawns were a closely connected band of many dawns,—a supposition, which was found to be fully borne out by express passages in the Vedic literature, stating, in unambiguous terms, that the Vedic dawns were 30 in number, and that in ancient times a period of several days elapsed between the first appearance of light on the horizon and the rising of the sun. We have also found that the dawn is expressly described in the Ṛig-

Veda as moving round like a wheel, a characteristic, which is true only in the case of the Polar dawn. These facts sufficiently prove the acquaintance of the Vedic bards with the physical phenomena, witnessible only in the Arctic regions. But to make the matter more certain, I have, in the last three chapters, quoted and discussed Vedic passages, which go to prove that the long Arctic nights and the corresponding long days of varying duration, as well as, a year of ten months or five seasons, were equally known to the poets of the Ṛig-Veda. An examination of the ancient sacrificial system, and especially of the annual *Sattras* and night-sacrifices, further showed that in old times yearly sacrificial sessions did not last for twelve months as at present, but were completed in nine or ten months; and the hundred night-sacrifices were, at that time, really performed, as their name indicates, during the darkness of the long night. The legends of Dīrghatamas and Aditi's sons, and the tradition about the sacrificial sessions of the Navagvas and the Dashagvas also pointed to the same conclusion. Our case does not, therefore, depend on an isolated fact here and an isolated fact there. We have seen that the half-year-long day and night, the long dawn with its revolving splendours, the long continuous night matched by the corresponding long day and associated with a succession of ordinary days and nights of varying lengths, and the total annual period of sunshine of less than twelve months are the principal peculiar characteristics of the Polar or the Circum-Polar calendar; and when express passages are found in the Vedas, the oldest record of early Aryan thoughts and sentiments, showing that each and every one of these characteristics was known to the Vedic bards, who themselves lived in a region where the year was made up of three hundred and sixty or three hundred and sixty five days, one is irresistibly led to the conclusion that the poets of the Ṛig-Veda must have known these facts by tradition and that their ancestors must have lived in regions where such phenomena were possible. It is not to be expected that the evidence on each and every one of these points will be equally conclusive, especially as we are dealing with facts which existed thousands of years ago. But if we bear in mind that the facts are astronomically connected in such a way that if one of them is firmly established all the others follow from it as a matter of course, the cumulative effect of the evidence discussed in the previous chapters cannot fail to be convincing. It is true that many of the passages, quoted in support of the Arctic theory, are interpreted, in the way I have done, for the first time; but I have already pointed out that this is due to the fact that the real key to the interpretation of these passages was discovered only during the last 30 or 40 years. Yâska and Sâyaṇa knew nothing definite about the circum-polar or the Arctic regions, and when a Vedic passage was found not to yield a sense intelligible to them, they either contented themselves with barely explaining the verbal texture of the passage, or distorted it to suit their own ideas. Western scholars have corrected some of these mistakes, but as the possibility of an Arctic home in pre-glacial times was not admitted 30 or 40 years back, the most explicit references, whether in the Avesta or the Ṛig-Veda, to a primeval home in the extreme north, have been either altogether ignored, or somehow or other explained away, even by Western scholars. Many of the passages cited by me fall under this class; but I trust that if my interpretations are examined without any bias and in the light of the latest scientific researches, they will be found to be far more natural and simple than those in vogue at present. In some cases no new interpretations were, however, necessary. The passages have heen correctly interpreted; but in the absence of the true key to their meaning, their real import was either altogether missed, or but imperfectly understood. In such cases I have had to exhibit the passages in their true light or colours, giving in each case, my reasons for doing the same. This has sometimes rendered it necessary to introduce certain topics not directly relevant to the question in hand; but on the whole, I think, it will be found that I have, as far as possible, tried to confine myself to the discussion of the direct evidence bearing on the points in issue, and have examined it according to the strict method of historic or scientific investigation. I did not start with any preconceived notion in favour of the Arctic theory, nay, I regarded it as highly improbable at first; but the accumulating evidence in its support eventually forced me to accept it, and, in all probability, the evidence cited in the previous chapters, will, I think, produce the same impression on the reader's mind.

But the evidence, which I am now going to cite in support of the Arctic theory, is of a different character. If the ancestors of the Vedic bards ever lived near the North Pole, the cosmical or the meteorological conditions of the place could not have failed to influence the mythology of these people; and if our theory is true, a careful examination of the Vedic myths ought to disclose facts, which cannot be accounted for by any other theory. The probative value of such evidence will manifestly be inferior to that of the direct evidence previously cited, for myths and legends are variously explained by different scholars. Thus Yâska mentions three or four different schools of interpretation, each of which tries to explain the nature and character of the Vedic deities in a different way. One of these schools would have us believe that many of the deities were real historical personages, who were subsequently apotheosized for their supernatural virtues or exploits. Other theologians divide the deities into *Karma-devatâs* or those that have been raised to the divine rank by their own deeds, and *Âjânadevatâs* or those that were divine by birth; while the Nairuktas (or the etymologists) maintain that the

Vedic deities represent certain cosmical and physical phenomena such as the appearance of the dawn or the breaking up of the storm-clouds by the lightning. The Adhyâtmikas, on the other hand, try to explain certain Vedic passages in their own philosophical way; and there are others, who endeavour to explain Vedic myths in other different ways. But this is not the place where the relative merits of these different schools can be discussed or examined. I only wish to point out that those, who explain the Vedic myths on the supposition that they represent, directly or allegorically, ethical, historical or philosophical facts, are not likely to accept any inference based upon the theory which interprets the Vedic myths as referring to certain cosmical and physical phenomena. It was for this reason that I reserved the discussion of the mythological evidence for consideration in a separate chapter, after all the evidence directly bearing on the subject has been examined. The evidence, which proves the existence of a long continuous dawn, or a long continuous day or night, is not affected by the different theories regarding the interpretation of the Vedic myths, and may, therefore, be termed, what the lawyers call, *direct* ; but in the case of the mythological evidence only those, who accept the Nairukta method of interpretation, will admit the validity of any inference based upon the consideration of these myths. It is true that the Nairukta school of interpretation dates from ancient times, and that modern scholars have accepted the method almost without reserve, though they might differ from the ancient Nairuktas, like Yâska, in the details of the explanation suggested by them. But still when a new theory is to be established, I thought it safer to separate the mythological from the direct evidence bearing upon the points at issue, even when the two lines of investigation seemed to converge towards the same point.

Now it has been recorded by Yâska that the Nairuktas explain most of the Vedic legends on the theory that they represent either the daily triumph of light over darkness, or the conquest of the storm-god over the dark clouds that imprison the fertilising waters and the light of the sun. Thus when the Ashvins are said to have rescued a quail (*Vartikâ*) from the jaws of a wolf, Yâska interprets the legend to mean the release and bringing out of the dawn or light from the darkness of the night (Nir. V, 21). His explanation of the character of Vṛitra is another instance in point. Speaking of the nature of the demon, he thus refers (Nir. II, 16) to the opinions of the different schools, "Who was Vṛitra ? 'A cloud,' say the Nairuktas ; 'an Asura, son of Tvashṭṛi,' say the Aitihâsikas. The fall of rain arises from the mingling of the waters and of light. This is figuratively depicted as a conflict. The hymns and the Brâhmaṇas describe Vṛitra as a serpent. By the expansion of his body, he blocked up the streams. When he was destroyed the waters flowed forth."[1] The Storm and the Dawn theories thus formed the basis of the Nairukta school of interpretation, and though Western scholars have improved upon it, yet the credit of suggesting this method of interpretation will always rest with the ancient Nairuktas, who, as observed by Prof. Max Muller, had carefully thought out the true character of the Vedic gods several centuries before the Christian era. Thus the legend of Prajâpati loving his own daughter is explained in the Aitareya Brâhmaṇa as referring to the sun running after the dawn or the heaven above (Ait. Br. III, 33); while Kumârila extends this theory to the case of Indra and Ahalyâ, which according to him represent the sun and the night. But though the Nairuktas fully accepted the theory, which explained the Vedic myths as representing cosmical and

1. See Nir. II, 16 :—तत्को वृत्रः । मेघ इति नैरुक्ताः । त्वाष्ट्रोऽसुर इत्यैतिहासिकाः । अपां च ज्योतिषश्च मिश्रीभावकर्मणो वर्षकर्म जायते । तत्रोपमार्थेन युद्धवर्णा भवंति । अहिवत्तु खलु मंत्रवर्णाः ब्राह्मणवादाश्च । विवृद्ध्या शरीरस्य स्रोतांसि निवारयांचकार । तस्मिन्हते प्रसस्यन्दिरे आपः । Cf. Muir's O. S. T. Vol. II, p. 175.

physical phenomena, yet as their knowledge of the physical world was very limited in those days, they were not able to explain every Vedic myth or legend by this method. For example, out of the various legends about the Ashvins Yâska could explain only one by the Dawn theory, namely, that of the quail being rescued from the jaws of the wolf. This defect has now been partially removed by Western scholars, who, living in the more northern regions, are familiar with the decay in the power of the sun during the cold season, or the eventual triumph of spring over winter, or the restoration of the decayed powers of the sun in summer. This phenomenon has, therefore, been used by them to explain the origin of certain Vedic myths, which have been left unexplained either by the Dawn or the Storm theory. Upto now, we have, thus, three theories for explaining the Vedic myths according to the Nairukta school of interpretation; and it is necessary to describe them briefly before we proceed to show how they fail to account for all the incidents in the myths and legends to which they are applied.

According to the Dawn theory, "the whole theogony and philosophy of the ancient world is centered in the Dawn, the mother of the bright gods, of the sun in his various aspects, of the morn, the day, the spring; herself the brilliant image and visage of immortality." Prof. Max Muller, in his *Lectures on the Science of Language*, further remarks[1] that "the dawn, which to us is a merely beautiful sight, was to the early gazers and thinkers the problem of all the problems. It was the unknown land from whence rose every day those bright emblems of divine powers, which left in the mind of man the first impression and intimation of another world, of power above, of order and wisdom. What we simply call the sun-rise, brought before their eyes every day the riddle of all riddles, the riddle of existence. The days of their life sprang from that dark

1. See Lectures on the Science of Language, Vol. II, p. 545, ff.

abyss, which every morning seemed instinct with light and life." And again "a new life flashed up every morning before their eyes, and the fresh breezes of the dawn reached them like greetings wafted across the golden threshold of the sky from the distant lands beyond the mountains, beyond the clouds, beyond the dawn, beyond 'the immortal sea which brought us hither.' The dawn seemed to them to open golden gates for the sun to pass in triumph, and while those gates were open their eyes and their minds strove in their childish way to pierce beyond the finite world. That silent aspect awakened in the human mind the conception of the Infinite, the Immortal, the Divine, and the names of dawn became naturally the names of higher powers." This is manifestly more poetic than real. But the learned Professor explains many Vedic myths on the theory that they are all Dawn-stories in different garbs. Thus, if Saraṇyu, who had twins from Vivasvat, ran off from him in the form of a mare, and he followed her in the form of a horse, it is nothing but a story of the Dawn disappearing at the approach of the Sun and producing the pair of day and night. The legend of Suryâ's marriage with Soma, and of Vṛishâkapâyî, whose oxen (the morning vapours) were swallowed by Indra, or of Aditi giving birth to the Âdityas are again said to be the stories of the Dawn under different aspects. Saramâ, crossing the waters to find out the cows stolen by Paṇis, is similarly the Dawn bringing with her the rays of the morning, and when Urvashî says that she is gone away and Purûravas calls himself Vasiṣhṭha or the brightest, it is the same Dawn flying away from the embrace of the rising Sun. In short, the Dawn is supposed to have been everything to the ancient people, and a number of legends are explained in this way, until at last the monotonous character of these stories led the learned professor to ask to himself the question, "Is everything the Dawn? Is everything the Sun?" —a question, which he answers by informing us that so far as his researches were concerned they had led him again and again to the Dawn and the Sun as the chief burden of the myths of the Aryan race. The dawn here referred to is the *daily* dawn as we see it in the tropical or the temperate zone, or, in other words, it is the *daily* conquest of light over darkness that is here represented as filling the minds of the ancient bards with such awe and fear as to give rise to a variety of myths. It may be easily perceived how this theory will be affected by the discovery that Ushas, or the goddess of the dawn in the Rig-Veda does not represent the evanescent dawn of the tropics, but is really the long continuous dawn of the Polar or the Circum-Polar regions. If the Arctic theory is once established, many of these mythological explanations will have to be entirely re-written. But the task cannot be undertaken in a work which is devoted solely to the examination of the evidence in support of that theory.

The Storm theory was originally put forward by the Indian Nairuktas as a supplement to the Dawn theory, in order to account for myths to which the latter was obviously inapplicable. The chief legend explained on this theory is that of Indra and Vritra, and the explanation has been accepted almost without reserve by all Western scholars. The word Indra is said to be derived from the same root which yielded *indu*, that is, the rain drop; and Vritra is one, who covers or encompasses (*vri*, to cover) the waters of the rain-cloud. The two names being thus explained, everything else was made to harmonise with the Storm theory by distorting the phrases, if the same could not be naturally interpreted in conformity therewith. Thus when Indra strikes *parvata* (*i. e.*, a mountain) and delivers the rivers therefrom, the Nairuktas understood *parvata* to be a storm-cloud and the rivers to be the streams of rain. Indra's wielding the thunderbolt has been similarly interpreted to mean that he was the god of the thunderstorm, and thunderstorm implied rain as a matter of course. If the Maruts helped Indra in the battle, it was easily explained by the Storm theory, because a thunderstorm or rain was always accompanied by stormy weather. But a more difficult point in the legend, which required explanation, was the hemming in or the captivating of the waters by Vṛitra or Ahi. In the case of waters in the clouds it was easy to imagine that they were kept captive in the cloud by the demon of drought. But the Ṛig-Veda often speaks of *sindhus* or streams being released by the slaughter of Vṛitra ; and if the streams or rivers really represented, as conceived by the advocates of this theory, the rivers of the Panjaub, it was rather difficult to understand how they could be described as being hemmed in or kept captive by Vṛitra. But the ingenuity of Vedic scholars was quite equal to the occasion, and it was suggested that, as the rivers in India often entirely dried up in summer, the god of the rainy season, who called them back to life, could be rightly described as releasing them from the grasp of Vṛitra. The Indian Nairuktas do not appear to have extended the theory any further. But in the hands of German mythologians the Storm theory became almost a rival to the Dawn theory; and stories, like that of Saraṇyu, have been explained by them as referring to the movements of dark storm-clouds hovering in the sky. "Clouds, storms, rains, lightning and thunder," observes Prof. Kuhn, "were the spectacles that above all others impressed the imagination of the early Aryans and busied it most in finding terrestrial objects to compare with their ever-varying aspects. The beholders were at home on the earth, and the things on the earth were comparitively familiar to them ; even the coming and going of the celestial luminaries might often be regarded by them with more composure, because of their regularity ; but they could never surcease to feel the liveliest interest in those wonderful meteoric changes, so lawless and mysterious in their visitations, which wrought such immediate and palpable effects for good or ill upon the lives and fortunes of the beholders."[1] For this reason Prof. Kuhn thinks that these meteorological phenomena are the principal ground-work of all Indo-European mythologies and superstitions; and in accordance with this creed Prof. Roth explains Saraṇyu as the dark storm-cloud soaring in the space in the beginning of all things and takes Vivasvat as representing the light of heavens.

The third theory, like the first, is solar in origin, and attempts to explain certain Vedic myths on the supposition that they represent the triumph of spring over snow and winter. Yâska and other Indian Nairuktas lived in regions where the contrast between spring and winter was not so marked as in the countries still further north; and it was probably for this reason that the Vernal theory was not put forward by them to explain the Vedic myths. Prof. Max Muller has tried to explain most of the exploits of the Ashvins by this theory.[2] If the Ashvins restored Chyavâna to youth, if they protected Atri from the heat and darkness, if they rescued Vandana from a pit where he was buried alive, or if they replaced the leg of Vishpalâ, which she had lost in battle, or restored to Ṛijrâshva his eye sight, it was simply the Sun-god restored to his former glory after the decay of his powers in winter. In short the birth of the vernal Sun, his fight against the army of winter, and his final victory at the beginning of the spring is, on this theory, the true key to the explanation of many myths where the Sun-god is represented as dying, decaying or undergoing some other affliction. As contrasted with the Dawn theory the physical phenomena, here referred to, are annual. But both are solar theories, and as such may be contrasted with the Storm theory which is meteorological in origin.

---

1. See Max Muller's Lectures on the Science of Language, Vol. II, p. 566.

2. See Contributions to the Science of Mythology, Vol. II, pp. 579-605.

Besides these three theories, the Dawn, the Storm and the Vernal, Mr. Nârâyaṇa Aiyangâr of Bangalore has recently attempted to explain a number of Vedic myths on the hypothesis that they refer to Orion and Aldebaran. This may be called the Astral theory as distinguished from others. But all these theories cannot be discussed in this place; nor is it necessary to do so, so far as our purpose is concerned. I wish only to show that in spite of the various theories started to explain the Vedic myths, a number of incidents in several important legends have yet remained unexplained; and mythologists have either ignored them altogether, or pushed them out of the way as insignificant or immaterial. If everything could be explained by the Dawn or the Storm theory, we may indeed hesitate to accept a new theory for which there would then be very little scope; but when a number of facts, which have yet remained unexplained, are satisfactorily and appropriately accounted for only by the Arctic theory, we shall be perfectly justified in citing these legends as corroborative evidence in support of our new theory. It is from this point of view that I mean to examine some of the important Vedic myths in this and the following chapter, and shall now begin with the legend of Indra and Vṛitra, or of captive waters, which is generally believed to have been satisfactorily explained by the Storm theory.

The struggle between Indra and Vṛitra is represented in the Vedas as being four-fold in character. *First*, it is a struggle between Indra and Vṛitra, the latter of whom appears also under the names of Namuchi, Shushṇa, Shambara, Vala, Pipru, Kuyava and others. This is *Vṛitra-tûrya*, or the fight or struggle with Vṛitra. *Secondly*, it is a fight for the waters, which, either in the form of *sindhus* (rivers) or as *âpaḥ* (simple floods), are often described as released or liberated by the slaughter of Vṛitra. This is *ap-tûrya* or the struggle for waters; and Indra is called *apsu-jit* or conquering in the waters, while Vṛitra is described as encompassing them (*âpaḥ pari-shayânam*). *Thirdly*, it is a struggle to regain the cows (*go-ishṭi*); and there are several passages in the Ṛig-Veda where the cows are said to have been released by Indra after having overthrown Vṛitra. *Fourthly*, it is a fight to regain the day-light or heaven called (*div-ishṭi*), or the striving for day; and in many places the sun and the dawn are said to be brought out by Indra after killing Vṛitra.[1] The following extracts from Macdonell's *Vedic Mythology* give the requisite authorities from the Ṛig-Veda for this four-fold character of the struggle between Indra and Vṛitra. Speaking of the terrible conflict, he thus sums up the principal incidents thereof as mentioned in the Ṛig-Veda :—

"Heaven and earth tremble with fear when Indra strikes Vṛitra with his bolt (I, 80, 11; II, 11, 9-10; VI, 17, 9); even Tvashṭṛi, who forged the bolt, trembles at Indra's anger (I, 80, 14). Indra shatters Vṛitra with his bolt (I, 32, 5); and strikes his face with his pointed weapon (I, 52, 15). He smote Vṛitra, who encompassed the waters (VI, 20, 2), or the dragon that lay around (*pari-shayânam*) the waters (IV, 19, 2); he overcame the dragon lying on the waters (V, 30, 6). He slew the dragon hidden in the water and obstructing the waters and the sky (II, 11, 5), and smote Vṛitra, who enclosed the waters, like a tree, with the bolt (II, 14, 2). Thus 'con-

1. The exploits of Indra are very pithily summed up in the *Nivids* or short sûtras or sentences used in offering oblations to the gods. These will be found collected in a separate chapter amongst the *Pari-shishṭas* or supplements to the Ṛig-Veda Saṁhitâ text published in Bombay (Tatva-vivechaka Press). According to Dr. Haug these *Nivids* are the originals of the Vedic *Suktas* or hymns. The *Nivids*, relating to Indra's exploits contain the following :—इंद्रो मरुत्वान् सोमस्य पिबतु ।...। अन्वृधासृजदपः । मरुतामोजसा सह ।...। अप्तूर्ये वृत्रतूर्ये । शंबरहत्ये गविष्टौ ।...। परमस्वां परावति ।...। वज्रस्य भर्ता । पुरां भेत्ता ।...। अपां स्रष्टा । अपां नेता । As regards the meaning of *Div-ishṭi* see Oldenberg's Vedic Hymns (I, 45, 7), S. B. E. Series, Vol. XLVI. p. 44.

quering in the waters (*apsu-jit*)' is his exclusive attribute (VIII, 36, 1)."[1]

As regards the abode of Vṛitra, we have (§ 68, A) :—

"Vṛitra has a hidden (*niṇya*) abode, whence the waters, when released by Indra, escape, overflowing the demon (I, 32, 10). Vṛitra lies on the waters (I, 121, 11 ; II 11, 19), or enveloped by the waters, at the bottom (*budhna*) of the *rajas* or aerial space (I, 52, 6). He is also described as lying on a summit (*sânu*), when Indra made the waters to flow (I, 80, 5). Vṛitra has fortresses, which Indra shatters when he slays him (X, 89, 7), and which are ninety-nine in number (VIII, 93, 2; VII, 19, 5). He is called *nadi-vrit*, or encompasser of rivers (I, 52, 2), and in one passage *parvata* or cloud is described as being within his belly (I, 57, 6)."

There are again passages (V, 32, 5 & 6) where Indra is said to have placed Shushṇa, who was anxious to fight, "in the darkness of the pit," and slaughtered him "in the darkness, which was unrelieved by the rays of the sun," (*asûrye tamasi*). In I, 34, 10, darkness is said to have prevailed in Vṛitra's hollow side, and in II, 23, 18, Bṛihaspati, with Indra, is said to have hurled down the ocean, which was "encompassed in darkness," and opened the stall of kine. Finally in I, 32, 10, Vṛitra's body is said to have sunk in "long darkness," being encompassed with waters. This shows that the waters of the ocean, which was encompassed by Vṛitra, were not lighted by the rays of the sun. In other words, the ocean (*arṇaḥ*) which Vṛitra is said to have encompassed was different from the 'bright ocean' (*shukram arṇaḥ*), which the sun is said to have ascended in V, 45, 10. Vṛitra's ocean (*arṇava*) was enveloped in darkness (*tamasâ parivṛitam*, II, 23, 18), while the ocean, which the sun ascended, was bright and shining (*shukram*). Indra is again described as going to a very

1. See Macdonell's Vedic Mythology, in Grundriss der Indo-Arischen Philologie und Altertumskunde, § 22 (Indra), pp. 58-61.

distant (*parâvat*) region to kill Vṛitra or Namuchi, (I, 53, 7; VIII, 12, 17; VIII, 45, 25). If we combine all these statements regarding the scene of the struggle between Indra and Vṛitra, we are led to the conclusion that the fight took place in a dark, distant and watery region. In VIII, 32, 26, Indra is said to have killed Arbuda with ice (*hima*); and in X, 62, 2, the Aṅgirases, who were the assistants of Indra in his conquest of the cows, are said to have struck Vala at the end of the year (*parivatsare*). There is another statement in the Ṛig-Veda, which gives us the date of Indra's fight with Shambara, but we shall discuss it later on. It is stated above that the number of Vṛitra's forts destroyed by Indra is given as ninety-nine; but in other passages it is said to be ninety or one hundred (I, 130, 7; IV, 30, 20). These fortresses or cities (*puraḥ*) are described as made of stone or iron (IV, 30, 20; IV, 27, I), and in some places they are said to be autumnal (*shâradîḥ*, I, 130, 7; 131, 4; VI, 20, 10). The importance of these facts, in the interpretation of the legend, will be discussed later on.

We have seen that the release of cows and the bringing up of the dawn and the sun are the simultaneous effects of Indra's conquest of Vṛitra. The following extracts from Macdonell's *Vedic Mythology* (p. 61) give the necessary authorities on the point:—

"With the liberation of waters is connected the winning of light, sun and dawn. Indra won light and the divine waters (III, 34, 8). The god is invoked to slay Vṛitra and win the light (VIII, 89, 4). When Indra had slain the dragon Vṛitra with his metallic bolt releasing the waters for man, he placed the sun visibly in the heavens (I, 51, 4; 52, 8). Indra, the dragon-slayer, set in motion the flood of waters of the sea, generated the sun, and found the cows (II, 19, 3). He gained the sun and the waters after slaying the demon (III, 34, 8-9). When Indra slew the chief of the dragons and released the waters from the mountain, he generated the sun, the sky and the dawn (I, 32, 4; VI, 30, 5). The cows are also mentioned along with the sun and the dawn (I, 62, 5; II, 12, 7; VI, 17, 5), or with the sun alone (I, 7, 3; II, 19, 3; X, 138, 2), as being found, delivered or won by Indra."

Indra is described in other passages as having released the streams pent up by the dragon (II, 11, 2), and he is said to have won the cows and made the seven rivers flow (I, 32, 12; II, 12, 12). In II, 15, 6, the streams released by him have been described as flowing *upwards* (*udañcham*). It may be further noticed that in all these passages the clouds are not referred to under their ordinary name *abhra*; but the words used are *parvata*, *giri*, *adri*, (which primarily mean a mountain), or *ûdhas* (udder), *utsa* (spring), *kabandha* (cask) or *kosha* (pail). All these words have been interpreted by the Nairuktas as meaning a cloud, and this interpretation has been accepted by Western scholars. The word *go*, which generally means a cow, is also interpreted in some cases to mean the waters released by Indra. Thus when Indra is said to have released the cows, which were fast within the stone (VI, 43, 3), or when he is said to have moved the rock, which encompassed the cows, from its place (VI, 17, 5), it is understood that the reference is to a cloud-rock, which imprisons the rain-waters. Maruts are the usual companions of Indra in this fight; but Vishṇu, Agni and Bṛihaspati are also spoken of as assisting him in the rescue of the cows from the grip of Vala. Bṛihaspati's conquest of Vala, who had taken shelter in a rock, is thus taken to be a paraphrase of Indra's conquest over Vṛitra. In X, 62, 2 and 3, the Aṅgirases are also described as driving out the cows, piercing Vala and causing the sun to mount the sky,—exploits, which are usually attributed to Indra. There are other versions of the same story to be found in the Ṛig-Veda, but for the purpose in hand, we need not go beyond what has been stated above.

Now whosoever reads this description of Indra's fight with Vṛitra cannot fail to be struck with the fact that there are *four simultaneous effects* said to have been produced by the conquest of Indra over Vṛitra, namely, (1) the release of the cows, (2) the release of the waters, (3) the production of the dawn and (4) the production of the sun. Let us now see if the Storm theory satisfactorily explains the *simultaneous* production of these results from the destruction of Vṛitra. Vṛitra is a cloud, a storm-cloud, or a rain-cloud, hovering in the sky, and by smiting it with his thunder-bolt Indra may well be described as releasing the waters imprisoned therein. But where are the cows, which are said to be released along with the waters? The Nairuktas interpret cows to mean waters; but, in that case, the release of the waters and the release of the cows cannot be regarded as two distinct effects. The recovery of the dawn and the sun, along with the release of waters, is, however, still more difficult to explain by the Storm theory, or, we might even say, that it cannot be explained at all. Rain-clouds may temporarily obscure the sun, but the phenomenon is not one which occurs regularly, and it is not possible to speak of the production of the light of the sun as resultiug from the breaking up of the clouds, which may only occasionally obscure the sun. The recovery of the dawn, as a prize of the conflict between Indra and Vṛitra, simultaneously with the release of waters, is, similarly, quite inexplicable by the Storm theory. The rain-clouds usually move in the heavens, and though we may occasionally find them on the horizon, it is absurd to say that by striking the clouds Indra brought out the dawn. I know of no attempt made by any scholar to explain the four simultaneous effects of Indra's fight with Vṛitra by any other theory. The Storm theory appears to have been suggested by the Nairuktas, because the release of waters was supposed to be the principal effect of the conquest, and waters were naturally understood to mean the waters, which we see every day. But in spite of the efforts of the Nairuktas and Western scholars, the simultaneous winning of light and waters still remains unexplained. Macdonell (*Ved. Myth.* p. 61) referring to this difficulty observes, "There appears to be a confusion between the notion of the restoration of the sun after the darkness of the thunderstorm, and the recovery of the sun from the darkness of the night at dawn. The latter trait in the Indra myth is most probably only an extension of the former." If this means anything, it is only a confession of the inability of Vedic scholars to explain the four simultaneous effects of Indra's conquest over Vṛitra by the Storm theory ; and, strange to say, they seem to attribute their failure, not to their own ignorance or inability, but to the alleged confusion of ideas on the part of the Vedic bards.

These are not, however, the only points, in which the Storm theory fails to explain the legend of Indra and Vṛitra. It has been pointed out above that Vṛitra was killed in distant regions, in which ghastly darkness reigned, and which abounded in waters; while in X, 73, 7, Indra by killing Namuchi, *alias* Vṛitra, is said to have cleared the gates of the Devayâna path, evidently meaning that Vṛitra was killed at the gates of the path leading to the region of the gods. Even in the Avesta, the fight between Apaosha and Tishtrya is said to have taken place in the sea of Vouru-Kasha, and Tishtrya is described as moving along the path made by Mazda after his fight with Apaosha. Vṛitra's abode is similarly described as 'hidden' and 'enveloped by waters' at the bottom of *rajas* (I, 52, 6). None of these conditions is satisfied by making the storm-cloud, the scene of the battle between Indra and Vṛitra ; for a cloud cannot be said to be the ocean of waters, nor can it be described as lying in a distant (*parâvat*) region, or at the threshold of the Devayâna or the path of the gods. In the Ṛig-Veda *parâvat* is usually contrasted with *arvâvat*, and it means a distant region on the other side, as contrasted with the region on this or the nearer side. The Devayâna is similarly constrasted with the Pitṛiyâna, and means the northern celestial hemisphere. The clouds over the head of the observer cannot be said to be either in the distant region, or at the gate of the Devayâna; nor can we speak of them as enveloped by sun-less darkness. It is, therefore, highly improbable that the rain-clouds could have been the scene of battle between Indra and Vṛitra. It was the sea on the other side, the dark ocean as contrasted with the bright ocean(*shukram arṇaḥ*) which the sun mounts in the morning, where the battle was fought according to the passages referred to above; and the lescription is appropriate only in the case of the nether world, the celestial hemisphere that lies underneath, and not in the case of clouds moving in the sky above. I do not mean to say that Indra may not have been the god of rain or thunderstorm, but as *Vṛitrahan*, or the killer of Vṛitra, it is impossible to identify him with the god of rain, if the description of the fight found in the Vedic passages is not to be ignored or set aside.

The third objection to the current interpretation of the Vṛitra myth, is that it does not satisfactorily explain the passages, which give the time of Indra's fight with the demon. On the Storm theory, the fight must be placed in the rainy season or *Varṣhâ*; but the forts of Vṛitra, which Indra is said to have destroyed and thus acquired the epithet *purabhid* or *purandara*, are described in the Ṛig-Veda as autumnal or *shâradîḥ*, *i. e.*, belonging or pertaining to *Sharad*, the season which follows *Varṣhâ*. The discrepancy may be accounted for, by supposing that *Varṣhâ* and *Sharad* were once included under one season which was named not *Varṣhâ* but *Sharad*. But the explanation is opposed to another passage in the Ṛig-Veda (X, 62, 2), which says that Vala was killed at the end of the year (*parivatsare*), unless we again suppose that the year commenced with *Sharad* in those days. Nor can we explain how

Arbuda is said to be killed with *hima* (ice) by Indra. Again, as previously stated, the dawn could not be considered as a prize of the conflict, nor could the fight be said to have been fought in darkness, if we choose the rainy season as the time for the battle of Indra with Vṛitra. It will thus be seen that the Storm theory does not satisfactorily explain the statements regarding the time of the struggle between Indra and Vṛitra.

The fourth objection against the Storm theory, as applied to the story of Vṛitra, is that many words like *parvata*, *giri*, or *adri*, which do not signify a cloud, either primarily or secondarily, have to be interpreted as referring figuratively to the rain-cloud. This sounds harsh in many a passage where Indra or Bṛihaspati is described as piercing a mountain or breaking open a *stone*-cave and liberating the waters or the cows confined therein. In the absence of any other theory, we had to interpret these passages by the Storm theory, as the Nairuktas have done, by assigning to any and every word, used to denote the prison-house of waters or the cows, the meaning of a rain-cloud moving in the sky. But though we could thus temporarily get over the difficulty, the fact, that we had to strain the words used, or to assign unnatural meanings to them, was always a drawback, which detracted from the value of our interpretation. It was probably for this reason that Prof. Oldenberg was led to suggest that Indra's piercing the mountain and liberating the waters therefrom should be understood to refer not to the rain-could, but to the actual striking of the mountains with the thunder-bolt and making the rivers flow forth from them. But, as observed by Max Muller, "the rivers do not gush out of rocks even when they have been struck by lightning"; and so Prof. Oldenberg's explanation, though it gets us out of one difficulty, lands us on another, which, to say the least, is equally puzzling. If we, therefore, cannot suggest a better explanation, we might as well accept the device of the Nairuktas and interpret *parvata*, or whatever other word or words may be found used to denote the place of the confinement of waters, as meaning a cloud, and explain the legend of Vṛitra by the Storm theory as best as we can.

It will be found from the foregoing discussion regarding the Storm theory as applied to the legend of Indra and Vṛitra, that it explains neither the simultaneous effects of Indra's conquest over Vṛitra, nor the statements regarding the seat of the battle between them, nor those regarding the time when it took place, nor again does it allow us to take the words, used in certain Vedic passages, in their natural sense; and yet we find that the theory has been accepted as the basis of the legend from the times of the Nairuktas upto the present. Why should it be so ?—is a question, which would naturally occur to any one, who examines the subject. It is true that the Storm theory fully explains the release of waters as a result of the fight; but the release of waters is not the only consequence, which we have to account for. There are four simultaneous effects of the war, the release of the waters, the release of the cows, the recovery of the dawn and the production of the sun. The Storm theory explains the first two and the Dawn theory the last two of these ; but the whole set of four is explained by neither, nor could the theories be so combined as to explain all the four effects, unless, like Prof. Macdonell, we suppose that the Vedic bards have confused the two entirely different ideas, *viz.*, the restoration of the sunlight after thunderstorm, and the recovery of light from the darkness of night. Of the two theories, the Storm and the Dawn, the ancient Nairuktas, therefore, seem to have adopted that which adequately accounted for the release of the waters and which suited better with their notion of Indra as a thunder-god, on the principle that half a loaf is better than none, and have ignored the remaining incidents in the legend as inexplicable, unimportant, or immaterial. The same theory has also been adopted by Western scholars, and it is the only theory in the field at present. But it is so manifestly inadequate that if a better theory could be found which will explain most of, if not all, the incidents in the legend, no one would hesitate to abandon the Storm theory in favour of the latter.

It is, in my opinion, a mistake to suppose that the struggle between Indra and Vṛitra *originally* represented the conflict between the thunder-god and the rain-cloud. It is really a struggle between the powers of light and darkness, and we find traces of it in the Aitareya Brâhmaṇa (IV, 5), where Indra alone of all gods is described as having undertaken the task of driving out Asuras from the darkness of the night. That Indra is the god of light is also evident from many other passages in the Ṛig-Veda, where, without any reference to the Vṛitra fight, Indra is said to have found the light (III, 34, 4; VIII, 15, 5; X, 43, 4) in the darkness (I, 108, 8; IV, 16, 4), or to have produced the dawn as well as the sun (II, 12, 7; 21, 4; III, 31, 15), or opened the darkness with the dawn and the sun (I, 62, 5). It was he, who made the sun to shine (VIII, 3, 6), and mount in the sky (I, 7, 3), or prepared a path for the sun (X, 111, 3), or found the sun in 'the darkness in which he resided' (III, 39, 5). It is evident from these passages that Indra is the winner of light and the sun, and this character of his was well understood by scholars, for Indra as *apavaryan*, or the recoverer (fr. *apa-vṛi*) of light, is compared by Max Muller with Apollon in the Greek mythology. But scholars have found it difficult to explain why this character of Indra should be mentioned in conjunction with other exploits, such as the conquest of Vṛitra and the liberation of the waters. In fact that is the real difficulty in the explanation of the legend either by the Storm or by the Dawn theory. Indra liberated the waters and brought about the dawn by killing Vṛitra,—is undoubtedly the burden of the whole story; but no explanation has yet been found by which the simultaneous recovery of light and waters could satisfactorily be accounted for. We have seen that by the Storm theory we can account for the release of waters, but not the recovery of the dawn; while if the legend is taken to represent a struggle between light and darkness, as implied by the Dawn theory, we can account for the recovery of the dawn and the sun, but not for the release of waters. Under these circumstances it is necessary to examine the nature and character of waters as described in the Vedas, before we accept or reject either or both of the above-mentioned theories.

It has been noticed above that the passages, where waters are said to be released by Indra after killing Vṛitra do not refer expressly to the rain-cloud. The words *parvata*, *giri*, and the like are used to denote the place where the waters were confined, and *âpaḥ*, or *sindhus*, to denote the waters themselves. Now *âpaḥ*, or waters generally, are mentioned in a number of places in the Ṛig-Veda, and the word in many places denotes the celestial or aerial waters. Thus we are told that they follow the path of the gods, and are to be found beside the sun, who is with them (I, 23, 17). In VII, 49, 2, we have an express statement that there are waters, which are celestial (*divyâḥ âpaḥ*), and also those that flow in earthly channels (*khanitrimâḥ*), thus clearly distinguishing between terrestrial and celestial waters. In the same verse they are said to have the sea or the ocean for the goal; and in VIII, 69, 12, the seven rivers are said to flow into the jaws of Varuṇa as into a surging abyss. Varuṇa again is described as the god, who, like Indra, makes the rivers flow (II, 28, 4); and we have seen that the sage Dîrghatamas is said to have been borne on the waters wending to their goal (I, 158, 6). But it is needless to cite more authorities on this point, for scholars are agreed that both celestial and terrestrial waters are mentioned in the Ṛig-Veda. The nature, the character, or the movements of celestial waters appear, however, to be very imperfectly understood; and this is the sole reason why scholars have not yet been able to connect the release of the waters with the recovery of the dawn in the Vṛitra legend. It seems to have been supposed that when the Ṛig-Veda speaks of the celestial waters (*divyâḥ âpaḥ*) only the rain-waters are intended. But this is a mistake; for, in passages which speak of the creation of the world (X, 82, 6; 129, 3), the world is said to have once consisted of nothing but undifferentiated waters. In short, the Ṛig-Veda, like the Hebrew Testament, expressly states that the world was originally full of waters, and that there were the waters in the firmament above and waters below. The Shatapatha Brâhmaṇa (XI, 1, 6, 1), the Aitareya Upanishad (I, 1,) and Manu (I, 9), all say that the world was created from watery vapours. There can, therefore, be no doubt that the idea of celestial waters was well-known to the ancestors of the Vedic bards in early days; and as the celestial waters were conceived to be the material out of which the universe was created, it is probable that the Vedic bards understood by that phrase what the modern scientists now understand by 'ether' or 'the nebulous mass of matter' that fills all the space in the universe. We need not, however, go so far. It is enough for our purpose to know that the celestial waters (*divyâḥ âpaḥ*), or the watery vapours (*purîsham*), are mentioned in the Ṛig-Veda, and that the Vedic bards considered the space or the region above, below, and around them to be full of these celestial vapours which are said to be co-eval with the world in X, 30, 10.

It is, however, alleged by Wallis in his *Cosmology of the Ṛig-Veda* (p. 115) that the Vedic bards were not acquainted with the regions below the earth, and that every thing, which is described in the Vedas as occurring in the atmosphere, including the movements of the sun during night and day, must be placed in the regions of the sky, which were over the head of these bards. This view appears to be adopted by Macdonell in his *Vedic Mythology*; and if it be correct, we shall have to place all the waters in the upper heaven. But I do not think that Wallis has correctly interpreted the passages quoted by Prof. Zimmer in support of his theory that a *rajas* (region) exists below the earth; and we cannot, therefore, accept Wallis' conclusions, which are evidently based upon prepossessions derived most probably from the Homeric controversy. Prof. Zimmer refers to three passages (VI, 9, 1; VII, 80, 1; V, 81, 4) to prove that a *rajas* beneath the earth was known to the Vedic people. The first of these passages is the well-known verse regarding the bright and the dark day. It says, "the bright day and the dark day, both roll the two *rajas* by the well-known paths." Here the two *rajas* are evidently the upper and the lower celestial hemisphere; but Wallis asks us to compare this verse with I, 185, 1, where day and night are said "to revolve like two wheels," that is, to circle round from east to west, the one rising as the other goes down, and observes that "we are in no way obliged to consider that the progress of either is continued below the earth." I am unable to understand how we can draw such an inference from these passages. In VI, 9, 1, quoted by Zimmer, two *rajas* or atmospheres are mentioned, and the bright and the dark day are said to roll along both these *rajas* or regions. But if we hold with Wallis that the progress of either begins in the east and stops in the west, without going below the earth, the whole movement becomes confined to one *rajas* or region and does not extend over the two. Zimmer's interpretation is, therefore, not only more probable, but the only one that explains the use of *rajasî* (in the dual), or the two regions, in the verse. The next passage (VII, 80, 1) is also misunderstood by Wallis. It describes the dawn as "unrolling the two regions (*rajasî*), which border on each other (*samante*), revealing all things." Now the dawn always appears on the horizon and the two *rajas*, which it unrolls and which are said to border on each other, must meet on this horizon. They can, therefore, only represent the lower and the upper celestial sphere. But Wallis would have us believe that both these *rajasî* are above the earth, and that narrowing down together towards east and west they meet on the horizon like two arched curves over one's head! The artificial character of this explanation is self-evident, and I see no reason why we should adopt it in preference to the simple and natural explanation of Zimmer, unless we start with a preconceived notion that references to the regions below the earth ought not to be and cannot be found in the Ṛig-Veda. The third passage pointed out by Zimmer is V, 81, 4, which says "O Savitṛi! Thou goest round (*pariyase*) the night, on both sides (*ubhayataḥ*)." Here Wallis proposes to translate *pariyase* by 'encompassest'; but *pariyase* ordinarily means 'goest round,' and there is no reason why the idea of motion usually implied by it should be here abandoned. It will thus be seen that the conclusion of Wallis is based upon the distortion of passages which Zimmer interprets in a simpler and a more natural way; and that Zimmer's view is more in accordance with the natural meaning of these texts. But if an express passage be still needed to prove conclusively that the region below the earth was known to the Vedic bards, we refer to VII, 104, 11, where the bard prays for the destruction of his enemies and says, "Let him (enemy) go down *below* the *three* earths, (*tisraḥ pṛithivîḥ adhaḥ*)." Here the region below the three earths is expressly mentioned; and since the enemy is to be condemned to it, it must be a region of torment and pain like the Hades. In X, 152, 5, we read, "One, who injures us, let him be sent to the nether darkness (*adharam tamaḥ*)," and, comparing this with the last passage, it is evident that the region below the earth was conceived as dark. In III, 53, 21, we have, "Let him, who hates us, fall downwards (*adharaḥ*)," and in II, 12, 4, the brood of the Dasyu, whom Indra killed, is said to be "sent to the unknown nether world (*adharam guhâkaḥ*)." These passages directly show that region below the earth was not only known to the Vedic bards, but was conceived as filled with darkness, and made the scene of Indra's fight with Vṛitra. It may, however, be alleged that "below the three earths" may simply mean underneath the surface of the earth. But, in that case, it was not necessary to speak of all the *three* earths; and since we are told that the region is below *all the three* earths, it can refer only to the nether world. This is further proved by the passage which describes what is above the three earths. The expression, corresponding to *tisraḥ pṛithivîḥ adhaḥ* or "the region below the three earths," will be *tisraḥ pṛithivîḥ upari* or "the region above the three earths," and as a matter of fact this expression is also found in the Ṛig-Veda. Thus in I, 34, 8, we are told that "the Ashvins, moving *above* the *three* earths (*tisraḥ pṛithivîḥ upari*), protect the vault or the top of heaven (*divo nâkam*) through days and nights"; and Ashvins are said to have come on their car from a distant region (*parâvat*) in the preceding verse of the same hymn. The phrase *divo nâkam* occurs several times in the Ṛig-Veda and means the top or the vault of the heaven. Thus in IV, 13, 5, the sun is said to guard (*pâti*) the vault of the heaven (*divo nâkam*); and as regards the three-fold division of the earth it is mentioned in several places in the Ṛig-Veda (I, 102, 8, IV, 53, 5; VII, 87, 5), and also in the Avesta (Yt. XIII, 3; Yasna, XI, 7). In IV, 53, 5, this three-fold division is further extended to *antarikṣha*, *rajas*, *rochana* and *dyu* or heaven. This shows what we are to understand by 'three earths.' It is the one and the same earth, regarded as three-fold; and since the Ashvins are described as protecting the vault of heaven by moving "above the three earths," it is clear that in contrast with the vault above, a nether region, as far below the three earths as the heaven is above them, must have been conceived and denoted by the phrase "below the three earths," and that the latter expression did not merely mean an interterranean ground. When we meet with two such phrases as the heaven "above the three earths," and the region "below the three earths," in the Ṛig-Veda, phrases, which cannot be mistaken or misunderstood, the hypothesis that the Vedic bards were not acquainted with the nether world at once falls to the ground.

Mr. Wallis seems to think that since *rajas* is said to be divided three-fold, like the earth, and since the highest *rajas* is mentioned as the seat of waters, there is no scope in the Vedic division of *rajas* for a region beneath the earth; for the three *rajas* are exhausted by taking them as the *rajas* of the earth (*pârthivam*), the *rajas* of the sky (*divo rajaḥ*) and the highest (*paramam*) *rajas*, the seat of waters. But this objection is quite untenable, inasmuch as six different *rajas*, are also mentioned in the Ṛig-Veda (I, 164, 6). We can, therefore, suppose that there were three *rajas* above the earth and three below it, and so meet the apparent difficulty pointed out by Wallis. The three *rajas* can in some places be also interpreted to mean the earthly *rajas*, the one above the earth and the one below it, (X, 82, 4,). In I, 35, 2, the Savitṛi is described as moving through the dark *rajas* (*kṛishṇena rajasâ*), and in the next verse we are told that he comes from the distant (*parâvat*) region, which shows that the dark *rajas* and the *parâvat* region are synonymous, and that the sun ascends the sky after passing through the dark *rajas*. Again the use of the word 'ascend'(*ud-yan* or *ud-âcharat*, I, 163, 1; VII, 55, 7), to describe the rising of the sun in the morning from the ocean, shows, by contrast, that the ocean which the sun is said to enter at the time of setting (X, 114, 4) is really an ocean underneath the earth. In I, 117, 5, the sun is described as sleeping in "the lap of *Nir-ṛiti*," and "dwelling in darkness"; while in I, 164, 32 and 33, the sun is said to have travelled in the interior of heaven and earth and finally gone into *Nir-ṛiti*, or as Prof. Max Muller renders it, 'the exodus in the west.' Now, in X,

114, 2, there are three *Nir-ṛitis* mentioned, evidently corresponding to the three earths and three heavens; and in X, 161 2, the lap of *Nir-ṛiti* is identified with the region of death. Purûravas is again said (X, 95, 14) to have gone to the distant region (*param parâvatam*) and there made his bed on the lap of *Nir-ṛiti* ; while the Maruts are described as *mounting up* to the firmament from the bottom-less *Nir-ṛiti* in VII, 58, 1. All these passages taken together show that *Nir-ṛiti*, or the land of dissolution and death, commenced in the west, that the sun lying in darkness travelled through the distant region (*parâvat*) and eventually rose in the east from the lap of *Nir-ṛiti*, and that the whole of this movement was placed not in the upper heaven, but on the other side of the vault through which the sun travelled before he entered into *Nir-ṛiti*. In other words, the *Nir-ṛitis* extended below the earth from west to east; and since the region below the three earths is expressly mentioned in the Ṛig-Veda, the three *Nir-ṛitis* must be understood to mean the three regions below the earth corresponding to the three-fold division of the earth or of the heaven above it. Zimmer is, therefore, correct in stating that the sun moved through the *rajas* below the earth during night and that the Vedic poets knew of this nether *rajas*.

There are other passages in the Ṛig-Veda which fully support the same view. Thus corresponding to the *rajasî*, or the two *rajas*, we have another expression in the dual, namely, *ubhau ardhau*, which literally denotes 'the two halves,' and when applied to heaven, 'the two celestial hemispheres.' The expression *ardhau* occures in II, 27, 15, and the two halves are there asked to be propitious to the sacrificer. Wallis, however, interprets *ubhau ardhau* to mean 'heaven and earth'. But this is a mistake for there is a passage in the Ṛig-Veda where we have the phrases *pare ardhe* (in the farther half) and *upare ardhe* (in the nearer half) of heaven (*divaḥ*), showing that the heaven alone (and not heaven and earth) was conceived as divided into two halves (I, 164, 12). A few verses later on (I, 164, 17), the cow with her calf (the dawn with the sun) is described as having appeared below the upper and above the lower realm, *i. e.*, between heaven and earth, and a question is then asked "To what half (*ardham*) has she departed ?" which again shows that the *ardham* here referred to is quite distinct from heaven and earth. In the Atharva Veda, X, 8, 7 and 13, the 'two halves' are referred to, and the poet asks, "Prajâpati with one half (*ardham*) engendered all creation; what sign is there to tell us of the other half ?" Here the other half cannot mean the earth; and Griffith accordingly explains it as referring to the sun at night. Another expression used to denote the upper and the lower world is *samudrau*, or the two oceans, (X, 136, 5). These two oceans are said to be one on this side (*avara*) and one on the other (*para*) side in VII, 6, 7; and a yonder ocean (*parâvati samudre*) is mentioned in VIII, 12, 17. I have already quoted above the passages which speak of the bright *arṇaḥ* or ocean (V, 45, 10), and of *arṇava* or an ocean pervaded with darkness (I, 23, 18). The two words *parastât* and *avastât* are also employed to convey the same idea. They denote a region on the nearer side and a region on the farther side. Thus in VIII, 8, 14, *parâvat* region is contrasted with *ambara* or the heaven above, and in III, 55, 6, the sun is described as sleeping in the *parâvat* region. We have seen above that Savitṛi is said to come up from the *parâvat* region, and that he moves through the dark region before ascending the sky. The two words *parâvat* and *arvâvat* thus separately denote the same regions that are jointly denoted by the dual words *rajasî*, *ardhau* or *samudrau*; and when both the upper and the lower hemispheres were intended the word *ubhayataḥ* was employed. Thus in III, 53, 5, we read, "O Maghavan ! O brother Indra ! go beyond (*parâ*) and come hither (*â*), you are wanted in both places, (*ubhayatra*)." The passages where

Savitṛi is described as going round the night on both sides is already referred to above.

With these passages before us, we cannot reasonably hold that the Vedic bards were ignorant of the lower celestial hemisphere, as supposed by Wallis and some other scholars. Nor is the hypothesis *a priori* probable, for I have shown elsewhere that the Vedic bards knew enough of astronomy to calculate the movements of the sun and the moon tolerably correct for all practical purposes; and the people, who could do this, could not be supposed to be so ignorant as to believe that the sky was nailed down to the earth at the celestial horizon, and that when the sun was not seen during the night, he must be taken to have disappeared somewhere in the upper regions of the heaven. The passage from the Aitareya Brâhmaṇa (III, 44), which is quoted by Wallis' and which tells us that the sun, having reached the end of the day, turns round as it were, and makes night where there was day before and day on the other side, and *vice versa*, is very vague and does not prove that the sun was believed to return by night through a region, which is somewhere in the upper heaven. The words used in the original are *avastât* and *parastât*; and Dr. Haug correctly translates *parastât* by 'what is on the other side.' Muir and others, however, interpret *parastât* to mean 'upper,' thus giving rise to the hypothesis that the sun returns during night by a passage through the upper region of the heaven. But in the face of the express passages in which regions below and above all the three earths are unmistakably mentioned, we cannt accept a hypothesis based upon a doubtful translation of a single word. It is a hypothesis that has its origin either in the preconceived notion regarding the primitive man, or in a desire to import into the Vedas the speculations of the Homeric cosmography. The knowledge of the Vedic bards regarding the nether world may not have been as exact as that of the modern astronomers, and we therefore, meet with such questions in the Ṛig-Veda (I, 35, 7) as "Where is Sûrya now (after sunset) and which celestial region his rays now illumine?" But there is enough explicit evidence to prove that the Vedic people knew of the existence of a region below the earth, and if some of their notions about this underworld were not very distinct, that does not, in the least, affect the value of this evidence.

If we, therefore, dismiss from our mind the idea that the lower world was not known to the Vedic people,—an assumption, which is quite gratuitous, the movements and character of the celestial waters become at once plain and intelligible. The ancient Aryans, like the old Hebrews, believed that the subtle matter, which filled the whole space in the universe, was nothing but watery vapours; and secondly that the movements of the sun, the moon and other heavenly bodies were caused by these vapours which kept on constantly circulating from the nether to the upper and from the upper to the lower celestial hemisphere. That is the real key to the explanation of many a Vedic myth; and unless we grasp it thoroughly, we cannot rightly understand some of the utterances of the Vedic poets. These waters were sometimes conceived as rivers or streams, moving in the heaven, and eventually falling into the mouth of Varuṇa, or the nether ocean (VII, 49, 2; VIII, 69, 12). The nether world was, so to say, the seat or the home of these waters, called *yahvatîḥ* or the eternal (IX, 113, 8); and they formed the kingdom of Varuṇa and Yama, as well as the hidden (*niṇya*) abode of Vṛitra. This movement of waters is very clearly expressed in the Parsi scriptures. In the Vendidad, XXI, 4-5 (15-23), the waters are described as follows,—"As the sea Vouru-Kasha is the gathering place of waters, rise up, go up the aerial way and go down on the earth; go down on the earth and go up the aerial way. Rise up and roll along! thou in whose rising and growing Ahura Mazda made the aerial way. Up! rise up and roll along! thou swift-horsed sun, above Hara Berezaiti, and produce light for the world, and mayest thou rise up there, if thou art to abide in Garo-nmânem, along the path made by Mazda, along the way made by the gods, the watery way they opened." Here the aerial waters are said to start from their gathering place, the sea Vouru-Kasha, go up into heaven and come back again to the sea to be purified before starting on a second round. Prof. Darmesteter in a note on this passage observes that "waters and light are believed to flow from the same spring and in the same bed," and quotes Bundahish, XX, 4, which says, "just as the light comes in through Albûrz (Hara Berezaiti, the mountain by which the earth is surrounded) and goes out through Albûrz, the water also comes out through Albûrz and goes away through Albûrz." Now waters are described in the Ṛig-Veda as following the path of the gods (VII, 47, 3), much in the same way as the waters in the Avesta are said to follow the path made by Mazda or the way made by the gods. Like the Avestic waters, the waters in the Ṛig-Veda have also the sea for their goal, and going by the aerial way eventually fall into the mouth of Varuṇa. But the Avesta supplies us with the key which establishes the connection of waters and light in unambiguous terms, for, as remarked by Prof. Darmesteter, it states clearly that both of them have the same source, and, in the passage quoted above, the swift-horsed sun is accordingly asked to go along the watery way in the skies above. In the Aban Yasht (V, 3), the river Ardvi Sûra Anâhita is described as running powerfully from the height Hukairya down to the sea Vouru-Kasha, like the river Sarasvatî, which is described in the Ṛig-Veda as tearing the peaks of mountains, and is invoked to descend from the great mountain in the sky to the sacrifice (V, 43, 11). Both are aerial rivers, but by coming down upon the earth they are said to fill up all the terrestrial streams. The terrestrial waters, nay, all things of a liquid nature on the earth, *e. g.*, the plant-sap, the blood, &c., were thus supposed to be produced from the aerial waters above by the agency of clouds and rain. The Parsi scriptures further tell us that between the earth and the region of infinite light (the *parame vyoman* of the Ṛig-Veda), there are three intermediate regions, the star region, which has the seeds of waters and plants, the moon region, and the sun region, the last being the highest (Yt. XII, 29-32). When the Ṛig-Veda, therefore, speaks of the highest *rajas* as being the seat of waters, it is not to be understood, as supposed by Wallace, that there are no nether waters, for it is the nether waters that come up from the lower world and moving in the uppermost region of the heaven produce terrestrial waters by giving rise to rain and clouds. Thus Ardvi Sûra Anâhita is said to run through the starry region (cf. Yt. VIII, 47), and has to be worshipped with sacrifice in order that her waters may not all run up into the region of the sun, thereby producing a drought on the surface of the earth, (Yt. V, 85 and 90). In the Ṛig-Veda, the Sarasvatî is similarly described as filling the earthly region and the wide atmospheric space (VI, 61, 11), and is besought to come swelling with streams, and along with waters. But the most striking resemblance between Ardvi Sûra Anâhita and Sarasvatî is that while the latter is described as Vṛitra-slayer or *Vṛitra-ghnî* in Ṛig. VI, 61, 7, Ardvi Sûra Anâhita is described in the Aban Yasht (V, 33 and 34) as granting to Thrâetaona, the heir of the valiant Âthwya clan (Vedic Trita Âptya), who offered up a sacrifice to her, a boon that he would be able to overcome Azi Dahâk, the three-mouthed, three-headed and six-eyed monster. This is virtually the same story which is found in the Ṛig-Veda X, 8, 8, where Trita Âptya, knowing his paternal weapons and urged by Indra, is said to have fought against and slew the three-headed son of Tvashṭṛi and released the cows. This clearly establishes the connection between waters, as represented by

Ardvi Sûra Anâhita or Sarasvatî, and the slaughter of Vṛitra. Many Vedic scholars have tried to identify Sarasvatî with the river of that name in the Panjaub: but as the latter is an insignificant stream, the identification has not been generally accepted. The above comparison now shows that the mighty Sarasvatî, like Ardvi Sûra Anâhita, is an aerial stream, which rises up from the nether store-house of waters, travels over the sky and again falls back into the lower ocean. A portion of these waters is brought down upon the earth in the form of rain by the sacrifices offered to the river, and along with it come the seeds of all the plants growing upon the surface of the earth. Thus in the Vendidad, V, 19 (56), the tree of all the seeds is described as growing in the middle of the sea Vouru-Kasha, and the seeds are then said to be brought up by the aerial rivers and sent down by them to the earth by means of rain, an idea similar to that found in the Ṛig-Veda, I, 23, 20, where the sacrificer informs us that Soma has told him that all medicines (medicinal herbs) are contained in the waters. We have thus a complete account of the cosmic circulation of the aerial waters and the production of the terrestrial waters and plants therefrom. The nether world or the lower celestial hemisphere is the home of these waters, and it is expressly said to be bounded on all sides by a mountainous range like that of Hara Berezaiti. When the aerial waters are allowed to come up through this mountain, they travel over the upper hemisphere and again fall into the sea Vouru-Kasha, or the lower ocean, producing, during their course, rains which fertilise the earth and make the plants grow upon its surface. But instead of descending down in the form of rain, these aerial waters were, it was apprehended, apt to turn away into the region of the sun and deprive us of rain. It was, therefore, necessary to worship them with sacrifices and invoke their blessings.

It is impossible to grasp the real meaning of the Vṛitra legend, without first realising the true nature and importance of the movements of the aerial waters as conceived by the ancestors of the Indo-Iranian people. As observed by Darmesteter, celestial waters and light were believed to flow from the same spring or source, and they both ran a parallel course. It was these aerial waters that made the heavenly bodies move in the sky, just as a boat or any other object is carried down by the current of a stream or river. If the waters, therefore, ceased to flow, the consequences were serious; for the sun, the moon, the stars, would then all cease to rise, and the world would be plunged in darkness. We can now fully understand the magnitude of the mischief worked by Vṛitra by stopping the flow of these waters. In his hidden home, at the bottom of *rajas*, that is, in the lower hemisphere, he encompassed the waters in such a way as to stop their flow *upwards* through the mountain, and Indra's victory over Vṛitra meant that he released these waters from the clutches of Vṛitra and made them flow *up* again. When the waters were thus released, they naturally brought with them, the dawn, the sun and the cows, *i.e.*, either days or the rays of the morning; and the victory was thus naturally described as four-fold in character. Now we can also understand the part played by *parvatas*, or mountains, in the legend. It was the mountain Albûrz, or Hara Berezaiti; and as Vṛitra, by stretching his body across, closed all the apertures in this mountainous range, through which the sun and the waters came up, Indra had to uncover or open these passages by killing Vṛitra. Thus the Bundahish (V, 5) mentions 180 apertures in the east and 180 in the west through Albûrz; and the sun is said to come and go through them every day, and all the movements of the moon, the constellations and the planets are also said to be closely connected with these apertures. The same idea is also expressed in the later Sanskrit literature when the sun is said to rise above the mountain in the east and set below the mountain in the west. The mountain on which Indra is said to have found Shambara (II, 12, 11), and the rock of Vala wherein the cows were said to have been imprisoned by the demon (IV, 3, 11; I, 71, 2) and which was burst open by Aṅgirases, also represent the same mountainous range, which separated the upper from the lower celestial hemisphere, or the bright from the dark ocean. This explanation of the Vṛitra legend may sound strange to many scholars, but it should be borne in mind that the co-relation between the flow of water and the rising of the dawn and the sun, here described, is not speculative. If the Vedic works do not express it in unambiguous terms, the deficiency is fully made up by the Parsi scriptures. Thus in Khorshed Yasht (VI, 2 and 3,) we are told that "When the sun rises up, then the earth becomes clean, the running waters become clean. ... ... Should the sun not rise up, then the Daevas would destroy all the things that are in the seven Karshvarees." The passages in the Farvardîn Yasht are still more explicit. This Yasht is devoted to the praise of the Fravashis, which correspond to the Pitṛis of the Ṛig-Veda. These ancient fathers are often described, even in the Ṛig-Veda, as taking part, along with the gods, in the production of the cosmical phenomena. Thus the Pitṛis are said to have adorned the sky with stars, and placed darkness in the night and light in the day (X, 68, 11), or to have found the hidden light and generated the dawn (VII, 76, 4 ; X, 107, 1). The Fravashis in the Parsi scriptures are said to have achieved the same or similar exploits. They are described (Yt. XIII, 53 and 54) as having " shown the beautiful paths to the waters, which had stood before for a long time in the same place, without flowing "; and the waters are then said to have commenced to flow " along the path made by Mazda, along the way made by the gods, the watery way appointed to them. " Immediately after (Yt. XIII, 57), the Fravashis are said to have similarly showed "the paths to the stars, the moon, the sun and the endless lights, that had stood before, for a long time, in the same place, without moving forward, through the oppression of the Daevas and the assaults of the Daevas." Here we have the co-relation between the flowing of waters and the moving forward of the sun distinctly ennunciated. It was the Fravashis, who caused to move onwards the waters and the sun, both of which "had stood still for a long time in the same place." Prof. Darmesteter adds a note saying that it was 'in winter' that this cessation of motion occurred, (Cf. Vend. V, 10-12; VIII, 4-10, cited and discussed *infra*). The Fravashis are further described (Yt. XIII, 78) as "destroying the malice of the fiend Angra Mainyu (the Avestic representative of Vṛitra), so that the waters did not stop flowing, nor did the plants stop growing." In Yasna LXV (Sp. LXIV), 6, the Fravashis, who had "borne the waters *up* stream from the nearest ones," are invoked to come to the worshipper; and a little further on the waters are asked to "rest still within their places while the Zaota (Sans. *Hotâ*) shall offer," evidently meaning that it is the sacrifice offered by the invoking priest that eventually secures the release or the flow of waters. There are other references to the flowing of waters (Yt. X, 61) in the Parsi scriptures, but those cited above are sufficient to prove our point. The main difficulty in the rational explanation of the Vṛitra legend was to connect the flow of waters with the rising of the dawn, and the passages from the Farvardîn Yasht quoted above furnish us with a clue by which this connection can be satisfactorily established.

There are two passages in the Vendidad, which give us the period during which these aerial waters ceased to flow, and it is necessary to quote them here, inasmuch as they throw further light on the circulation of aerial waters. It has been stated above that according to Prof. Darmesteter these waters ceased to flow during winter; but the point is made perfectly clear in Fargards V and VIII of the Vendidad, where Ahura Mazda declares how the corpse of a person dying during winter is to be dealt with, until it is finally disposed of according to the usual rites at the end of the season. Thus in Fargard V, 10 (34), Ahura Mazda is asked, "If the summer is passed and *the winter has come*, what shall the worshipper of Mazda do?" To which Ahura Mazda answers, "In every house, in every borough they shall raise three *Katas* for the dead, large enough not to strike the skull, or the feet or the hands of the man; ... and they shall let the lifeless body lie there for *two nights, three nights* or *a month long*, until the birds begin to fly, the plants to grow, the floods to flow, and the wind to dry up the waters from off the earth. And as soon as the birds begin to fly, and the plants to grow, and the floods to flow, and the wind to dry up the waters from off the earth, then the worshipper of Mazda shall lay down the dead (on the Dakhma), his eyes towards the sun." I have referred to this passage previously, but as the theory of the circulation of aerial waters was not then explained, the discussion of the passage had to be postponed. We now clearly see what is meant by the phrases like 'floods to flow' and 'plants to grow'. They are the same phrases, which are used in the Farvardîn Yasht and are there connected with the moving forward of the sun and the moon, that had stood still, or without moving, in the same place for a long time. In other words, the waters, as well as the sun, ceased to move during winter, and the worshipper of Mazda is ordered not to dispose of the corpse until the floods began to flow and the sun to move, be it for *two nights, three nights*, or *a month long*. The Mazda-worshippers believed that the corpse was cleansed by its exposure to the sun, and dead bodies could not, therefore, be disposed of during night. The passage from the Vendidad, above referred to, therefore, clearly indicates that the season of winter was once marked by long darkness extending over two nights, three nights, or a month; and that during the period, the floods ceased to flow and the plant to grow. It was during such a winter that the difficulty of disposing the corpse arose, and Ahura Mazda is asked what the faithful should do in such cases. The question has no meaning otherwise, for, if in the ancient home of the Mazdayasnians the sun shone every day during winter, as he does with us in the tropical regions, there would have been no difficulty in the disposal of the corpse by exposing it to the sun the next morning; and it would be absurd to ask the faithful to keep the uncleanly dead body in his house for two nights, three nights, or a month long, until the winter passed away. The passage from Fargard V quoted above makes no mention of darkness, though it can be easily inferred from the statement that the body is, at last, to be taken out and laid down on the Dakhma with its eyes towards the sun, evidently meaning that this ceremony was impossible to be performed during the time the dead body was kept up in the house. But Fargard VIII, 4 (11), where the same subject is again taken up, mentions darkness distinctly. Thus Ahura Mazda is asked "If in the house of the worshipper of Mazda a dog or a man happens to die, and it is raining, or snowing, or blowing, or the *darkness* is coming on, when the flocks and the men lose their way, what shall the worshipper of Mazda do?" To this Ahura Mazda gives the same reply as in Fargard V. The faithful is directed, VIII, 9, (21), to dig a grave in the house, and there "let the lifeless body lie for two nights, three nights, or a month long, until the birds begin to fly, the plants to grow, the floods to flow, and the wind to dry up the waters from off the earth." Here in the question asked to Ahura Mazda darkness is distinctly mentioned along with snowing and blowing; and in the Farvardîn Yasht we have seen that the flowing of waters and the moving of the sun are described as taking place at the same time. The passage from Tîr Yasht, where the appointed time for the appearance of Tishtrya after conquering Apaosha in the watery regions is described as one night, two nights, fifty, or one hundred nights, has already been referred to in the last chapter. From all these passages taken together, it inevitably follows that it was during winter that the water ceased to flow, and the sun to move, and that the period of stagnation lasted from one night to a hundred nights. It was a period of long darkness, when the sun was not seen above the horizon; and if a man died during the period, his corpse had to be kept in the house until the waters again commenced to flow, and the sun appeared on the horizon along with them. I have pointed out previously how the Hindu belief that it is inauspicious to die in the Dakshiṇâyana must be traced to this primeval practice of keeping the dead body undisposed of during the long Arctic night. The word *Kata* which is used for 'grave' in the Parsi scriptures occurs once in the Ṛig-Veda, I, 106, 6, where the sage Kutsa, lying in *Kâṭa* is described as invoking the Vṛitra-slaying Indra for his protection; and I think that we have here, at least, an indirect reference to the practice of keeping dead bodies in a *Kâṭa*, until Vṛitra was killed, and the waters and the sun made free to run their usual course. We are, however, concerned here only with the circulation of the celestial waters; and from the Avestic passages quoted above, it is clear that the aerial waters ceased to flow during winter for several days or ṛather nights, and that, since light sprang from the same source as waters, the sun also ceased to move during the period and stood still in the watery regions, until the Fravashis, who helped the gods in their struggle for waters or in their conflict with powers of darkness, made the waters and the sun move onwards to take their usual course in the upper celestial hemisphere. We can now understand why Indra is described as moving by his might the stream upwards (*udañcha*) in II, 15, 6, and how the rivers are said to be set free to move on (*sartave*) by killing

Vṛitra (I, 32, 12), or how in I, 80, 5, Indra is said to have made the lights of heaven shine forth without obstruction and set the waters (*apaḥ*) free to flow (*sarmâya*). There are many other passages in the Ṛig-Veda, where the flowing of waters and the appearance of the sun or the dawn are spoken of as taking place simultaneously, as may be seen from the quotations from Macdonell's *Vedic Mythology* given above. All these passages become intelligible only when interpreted on the theory of the cosmic circulation of aerial waters through the upper and the lower celestial hemispheres. But as the theory was little understood or studied in this connection, the Vedic scholars, ancient and modern, have hitherto failed to interpret the Vṛitra legend in a rational and intelligible way, especially the four simultaneous effects of the conquest of Indra over Vṛitra mentioned therein.

The cosmic circulation of aerial waters described above, is not peculiar to the Indo-Iranian mythology. Dr. Warren, in his *Paradise Found*, states that a similar circulation of aerial waters is mentioned in the works of Homer. Homer describes the sun as returning to the flowing of the ocean, or sinking into it, and again rising from it and mounting the sky. All rivers and every sea and all fountains and even deep wells are again said to arise from the deep flowing ocean, which was believed to encircle the earth. [1] Hêlios or the sun is further described as sailing from west to east in a golden boat or cup, evidently meaning that the underworld was supposed to be full of waters. But Homeric scholars seem to have raised unnecessary difficulties in the proper interpretation of these passages by assuming that Homer conceived the earth to be flat and that as the Hades was a region of complete darkness, the sun could not be said to go there even after his setting. Dr. Warren has, however, shown that the assumption is entirely ground-

1. See Dr. Warren's Paradise Found, 10th Edition (1893), Part V, Chap. V, pp. 250-260.

less, and that Homer's earth was really a sphere and that the underworld was full of aerial waters. We have seen above, how some Vedic scholars have raised similar difficulties in the interpretation of the Vṛitra myth by supposing that the lower celestial hemisphere was unknown to the Vedic bards. This is probably a reflection of the Homeric controversy, but as pointed out by Dr. Warren,[1] these baseless assumptions are due mainly to a prejudice with which many scholars approach the question of the interpretation of ancient myths. It is assumed that the early man could not possibly have known anything about the world, beyond what the rudest savages know at present; and plain and explicit statements are sometimes put aside, distorted, or ignored by scholars, who, had they not been blinded by prejudice, would certainly have interpreted them in a different way. It is impossible to do justice to the subject in this place, and I would refer the reader for further details to Dr. Warren's instructive works on the subject. Dr. Warren also states that Euripides, like Homer, held the view that there was one fountain of all the world's water, and that the same conception is expressed by Hesiod in his *Theogony*, where all rivers as sons, and all fountains and brooks as daughters, are traced back to Okeanos. Then we have the constant descending movement of all waters until they reach the world-surrounding Ocean-river at the equator, beyond which is the underworld, similar to the movements of aerial waters described in the Avesta. Aristotle, in his *Meteors*, is said also to have mentioned "a river in the air constantly flowing betwixt the heaven and the earth and made by the ascending and the descending vapours."[2] It is again pointed by Grill that the ancient Germans had a similar world-river, and the descending Ukko's stream and the ascending Amma's stream in the Finnish mythology are similarly believed to be the traces of a like cosmic water-circulation.

1. Paradise Found, p. 333*f*. 2. Paradise Found, p. 51, and 256, notes.

We read of a golden boat also in the Lettish mythology; and Prof. Max Muller, referring to it, says, "What the golden boat is that sinks into the sea and is mourned for by the daughter of the sky, however, doubtful it may be elsewhere, is not to be mistaken in the mythology of the Lets. It is the setting sun, which in the Veda has to be saved by the Ashvins; it is the golden boat in which Hêlios and Hêracles sail from west to east. Sometimes it is the Sun-daughter herself that is drowned like Chyavâna in the Veda, and as Chyavâna and similar heroes had to be saved in the Veda by the Ashvins, the Lets also call upon the God-sons to row in a boat and save the Sun-daughter."[1] In connection with this, it may be here observed that the Ashvins are described in the Ṛig-Veda as saving their proteges in boats (I, 116, 3; I, 182, 6), and that though Ashvins' boats are not described as golden, their chariot is said to be *hiraṇyayî* or golden in VIII, 5, 29; while the boats of Pûṣhan, in which he crosses the aerial ocean (*samudra*), are actually said to be golden in VI, 58, 3. In I, 46, 7, the Ashvins are again spoken of as having both a chariot and a boat, as a sort of double equipment; and their chariot is said to be *samâna yojana*, or traversing, without distinction, both the heaven and the watery regions in I, 30, 18. The word *samâna* is meaningless unless there is some difficulty in traversing over one part of the celestial sphere as distinguished from the other. The Vedic gods used these boats especially in crossing the lower world, the home and seat of aerial waters; and when they appeared above the horizon, they are described as traversing the upper sphere by means of their chariots. But sometimes the waters are said to carry them even across the sky above, just as the chariot is described as going over the lower world. For instance in the legend of Dîrghatamas, discussed previously, he is said to be borne on waters for ten

1. See Max Muller's Contributions to the Science of Mythology, Vol. II, p. 433.

months and then growing old was about to die or reach the ocean, to which the waters were speeding. In other words, this means that the sun, who was borne on waters for ten months, was about to go into the lower watery regions as explained in the chapter VI. But to proceed with the subject in hand, the idea of the cosmic circulation of aerial waters, is not confined to the Indian, the Iranian or the Greek mythology. In the Egyptian mythology, Nu-t, the goddess of the sky, is sometimes "represented by a figure in which the band of stars is accompanied by a band of water"; and Sir Norman Lockyer tells us that "not only the Sun-gods, but the stars, were also supposed to travel in boats across the firmament from one horizon to the other."[1] The Jewish idea of the firmament in the midst of waters, the waters above being afterwards separated from the waters below the firmament, is already referred to above. There is, therefore, nothing strange or surprising if we find in the Vedas and in the Avesta more or less clear references to the circulation of aerial waters through the upper and the lower celestial hemispheres of the universe. It is an idea which is found in the ancient mythology of every other nation, and nothing but false prejudice can deter us from interpreting the simultaneous movements or the liberation of waters and light, described in the Vedic hymns, on the theory of the cosmic circulation of aerial waters.

But even after accepting the theory of the cosmic circulation of celestial waters and the simultaneous release of waters and dawn, it may be asked how the Arctic theory comes in, or is in any way required, to explain the Vṛitra legend. We may admit that the waters imprisoned by Vṛitra, by shutting up the passages through the rocky walls that surround them, may be taken to mean the celestial waters in the world below the three earths; but still, the struggle between Indra and Vṛitra may, for aught we know, represent

1. See Lockyer's Dawn of Astronomy, p. 35.

the *daily* fight between light and darkness, and it may be urged, that there is no necessity whatever, for bringing in the Arctic theory to explain the legend. A little reflection will, however, show that all the incidents in the legend cannot be explained on the theory of a daily struggle between light and darkness. In X, 62, 2, the Aṅgirases, who are the assistants of Indra in his conquest of cows, are said to have defeated Vala at the end of the year (*parivatsare*). This shows that the struggle was annual and did not take place every day. Then we have the passage (VIII, 32, 26), where Arbuda, the watery demon, is said to have been killed by Indra with ice (*hima*), and not with a thunderbolt as usual. In addition to the fact that the struggle was an yearly one, we must, therefore, hold that the conflict took place during winter, the season of ice and snow; and this is corroborated by the statement in the Avesta, that it was during winter that the waters, and with them the sun, ceased to move onwards. Vṛitra's forts are again described as autumnal or *shâradîḥ*, showing that the fight must have commenced at the end of *Sharad* (autumn) and continued during winter. We have further seen that there are a hundred night-sacrifices, and the duration of Tishtrya's fight with Apaosha is described as varying from one to a hundred nights in the Tîr Yasht. All these incidents can be explained only by the Arctic theory, or by the theory of the long autumnal night, and not on the hypothesis of a daily struggle between light and darkness.

We have come to the conclusion that Indra's fight with Vṛitra must have commenced in *Sharad*, and lasted till the end of *Shishira* in the watery regions of the nether world. Fortunately for us this conclusion is remarkably borne out by an important passage preserved in the Ṛig-Veda, which gives us, what may be called, the very date of the commencement of Indra's conflict with Vṛitra, though the true bearing of the passage has yet remained unexplained owing to the absence of the real key to its meaning. In II, 12, 11, we read, "Indra found Shambara dwelling on the mountains (in) *chatvârimshyâm sharadi*."[1] Now *chatvârimshyâm* is an ordinal numeral in the feminine gender and in the locative case, and similarly *sharadi* is the locative of *sharad* (autumn), which also is a word of feminine gender in Sanskrit. The phrase *chatvârimshyâm sharadi* is, therefore, capable of two interpretations or constructions, though the words are simple in themselves. *Chatvârimshyâm* literally means 'in the fortieth,' and *sharadi* 'in autumn.' If we now take *chatvârimshyâm* (in the fortieth) as an adjective qualifying *sharadi* (in autumn), the meaning of the phrase would be "in the fortieth autumn"; while if the two words are taken separately the meaning would be "on the fortieth, in autumn." Sâyaṇa and Western scholars have adopted the first construction, and understand the passage to mean, "Indra found Shambara dwelling on the mountains *in the fortieth autumn*, that is, in the fortieth year"; for the words indicating seasons, like *Vasanta* (spring), *Sharad* (autumn), or *Hemanta* (winter), are understood to denote a year, especially when used with a numeral adjective meaning more than one. This construction is grammatically correct, for *chatvârimshyâm* and *sharadi* being both in the feminine gender and in the locative case, the two words can be taken together, and understood to mean "in the fortieth autumn or year." But what are we to understand by the statement, that Shambara was found in the fortieth year by Indra? Are we to suppose that Indra was engaged in searching out the demon for 40 years, and it was only at the end of this long period that the enemy was, at last, found dwelling on the mountains? If so, Indra's conflict with Shambara cannot be daily or yearly, but must be supposed to have taken place only once in 40 years, an inference, which is

1. Ṛig. II, 12, 11,—यः शंबरं पर्वतेषु क्षियंतं चत्वारिंश्यां शरद्यन्वविंदत् । ओजायमानं यो अहिं जघान दानुं शयानं स जनास इंद्रः ॥

directly opposed to the statement (X, 62, 2) that "Vala was killed at the end of the year (*parivatsare*)." Some scholars try to get out of the difficulty by suggesting that the passage may be taken as referring to a famine or drought that occurred after 40 years, or that it may represent a forty years' war between the Aryans protected by Indra, and Shambara, the chief of the aboriginal races dwelling on the mountains ! But both these explanations are too far-fetched and imaginary to deserve any serious attention or refutation. The story of Shambara is mentioned in a number of places in the Ṛig-Veda, and everywhere it represents Indra's conflict with Vṛitra.[1] It is, therefore, preposterous to hold that a forty years' war with the aboriginies is referred to in this single passage, especially when the passage *is* capable of being interpreted differently without straining the words used. It is the most ordinary Sanskrit idiom to use the locative case in mentioning the month, the day, the season or the year, when a particular incident is said to have taken place. Thus, even now, we say, "*Kârttike, shukla-pakṣhe, trayodashyâm*," meaning "in the month of Kârttika, in the bright half, on the thirteenth (*titki* or day)." The feminine ordinal numerals, like *chaturthi*, *ekâdashî*, *trayodashî*, are always used, without any noun, to denote the *tithi* or the day of the month, or the fortnight, as the case may be. Thus in the Taittirîya Brâhmaṇa (I, 1, 9, 10), we have the expression "*yadi saṁvatsare na âdadhyât dvâdashyâm purastât âdadhyât*," meaning that "if the sacrificial fire is not consecrated at the end of the year (*saṁvatsare*), it should be consecrated on the twelfth (*dvâdashyâm*) afterwards." Here *dvâdashyâm* is a feminine ordinal in the locative case used by itself, and means "on the twelfth *tithi* or day" after the end of the year mentioned in the preceding sentence.

1. See the *Nivids*, quoted *supra* (p. 246). *Shambara-hatya* or the fight with Shambara, and *go-ishṭi* or the struggle for cows are declared to be the one and the same in these *nivids*.

Chatvârimshyâm, in the Vedic passage under discussion, may be similarly taken to denote the *fortieth tithi* or day, and *sharadi* the season at the time, the two words being taken as independent locatives. The passage would then mean "Indra found Shambara dwelling on the mountains on the *fortieth* (scil. *tithi* or day) in autumn."

Now *Sharad* is the fourth season of the year, and the fortieth day of *Sharad* would mean seven months and ten days, or 220 days, after the first day of *Vasanta* or the spring, which commenced the year in old times. In short, the passage means that Indra's fight with Shambara, or the annual conflict between light and darkness, commenced on the tenth day of the eighth month of the year, or on the 10th of October, if we take the year to have then commenced with March, the first month in the old Roman calendar. In I, 155, 6, Vishṇu, like a rounded wheel, is said to have set in swift motion his ninety racing steeds together with the four, and the reference is evidently to a year of four seasons of ninety days each. If we accept this division, each season would be of three months' duration, and *Sharad* being the third (cf. X, 90, 6), the fortieth day of *Sharad* would still mean the 10th day of the eighth month of the year. The passage thus gives the very date of Indra's annual fight with Vṛitra; and if it had been correctly understood, much useless speculation about the nature of Vṛitra's legend would have been avoided. We have seen previously that the seven Âdityas, or monthly Sun-gods, the sons of Aditi, were presented by her to the gods in a former *yuga*, and that she cast away the eighth, the Mârtâṇḍa, because he was born in an undeveloped state. In other words, the Sun-god of the eighth month is here said to have died soon after he was born, evidently meaning, that the Sun went below the horizon in the beginning of the eighth month; and by fixing the date of the commencement of Indra's fight with Vṛitra as the fortieth day in *Sharad*, or the 10th day of the eight month, we arrive at the same conclusion. The legend of Aditi and the date of the commencement of Indra's fight with Shambara, as given in II, 12, 11, thus corroborate each other in a remarkable way; and as the current interpretation of the passage does not yield any intelligible sense, there is no course left for us but to accept the only other possible interpretation.

According to this interpretation *Sharad* becomes the last season of sunshine, and it may be here remarked that the etymological meaning of the word further supports the same view. For *Sharad* is derived from *shṛî*, to wither or waste away, (Uṇâdi 127), and the word thus primarily signifies the 'season of decay or withering'; and the decay here referred to is evidently the decay of the power of the sun, and not the withering of grass, as suggested by Sâyaṇa in his commentary on III, 32, 9. Thus we find in the Taittirîya Saṁhitâ, II, 1, 2, 5, that "There are three lustres or powers of the sun; one in *Vasanta*, that is, in the morning; one in *Grîshma* or the mid-day; and one in *Sharad* or the evening."[1] We cannot suppose that the words, morning, mid-day and evening, are here used in their primary sense. The three stages of the day represented by them are predicated of the yearly sun, and *Sharad* is said to be the evening, *i.e.*, the time of decline in his yearly course. It follows, therefore, that after *Sharad* there was no period of sunshine in ancient times; and a Vedic passage,[2] quoted by Shabara in his commentary on Jaimini Suttras VI, 7, 40, says, "The sun is all the seasons; when it is morning (*uditi*), it is *Vasanta*; when the milking time (*saṅgava*), it is *Grîshma*;

1. Taitt. Saṁ. II, 1, 2, 5,—त्रीणि वा आदित्यस्य तेजांसि वसंता प्रातर्ग्रीष्मे मध्यंदिने शरद्यपराह्णे । यावंत्येव तेजांसि तान्येवावरुंधे । Also compare Taitt. Saṁ. II, 1, 4, 2.

2. Shabara or Jaimini VI, 7, 40, quotes, आदित्यो वा सर्वे ऋतवः स यदैवोदेत्यथ वसंतो यदा संगवोऽथ ग्रीष्मो यदा मध्यंदिनोऽथ वर्षा यदाऽपराह्णोऽथ शरद् यदास्तमेत्यथ हेमंतशिशिरौ । I have not been able to trace the passage; but it clearly states that the last two seasons formed the night of the yearly sun.

when mid-day (*madhyan-dina*), it is *Varshâ*; when evening (*aparâhṇa*), it is *Sharad*; when it sets (*astam eti*), it is the dual season of *Hemanta* and *Shishira*." If this passage has any meaning, it shows that the powers of the sun declined in *Sharad*, and the end of *Sharad* (autumn), therefore, represented his annual succumbing to the powers of darkness; or, in short, the dual season of *Hemanta* and *Shishira* represented the long night when the sun went below the horizon. It may also be mentioned that the word *himyâ* (*lit.* wintry) is used in the Ṛig-Veda for night (I, 34, 1), implying that the wintry season was the season of special darkness.

But it may be urged that we have no authority for holding that, in ancient days, time was reckoned simply by seasons and days; and *chatvârimshyâm sharadi* cannot, therefore, be interpreted to mean "On the 40th (day) in *Sharad*." The objection is not, however, well-founded; for in ancient inscriptions we find many instances where dates of events are recorded only by reference to seasons. Thus in the book on the *Inscriptions from the Cave-Temples of Western India*, by Dr. Burgess and Paṇḍit Bhagwânlâl Indrâji, published by the Government of Bombay in 1881, the date of inscription No. 14 is given as follows:—"Of king (*raño*) Vâsiṭhîputa, the illustrious lord (*sâmi-siri*) [Puḷumâyi] in the year seventh (7), of *Grîshma* the fifth (5) fortnight, and first (1) day." Upon this Dr. Burgess remarks that "the mention of the 5th fortnight of *Grîshma* shows that the year was not divided into six seasons (*ṛitu*) but into three, namely, *Grîshma*, *Varshâ* and *Hemanta*." But what is important for our purpose in this inscription is the method of giving the date by seasons, fortnights and days, without any reference to the month. This inscription is followed in the same book by others, one of which (No. 20) is thus dated:—"In the twenty-fourth year (24) of the king Vâsiṭhîputa, the illustrious Puḷimâvi, in the third (3) fortnight of the winter (*hemanta*) months, on the second (2) day"; and another is said to be inscribed "On the tenth day, in the sixth fortnight of *Grishma*, in the eighth year of king Mâḍhariputta, the lord Sîrisena."[1] Dr. Bhâṇḍârkar, in his *Early History of the Deccan*, has ascertained that Mâḍhariputta reigned in the Mahârâshṭra from about A. D. 190 to 197, and Puḷumâyi was on the throne of the Mahârâshṭra about 60 years earlier, that is, from A. D. 130 to 154. All the inscriptions noted above, therefore, belong to the 2nd century of the Christian era, that is, a long time before the date of Ârya Bhaṭṭa or Varâhamihira, whose works seem to have established, if not introduced, the present system of measuring time by seasons, months, fortnights and days. It is, therefore, clear that eighteen hundred years ago, dates of events were recorded and ascertained by mentioning only the season, the fortnight and the day of the fortnight, without any reference to the month of the year; and we might very well suppose that several centuries before this period these dates were given by a still more simple method, namely, by mentioning only the season and the day of that season. And, as a matter of fact, we do find this method of measuring time, *viz.*, by seasons and days, adopted in the Avesta to mark the particular days of the year. Thus in the Âfrigân Gâhanbâr (I, 7-12), as written in some manuscripts mentioned by Westergaard in his notes on the Âfrigân, there is a statement of the dif-

1. Inscription No. 14 of Kârle inscriptions runs thus :—रञो वासिठिपुतस सामिसिरि पुकुमाविस सवछरे सतमे ७ गिम्हपंखे पचमे ५ दिवसे पथमे १; (or in Sanskrit—राज्ञो वासिठीपुत्रस्य स्वामिश्री पुकुमाविनः संवत्सरे सप्तमे ७, ग्रीष्मपक्षे पंचमे ५, दिवसे प्रथमे १).

Inscription No. 20 of the same section runs thus :—सिधं रञो वासिठिपुतस सिरिपुळुमाविस सवछरे चतुविसे २४ हेमतान पखे ततिये ३ दिवसे बितिये २; (or in Sanskrit—सिद्धम्। राज्ञो वासिष्ठीपुत्रस्य श्रीपुळुमावेः संवत्सरे चतुर्विंशे २४, हैमन्तानां पक्षे तृतीये ३, दिवसे द्वितीये २).

An inscription from the Kânheri cave (p. 60) is as follows :—सिधं रञो माढरीपुतस स्वामिसिरिसेनस सवछरे ८ गिप ५ दिव १०; (or in Sanskrit—सिद्धम्। राज्ञो माढरिपुत्रस्य स्वामिश्रीसेनस्य संवत्सरे ८, ग्री.प. ५, दिव. १०).

ferent rewards which a Mazdayasnian receives in the next life for what he gives as present in this to the Ratu (religious head); and we have therein such expressions as "On the 45th (day) of Maidhyô-Zaremya, *i. e.*, on (the day) Dae of (the month) Ardibehest;" or "On the 60th (day) of Maidhyôshma, *i.e.*, on (the day) Dae of (the month) Tîr;" and so on. Here each date is given in two different ways: *first*, by mentioning the Gâhanbâr or the season (the year being divided into six Gâhanbârs), and the day of that season; and *secondly*, by mentioning the month and the day of that month. Strictly speaking there is no necessity to adopt this double method of marking the days of the year, for either of them is enough to accurately define the day required. It is, therefore, highly probable, as remarked by Mr. Ervad Jamshedji Dadabhai Nadershah, that the method of counting by seasons and days is the older of the two, and the phrases containing the names of months and days are later interpolations, made at a time when the older method was superseded by the latter.[1] But even supposing that the double phrases were used originally, we can, so far as our present purpose is concerned, safely infer from these passages that the method of marking the days of the year by mentioning the season and the day thereof was in vogue at the time when the Âfrigân was written; and if the method is so old, it fully warrants us in interpreting *chatvârimshyâm sharadi* to mean "On the 40th (day) in *Sharad* (autumn)." There can be little doubt that the Vedic bards have recorded in this passage the exact date of the commencement of Indra's fight with Shambara, but in the absence of the true key to its meaning the passage has been so long unfortunately misunderstood and misinterpreted both by Eastern and Western scholars. The grammatical possibility of connecting *chatvârimshyâm*, as an adjective, with *sharadi* helped on

1. See his essay on "The Zoroastrian months and years with their divisions in the Avestic age" in the *Cama Memorial Volume*, pp. 251-254.

this misconception; and though Vedic scholars were unable to explain why Shambara, according to their interpretation, should be described as having been found in the 40th year, yet they seemed to have accepted the interpretation because no other meaning appeared possible to them. The alternative construction proposed by me above is very simple. Instead of taking *chatvârimshyâm* as an adjective qualifying *sharadi*, I take the two words as independent locatives, but the change in the meaning caused thereby is very striking and important; and so long as the Arctic theory was unknown, the attention of scholars was not likely to be drawn to this alternative construction.[1] But now we can very well understand why Indra is said to have found Shambara on the 40th (day) of *Sharad*, and why the forts, which gave shelter to the demon, are described as *shâradîḥ*, as well as why Arbuda or the watery demon is said to be killed by ice (*hima*). I have stated before that the forts (*puraḥ*) of Shambara must be understood to mean 'days,' and the adjective *shâradîḥ* only serves to streng-

1. A similar phrase is found also in the Atharva Veda (XII, 3, 34 and 41). The hymn describes the preparation of *Brahmaudana*, or the porridge given as a fee to the Brâhmans, and in the 34th verse it is stated that "The treasurer shall fetch it in sixty autumns, (*shashṭyâm sharatsu nidhipâ abhîchhât*)." But, as remarked by Prof. Bloomfield (*vide* his translation of A.V. with notes in S. B. E. Series, Vol. XLII, p. 651), the meaning of the phrase "sixty autumns" is obscure; and the only other alternative possible is to take *shashṭyâm* as the locative of *shashṭî* (feminine form, in long *î*, of *shashṭa*) meaning "the 60th"; and interpret the original phrase to mean "On the 60th (*tithi*) in autumns." The word *shashṭa* cannot be used in classical Sanskrit as an ordinal numeral according to Pâṇini (V, 2, 58); but the rule does not seem to hold strictly in Vedic Sanskrit (*See* Whitney's Grammar, § 487). Even in the post-Vedic literature we meet with such ordinal forms as *shashṭa*, *ashṭta*, &c. Thus the colophon of the 60th chapter of the Sabhâ- and the Udyoga-parvan of the Mahâbhârata (Roy's Cal. Ed.) reads thus:—*Iti...shashṭaḥ adhyâyaḥ*, shewing that *shashṭa* was used at the time as an ordinal numeral, (*See* Pet. Lex. s. v. *shashṭa*). The *Brahmaudana* is, according to this interpretation, to be cooked on the 60th day in autumns, *i. e.*, at the end of *Sharad* every year.

then the same view. The disappearance of the sun below the horizon in the beginning of the 8th month in autumn, followed by a long twilight, a continuous dark night of about 100 days, and a long dawn of 30 days in the Arctic regions, is the basis of the legend, and every incident therein can be naturally and intelligibly explained only on this theory.

There is one more incident in the Vṛitra legend which requires to be considered before we close its examination. We have seen that water and light are described as having been simultaneously liberated by Indra after slaughtering Vṛitra. These waters are sometimes spoken of as streams or rivers (II, 15, 3; 11, 2), which flow *upwards* or *udañcha* (II, 15, 6), and are said to be *seven* in number (I, 32, 12; II, 12, 12). The theory of the cosmic circulation of aerial waters explains why these waters are described as flowing *upwards* simultaneously with the dawn, for as the sun was believed to be carried in the sky by aerial currents, the light of the sun appeared above the horizon when the aerial rivers began to flow *up* from the nether world where they had been blocked before by Vṛitra. The waters or the rivers were, therefore, aptly described as flowing upwards and bringing the light of the sun with them. But we have still to answer the question why the rivers or waters are described as *seven* in number, and it is alleged that the Storm theory supplies us with a satisfactory reply to this question. Thus it has been suggested by Western scholars that the seven rivers, here referred to, are the seven rivers of the Panjaub which are flooded during the rainy season by waters released by Indra from the clutches of the demon who confines them in the storm-cloud. The rivers of the Panjaub may therefore, it is urged, be well described as being set free to flow (*sartave*) by Indra himself, and in support of this explanation we are referred to the Ṛig-Veda X, 75, and to the phrase *hapta-hindu* occurring in Fargard I of the Vendidad, where it is said to denote the Panjaub or India. But the hypothesis, howsoever tempting it may seem at the first sight, is quite inadequate to explain the seven-fold division of waters in a satisfactory way. It has been pointed out above that the simultaneous release of waters and light can be accounted for only on the theory of the cosmic circulation of aerial waters; and if this is correct, we cannot identify the seven rivers, set free to flow *upwards* (*udañcha*) by Indra, with any terrestrial rivers whether in the Panjaub or elsewhere. The Panjaub is, again, as its name indicates, a land of *five* and not of seven rivers; and it is so described in the Vâjasaneyî Saṁhitâ.* The term *pañcha-nada* is, therefore, more appropriate in the case of the Panjaub, than *sapta sindhavaḥ* or the *Hapta-hindu* of the Avesta. But we might get over the difficulty by supposing that Kubhâ and Sarasvatî, or any other two tributaries of the Indus were included in the group by the Vedic bards, when they spoke of seven rivers. In the Ṛig-Veda (X, 75), about fifteen different rivers are mentioned, including the Gaṅgâ, the Yamunâ, the Kubhâ, the Krumu, the Gomatî, the Rasâ, and the five rivers of the Panjaub; but nowhere do we find what specific rivers were included in the group of seven rivers. This has given rise to a difference of opinion amongst scholars. Thus Sâyaṇa includes the Ganges and the Jamuna in the group, which, according to Prof. Max Muller, is made up by adding the Indus and the Sarasvatî to the five rivers of the Panjaub. On the other hand, Lassen and Ludwig hold that the Kubhâ must be included in the group at the cost of the Sarasvati. This shows that we are not on a safe ground in supposing that the expression "seven rivers" once meant what is, by nature, "the land of five rivers." The expression *sapta sindhavaḥ* occurs in about a dozen places in the Ṛig-Veda, and in five of these it distinctly denotes the seven rivers set free by

* See Vâj. Saṁ. XXXIV, 11,—पंच नद्यः सरस्वतीमपि यंति सस्रोतसः। सरस्वती तु पंचधा सो देशेऽभवत् सरित्॥ Here सो is equal to सा and उ:

Indra along with the release of cows or the recovery of dawn (I, 32, 12 ; II, 12, 3 and 12 ; IV, 28, 1, &c.) ; and for reasons given above, we cannot suppose that they represent any terrestrial rivers in these passages. In the remaining cases, there is not a single instance where the expression may be said to decisively denote only the terrestrial rivers; nay, it is more likely that celestial rivers are referred to everywhere by the expression of *sapta sindhavaḥ*. I do not mean to say that *sapta sindhavaḥ, sapta pravataḥ*, or *sapta sravataḥ* can in no case denote any terrestrial rivers. For there are three groups of seven rivers mentioned in the Ṛig-Veda,—the celestial, the terrestrial and the infernal. Thus in X, 64, 8, "thrice three wandering rivers" are mentioned ; while the waters are said "to flow forward triply, seven and seven" in X, 75, 1. It is, therefore, clear that like the Ganges in the Purâṇas, the Vedic bards conceived a group of seven rivers in the heaven, another on the earth, and a third in the nether world, somewhat after the manner of the eleven gods in the heaven, eleven on the earth, and eleven in the waters (I, 139, 11; 134, 11; X, 65, 9). If so, we cannot say that a seven-fold division of the terrestrial rivers was not known to the Vedic bards. But, for reasons given above, we cannot hold that this seven-fold division was suggested by the rivers of the Panjaub ; and then extended to the upper and the lower celestial hemisphere. The Panjaub, as remarked above, is a land of five rivers and not seven ; and though we might raise the number to seven by adding to the group *any two* insignificant tributaries according to our fancy, yet the artificial character of the device is too apparent to justify us in holding that the expression *sapta sindhavaḥ* was *originally* suggested by the rivers of the Panjaub. We must again bear in mind that the seven-fold division of waters does not stand by itself in the Ṛig-Veda ; but is only a particular case of a general principle of division adopted therein. Thus we have seven earthly abodes (I, 22, 16), seven mountains (VIII,96, 2), seven rays or horses of the sun (I, 164, 3), seven *hotṛis* (VIII, 60, 16), seven regions (*dishaḥ*) and seven Âdityas (IX, 114, 3), seven *dhîtis* or devotions (IX, 8, 4), seven sisters or *maryâdâḥ*, (X, 5, 5-6), and possibly seven and seven gods (X, 55, 3), in the Ṛig-Veda; while in the later Sanskrit literature we have the seven heavens, seven earths, seven mountains, seven oceans and seven nether worlds. This seven-fold division is also found in other Aryan mythologies, as, for instance, in the Avesta, where the earth is said to be divided into seven Karshavares (Yt. X, 16 and 64), and in the Greek mythology, which speaks of the seven layers of heaven over one another. It follows, therefore, that the seven-fold division must be traced back almost to the Indo-European period; and if so, we cannot maintain that the seven-fold division of waters, which is only a particular case of the general principle, was suggested by the rivers of the Panjaub, for, in that case, we shall have to make the Panjaub the home of the Aryans before they separated. But if the rivers set free to flow *up* by Indra are not terrestrial, and if the expression *sapta sindhavaḥ* was not originally suggested by the rivers of the Panjaub, it may be asked how we account for the number of rivers and the origin of the phrase *Hapta-hindu* occurring in the Avesta. The true key to the solution of the question will be found in the simultaneous release of waters and light effected by Indra after conquering Vṛitra. In II, 12, 12, Indra, who caused the seven rivers to flow, is described as *sapta-rashmiḥ*, or seven-rayed, suggesting that seven rays and seven rivers must have, in some way, been connected. We have also seen that the waters and the sun are said to move at the same time in the Parsi scriptures. If so, what can be more natural than to suppose that the seven suns required seven horses or seven aerial rivers to carry them over the sky, much in the same way as Dîrghatamas is said to have been borne upon waters in I, 158, 6? Again according to the legend of Aditi, there were seven suns or month-gods located in seven different regions and producing seven months of sun-shine of different temperatures. But how could the seven suns move in seven different parts of heaven except by the agency of seven different aerial rivers coming up from the nether world, each with its own sun? In short, when the close connection between waters and light is once established, it is not difficult to perceive why the waters and light are each said to be seven-fold. The seven celestial rivers are expressly mentioned in the Ṛig-Veda (IX, 54,2), and the flowing forth of the seven rivers and the appearance of the dawn on the horizon are described as simultaneous in many passages, some of which have been already referred to above. Neither the Storm theory, nor the geography of the Panjaub, satisfactorily accounts for the simultaneous happening of these events; and so long as this difficulty is not solved, except by the Arctic theory and the cosmic circulation of aerial waters, we cannot accept the hypothesis of Western scholars referred to above, howsoever eloquently expounded it may be. As regards the origin of the phrase *Hapta-hindu*, which is believed to denote India in the Avesta, I think, we can explain it by supposing that the expression *sapta sindhavaḥ* was an old one, carried by the Aryans with them to their new home, and there applied to new places or countries, just as the British colonists now carry the old names of their mother country to their new places of settlement. *Hapta-hindu* is not the only expression which occurs in the Avesta in the enumeration of the Aryan countries. We have, Vârena, Haêtumant, Rangha and Harahvaiti in the list, which are the Zend equivalents of Varuṇa, Setumat, Rasâ and Sarasvatî.[1] But it is never argued from it

1. Darmesteter, in his introduction to Fargard I of the Vendidad, observes that "names, originally belonging to mythical lands, are often, in later times, attached to real ones." If this is true of Varena, Rangha (Rasâ), and other names, there is no reason why *Hapta-hindu* should not be similarly explained, especially when it is now clear that the phrase *sapta sindhavaḥ* denotes celestial rivers in the Vedas.

that the Vedic deity, Varuṇa, was so named from the country called Varena by the worshippers of Mazda; and the same may be said of Rasâ and Sarasvatî. Rasâ and Sarasvatî sometimes denote the terrestrial rivers even in the Ṛig-Veda. But there is ample evidence to show that they were originally the aerial rivers. It is, therefore, more natural to hold that all these were ancient mythological names brought with them by they Aryan settlers to their new home and there applied to new places or objects. There are places in Burma which are named Ayodhya, Mithila, &c., and this is explained on the ground that they were so named by the Indian settlers in Burma after the well-known places in their native land. There is no reason why the same theory should not be applied in the case of *Hapta-hindu*, especially when we see that the rivers set free by Indra by slaughtering Vṛitra cannot but be celestial.

It will be seen from the foregoing discussion that the true nature and movements of waters released by Indra from the grasp of Vṛitra has been misunderstood from the days of the most ancient Nairuktas, or, we might say, even from the days of the Brâhmaṇas. There are passages in the Ṛig-Veda where Pûshan is said to cross the upper celestial hemisphere in boats; but the Ashvins and Sûrya are generally described as traversing the heaven in their chariots. This led the ancient Nairuktas to believe that the upper celestial hemisphere was not a seat of aerial waters, and that when Indra was described as releasing waters by slaughtering Vṛitra, the waters referred to could not but be the waters imprisoned in the rain-clouds. The seven rivers set free to flow by killing Vṛitra were similarly understood to be the rivers of India, like the Ganges, the Jamuna, &c., while the piercing of the mountains was explained away by distorting or straining the meaning of such words as, *parvata*, *giri*, &c., as stated above. It was at this stage that the subject was taken in hand by Western scholars, who, taking their cue from the *Hapta-hindu* of the Avesta, eloquently advanced the theory that the seven rivers, set free by Indra, were the rivers of the Panjaub. This explanation, when first started, was regarded as an important historical discovery; and so it would have been, if it had been a real fact. But, as pointed out above, the Panjanb is, by nature, a land of five rivers and not seven; and it is so described in the Vâjasaneyî Saṁhitâ. It is also evident that as the seven rivers, set free to flow by Indra, were released simultaneously with the dawn, they could not be the rivers of the Panjaub. We do not mean to say that the Panjaub was not an Aryan settlement at the time when the Vedic hymns were sung, for the rivers of the Panjaub are expressly mentioned in the Ṛig-Veda. But the rivers of the Panjaub were not the seven rivers mentioned in the *Vedas*; and if so, a new explanation of the Vṛitra legend becomes necessary, and such an explanation is furnished only by the theory of the cosmic circulation of aerial waters or rivers through the lower and the upper world, carrying along with them the sun, the moon and the other heavenly bodies. We can now very well explain how Vṛitra, by stretching his body cross, closed the passages in the mountainous ranges (*parvatas*), which, on the analogy of mountains usually seen on the horizon, were believed to lie between the upper and the lower world; and how the waters, and with them the sun and the dawn, were prevented from coming up from the nether world for a long time in the Arctic home of the ancestors of the Vedic bards. Another point elucided by the present theory is the four-fold character of the effects of Indra's conquest over Vṛitra, a point which has been entirely neglected by ancient and modern Nairuktas, not because it was unknown but because they were unable to give any satisfactory explanation of the same, except on the hypothesis that different effects have been confounded with each other by the poets of the Ṛig-Veda. But the theory of the cosmic circulation of aerial waters, a theory which is also found in the mythology of many other nations, now clears up the whole mystery. If Indra is described as the leader or the releaser of waters (*apâm netâ*, or *apâm srashṭâ*), the waters do not mean the waters in the clouds, but the waters or the watery vapours which fill the universe, and formed the material out of which the latter was created. In other words, the conquest over waters was something grander, something far more marvelous and cosmic in character than the mere breaking up of the clouds in the rainy season; and under these circumstances it was naturally considered to be the greatest of Indra's exploits, when, invigorated by a hundred nightly Soma sacrifices, he slew with ice the watery demon of darkness, shattered his hundred autumnal forts, released the waters or the seven rivers upstream to go along their aerial way and brought out the sun and the dawn, or the cows, from their place of confinement inside the rocky caves, where they had stood still since the date of the war, which, according to a Vedic passage, hitherto misread and misunderstood, commenced in higher latitudes every year on the 40th day of *Sharad* or autumn and lasted till the end of winter. It is not contended that Indra had never been the god of rain. There are a few passages in the Ṛig-Veda (IV, 26, 2; VIII, 6, 1), where he is expressly mentioned as sending down rain, or is compared to a rain-god. But as Vṛitra-han or the killer of Vṛitra and the releaser of waters and the dawn, it is impossible to identify him with the god of rain. The story of the release of captive waters is an ancient story; for Vṛitra appears as Orthros in the Greak mythology, and Vṛitra-han, as Verethragna, is the god of victory in the Parsi scriptures. Now this Vṛitra-han may not have been originally the same as Indra, for the word *Indra* does not occur in European Aryan languages, and it has, therefore, been suggested by some comparative mythologians that the conquest of waters, which was originally the exploit of some other

Aryan deity, was probably ascribed to Indra in the Vedic mythology, when Indra became the principal deity in the Vedic pantheon. The fact that Tishtrya, and not Verethraghna, is said to be the releaser of waters and light in the Avesta, lends some support to this theory. But whichever view we adopt, it does not affect the conclusion we have come to above regarding the true explanation of the Vṛitra legend. Clouds and rain cannot constitute the physical basis of the legend, which is evidently based on the simple phenomenon of bringing light to the people who had anxiously waited for it during the darkness of the long night in the Arctic regions; and it is a pity that any misconception regarding Vedic cosmography, or the nature of waters and their cosmic movements, should have, for sometime at least, stood in the way of the true interpretation of this important legend. Indra may have become a storm-god afterwards; or the conquest over Vṛitra, originally achieved by some other deity, may have come to be ascribed to Indra, the rain-god in later times. But whether the exploits of *Vṛitra-han* were subsequently ascribed to Indra, or whether Indra, as the releaser of captive waters, was afterwards mistaken for the god of rain, like Tishtrya in the Avesta, one fact stands out boldly amidst all details, *viz.*, that captive waters were the aerial waters in the nether world, and that their captivity represented the annual struggle between light and darkness in the original home of the Aryans in the Arctic region; and if this fact was not hitherto discovered, it was because our knowledge of the ancient man was too meagre to enable us to perceive it properly.

VṚITRA TRIUMPHANT.

(WATERS AND THE SUN CONFINED)

1. Varuṇa's tree. 2. Waters.

VṚITRA SLAIN.

(WATERS AND THE SUN SET FREE TO MOVE)

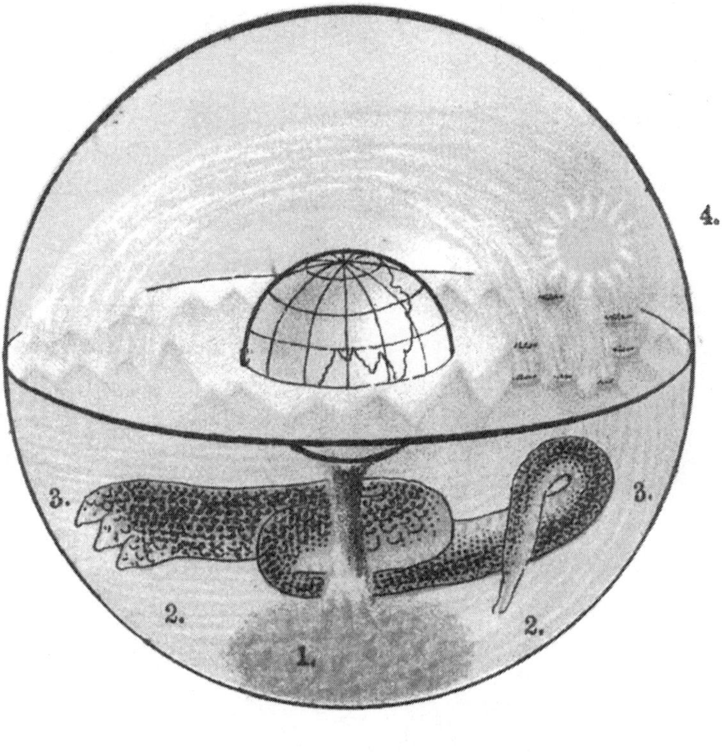

3. Vṛitra, as a Serpent. 4. The Sun.

CHAPTER X.

VEDIC MYTHS—THE MATUTINAL DEITIES.

Vernal theory and the legends of the Ashvins —The part played by the Ashvins in the struggle for waters and light —Intelligible only on the Arctic theory —Their exploits and legends —Saving or rejuvenating, rescuing from the ocean, or restoring the eye-sight or light, to Chyavâna, Rebha, Bhujyu, Atri, Vandana &c.—All explained at present as referring to the rescue of the daily dawn or the vernal restoration of the powers of the winter sun —But the theory fails to explain references to blindness or darkness in several legends —Nor does it account for the duration of the distress of the Ashvins' proteges —Nor for the character of the place of distress from which the proteges were saved —Bottomless and dark ocean really means the nether world —A bowl with bottom up and mouth downwards indicates the inverted hemisphere of the Hades —Legend of Rijrâshva —The slaughter of a hundred sheep represents the conversion of a hundred days into so many nights —The story of Saptavadhri or the seven-eunuch, praying for safe delivery after ten months of gestation —Remains unexplained up to the present —The interior of heaven and earth is conceived in the Veda as the womb in which the sun moves when above the horizon —Ten months' gestation thus represents the ten months when the Sun is above the horizon —Prayer for safe delivery indicates the perils of the long night —Riddle or paradox of a child becoming invisible as soon as born —The story of the hidden Agni refers to the same phenomenon —Probable origin of the Purânic story of Kumâra or Kârttikeya —Superiority of the Arctic over the Vernal theory in explaining the legends of the Ashvins —The legend of Indra's stealing Sûrya's wheel —The meaning of *dasha-prapitve* discussed —Indicates darkness on the completion of ten months —Vishnu's three strides —Different opinions about their nature quoted —Vishnu's strides represent the yearly course of the sun —And his third invisible step represents the nether world —Vishnu's opprobrious name, Shipivishta —Represents the dark or the diseased sun during the long Arctic night —The three abodes of Savitri, Agni and the Ashvins compared to Vishnu's third step —The legend of Trita A'ptya —Trita, or the third, represents the third part of the year —The Indo-Germanic origin of the legend —The A'pas —Their character and nature described —Seven-fold and ten-fold division of things in the Vedic literature —Various instances of seven-fold and ten-fold division collected —This two-fold division probably due to the seven and ten months' period of sunshine in the Arctic region —The Dâsharâjna fight —Represents struggle with the ten-fold division of darkness —Brihaspati and his lost wife in the Rig-Veda —The ten non-sacrificing kings and Râvana compared —Mythical element in the Râmâyana probably derived from the Vedic mythology —Hanumân and Vrishâkapi —Was Râmâyana copied from Homer —Both may have a common source —Conclusion.

THE inadequacy of the Storm theory to explain the legend of Indra and Vṛitra has been fully set forth in the last chapter; and we have seen how a number of points therein, hitherto unintelligible, can be explained by the Arctic theory, combined with the true conception of the circulation of aerial waters in the upper and the nether world. We shall now take up the legends that are usually explained on the Vernal theory, and show how, like the Storm theory, it fails to account satisfactorily for the different features of these legends. Such legends are to be found amongst the achievements of the Ashvins, the physicians of the gods. These achievements are summed up as it were in certain hymns of the Ṛig-Veda (I, 112; 116; 117; 118), each of which briefly refers to the important exploits of these twin gods. As in the case of Vṛitra, the character of the Ashvins and their exploits are explained by different schools of interpreters in different ways. Thus Yâska (Nir. XII,1) informs us that the two Ashvins are regarded by some as representing Heaven and Earth, by others as Day and Night, or as Sun and Moon; while the Aitihâsikas take them to be two ancient kings, the performers of holy acts. But as before, we propose to examine the legends connected with the Ashvins only according to the naturalistic or the Nairukta school of interpretation. Even in this school there are, however, a number of different views held regarding the nature and the character of these two gods. Some believe that the natural basis of the Ashvins must be the morning star, that being the only morning-light visible before fire, dawn and sun; while others think that the two stars in the constellation of Gemini were the original representatives of the twin gods. The achievements of these gods are, however, generally explained as referring to the restoration of the powers of the sun decayed in winter; and an elaborate discussion of the Ashvins' exploits on this theory will be found in the *Contributions to the Science of Mythology*, (Vol. II, pp. 583-605), by Prof. Max Muller, published a few years ago. It is beyond the scope of this work to examine each one of the different legends connected with the Ashvins, as Prof. Max Muller has done. We are concerned only with those points in the legends which the Vernal or the Dawn theory fails to explain, and which can be well accounted for only by the Arctic theory; and these we now proceed to notice.

Now, in the first place, we must refer to the part played by the Ashvins in the great struggle or fight for waters and light, which has been discussed in the previous chapter. The Ashvins are distinctly mentioned in the sacrificial literature as one of the deities connected with the Dawn (Ait. Br. II, 15); and we have seen that a long laudatory song recited by the Hotṛi before sunrise is specially devoted to them. The daughter of Sûrya is also described as having ascended their car (I, 116, 17; 119, 5), and the Aitareya Brâhmaṇa, (IV, 7-9), describes a race run by the gods for obtaining the *Âshvina-shastra* as a prize; and the Ashvins, driving in a carriage drawn by donkeys, are said to have won it in close competition with Agni, Uṣhas and Indra, who are represented as making way for the Ashvins, on the understanding that after winnig the race the Ashvins would assign to them a share in the prize. The kindling of the sacrificial fire, the break of the dawn, and the rise of the sun are again spoken of as occurring simultaneously with the appearance of the Ashvins (I, 157, 1; VII, 72, 4); while in X, 61, 4, the time of their appearance is said to be the early dawn when "darkness still stands amongst the ruddy cows." Their connection with the dawn and their appearance in the interval between dawn and sunrise are thus taken to be clearly established; and whatever theory we may adopt to explain the character of the Ashvins on a physical basis, we cannot lose sight of the fact that they are matutinal deities, bringing on the dawn or the light of the morning along with them. The two epithets which are peculiar to Indra, *viz. Vṛitrahan*, and *Shata-kratu* are applied to them (*Vṛitrahantamâ*, VIII, 8, 22; *Shata-kratû*, I, 112, 23); and in I, 182, 2, they are expressly said to possess strongly the qualities of Indra (*Indra-tamâ*), and of the Maruts (*Marut-tamâ*) the associates of Indra in his struggle with Vṛitra. Nay, they are said to have protected Indra in his achievements against Namuchi in X, 131, 4. This leaves no doubt about their share in the Vṛitra-fight; and equally clear is their connection with the waters of the ocean. In I, 46, 2, they are called *sindhu-mâtarâ*, or having the ocean for their mother, and their car is described as turning up from the ocean in IV, 43, 5; while in I, 112, 13, the Ashvins in their car are said to go round the sun in the distant region (*parâvati*). We also read that the Ashvins moved the most sweet *sindhu* or ocean, evidently meaning that they made the waters of the ocean flow forward (I, 112, 9); and they are said to have made Rasâ, a celestial river, swell full with water-floods, urging to victory the car without the horse (I, 112, 12). They are also the protectors of the great Atithigva and Divodâsa against Shambara; and Kutsa, the favourite of Indra, is also said to have been helped by them (I, 112, 14 and 23). In verse 18 of the same hymn, the Ashvins are addressed as Aṅgirases, and said to have triumphed in their hearts and went onwards to liberate the flood of milk; while in VIII, 26, 17, we read that they abide in the sea of heaven (*divo arṇave*). Taking all these facts together, we can easily see that the Ashvins were the helpers of Indra in his struggle for waters and light; and we now know what that struggle means. It is the struggle between the powers of light and darkness, and the Ashvins, in their character as divine physicians, were naturally the first to help the gods in this distress or affliction. It is true that Indra was the principal actor or hero in this fight; but the Ashvins appear to have stood by him, rendering help whenever necessary, and leading the van in the march of the matutinal deities after the conquest. This character of the Ashvins is hardly explained by the Vernal theory; nor can it be accounted for on the theory of a daily struggle between light and darkness, for we have seen that the dawn, during which the *Âshvina-shastra* is recited, is not the evanescent dawn of the tropics. The Arctic theory alone can satisfactorily interpret the facts stated above; and when they are interpreted in this way, it is easy to perceive how the Ashvins are described as having rejuvenated, cured, or rescued a number of decrepit, blind, lame or distressed proteges of theirs in the various legends ascribed to them.

The important achievements of the Ashvins have been summed up by Macdonell in his *Vedic Mythology* (§ 21) as follows :—

"The sage Chyavâna, grown old and deserted, they released from his decrepit body; they prolonged his life, restored him to youth, rendered him desirable to his wife and made him the husband of maidens (I, 116, 10 &c). They also renewed the youth of the aged Kali, and befriended him when he had taken a wife (X, 39, 8; I, 112, 15). They brought, on a car, to the youthful Vimada wives or a wife named Kamadyû (X, 65, 12), who seems to have been the beautiful spouse of Purumitra (I, 117, 20). They restored Vishṇâpû, like a lost animal, to the sight of their worshipper Vishvaka, son of Kṛishṇa (I, 116, 23 ; X, 65, 12). But the story most often referred to is that of the rescue of Bhujyu, son of Tugra, who was abandoned in the midst of ocean (*samudre*), or in the water-clouds (*udameghe*), and who, tossed about in darkness, invoked the aid of the youthful heroes. In the ocean which is without support (*anârambhaṇe*), they took him home in a hundred-oared (*shatâritram*) ship (I, 116, 5). They rescued him with animated water-tight ships, which traversed the air (*antarikṣha*), with four ships, with an animated winged boat, with three flying cars having a hundred feet and six horses. In one passage Bhujyu is described as clinging to a log in the midst of water (*arṇaso madhye*, I, 182, 7). The sage Rebha stabbed, bound, hidden by the malignant, overwhelmed in waters for ten nights and nine days, abandoned as dead, was by the Ashvins revived and drawn out, as Soma juice is raised with a ladle (I, 116, 24 ; I, 112, 5). They delivered Vandana from his calamity and restored him to the light of the sun. In I, 117, 5, they are also said to have dug up for Vandana some bright buried gold of new splendour 'like one asleep in the lap of Nir-ṛiti,' or like 'the sun dwelling in darkness.' They succoured the sage Atri Sapta-vadhri, who was plunged in a burning pit by the wiles of a demon, and delivered him from darkness (I, 116, 8 ; VI, 50, 10). They rescued from the jaws of a wolf a quail (*vartikâ*), who invoked their aid (I, 112, 8). To Ṛijrâshva, who had been blinded by his cruel father for killing one hundred and one sheep and giving them to a she-wolf to devour, they restored his eyesight at the prayer of the she-wolf (I, 116, 16; 117, 17) ; and cured Parâvṛij of blindness and lameness (I, 112, 8). When Vishpalâ's leg had been cut off in the battle like the wing of a bird, the Ashvins gave her an iron one instead (I, 116, 15). They befriended Ghoṣhâ when she was growing old in her father's house by giving her a husband (1, 117, 7 ; X, 39, 3). To the wife of a eunuch

(Vadhrimatî) they gave a son called Hiraṇya-hasta (I, 116, 13; VI, 62, 7). The cow of Shayu which had left off bearing they caused to give milk (I, 116, 22); and to Pedu they gave a strong swift dragon-slaying steed impelled by Indra which won him unbounded spoils (I, 116, 6)."

Besides these there are many other exploits mentioned in I, 112, 116-119; and the Ashvins are described as having saved, helped, or cured a number of other persons. But the above summary is sufficient for our purpose. It will be seen from it that the Ashvins bear the general character of helping the lame, the blind, the distressed, or the afflicted; and in some places a reference to the decayed powers of the sun is discernible on the face of the legends. Taking their clue from this indication, many scholars, and among them Prof. Max Muller, have interpreted all the above legends as referring to the sun in winter and the restoration of his power in spring or summer. Thus Prof. Max Muller tells us that Chyavâna is nothing but the falling sun (*chyu*, to fall), of which it might well be said that he had sunk in the fiery or dark abyss from which the Ashvins are themselves said to come up in III, 39, 3. The Vedic Ṛishis are again said to have betrayed the secret of the myth of Vandana by comparing the treasure dug for him by the Ashvins to the sun 'dwelling in darkness.' Kali is similarly taken to represent the waning moon, and Vishpalâ's iron leg, we are told, is the first quarter or *pâda* of the new moon, called 'iron' on account of his darkness as compared with the golden colour of the full moon. The blindness of Ṛijrâshva is explained on this theory as meaning the blindness of night or winter; and the blind and the lame Parâvṛij is taken to be the sun after sunset or near the winter solstice. The setting sun thrown out of a boat into waters is similarly understood to be the basis of the legend Bhujyu or Rebha. Vadhrimati, the wife of the eunuch, to whom Hiraṇya-hasta or the gold-hand is said to be restored, is, we are further told, nothing but the dawn under a different name. She is called the wife of the eunuch because she was separated from the sun during the night. The cow of Shayu, (derived from *shî*, to lie down) is again said to be the light of the morning sun, who may well be described as sleeping in the darkness from which he was brought forth by the Ashvins for the sake of Vandana. In short, each and every legend is said to be a story of the sun or the moon in distress. The Ashvins were the saviours of the morning-light, or of the annual sun in his exile and distress at the time of the winter solstice; and when the sun becomes bright and brisk in the morning every day, or vigorous and triumphant in the spring, the miracle, we are told, was naturally attributed to the physicians of the gods.

This explanation of the different legends connected with the Ashvins is no doubt an advance on that of Yâska, who has explained only one of these legends, *viz.*, that of the quail, on the Dawn theory. But still I do not think that all the facts and incidents in these legends are explained by the Vernal theory as it is at present understood. Thus we cannot explain why the proteges of the Ashvins are described as being delivered *from darkness* on the theory that every affliction or distress mentioned in the legend refers to mere decrease of the power of the sun in winter. Darkness is distinctly referred to when the treasure dug up for Vandana is compared to the "sun dwelling in darkness" (I, 117, 5), or when Bhujyu is said to have been plunged in waters and sunk in bottomless darkness (*anârambhaṇe tamasi*), or when Atri is said to have been delivered from darkness (*tamas*) in VI, 50, 10. The powers of the sun are no doubt decayed in winter, and one can easily understand why the sun in winter should be called lame, old, or distressed. But blindness naturally means darkness or *tamas* (I, 117, 17); and when express references to darkness (*tamas*) are found in several passages, we cannot legitimately hold that the story of curing the blind refers to the restoration of the decayed powers of the winter sun. The darkness referred to is obviously the real darkness of the night ; and on the theory of the daily struggle between light and darkness we shall have to suppose that these wonders were achievede very day. But as a matter of fact they are not said to be performed every day, and Vedic scholars have, therefore, tried to explain the legends on the theory of the yearly exile of the sun in winter. But we now see that in the latter case references to blindness or darkness remain unintelligible ; and as the darkness is often said to be of several days' duration, we are obliged to infer that the legends refer to the long yearly darkness, or, in other words, they have for their physical basis the disappearance of the sun below the horizon during the long night of the Arctic region.

The Vernal theory cannot again explain the different periods of time during which the distress experienced by the Ashvins' proteges is said to have lasted. Thus Rebha, who was overwhelmed in waters, is said to have remained there for ten nights and nine days (I, 116, 24) ; while Bhujyu, another worshipper of theirs, is described as having been saved from being drowned in the bottomless sea or darkness, where he lay for three days and three nights (I, 116, 4). In VIII, 5, 8, the Ashvins are again described as having been in the *parâvat* or distant region for three days and three nights. Prof. Max Muller, agreeing with Benfey, takes this period, whether of ten or three days, as representing the time when the sun at the winter solstice seems bound and to stand still (hence called *solstice*), till he jumps up and turns back. But ten days is too long a period for the sun to stand still at the winter solstice, and even Prof. Max Muller seems to have felt the difficulty, for immediately after the above explanation he remarks that "whether this time lasted for ten or twelve nights would have been difficult to settle even for more experienced astronomers than the Vedic Ṛishis." But even supposing that the period of ten days may be thus accounted for, the explanation entirely fails in the case of the legend of Dîrghatamas who is said to have grown old in the tenth *yuga* and rescued by the Ashvins from the torment to which he was subjected by his enemies. I have shown previously that *yuga* here means a month; and if this is correct, we shall have to suppose that Dîrghatamas, representing the annual course of the sun, stood still at the winter solstice for two months! The whole difficulty, however, vanishes when we explain the legends on the Arctic theory, for the sun may then be supposed to be below the horizon for any period varying from one to a hundred nights, or even for six months.

The third point, left unexplained by the Vernal theory, is the place of distress or suffering from which the proteges are said to have been rescued by the Ashvins. Bhujyu was saved not on land, but in the watery region (*apsu*) without support (*anârambhaṇe*) and unillumined (*tamasi*) by the rays of the sun (I, 182, 6). If we compare this description with that of the ocean said to have been encompassed by Vṛitra, or of the dark ocean which Bṛihaspati is said to have hurled down in II, 23, 18, we can at once recognize them as identical. Both represent the nether world which we have seen is the home of aerial waters, and which has to be crossed in boats by the drowned sun in the Ṛig-Veda or by Hêlios in the Greek mythology. It can not, therefore, be the place where the sun goes in winter; and unless we adopt the Arctic theory, we cannot explain how the proteges of the Ashvins are said to have been saved from being drowned in a dark and bottomless ocean. In VIII, 40, 5, Indra is said to have uncovered the seven-bottomed ocean having a side-opening (*jimha-bâram*), evidently referring to the fight for waters in the nether world. The same expression (*jimha-bâram*) is used again in I, 116, 9, where the Ashvins are described as having lifted up a well "with bottom up and opening in the side or downwards;"

and in I, 85, 11, a well lying obliquely (*jimha*) is said to have been pushed up by the Ashvins for satisfying the thirst of Gotama. These words and phrases are not properly explained by the commentators, most of whom take them as referring to the clouds. But it seems to me that these phrases more appropriately describe the antepodal region, where every thing is believed to be upside down in relation to the things of this world. Dr. Warren tells us that the Greeks and the Egyptians conceived their Hades, or things therein, as turned upside down, and he has even tried to show that the Vedic conception of the nether world corresponds exactly with that of the Greeks and the Egyptians.[1] The same idea is also found underlying the Hades conception of many other races, and I think Dr. Warren has correctly represented the ancient idea of the antepodal under-world. It was conceived by the ancients as an inverted tub or hemisphere of darkness, full of waters, and the Ashvins had to make an opening in its side and push the waters up so that after ascending the sky they may eventually come down in the form of rain to satisfy the thirst of Gotama. The same feat is attributed to the Maruts in I, 85, 10 and 11, and there too we must interpret it in the same way. The epithets *uchchâ-budhna* (with the bottom up) and *jimha-bâra* (with its mouth downwards or sidewards), as applied to a well (*avata*), completely show that something extraordinary, or the reverse of what we usually see, is here intended; and we cannot take them as referring to the clouds, for the well is said to be pushed *up* (*ûrdhvam nunudre*) in order to make the waters flow from it hitherward. It may also be observed that in I, 24, 7, the king Varuṇa of hallowed might is said to sustain "erect the Tree's stem in the bottomless (*abudhna*) region," and "its rays which are hidden from us have," we are told, "their bottom up and flow downwards (*nichînâḥ*)." This description of the region of Varuṇa exact-

1. See Paradise Found, pp. 481-82.

ly corresponds with the conception of the Hades in which every thing is turned upside down. Being regarded as an inverted hemisphere, it is rightly described, from the point of view of persons in this world, as a supportless region with bottom up and mouth downwards; and it was this bottomless darkness (I, 182, 6), or the bottomless and supportless ocean, in which Bhujyu was plunged, and which he crossed without distress by means of the boats graciously provided by the Ashvins. In the Atharva Veda X, 8, 9, a bowl with mouth inclined or downwards (*tiryag-bilaḥ*), and bottom upwards (*ûrdhva-budhnaḥ*) is said to hold within it every form of glory; and there seven Ṛishis, who have been this Mighty One's protectors, are described as sitting together.[1] The verse occurs also in the Bṛih. Arṇ. Up. II, 3, 3, with the variant *arvâg-bilaḥ* (with its mouth downwards) for *tiryag-bilaḥ* (with its mouth inclined) of the Atharva Veda. Yâska (Nir. XII, 38) quotes the verse and gives two interpretations of the same, in one of which the seven Ṛishis are taken to represent the seven rays of the sun, and the bowl the vault above; while in the second the bowl is said to represent the human head with its concave cup-like palate in the mouth. But it seems to me more probable that the description refers to the nether world rather than to the vault above or to the concave human palate. The glory referred to is the same as the Hvarenô of the Parsi scriptures In the Zamyâd Yasht, this Hvarenô or Glory is said to have thrice departed from Yima and was restored to him once by Mithra, once by Thraêtaona who smote Azi Dahâka, and finally by Keresâspa and Atar, who defeated Azi Dahâka. The fight took place in the sea Vouru-Kasha in the bottom of the deep river, and we have seen that this must be taken to mean the world-surrounding Okeanos. The Hvarenô (Sans. *swar*) or Glory is properly the light, and one who possessed it reigned

1. See Atharva Veda, X, 8, 9,—तिर्यग्बिलश्चमस ऊर्ध्वबुध्नस्तस्मिन्यशो निहितं विश्वरूपम् । तदासत ऋषयः सप्त साकं ये अस्य गोपा महतो बभूवुः ॥

supreme and one who lost it fell down. Thus "when Yima lost his Glory he perished and Azi Dahâka reigned; as when light disappears, the fiend rules supreme."[1] It may also be noticed that amongst the persons to whom the glory belonged in ancient days are mentioned the seven Amesha Spentas, all of one thought, one speech and one deed. We have thus a very close resemblance between the glory said to have been placed in a bowl with bottom up and guarded by the seven Ṛishis in the Vedas, and the Hvarenô or the glory mentioned in the Avesta, which once belonged to the seven Amesha Spentas, and which thrice went away from Yima and had to be restored to him by fighting with Azi Dahâka, the Avestic representative of the Ahi Vṛitra, in the sea Vouru-Kasha; and this strengthens our view that the bowl with the bottom up and the mouth downwards is the inverted hemisphere of the nether world, the seat of darkness and the home of aerial waters. It was this region wherein Bhujyu was plunged and had to be saved by the intervention of the Ashvins.

Now if Bhujyu was plunged in this bottomless darkness and ocean for three nights and three days (I, 116, 4), or Rebha was there for ten nights and nine days (I, 116, 24), it is clear that the period represents a continuous darkness of so many days and nights as stated above; and I think, the story of Ṛijrâshva, or the Red-horse, also refers to the same incident, *viz.*, the continuous darkness of the Arctic region. Ṛijrâshva, that is, the Red-horse, is said to have slaughtered 100 or 101 sheep and gave them to the Vṛikî, or the she-wolf, and his own father being angry on that account is said to have deprived him of his sight. But the Ashvins at the prayer of the she-wolf restored to Ṛijrâshva his eyesight and thus cured him of his blindness. Prof. Max Muller thinks that the sheep may here mean the stars, which may be said to have been slaughtered by the rising sun. But we have

1. See S. B. E. Series, Vol. IV, Introd. p. lxiii.

seen that the 350 sheep of Hêlios are taken to represent 350 nights, while the corresponding 350 days are said to be represented by his 350 oxen. In short, the Greek legend refers to a year of 350 days and a continuous night of ten days; and the period of 10 nights mentioned in the legend of Rebha well accords with this conception of the ancient Aryan year, inferred from the story of Hêlios. This resemblance between the two stories naturally leads us to inquire if any clue cannot be found to the interpretation of the legend of Ṛijrâshva in the story of Hêlios; and when we examine the subject from this point of view, it is not difficult to discover the similarity between the slaughter of sheep by Ṛijrâshva and the consuming of the oxen of Hêlios by the companion of Odysseus. The wolf, as observed by Prof. Max Muller, is generally understood in the Vedic literature to be a representative of darkness and mischief rather than of light, and therefore the slaughter of 100 sheep for him naturally means the conversion of hundred days into nights, producing thereby a continuous darkness for a hundred nights of 24 hours each. Ṛijrâshva or the Red-sun may well be spoken of as becoming blind during these hundred continuous nights, and eventually cured of his blindness by the Ashvins, the harbingers of light and dawn. The only objection that may be urged against this interpretation is that hundred days should have been described as oxen or cows and not as sheep. But I think, that such nice distinctions cannot be looked for in every myth, and that if hundred days were really converted into so many nights we can well speak of them as "sheep." The slaughter of 100 or 101 sheep can thus be easily and naturally explained on the theory of long continuous darkness, the maximum length of which, as stated in the previous chapter, was one hundred days, or a hundred periods of 24 hours. In short, the legends of the Ashvins furnish us with evidence of three, ten, or a hundred continuous nights in ancient times; and the incidents which lead us to this inference, are, at best, but feebly explained by the Vernal or the Dawn theory as at present understood.

But the most important of the Ashvins' legends, for our purpose, is the story of Atri Saptavadhri. He is described as having been thrown into a burning abyss and extricated from this perilous position by the Ashvins, who are also said to have delivered him from darkness (*tamasaḥ*) in VI, 50, 10. In I, 117, 24, the Ashvins are represented as giving a son called Hiraṇya-hasta, or the Gold-hand, to Vadhrimatî or the wife of a eunuch ; while in V, 78, a hymn, whose seer is Saptavadhri himself, the latter is represented as being shut up in a wooden case, from which he was delivered by the Ash vins. Upon this Prof. Max Muller observes, "If this tree or this wooden case is meant for the night, then, by being kept shut up in it, he (Saptavadhri) was separated from his wife, he was to her like a Vadhri (eunuch), and in the morning only when delivered by the Ashvins he became once more the husband of the dawn." But the learned Professor is at a loss to explain why Atri, in his character of the nocturnal sun, should be called not only a Vadhri but Saptavadhri, or a seven-eunuch. Vadhri, as a feminine word, denotes a leathern strap, and, as pointed out by Prof. Max Muller, Sâyaṇa is of opinion that the word can be used also in the masculine gender (X, 102, 12). The word Saptavadhri may, therefore, denote the sun caught in a net of seven leather straps. But the differ ent incidents in the legend clearly point out that a seven-eunuch, and not a person caught in seven leather straps, is meant by the epithet Saptavadhri as applied to Atri in this legend.

It is stated above that a whole hymn (78) of nine verses in the 5th Maṇḍala of the Ṛig-Veda is ascribed to Atri Saptavadhri. The deities addressed in this hymn are the Ashvins whom the poet invokes for assistance in his miserable plight. The first six verses of the hymn are simple and intelligible. In the first three, the Ashvins are invoked to come to the sacrifice like two swans; and in the fourth, Atri, thrown into a pit, is said to have called on them, like a wailing woman, for assistance. The 5th and the 6th verses narrate the story of Saptavadhri, shut up in a tree or a wooden case, whose sides are asked to tear asunder like the side of her who bringeth forth a child. After these six verses come the last three (the hymn containing only nine verses), which describe the delivery of a child that was in the womb for 10 months; and Vedic scholars have not as yet been able to explain what rational connection these three verses could possibly have with the preceding six verses of the hymn.[1] According to Sâyaṇa, these three verses constitute what is called the Garbhasrâviṇî-upanishad or the liturgy of child-birth; while Ludwig tries to explain the concluding stanzas as referring to the delivery of a child, a subject suggested by the simile of a wailing woman in the 4th verse, or by the comparison of the side of the tree with the side of a parturient woman. It seems, however, extraordinary, if not worse, that a subject, not relevant except as a simile or by way of comparison, should be described at such length at the close of the hymn. We must, therefore, try to find some other explanation, or hold with Sâyaṇa that an irrelevant matter, *viz.*, the liturgy of child-birth, is here inserted with no other object but to make up the number of verses in the hymn. These verses may be literally translated as follows:—

"7. Just as the wind shakes a pool of lotuses on all sides, so may your embryo (*garbha*) move (in your womb), and come out after being developed for ten months (*dashamâsyaḥ*)."

1. The last five verses of the hymn are as follows:—वि जिहीष्व वनस्पते योनिः सूष्यन्त्या इव । श्रुतं मे अश्विना हवं सप्तवध्रिं च मुञ्चतम् ॥ ५ ॥ भीताय नाधमानाय ऋषये सप्तवध्रये । मायाभिरश्विना युवं वृक्षं सं च वि चाचथः ॥ ६ ॥ यथा वातः पुष्करिणीं समिङ्गयति सर्वतः । एवा ते गर्भ एजतु निरैतु दशमास्यः ॥ ७ ॥ यथा वातो यथा वनं यथा समुद्र एजति । एवा त्वं दशमास्य सहावेहि जरायुणा ॥ ८ ॥ दश मासाञ्छशयानः कुमारो अधि मातरि । निरैतु जीवो अक्षतो जीवो जीवन्त्या अधि ॥ ९ ॥

"8. Just as the wind, just as the forest, just as the sea moves, so O ten-monthed (embryo)! come out with the outer cover (*jarâyu*)."

"9. May the child (*kumâra*), lying in the mother's (womb) for ten months, come out alive and unhurt, alive for the living mother."

These three verses, as observed above, immediately follow the verses where the wooden case is said to be shut and opened for Saptavadhri, and naturally they must be taken to refer to, or rather as forming a part of the same legend. But neither the Vernal nor the Dawn theory supplies us with any clue whatsoever to the right interpretation of these verses. The words used present no difficulty. A child full-grown in the womb for ten months is evidently intended, and its safe delivery is prayed for. But what could this child be? The wife of the eunuch Vadhrimatî is already said to have got a child Hiraṇya-hasta through the favour of the Ashvins. We cannot, therefore, suppose that she prayed for the safe delivery of a child, nor can Saptavadhri be said to have prayed for the safe delivery of his wife, who never bore a child to him. The verses, or rather their connection with the story of Saptavadhri told in the first six verses of the hymn, have, therefore, remained unexplained up to the present day, the only explanations hitherto offered being, as observed above, either utterly unsatisfactory or rather no explanations at all.

The whole mystery is, however, cleared up by the light thrown upon the legend by the Arctic theory. The dawn is sometimes spoken of in the Ṛig-Veda as producing the sun (I, 113, 1; VII. 78, 3). But this dawn cannot be said to have borne the child for ten months; nor can we suppose that the word *dasha-mâsyaḥ* (of ten months), which is found in the 7th and the 8th, and the phrase *dasha mâsân* found in the 9th verse of the hymn were used without any specific meaning or intention. We must, therefore, look for some other explanation, and this is supplied by the fact that the sun is said to be pre-eminently the son of Dyâvâ-prithivî, or simply of Dyu in the Ṛig-Veda. Thus in X, 97, 1, the sun is called *divas-putra* or the son of Dyu, and in I, 164, 33, we read, "Dyu is the father, who begot us, our origin is there; this great Earth is our parent mother. The father laid the daughter's embryo (*garbham*) within the womb of the two wide bowls (*uttânayoḥ chamvoḥ*)". In the preceding verse, we have, "He (the sun) yet enveloped in his mother's womb, having various offsprings, has gone into the (region of) Nir-ṛiti"; and further that "he, who had made him, does not know of him; surely is he hidden from those who saw him." In I, 160, 1, we similarly find that "These Heaven and Earth, bestowers of prosperity and all, the wide sustainers of the regions, the two bowls of noble birth, the holy ones: between these two goddesses, the refulgent sun-god travels by fixed decrees." These passages clearly show (1) that the sun was conceived as a child of the two bowls, Heaven and Earth, (2) that the sun moved like an embryo in the womb, *i.e.*, the interior of heaven and earth, and (3) that after moving in this way in the womb of the mother for some time, and producing various offsprings, the sun sank into the land of desolation (*Nir-ṛiti*), and became hidden to those that saw him before. Once the annual course of the sun was conceived in this way, it did not require any great stretch of imagination to represent the dropping of the sun into *Nir-ṛiti* as an exit from the womb of his mother. But what are we to understand by the phrase that 'he moved in the womb for ten months'? The Arctic theory explains this point satisfactorily. We have seen that Dîrghatamas was borne on waters for ten months, and the Dashagvas are said to have completed their sacrificial session during the same period. The sun can, therefore, be very well described, while above the horizon for ten months, as moving in the womb of his mother, or between heaven and earth for ten months. After this period, the sun was lost, or went out of the womb into the land of desolation, there to be shut up as in a wooden case for two months. The sage Atri, therefore, rightly invokes the Ashvins for his deliverance from the box and also for the safe delivery of the child, *i.e.*, himself, from the womb of his mother after ten months. In the Atharva Veda XI, 5, 1, the sun, as a Brahmachârin, is said to move between heaven and earth, and in the 12th verse of the same hymn we are told that "Shouting forth, thundering, red, white he carries a great penis (*bṛihach-chhepas*) along the earth." If the sun moving between heaven and earth is called *bṛihach-chhepas* he may well be called Vadhri (eunuch), when sunk into the land of *Nir-ṛiti*. But Prof. Max Muller asks us, why he should be called Saptavadhri or a seven-eunuch? The explanation is simple enough. The heaven, the earth and the lower regions are all conceived as divided seven-fold in the Ṛig-Veda, and, when the ocean or the waters are described as seven-fold (*sapta-budhnam arṇavam*, VIII, 40, 5; *sapta âpaḥ* X, 104, 8), or when we have seven Dânus or demons, mentioned in X, 120, 6, or when Indra is called *sapta-han* or the seven-slayer (X, 49, 8), or Vṛitra is said to have seven forts (I, 63, 7), or when the cowstead (*vraja*), which the two Ashvins are said to have opened in X, 40, 8, is described as *saptâsya*, the sun, who is *bṛihach-chhepas* and seven-rayed or seven-horsed (V, 45, 9) while moving between heaven and earth, may very well be described as Saptavadhri or seven-eunuch when sunk into the land of *Nir-ṛiti* or the nether world of bottomless darkness, from which he is eventually released by the Ashvins. The last three verses of V, 78, can thus be logically connected with the story of Saptavadhri mentioned in the immediately preceding verses, if the period of ten months, during which the child moves in the mother's womb, is taken to represent the period of ten months' sunshine followed by the long night of two months, the existence of which we have established by independent Vedic evidence. The point has long remained unexplained, and it is only by the Arctic theory that it can be now satisfactorily accounted for.

In connection with this subject it is necessary to refer to a riddle or a paradox, which arises out of it. The sun was supposed to move in the womb of his mother for ten months and then to drop into the nether world. In other words, as soon as he came out of the womb, he was invisible; while in ordinary cases a child becomes visible as soon as it is brought into the world after ten months of gestation. Here was an idea, or rather an apparent contradiction between two ideas, which the Vedic poets were not slow to sieze upon, and evolve a riddle out of it. Thus we have seen above (I, 164, 32) that the sun is described as being invisible to one who made him, evidently meaning his mother. In V, 2, 1, we again meet with the same riddle; for it says, "Young mother carries in secret the boy confined; she does not yield him to the father. People do not see before them his fading face, laid down with the Arâti."[1] In I, 72, 2, we further read, "All the clever immortals did not find the calf though sojouring round about us. The attentive (gods), wearying themselves, following his foot-steps, stood at the highest beautiful standing place of Agni;" and the same idea is expressed in I, 95, 4, which says, "Who amongst you has understood this secret? The calf has by itself given birth to its mother. The germ of many, the great seer moving by his own strength comes forward from the lap of the active one (*apasâm*)." It is the story of the hidden Agni, who is described in X, 124, 1, as having long (*jyok*) resided in

1. See Oldenberg's Vedic Hymns, S. B. E. Series, Vol. XLVI, pp. 366-68. The first two verses of the hymn are:—कुमारं माता युवतिः समुब्धं गुहा बिभर्ति न ददाति पित्रे। अनीकमस्य न मिनज्जनासः पुरः पश्यन्ति निहितमरतौ ॥ १ ॥ कमेतं त्वं युवते कुमारं पेषी बिभर्षि महिषी जजान। पूर्वीर्हि गर्भः शरदो ववर्धापश्यं जातं यदसूत माता ॥ २ ॥

the long darkness (*dirgham tamaḥ*), and who eventually comes out as the child of waters (*apâm napât*, I, 143, 1). The epithet *apâm napât* as applied to Agni is usually explained as referring to the lightening produced from the clouds, but this explanation does not account for the fact of his long residence in darkness. The puzzle or the riddle is, however, satisfactorily solved by the Arctic theory, combined with the cosmic circulation of aerial waters. The sun, who moves in the interior of heaven and earth for ten months, as in the womb of his mother, naturally suggested to the Vedic poets the parallel idea of the period of ten months' gestation; but the wonder was that while a child is visible to all as soon as it is born, the sun became invisible just at the time when he came out of the womb. Where did he go? Was he locked up in a wooden chest or bound down with leather straps in the region of waters? Why did the mother not present him to the father after he was safely delivered? Was he safely delivered? These questions naturally arise out of the story, and the Vedic poets appear to take delight in reverting again and again to the same paradox in different places. And what applies to Sûrya or the sun applies to Agni as well; for there are many passages in the Ṛig-Veda where Agni is identified with the sun. Thus Agni is said to be the light of heaven in the bright sky, waking at dawn, the head of heaven (III, 2, 14), and he is described as having been born on the other side of the air in X, 187, 5. In the Aitareya Brâhmaṇa (VIII, 28), we are further told that the sun, when setting, enters into Agni and is reproduced from the latter; and the same identification appears to be alluded to in the passages from the Ṛig-Veda, where Agni is said to unite with the light of the sun or to shine in heaven (VIII, 44 29). The story of concealing the child after ten months of gestation whether applied to Agni or to Sûrya is thus only a different version of the story of the disappearance of the sun from the upper hemisphere after ten months of sunshine.

But what became of the child (*Kumâra*) which disappeared in this way? Was he lost for ever or again restored to his parents? How did the father or even the mother obtain the child so lost? Some one must bring the child to them, and this task seems to have been entrusted to the Ṛibhus or the Ashvins in the Ṛig-Veda. Thus in I, 110, 8, the Ṛibhus are said to have united the mother with the calf, and in I, 116, 13, the Ashvins are described as giving to Vadhrimati a child called Hiraṇya-hasta. The story of restoring Vishṇâpu to Vishvaka (I, 117, 7) and of giving milk to Shayu's cow probably refer to the same phenomenon of bringing back the morning sun to the parents; and from this it is but a small step to the story of Kumâra (*lit.*, a child), one of the names of Kârttikeya in the Purâṇas. It was this Kumâra, or the once hidden (*guha*), or dropped (*skanda*) Child, rising along with the seven rivers or mothers (VIII, 96, 1) in the morning, that led the army of gods or light and walked victoriously along the Devayâna path. He was the leader of days, or the army of gods; and as Maruts were the allies of Indra in his conflict with Vṛitra, Kumâra or the Child, meaning the morning sun, may, by a turn of the mythological kaleidoscope, be very well called a son of Rudra, the later representative of the Maruts; or said to be born of Agni, who dwelt in waters; or described as the son of seven or six Kṛittikâs. As the morning sun has to pierce his way up through the apertures of Albûrz, temporarily closed by Vṛitra, this Kumâra can again be well termed Krauñcha-dâraṇa, or the piercer of the Krauñcha mountain, an epithet applied to him in the Purâṇas.[1] But we are not here concerned with the growth which Kumâra, or the child of the

1. For a further development of the idea see Mr. Nârâyan Ayangâr's Essays on Indo-Aryan Mythology, Part II, pp. 57-80. In the light of the Arctic theory we may have to modify some of Mr. Aiyangâr's views. Thus out of the seven rivers or mothers, which bring on the light of the sun, one may be regarded as his real mother and the other six as stepmothers.

morning, attained in later mythology. We took up the legends of the Ashvins with a view to see if there were any incidents in them which became intelligible only on the Arctic theory, and the foregoing examination of the legends shows that we have not searched in vain. The expression *dasha-mâsya* in the legend of Sapta-vadhri and *dashame yuge* in that of Dîrghatamas directly indicate a period of ten months' sunshine, and we have seen that three, ten, or a hundred continuous nights are also referred to directly or metaphorically in some of these legends. We have again such expressions as "the sun sleeping in darkness or in the lap of Nir-ṛiti," which show that actual and not metaphorical darkness was intended. In short, the sun, sunk in the nether world of waters and darkness, and not merely a winter sun, is the burden of all these legends, and the achievements of the Ashvins refer to the rescue of the sun from the dark pit of the nether world or from the bottomless ocean or darkness. The Vernal and Arctic theories are both solar in character, and in either case the legends are interpreted on the supposition that they represent some solar phenomenon. But the Arctic theory does not stop with the decay of the sun's power in winter, but goes a step further in making the long darkness of the circum-polar region, the natural basis of many important Vedic legends; and the foregoing discussion of the myths of the Ashvins clearly shows that a wider basis, like the one supplied by the Arctic theory, was not only desirable but necessary for a proper explanation of these legends—a fact, which, in its turn, further corroborates and establishes the new theory.

The Sûrya's Wheel.

We have already discussed the legend of the seven Âdityas with their still-born brother, and shewn that it represents seven months of sunshine in the ancient Aryan home. But this is not the only period of sunshine in the Arctic region, where, according to latitude, the sun is above the horizon from 6 to 12 months. The sacrificial session of the Navagvas and the Dashagvas thus lasted for nine or ten months, and amongst the Ashvins' legends, that of Saptavadhri is just shown to have been based on the phenomenon of ten months' sunshine. Is there any legend of Sûrya in the Ṛig-Veda, which refers to this phenomenon ?—is the question we have now to consider. The statement that ten horses are yoked to the carriage of the sun has been shewn to point out to a period of ten months' sunshine; but the legend of Indra's stealing the wheel of the sun is still more explicit. To understand it properly we must, however, first see in what relation Indra generally stands to Sûrya. It has been shown in the last chapter, that Indra is the chief hero in the fight between the powers of light and darkness. It is he, who causes the sun to rise with the dawn, or makes the sun to shine (VIII, 3, 6; VIII, 98, 2) and mount the sky (I, 7, 3). The sun, it is further stated, (III, 39 5), was dwelling in darkness, where Indra, accompanied by the Dashagvas found him and brought him up for man. It is Indra again who makes a path for the sun (X, 111, 3), and fights with the demons of darkness in order to gain back the light of the morning. In short, Indra is everywhere described as a friend and helper of Sûrya, and yet the Ṛig-Veda mentions a legend in which Indra is said to have taken away or stolen the wheel of Sûrya and thus vanquished him (I, 175, 4; IV, 30, 4; V, 31, 11; X, 43, 5). It has been supposed that the legend may refer either to the obscuration of the sun by a storm-cloud, or to his diurnal setting ; but the former is too uncertain an event to be made the basis of a legend like the present, nor can a cloud be said to be brought on by Indra, while we have no authority to assume, as presupposed in the latter case, that the legend refers to the daily setting of the sun. We must, therefore, examine the legend a little more closely, and see if we can explain it in a more intelligible way. Now

Sûrya's chariot is described in the Ṛig-Veda as having but one wheel (I, 164, 2), though the wheel is said to be seven-fold; and in later mythology it is distinctly stated that the chariot of the sun is *eka-chakra* or a monocycle. If this wheel is taken away, the progress of the sun must cease, bringing everything to a dead lock. It seems, however, that the wheel of the sun means the sun himself in the present legend. Thus in I, 175, 4, and IV, 30, 4, the phrase used is *sûryam chakrum*, evidently meaning that the solar orb itself is conceived as a wheel. When this wheel is said to be stolen, we must, therefore, suppose that the sun himself was taken away, and not that one of the two wheels of his carriage was stolen, leaving the carriage to run on one wheel as best as it could. What did Indra do with this solar wheel, or the sun himself, which he stole in this way? We are told that he used solar rays as his weapon to kill or burn the demons (VIII, 12, 9). It is, therefore, clear that the stealing of the solar wheel and the conquest over the demons are contemporaneous events. Indra's fight with the demons is mainly for the purpose of regaining light, and it may be asked how Indra can be described to have used the solar orb as a weapon of attack for the purpose of regaining Sûrya that was lost in darkness? For it amounts to saying that the solar orb was used as a weapon in recovering the sun himself, which was believed to be lost in darkness. But the difficulty is only apparent and is due to the modern notions of light or darkness. Sûrya and darkness, according to the modern notions, cannot be supposed to exist in the same place; but the Ṛig-Veda distinctly speaks of "the sun dwelling in darkness" in two places at least (III, 39, 5; I, 117, 5); and this can be explained only on the supposition that the Vedic bards believed that the sun was deprived of his lustre when he sank below the horizon, or that his lustre was temporarily obscured during his struggle with the demons of darkness. It is impossible to explain the expression *tamasi kshiyantam* (dwelling in darkness) on any other theory; and if this explanation is accepted, it is not difficult to understand how the solar orb could be said to be utilized by Indra in vanquishing the demons and regaining the morning light. In other words, Indra helps the sun in destroying the obstruction which marred or clouded his lustre, and when this obstruction is removed the sun regains his light and rises up from the nether ocean. Indra is, therefore, correctly described in IV, 17, 14, as having stopped the wheel of the sun, and, turning it round, flung it into the concealing darkness at the bottom of *rajas* or in the nether world of darkness. But the passage important for our purpose is VI, 31, 3. It reads as follows:—

> *Tvam Kutsena abhi Shushṇam Indra*
> *Ashusham yudhya Kuyavam gavishṭau* ।
> *Dasha prapitve adha Sûryasya*
> *mushâyas chakram avive rapâmsi* ॥

The first half of the verse presents no difficulty. It means "O Indra! in the striving for the cows, do you, with Kutsa, fight against Shushṇa, the Ashusha and the Kuyava."[1] Here Ashusha and Kuyava are used as adjectives to Shushṇa and mean 'the voracious Shushṇa, the bane of the crops.' The second hemistich, however, is not so simple. The last phrase *avive-rapâmsi* is split in the *Pada* text as *aviveḥ* and *rapâmsi*, which means "destroy calamities or mischiefs (*rapâmsi*)." But Prof. Oldenberg proposes to divide the phrase as *aviveḥ* and *apâmsi*, in conformity with IV, 19 10, and translates, "Thou hast manifested thy manly works (*apâmsi*)."[2] It is not, however, necessary for our present purpose to examine the relative merits of these two interpretations; and we may, therefore, adopt the older of the two, which translates the phrase as meaning, "Thou hast destroyed calamities or mischiefs,

1. See Ṛig. VI, 31, 3,—त्वं कुत्सेनाभि शुष्णमिंद्राशुषं युध्य कुयवं गविष्टौ। दश प्रपित्वे अध सूर्यस्य मुषायश्चक्रमविवेरपांसि ॥
2. See Oldenberg's Vedic Hymns, S. B. E. Series, Vol. XLVI, p. 69.

(*rapâṁsi*)." Omitting the first two words, *viz.*, *dasha* and *prapitve*, the second hemistich may, therefore, be rendered, "Thou hast stolen the wheel of Sûrya and hast destroyed calamities." We have now to ascertain the meaning of *dasha prapitve*. Sâyaṇa takes *dasha* as equivalent to *adashaḥ* (*lit.*, bittest, from *daṁsh*, to bite), and *prapitve* to mean "in the battle"—and translates, "Thou bittest him in the battle." But this is evidently a forced meaning, and one that does not harmonise with other passages, where the same legend is described. Thus in IV, 16, 12, we are told that Shushṇa was killed at *ahnaḥ prapitve*, and the last phrase evidently denotes the time when Shushṇa was defeated; while in V, 31, 7, Indra is described as having checked the wiles of Shushṇa by reaching *prapitvam*. By the side of the expression *dasha prapitve*, we thus have two more passages in the Ṛig-Veda, referring to the same legend, and in one of which Shushṇa is said to be killed at the *prapitva* of the day (*ahnaḥ prapitve*), while in the other, the wiles of the demon are said to be checked by Indra on reaching *prapitvam*. The three expressions, *dasha prapitve*, *ahnaḥ prapitve*, and *prapitvam yan*, must, therefore, be taken to be synonymous; and whatever meaning we assign to *prapitve*, it must be applicable to all the three cases. The word *prapitve* is used several times in the Ṛig-Veda, but scholars are not agreed as to its meaning. Thus Grassmann gives two meanings of *prapitva*. The first denoting "advance," and the second "the beginning of the day." According to him *ahnaḥ prapitve* means "in the morning" (IV, 16, 12). But he would render *prapitvam yan* simply by "advancing." In VI, 31, 3, he would also take *prapitve* as meaning "in the morning." The word *prapitve* also occurs in I, 189, 7, and there Prof. Oldenberg translates it by "at the time of the advancing day," and quotes Geldner in support thereof. Sâyaṇa in VIII, 4, 3, translates *âpitve* by 'friendship' and *prapitve* by 'having acquired,' (cf. Nir. III, 20). Under these circumstances it is, I think, safer to ascertain the meaning of *prapitve* direct from those Vedic passages where it occurs in contrast with other words. Thus in VII, 41, 4, (Vâj. Saṁ, XXXIV, 37) and VIII, 1, 29, we find *prapitve* very distinctly contrasted with *madhye* (the middle) and *uditâ* (the beginning) of the day; and in both these places *prapitve* can mean nothing but 'the decline or the end of the day.'[1] Mahîdhara, on Vâj. Saṁ. XXXIV, 37, explains *prapitve* as equivalent to *prapatane* or *astamaye*, meaning "the decline, fall, or end of the day." Adopting this meaning, the phrase *ahnaḥ prapitve ni barhîḥ*, in IV, 16, 12, would then mean that Shushṇa was killed 'when the day had declined.' Now if Shushṇa was killed when the day had declined the phrase *dasha prapitve* ought to be, by analogy, interpreted in the same way. But it is difficult to do so, so long as *dasha* is separated from *prapitve*, as is done in the *Pada* text. I propose, therefore, that *dasha-prapitve* be taken as one word, and interpreted to mean "at the decline of the ten," meaning that Shushṇa was killed at the end or completion of ten (months). In I, 141, 2, the phrase *dasha-pramatim* is taken as a compound word in the *Pada* text, but Oldenberg, following the Petersberg Lexicon, splits it into *dasha* and *pramatim*. I propose to deal exactly in the reverse way with the phrase *dasha prapitve* in the passage under consideration, and translate the verse thus :—"O Indra! in the striving for cows do thou, with Kutsa, fight against Shushṇa, the Ashusha and Kuyava. On the decline (or the completion) of the ten (*scil.* months), thou stolest the wheel of Sûrya and didst destroy calamities (or, according to Oldenberg, manifest manly works)." The passage thus becomes intelligible, and we are not required

1. Ṛig. VII, 41, 4,—उतेदानीं भगवन्तः स्यामोत प्रपित्व उत मध्ये अह्नां । उतोदिता मघवन्सूर्यस्य वयं देवानां सुमतौ स्याम ॥ Ṛig. VIII, 1, 29—मम त्वा सूर उदिते मम मध्यंदिने दिवः । मम प्रपित्वे अपिशर्वरे वसवा स्तोमासो अवृत्सत ॥ These two passages clearly prove that *prapitve*, used with reference to the day, denotes decline or the termination thereof.

to invent a new meaning for *dasha* and make Indra bite his enemy on the battle-field. If we compare the phrase *dasha-prapitve* with *ahnaḥ prapitve* occurring in IV, 16, 12, and bear in mind the fact that both are used in connection with the legendary fight with Shushṇa, we are naturally led to suppose that *dasha-prapitve* denotes, in all probability, the time of the contest, as *ahnaḥ prapitve* does in the other passage, and that *dasha prapitve* must be taken as equivalent to *dashânam prapitve* and translated to mean "On the completion of the ten," which can be done only by taking *dasha-prapitve* as a compound word. The grammatical construction being thus determined, the only question that remains is to decide whether *dasha* (ten) means ten days or ten months. A comparison with *ahnaḥ prapitve* may suggest "days," but the fight with Shushṇa cannot be regarded to have been fought every ten days. It is either annual or daily; and we are thus led to interpret *dasha* in the compound *dasha-prapitve* (or *dashânâm* when the compound is dissolved) as equivalent to ten months in the same way as the numeral *dvâdashasya* is interpreted to mean "of the twelfth month," or *dvâdashasya mâsasya* in VII, 103, 9. The passage thus denotes the exact time when the wheel of the sun, or the solar orb, was stolen by Indra and utilized as a weapon of attack to demolish the demons of darkness. This was done at the end of ten months, or at the end of the old Roman year, or at the close of the sacrificial session of the Dashagvas who with Indra are said to have found the sun dwelling in darkness. The construction of the passage proposed above is not only natural and simple, but the sense it gives is in harmony with the meaning of similar other passages relating to the fight of Shushṇa, and is far more rational than the current meaning which makes Indra bite his enemy in a rustic and unprecedented manner. It is the *Pada* text that is responsible for the present unnatural meaning; for if it had not split up the phrase into *dasha* and *prapitve*, its correct meaning might not have become so obscure as at present. But the *Pada* text is not infallible; and even Yâksa and Sâyaṇa have adopted amendments in certain cases (cf. I, 105, 18; X, 29, 1; and Nir. V, 21; VI, 28), and the same thing has been done rather more freely by Western scholars. We are not, therefore, following an untrodden path in giving up the *Pada* text, especially when the verse is more naturally and intelligently interpreted by taking *dasha-prapitve* as one compound word. When the verse is so interpreted we get a complete account of the annual course of the sun in the home of the Aryans in ancient days. It was Indra, who caused the sun to rise after his long fight with Vṛitra; and when the sun had shone for ten months, Indra stole the solar orb and took the sun with him into darkness to fight with the demons. That is the meaning of the whole legend; and when it can be so naturally explained only by the Arctic theory, the necessity of the latter becomes at once established.

Vishṇu's three strides.

There are a few more Vedic legends which indicate or suggest the Arctic conditions of climate or calendar, and I propose to briefly examine them in this chapter. One of these legends relates to Vishṇu and his three long strides, which are distinctly mentioned in several places in the Ṛig-Veda (I, 22, 17-18; I, 154, 2). Yâska (Nir. XII, 19) quotes the opinion of two older writers regarding the character of these three steps. One of these, *viz.*, Shâkapûṇi, holds that the three steps must be placed on the earth, in the atmosphere, and in the sky; while Aurṇavâbha thinks that the three steps must be located, one on the hill where the sun rises (*samârohaṇa*), another on the meridian sky (*Vishṇu-pada*), and the third on the hill of setting (*gaya-shiras*). Prof. Max Muller thinks that this three-fold stepping of Vishṇu is emblematic of the rising, the culminating and the setting of the sun; and Muir quotes a passage from the Râmâyaṇa (IV, 40, 64), which mentions *udaya-parvata*, or the mountain of sun-rise, and says that on the top of it is the peak Saumanasa, the place where Vishṇu's first step was planted. We are then told that his second step was placed on the summit of Meru; and that "when the sun had circled round Jambudvîpa by the north, he is mostly visible on that lofty peak." It seems, therefore, that according to the Râmâyaṇa the third step of Vishṇu was round Jambudvîpa, and was planted after sunset, whatever that may mean. In the Purâṇic literature, Vishṇu's three steps appear as the three steps of Vâmana, the fifth incarnation of Vishṇu. Bali, the powerful enemy of the gods, was celebrating a sacrifice, when, assuming the form of a dwarf, Vishṇu approached him, and begged for three paces of ground. No sooner the request was granted than Vishṇu assumed a miraculous form and occupied the whole earth by the first step and the atmosphere and everything above it with the second. Bali, who was the lord of the universe before, was surprised at the metamorphosis of the dwarf; but had to make good his own word by offering his head for the third step of Vâmana. The offer was accepted and Bali was pressed down under the third step into the nether world, and the empire of the earth and heavens above was again restored to Indra from whom it had been snatched away by Bali. Amongst these various interpretations one thing stands out very clear, *viz.*, that Vishṇu represents the sun in one form or another. But Vedic scholars are not agreed as to whether Vishṇu's strides represent the daily or the yearly course of the sun. We must, therefore, carefully examine the Vedic passages relating to Vishṇu, and see if any indication is found therein to decide which of these two views is more probable or correct. Now in I, 155, 6, Vishṇu is described as setting in motion, like a revolving wheel, his ninty steeds with their four names, evidently referring to 360 days, divided into four groups or seasons of 90 days each. This is good evidence to hold that the yearly course of the sun must be taken as the basis of the exploits of Vishṇu. The Ṛig-Veda further tells us that Vishṇu was the intimate friend of Indra (*yujyaḥ sakhâ*, I, 22, 19), and that he assisted Indra in his fight with Vṛitra. Thus in IV, 18, 11, we are told that "Indra about to kill Vṛitra said 'O friend Vishṇu! stride vastly,' (also cf. VIII, 12, 27)"; and in I, 156, 4, Vishṇu is said to have opened the cows' stable with the assistance of his friend, while both Indra and Vishṇu are described as having together vanquished Shambara, conquered the host of Varchins and produced the sun, dawn and the fire in VII, 99, 4 and 5. It is evident from these passages that Vishṇu was the associate of Indra in his fight with Vṛitra (cf. VIII, 63, 9); and if so, one of the three steps must be placed in regions where this fight was fought, that is, in the nether world. We can now understand why, in I, 155, 5, it is said that two of the three steps of Vishṇu are visible to man, but the third is beyond the reach of birds or mortals (also cf. VII, 99, 1). When the third step of Vishṇu is located in the nether world, it can well be said to be invisible, or beyond the reach of mortals. We have seen that the abode of Vṛitra is said to be hidden and filled with darkness and waters. If Vishṇu helped Indra in his fight with Vṛitra, his third step must be taken to correspond with the home of Vṛitra; in other words, Vishṇu's strides represent the annual course of the sun divided into three parts. During two of these the sun was above the horizon, and hence two of Vishṇu's three strides were said to be visible. But when in the third or the last part of the year the sun went below the horizon producing continuous darkness, Vishṇu's third step was said to be invisible. It was then that he helped Indra to demolish Vṛitra and bring back the dawn, the sun and the sacrifice. It has been shown in the last chapter that Indra's fight with Shambara commenced on the fortieth day of *Sharad* or in the eighth month after the beginning of the year with *Vasanta.* These eight months of sunshine and four of darkness may very well be represented by two visible and one invisible step of Vishṇu, and the Purâṇic story of Vishṇu's sleeping for four months in the year further supports the same view. It may also be noticed that Vishṇu is said to sleep on his serpent bed in the midst of the ocean; and the ocean and the serpent here alluded to are evidently the waters (*âpaḥ*) and Ahi or Vṛitra mentioned in the Vṛitra legend. It is said that the sleep of Vishṇu represents the rainy season of four months; but this is a later misrepresentation of the kind we have noticed in the last chapter in regard to waters. When the exploits of Indra were transferred from the last season of the year, *viz.*, *Hemanta*, to *Varshâ* or the rainy season, the period, during which Vishṇu lay dormant, must have been naturally misunderstood in the same way and identified with the rainy season. But originally Vishṇu's sleep and his third step must have been identical; and as the third step is said to be invisible, we cannot suppose that it was planted in the rainy season, which is visible enough. The long darkness of the winter night in the Arctic region can alone adequately represent the third step of Vishṇu or the period of his sleep; and the legend about the Phrygian god, who, according to Plutarch, was believed to sleep during winter and resume his activity during summer, has been interpreted by Prof. Rhys in the same way. The Irish *couvade* of the Ultonian heroes also points out to the same conclusion.*

But apart from the sleep of Vishṇu which is Purâṇic, we have a Vedic legend which has the same meaning. In the Ṛig-Veda (VII, 100, 6), Vishṇu is represented as having a bad name, *viz.*, *shipivishṭa.* Thus the poet says, "O Vishṇu!

---

* See Rhys' Hibbert Lectures, p. 632. The passage is quoted in full in Chap. XII, *infra.*

what was there to be blamed in thee when thou declaredest 'I am *shipivishṭa*'?" Yâska records (Nir. V, 7–9) an old tradition that according to Aupamanyava, Vishṇu has two names *Shipivishṭa* and *Vishṇu*, of which the former has a bad sense (*kutsitârthîyam*); and then quotes the aforesaid verse which he explains in two ways. The first of these two interpretations accords with that of Aupamanyava; and *shipivishṭa* is there explained by Yâska to mean *shepaḥ iva nirveshṭitaḥ*, or "enveloped like the private parts," or "with rays obscured" (*apratipanna-rashmiḥ*). Yâska, however, suggests an alternative interpretation and observes that *shipivishṭa* may be taken as a laudatory appellation, meaning "one whose rays (*shipayaḥ*) are displayed (*âvishṭâḥ*)." It is inferred by some scholars from this passage that the meaning of the word *shipivishṭa* had already become uncertain in the days of Yâska; but I do not think it probable, for even in later literature *shipivishṭa* is an opprobrious appellation meaning either "one whose hair has fallen off," or "one who is afflicted with an incurable skin disease." The exact nature of the affliction may be uncertain; but there can be no doubt that *shipivishṭa* has a bad meaning even in later Sanskrit literature. But in days when the origin of this phrase, as applied to Vishṇu, was forgotten, theologians and scholars naturally tried to divest the phrase of its opprobrious import by proposing alternative meanings; and Yâska was probably the first Nairukta to formulate a good meaning for *shipivishṭa* by suggesting that *shipi* may be taken to mean "rays." That is why the passage from the Mahâbhârata (Shânti-Parvan, Chap. 342, vv. 69-71), quoted by Muir, tells us that Yâska was the first to apply the epithet to Vishṇu; and it is unreasonable to infer from it, as Muir has done, that the writer of the Mahâbhârata "was not a particularly good Vedic scholar." In the Taittirîya Saṁhitâ, we are told that Vishṇu was worshipped as *Shipivishṭa* (II, 2, 12, 4 and 5), and that *shipi* means cattle or *pashavaḥ* (II, 5, 5,

2; Tân. Br. XVIII, 6, 26). *Shipivishṭa* is thus explained as a laudatory appellation by taking *shipi* equal to 'cattle,' 'sacrifice' or 'rays.' But these etymological devices have failed to invest the word with a good sense in Sanskrit literature; and this fact by itself is sufficient to show that the word *shipivishṭa* originally was, and has always been, a term of reproach indicating some bodily affliction, though the nature of it was not exactly known. The theological scholars, it is true, have tried to explain the word in a different sense; but this is due to their unwillingness to give opprobrious names to their gods, rather than to any uncertainty about the real meaning of the word. It was thus that the word *shipivishṭa*, which is originally a bad name (*kutsitârthîyam*) according to Aupamanyava, was converted into a mysterious (*guhya*) name for the deity. But this transition of meaning is confined only to the theological literature, and did not pass over into the non-theological works, for the obvious reason that in ordinary language the bad meaning of the word was sufficiently familiar to the people. There can, therefore, be little doubt that, in VII, 100, 5 and 6, *shipivishṭa* is used in a bad sense as stated by Aupamanyava. These verses have been translated by Muir as follows :— "I, a devoted worshipper, who know the sacred rites, today celebrate this thy name *shipivishṭa*; I, who am weak, laud thee who art strong and dwellest beyond this lower world (*kshayantam asya rajasaḥ parâke*). What, Vishṇu, hast thou to blame, that thou declaredest, 'I am *shipivishṭa*'? Do not conceal from us this form (*varpas*), since thou didst assume another shape in the battle." The phrase "dwelling in the lower world" (*rajasaḥ parâke*), or "beyond this world," furnishes us with a clue to the real meaning of the passage. It was in the nether world that Vishṇu bore this bad name. And what was the bad name after all? *Shipivishṭa*, or "enveloped like *shepa*," meaning that his rays were obscured, or that he was temporarily concealed in a dark cover. The poet, therefore, asks Vishṇu not to be ashamed of the epithet, because, says he, the form indicated by the bad name is only temporarily assumed, as a dark armour, for the purpose of fighting with the Asuras, and as it was no longer needed, Vishṇu is invoked to reveal his true form (*varpas*) to the worshipper. That is the real meaning of the verses quoted above, and in spite of the attempt of Yâska and other scholars to convert the bad name of Vishṇu into a good one by the help of etymological speculations, it is plain that *shipivishṭa* was a bad name, and that it signified the dark outer appearance of Vishṇu in his fight with the demons in the nether world. If the sun is called *bṛihach-chhepas* when moving in regions above the horizon, he can be very well described as *shipivishṭa* or "enveloped like *shepa*," when moving in the nether world; and there is hardly anything therein of which the deity or his worshippers should be ashamed of. Later Purâṇic tradition represents Vishṇu as sleeping during this period; but whether we take it as sleep or disease it means one and the same thing. It is the story of Vishṇu going down to the nether world, dark or diseased, to plant his third step on the head of the Asuras, or in a dark armour to help Indra in his struggle for waters and light, a struggle which, we have seen, lasted for a long time and resulted in the flowing of waters, the recovery of the dawn and the coming out of the sun in a bright armour after a long and continuous darkness.

A comparison with the abodes of other Vedic deities, who are said to traverse the whole universe like Vishṇu confirms the same view. One of these deities is Savitṛi, who in V, 81, 3, is described as measuring the world (*rajâṁsi*); and in I, 35, 6, we are told "There are three heavens (*dyâvaḥ*) of Savitṛi, two of them are near and the third, bearing the brave, is in the world of Yama." This means that two of Savitṛi's three abodes are in the upper heaven and one in the nether world or the kingdom of Yama. The second deity that traverses or measures the universe is Agni (VI, 7, 7). He has three stations, one in *samudra* or ocean, one in heaven (*divi*) and one in the waters or *apsu* (I, 95, 3). His light is spoken of as three-fold (III, 26, 7), he has three heads (I, 146, 1) and three seats, powers or tongues (III, 20, 2; VIII, 39, 8). Now although these three stations do not seem to be always conceived alike, yet one of them at any rate can be clearly identified with the third step of Vishṇu; for in X, 1, 3, we are told that the third station of Agni is known only to Vishṇu, while in V, 3, 3, Agni, with the *upama* (last or highest) step of Vishṇu, is said to guard the sacred cows. This description agrees well with I, 154, 5 and 6, where swift moving cows and a spring of honey are said to exist in the place where the highest step of Vishṇu is planted. It has been shown above that Agni sometimes represents the sun in the Ṛig-Veda, and that his hiding in the waters and coming out of them as *apâm napât* or the child of waters is only a different version of the sun sinking below the horizon for a long time and then emerging out of the nether ocean at the end of the long Arctic night. Vishṇu is also the same sun under a different name, and the third step of Vishṇu and the third or the hidden abode of Agni can, therefore, be easily recognised as identical in character. The third deity that traverses the universe is the Ashvins to whom the epithet *parijman* or 'going round' is applied several times in the Ṛig-Veda (I, 46, 14; I, 117, 6). The Ashvins are said to have three stations (VIII, 8, 23), and their chariot, which is said to go over both the worlds alike (I, 30, 18), has three wheels one of which is represented as deposited in a cave or a secret place, like the third step of Vishṇu, which is beyond the ken of mortals (cf. X, 85, 14–16). This coincidence between the third stations of the three different world-traversing gods cannot be treated as accidental; and if so, the combined effect of all the passages stated above will be clearly seen to point out to the conclusion that the third or the hidden place, dwelling or abode in each case must be sought for in the nether world, the world of the Pitṛis, of Yama, of waters and darkness.

Trita Âptya.

It has been stated above that the year divided into three parts of 4 months each represents the three steps of Vishṇu; and that the first two parts were said to be visible as contrasted with the third which was hidden, because in the ancient home of the Aryan people the sun was above the horizon only for about 8 months. If we personify these three parts of the year, we get a legend of three brothers, the first two of whom may be described as arranging to throw the third into a pit of darkness. This is exactly the story of Trita Âptya in the Ṛig-Veda or of Thrâetaona in the Avesta. Thus Sâyaṇa, in his commentary on I, 105, quotes a passage from the Taittirîya Brâhmaṇa (III, 2, 8, 10–11) and also a story of the Shâṭyâyanins giving the legend of three brothers called Ekata, Dvita and Trita, or the first, the second and the third, the former two of whom threw the last or Trita into a well from which he was taken out by Bṛihaspati. But in the Ṛig-Veda Ekata is not mentioned anywhere; while Dvita, which grammatically means the second, is met with in two places (V, 18, 2; VIII, 47, 16). Dvita is the seer of the 18th hymn in the fifth Maṇḍala, and in the second verse of the hymn he is said to receive maimed offerings; while in VIII, 47, 16, the dawn is asked to bear away the evil dream to Dvita and Trita. Grammatical analogy points out that Trita must mean the third, and in VI, 44, 23, the word *triteshu* is used as a numeral adjective to *rochaneshu* meaning "in the third region." As a Vedic deity Trita is called Âptya, meaning "born of or residing in waters" (Sây. on VIII, 47, 15); and he is referred to in several places, being associated with the Maruts and Indra in slaying the demon or the powers of darkness like Vṛitra. Thus in X, 8, 8, Trita, urged by Indra, is said to have fought against and slew the three-headed (*tri-shiras*) son of Tvashṭṛi and released the cows; while in X, 99, 6, we read that Indra subdued the loud-roaring six-eyed demon, and Trita, strengthened by the same draught, slew the boar (*varâha*) with his iron-pointed bolt. But the most important incident in the story of Trita is mentioned in I, 105. In this hymn Trita is described as having fallen into a *kûpa* or well, which is also called *vavra* or a pit in X, 8, 7. Trita then invoked the gods for help and Bṛihaspati hearing his prayers released him from his distress (I, 105, 17). Some of the verses in the hymn are very suggestive; for instance in verse 9, Trita tells us about his "kinship with the seven rays in the heaven. Trita Âptya knows it and he speaks for kinship." The ruddy Vṛika, or the wolf of darkness, is again described in verse 18 as having perceived Trita going by the way. These references show that Trita was related to the powers of light, but had the misfortune of being thrown into darkness. In IX, 102, 2, Trita's abode is said to be hidden or secret, a description similar to that of the third step of Vishṇu. The same story is found in the Avesta. There Thrâetaona, who bears the patronomic epithet Âthwya (*Sans.* Âptya), is described as slaying the fiendish serpent Azi Dahâka, who is said to be three-mouthed and six-eyed (Yt. XIX, 36–37; V, 33–34). But what is still more remarkable in the Avestic legend is that Thrâetaona in his expedition against the demon is said to have been accompanied by his two brothers who sought to slay him on the way.[1] The Avestic legend thus fully corroborates the story of the Shâṭyâyanins quoted by Sâyaṇa, and when the two accounts agree so well we cannot lightly set aside the story in the Brâhmaṇa,

1. See Spiegel, Die Arische Periode, p. 271, quoted by Macdonell in his Vedic Mythology, § 23. Also compare S. B. E. Series, Vol. XXXIII p. 222, note 2.

or hold that it was woven out of stray references in the Ṛig-Veda. But in the absence of the Arctic theory, or the theory of long darkness extending over nearly four months or a third part of the year, European Scholars have been at a loss to understand why the deity should have been named 'the Third'; and various ingenious theories have been started to explain how Trita, which ordinarily means the third, came to denote the deity that was thrown into a pit or well in a distant land. Thus Prof. Max Muller thinks that the name of the deity was originally Tṛita (तृत) and not Trita (त्रित); and he derives the former from the root *tṛî* (तॄ) to cross. Tṛita (तृत), which, by-the-by, is not a regular grammatical form though found in the Atharva Veda VI, 113, 1 and 3, would thus mean "the sun crossing the ocean," being in this respect comparable to *taraṇi* which means "the sun" in the later Sanskrit literature. In short, according to Prof. Max Muller, Tṛita (तृत) means the 'set sun'; and the story of Trita (त्रित) is, therefore, only a different version of the daily struggle between light and darkness. But Prof. Max Muller's theory requires us to assume that this misconception or the corruption of Tṛita (तृत) into Trita (त्रित) took place before the Aryan separation, inasmuch as in Old Irish we have the word *triath* which means the sea, and which is phonetically equivalent to Greek *triton*, Sanskrit *trita* and Zend *thrita*. Prof. Max Muller himself admits the validity of this objection, and points out that the Old Norse *Thridi*, a name of Odin, as the mate of Har and Jasnhar, can be accounted for only on the supposition that *tṛita* (तृत) was changed by a misapprehension into *trita* (त्रित) long before the Aryan separation. This shows to what straits scholars are reduced in explaining certain myths in the absence of the true key to their meaning. We assume, without the slightest authority, that a misapprehension must have taken place before the Aryan separation, because we cannot explain why a deity was called 'the Third,' and why *triath* in Old Irish was used to denote the sea. But the whole legend can be now very easily and naturally explained by the Arctic theory. The personified third part of the year, called Trita or the Third, is naturally described as going into darkness, or a well or pit, or into the waters of the nether world, for the sun went below the horizon during that period in the home of the ancestors of the Vedic people. The connection of Trita with darkness and waters, or his part in the Vṛitra fight, or the use of the word *triath* to denote the sea in Old Irish now become perfectly plain and intelligible. The nether world is the home of aerial waters, and Bṛihaspati, who is said to have released the cows from their place of confinement in a cave in the nether world, is naturally spoken of as rescuing Trita, when he was sunk in the well of waters. Speaking of the abode of Trita, Prof. Max Muller observes that "the hiding place of Trita, the *vavra*, is really the same *anârambhaṇam tamas*, the endless darkness, from which light and some of its legendary representatives, such as Atri, Vandana and others, emerged every day." I subscribe to every word of this sentence except the last two. It shows how the learned Professor saw, but narrowly missed grasping the truth, having nothing else to guide him except the Dawn and the Vernal theory. He had perceived that Trita's hiding place was in the endless darkness and that the sun rose out of the same dark region; and from this to the Arctic theory was but a small step. But whatever the reason may be, the Professor did not venture to go further, and the result is that an otherwise correct conception of the mythological incidents in Trita's legend is marred by two ominous words, *viz.*, "every day," at the end of the sentence quoted above. Strike off the last two words, put a full point after 'emerged,' and in the light of the Arctic theory we have a correct explanation of the legend of Trita as well as of the origin of the name, Trita or the Third.

Âpaḥ.

The nature and movement of aerial or celestial waters have been discussed at length in the last chapter and practically there is very little that remains to be said on this point. We have also seen how the nether world or the world of waters was conceived like an inverted hemisphere or tub, so that anyone going there was said to go to the region of endless darkness or bottomless waters. A mountainous range was again believed to extend over the borders of this ocean, forming a stony wall as it were between the upper and the lower world; and when the waters were to be freed to flow upwards, it was necessary to pierce through this mountainous range and clear the apertures which were closed by Vṛitra by stretching his body across them. In one place the well or *avata*, which Brahmaṇaspati opened, is said to be closed at its mouth with stones (*ashmâsyam*, II, 24, 4), and in X, 67, 3, the stony barriers (*ashmanmayâni nahanâ*) of the prison wherein the cows were confined are expressly mentioned. A mountain, *parvata*, is also said to exist in the belly of Vṛitra (I, 54, 10), and Shambara is described as dwelling on the mountains. We have seen how the word *parvata* occurring in this connection has been misunderstood ever since the days of the Nairuktas, who, though they did a yeoman's service to the cause of Vedic interpretation, seem to have sometimes carried their etymological method too far. The connection of the nether world of waters with mountains and darkness may thus be taken as established, and the legends of Vṛitra, Bhujyu, Saptavadhri, Trita, &c. further show that the nether waters formed not only the home of the evil spirits and the scene of fights with them, but that it was the place which Sûrya, Agni, Vishṇu, the Ashvins and Trita had all to visit during a portion of the year. It was the place where Vishṇu slept, or hid himself, when afflicted with a kind of skin-disease, and where the sacrificial horse, which represented the sun, was harnessed by Trita, and first bestrode by Indra (I, 163, 2). It was the place from which the seven aerial rivers rose up with the seven suns to illumine the ancient home of the Aryan race for seven months, and into which they again dropped with the sun after that period. It was the same waters that formed the source of earthly waters by producing rain by their circulation through the upper regions of heaven. These waters were believed to stretch from west to east underneath the three earths, thus forming at once the place of desolation and the place of the birth of the sun and other matutinal deities mentioned in the Ṛig-Veda. It was the place where Vṛitra concealed the cows in a stony stable, and where Varuṇa and Yama reigned supreme, and the fathers (Pitṛis) lived in comfort and delight. As regards the division of this watery region, we might say that the Vedic bards conceived the nether world as divided in the same way as the earth and the heaven. Thus there were three, seven or ten lower worlds to match with the three-fold, seven-fold or ten-fold division of the heaven and the earth. It will thus be seen that a right conception of the nether waters and their movement is quite necessary for understanding the real meaning of many a Vedic, and, we might even say, the Purâṇic legends, for the latter are generally based either upon the Vedic legends or some one or other incident mentioned in them. If this universal and comprehensive character of the waters be not properly understood many legends will appear dark, confused or mysterious; and I have, therefore, summed up in this place the leading characteristics of the goddesses of water as conceived by the Vedic poets and discussed in the foregoing pages. In the post-Vedic literature many of these characteristics are predicated of the sea of salt water on the surface of the earth, much in the same way as the Greek *Okeanos*, which has been shewn to be phonetically identical with the Sanskrit word *âshayâna* or enveloping, came to denote the ocean or the sea in European languages. Thus Bhartṛihari in his Vairâgya-shataka (v. 76) says:—"Oh! how extensive, grand and patient is the body of the ocean! For here sleeps Keshava (Vishṇu); here the clan of his enemies (Vṛitra and other demons of darkness); here lie also the host of mountains (the *parvata* of the Vedas) in search of shelter; and here too (lies) the Mare's fire (submarine fire) with all the Saṁvartakas (clouds)." This is intended to be a summary of the Purâṇic legends regarding the ocean, but it can be easily seen that every one of them is based upon the Vedic conception of the nature and movements of aerial waters, which formed the very material out of which the world was believed to be created. After this it is needless to explain why *Âpaḥ* occupied such an important place in the Vedic pantheon.

Seven-fold and Ten-fold.

It is stated above that the nether waters are divided after the manner of the heaven and the earth, either into three, seven or ten divisions. We have also seen that the ancient sacrificers completed their sacrificial session in seven, nine or ten months; and that the Navagvas and the Dashagvas are, therefore, sometimes mentioned together, sometimes separately and sometimes along with the seven sages or *vipras*. I have also briefly referred to the seven-fold division, which generally obtains not only in the Vedic, but also in other Aryan mythologies. But the subject deserves a fuller consideration, and I propose here to collect certain facts bearing upon it, which seem to have hitherto attracted but little attention. All that Yâska and Sâyaṇa tell us about the seven-fold division is that there are seven horses of the sun and seven tongues or flames of Agni, because the rays of the sun are seven in number; and the late Mr. S. P. Pandit goes so far as to assert that the seven rays here referred to may be the prismatic colours with which we are familiar in the science of optics, or the seven colours of the rainbow. All this appears to be very satisfactory at the first sight, but our complacency is disturbed as soon as we are told that along with the *seven* rays and horses of the sun, the Ṛig-Veda speaks of *ten* horses or *ten* rays of the same luminary. Yâska and Sâyaṇa get over the difficulty either by ignoring or by explaining away, in a tortuous manner, all references to the ten-fold division of this kind. But the places where it is mentioned are too many to allow us to lightly set aside the ten-fold division, which occurs along with the seven-fold one in the Ṛig-Veda; and we must find out why this double division is recorded in the Ṛig-Veda. But before inquiring into it, we shall collect all the facts and see how far this double division extends in the Vedic literature.

We begin with the sun. He is described as seven-horsed (*saptâshva*) in V, 45, 9, and his chariot is described as seven-wheeled, or yoked with seven horses, or one seven-named horse in I, 164, 3. The seven bay steeds (*haritaḥ*) are also mentioned as drawing the carriage of the sun in I, 50, 8. But in IX, 63, 9, the sun is said to have yoked ten horses to his carriage; and the wheel of the year-god is said to be carried by ten horses in I, 164, 14. In the Atharva Veda XI, 4, 22, the sun's carriage is, however, said to be eight-wheeled (*ashṭâ-chakra*).

Indra is called *sapta-rashmi* in II, 12, 12, and his chariot is also said to be seven-rayed in VI, 44, 24. But in V, 33, 8, ten white horses are said to bear him; while in VIII, 24, 23, Indra is said to be "the tenth new" (*dashamam navam*). In the Taittirîya Âraṇyaka III, 11, 1, Indra's self is said to be going about ten-fold (*Indrasya âtmânam dashadhâ charantam*); and corresponding to it, it may be here noticed, we have in the Bahrâm Yasht, in the Avesta, ten incarnations of Verethraghna (*Sans.* Vṛitrahan) specifically mentioned. Amongst the proteges of Indra we again have one called Dasha-dyu, or one shining ten-fold (I, 33, 14; VI, 26, 4); while Dashoṇi a being with ten arms or helpers, and Dasha-mâya, or a ten-wiled person, are mentioned amongst those whom Indra forced to submit to Dyotana in VI, 20, 8. Dashoṇya and Dasha-shipra are also mentioned to have been by the side of Indra when he drank Soma with Syûmarashmi in VIII, 52, 2.

The chariot of Soma and Pûṣhan is described as five-rayed and seven-wheeled in II, 40, 3. But Soma is said to have ten rays (*rashmayaḥ*) in IX, 97, 23.

Agni is described as *sapta-rashmi* or seven-rayed in I, 146, 1, and his rays are expressly said to be seven in II, 5, 2. His horses are similarly described as seven-tongued in III, 6, 2. ·But in I, 141, 2, Agni is said to be *dasha-pramati*, and his ten secret dwellings are mentioned in X, 51, 3. The adjective *navamam* or the ninth is also applied to the youngest (*naviṣhṭhâya*) Agni in V, 27, 3, much in the same way as *dashamam* is applied to the new (*nava*) Indra in VIII, 24, 23.

Seven *dhîtis*, prayers or devotions of sacrificial priests, are mentioned in IX, 8, 4. But in I, 144, 5, their number is said to be ten.

Foods are said to be seven in III, 4, 7. But in I, 122, 13, the food is described as divided ten-fold. In the Shatapatha Brâhmaṇa I, 8, 1, 34, *haviḥ*, or sacrificial oblation, is, however, described as made in ten ways.

Seven *vipras* (III, 7, 7,), or seven sacrificers (*hotâraḥ*), are mentioned in several places (III, 10, 4; IV, 2, 15; X, 63, 7). But in III, 39, 5, the number of the Dashagvas is expressly stated to be ten. Ten sacrificers (*hotâraḥ*) are also mentioned in the Taittirîya Brâhmaṇa II, 2, 1, 1, and II, 2, 4, 1.

Bṛihaspati, the first-born sacrificer, is described as seven-mouthed or *saptâsya* in IV, 50, 4, and the same verse occurs in the Atharva Veda (XX, 88, 4). But in the Atharva Veda IV, 6, 1, the first Brâhmaṇa Bṛhaspati is said to be *dashâsya*, or ten-mouthed, and *dasha-shirṣha*, or ten-headed. Seven heads of the Brâhmaṇa are not expressly mentioned in the

Ṛig-Veda, but in X, 67, 1, "our father," meaning the father of the Aṅgirases, is said to have acquired seven-headed (*sapta-shîrṣhṇî*) devotion or intelligence (*dhî*).

Seven divisions of the earth are mentioned in I, 22, 16. But the earths are said to be ten (*dashâvani*) in X, 94, 7, (also cf. I, 52, 11).

The cows' stable which the Ashvins opened is said to be *saptâsya* or seven-mouthed in X, 40, 8. But a ten-fold cows' stable (*dashavraja*) is mentioned in VIII, 8, 20; 49, 10; 50, 9.

In X, 93, 4, Aryaman, Mitra, Varuṇa, Rudra, Maruts, Pûṣhan and Bhaga are mentioned as seven kings. But ten gold-like (*hiraṇyasaṇdṛisha*) kings are referred to in VIII, 5, 38, and ten non-sacrificing (*ayajyavaḥ*) kings are mentioned in VII, 83, 7. The Atharva Veda, XI, 8, 10, further tells us that there were only ten ancient gods.

These references will make it clear that if the horses of the sun are mentioned as seven in one place, they are said to be ten in another; and so there are seven devotions and ten devotions; seven earths and ten earths; seven cowpens and ten cowpens, and so on. This double division may not be equally explicit in all cases; but, on the whole, there can be no doubt that the several objects mentioned in the above passages are conceived as divided in a double manner, once as seven-fold and once as ten-fold. To this double division may be added the three-fold division of the heaven, the earth and the nether world or Nir-ṛiti; and the eleven-fold division of gods in the heaven, the earth and waters mentioned previously. In the Atharva Veda XI, 7, 14, nine earths, nine oceans and nine skies are also mentioned, and the same division again occurs in the Atharvashiras Upaniṣhad, 6. Now it is evident that the theory started by Yâska cannot explain all these different methods of division. We might say that the three-fold division was suggested by the heaven, the earth and the lower world. But how are we to account for all kinds of division from seven to eleven? So far as I am aware there is no attempt made to explain the principle of division underlying these different classifications. But now the analogy of the seven priests, the Navagvas and the Dashagvas, suggests to us the probable reason of the different methods of division noticed above. The fact that the horses of the sun are once said to be seven and once ten, seems naturally to refer to seven months' and ten months' period of sunshine previously described; and if so, this helps us in understanding the real meaning of the different divisions. The seven-fold, nine-fold or ten-fold division of things is thus merely a different phase of the division of sacrificers into the seven Hotṛis, the Navagvas and the Dashagvas. Both seem to be the effects of the same cause. The mother land of the Aryan race in ancient times, lying between the North Pole and the Arctic circle, was probably divided into different zones according to the number of months for which the sun was seen above the horizon in each; and the facts, that the Navagvas and the Dashagvas are said to be the chief or the most prominent of the Aṅgirases, that *saptâshva* was the principal designation of Sûrya, and that the sons of Aditi who were presented to the gods were only seven in number, further show that in the ancient Arctic home a year of seven, nine, or ten months' sunshine must have been more prevalent than a year of 8 or 11 months. It may, however, be noticed that just as the Aṅgirases are said to be *virûpas*, Aryaman is described in X, 64, 5, as having a great chariot, and amidst his births of various forms (*viṣhu-rûpeṣhu*) he is said to be a seven-fold sacrificer (*sapta-hotṛi*), showing that though the seven-fold character of Aryaman was the chief or the principal one, yet there were various other forms of the deity. In X, 27, 15, seven, eight, nine and ten *Vîras* or warriors are said to rise from below, behind, in the front, or on the back, or, in other words, all round. This verse is differently interpreted by different scholars; but it seems to me to refer to the seven-fold, eight-fold, or nine-fold division of the sacrificers, or the Aṅgirases, who are actually described in III, 53,7, as "the *Vîras* or warriors of the Asura." It is, therefore, quite probable that the same *Vîras* are referred to in X, 27, 15. In VII, 4, 1, Indra is said to be worshipped by people in the front (east), behind (west), up (north), and down (south), meaning that his worshippers were to be found everywhere; and if the adjectives "below, behind &c." in X, 27, 15, be similarly interpreted the verse would mean that the seven-fold, eight-fold, nine-fold, or ten-fold division of sacrificers was to be met with in places all round. In other words, the different places in the Arctic region had each a group of sacrificers of its own, corresponding to the months of sunshine in the place. On no other theory can we account for the different divisions satisfactorily as on the Arctic theory, and in the absence of a better explanation we may, I think, accept the one stated above.

The ten Kings and Râvana.

It has been noticed above that ten gold-like kings (VIII, 5, 38), and ten non-sacrificing kings (VII, 83, 7), are mentioned in the Ṛig-Veda. But there is an important incident connected with the ten non-sacrificing kings which deserves more than a passing notice in this place. Sudâs, the son of Divodâsa Atithigva, is described as engaged in a fight with the ten non-worshipping (*ayajyavaḥ*) kings, and is said to have received help from Indra and Varuṇa (VII, 33, 3-5 ; 83, 6-8). It is known as the *Dâsharâjña* fight, and Vasiṣhṭha, as the priest of Sudâs, is said to have secured the assistance of Indra for him. On this slender basis some scholars have erected a stately edifice of the fight of the Aryan races with the ten non-Aryan or non-worshipping kings. But it seems to me that the *Dâsharâjña* fight can be more simply and naturally explained by taking it to be a different version of Indra's fight with the seven Dânus or demons (X, 120, 6). In X, 49, 8, Indra is called the seven-slayer (*sapta-han*) with reference either to the seven Dânus or demons (X, 120, 6,) or to the seven cities of Vṛitra (I, 174, 2), in the seven-bottomed ocean (VIII, 40, 5). Now if Indra is *sapta-han* on the seven-fold division, he may be easily conceived as *dasha-han*, or the ten-slayer, on the ten-fold method of division. The word *dasha-han* does not occur in the Ṛig-Veda, but the fight with the ten kings (*ayajyavaḥ dasha râjânaḥ*) practically amounts to the same thing. It has been stated above that amongst Indra's enemies we have persons like Dasha-mâya and Dashoṇi, who are obviously connected in some way with the number ten. The ten gold-like kings mentioned above again seem to represent the ten monthly sun-gods, and the fact that they are said to be given to the sacrificers further strengthens this view. One of Indra's proteges is, we further know, described as Dasha-dyu, or shining ten-fold. If all these facts are put together, we are naturally led to the conclusion that like the seven Dânus or demons, the powers of darkness were sometime conceived as ten-fold, and Indra's helping Sudâs in his fight with the ten non-worshipping kings is nothing more than the old story of the annual fight between light and darkness as conceived by the inhabitants of a place where a summer of ten months was followed by a long winter night of two months, or, in other words which formed the land of the Dashagvas.

But our interest in this remarkable fight does not come to an end with this explanation. For when we remember the fact that the word king was not confined to the warrior class in the Ṛig-Veda, and that in one place (I, 139, 7) it seems to be actually applied to the Aṅgirases, the expressions 'ten golden kings' and 'ten sacrificers' or 'ten-fold Aṅgirases,' or 'the ten Dashagvas sacrificing for ten months' become synonymous phrases. Now Bṛihaspati was the chief of the Aṅgirases, and as such may naturally be considered to be the representative of them all; and we have seen that he is represented once as seven-mouthed and seven-headed, and once as ten-mouthed and ten-headed (Ṛig. IV, 50, 4; A. V. IV, 6, 1). This Bṛihaspati is connected with the story of Saramâ and Paṇis, and is said to have helped Indra in recovering the cows, or is sometimes described as having performed the feat himself (I, 83, 4; X, 108, 6-11). Bṛihaspati is also represented in X, 109, as having lost his wife, who was restored to him by the gods. This is obviously the story of the restoration of the dawn to man, as represented by the chief sacrificer Bṛihaspati. In the Taittirîya Âraṇyaka I, 12, 3-4, Indra is described as the lover of Ahalyâ (*Ahalyâyai jâraḥ*), and the myth has been explained as referring to the dawn and the sun, by an old orthodox scholar like Kumârila. Ahalyâ in the later literature is the wife of the Ṛishi Gotama (*lit.* rich in cows); but it is not difficult to perceive that the story of Ahalyâ (which Prof. Max Muller derives from *ahan*, a day), was originally a dawn-story, or a different version of the legend of Brahmajâyâ narrated in X, 109.

These facts are very suggestive and call to mind some of the incidents in the story of the Râmâyaṇa. It is quite outside the scope of this book to fully enter into the question of the historical basis of this well-known Indian epic. We are concerned with Vedic myths and Vedic mythology, and if we refer to the Râmâyaṇa we do so simply to point out such resemblances as are too striking to be left unnoticed. The main story in the Râmâyaṇa is narrated in such detail that, on the face of it, it bears the stamp of a historic origin. But even then we have to explain why Râma's adversary was conceived as a ten-headed monster or an unnatural being, and why Râma's father was called Dasharatha or ten-carred. A ten-headed monster cannot ordinarily be regarded as a historical fact and it seems not unlikely that some of the incidents of Vedic myths may have been skilfully interwoven with the main story of the epic by its auther. We have seen above that some of the Indra's enemies are described as Dashoṇi or Dashamâya, and that in the *Dâsharâjña* fight there were ten non-sacrificing or demoniac kings opposed to Sudâs. These ten non-sacrificing kings may well be conceived as a single king with ten heads and spoken of as a ten-headed monster, much in the same way as Bṛihaspati, the chief of the ten Aṅgirases, is said to be ten-headed or ten-mouthed. The fact that the brother of this ten-headed monster slept continuously for six months in a year also indicates his Arctic origin. Prof. Rhys, in his *Hibbert Lectures*, quotes Plutarch to the effect that the Paphlagonians regarded their gods as shut up in a prison during winter and let loose in summer, and interprets the legend as indicating the temporary ascendancy of the powers of darkness over those of light during the continuous night of the Arctic region. If we adopt this view, we can easily explain how all the gods were said to be thrown into prison by Râvaṇa until they were released by Râma. Another fact in the Râmâyaṇa which is supposed to require explanation is the conception of the monkey-god Hanûmân. The Ṛig-Veda mentions a monkey (*kapi*), who, as Vṛishâkapi, has been elsewhere shown to represent the sun at the autumnal equinox, or according to the Arctic theory discussed in this book, at the time of going down below the horizon into the long darkness of the nether world. It is Dr. Pischel, who first threw out the hint that this Vṛishâkapi may probably be the ancestor of the Purâṇic Hanûmân; and the fact that Hanûmân was born at a time when the sun we said to be eclipsed goes to corroborate the view to a certain extent. Mr. Nârâyan Aiyangâr, in his Essays on Indo-Aryan mythology, further points out that Sitâ, the wife of Râma, may be traced to the Ṛig-Vedic *Sitâ*, meaning "a ploughed furrow" which is invoked to bestow wealth upon the worshipper in IV, 57, 6 and 7; and so far as the birth of Sitâ from the earth and her final disappearance into it are concerned the explanation appears very probable. It seems, therefore, very likely that the mythical element in the Râmâyaṇa was derived from the story of the restoration of the dawn or Brahmajâya to man as represented by the first sacrificer Bṛihaspati, or the fight of Indra with Vṛitra for the recovery of light. Whether we can go further than this cannot be decided without further research. Prof. Max Muller, in his Lectures on the Science of Language, has shown that many names in the Iliad can be traced back to the Vedas. For instance he derives Helen from Saramâ, Paris from Paṇis, and Briesis from Bṛisaya. But even then all the personages mentioned in the Iliad cannot be explained in this way. One thing, however, seems certain, that the story of the restoration of the Dawn-wife to her husband was an ancient inheritance both with the Greeks and the Indians ; and we need not, therefore, be surprised if we discover a few striking coincidences between the Iliad on the one hand and the Râmâyaṇa on the other ; for a common mythical element appears to have been interwoven with the main story, of course with a different local colouring, in each case. The question whether the Râmâyaṇa was copied from Homer is, therefore, entirely meaningless. The fact seems to be that both Homer and Vâlmîki have utilised a common mythological stock, and any resemblances between their works only go to prove the theory of their common origin. It has been pointed out by Prof. Weber that in the Buddhistic Dasharatha Jâtaka, Sîtâ is represented as the sister and not as the wife of Râma, and the learned Professor tells us that this must be an ancient version of the story, for a marriage with one's sister must be considered to be as primeval as Adam himself. The late Mr. Telang was of opinion that the Buddhists must have deliberately misrepresented the story of the Brahmanical epic, and such a perversion is not improbable. But on the theory that certain features of the Vedic dawn-myths were probably interwoven with the main historic story of the epic, we may explain the Buddhistic account by supposing that it was the out-come of an unsuccessful attempt made in pre-Buddhistic time to identify Râma with Sûrya in the Ṛig-Veda, the latter of whom is described both as the brother and the lover of the Dawn (VII, 75, 5; VI, 55, 4 and 5; X, 3, 3). I have already stated that the subject is too vast to be treated here at any length. My object was to point out a few resemblances between the story of the Râmâyaṇa and the Vedic myths as they occurred to me. But the question, howsoever interesting, is not relevant to the subject in hand, and I must give up the temptation of going into it more fully in this place. The question of ten incarnations is also similarly connected with the ten golden kings, or the ten gods mentioned in the Atharva Veda, or the ten incarnations of Verethreghna in the Avesta. The ten incarnations in the Avesta (Yt. XIV) are, a wind, a bull, a horse, a camel, a boar, a youth, a raven, a ram, a buck and a man; and four of them, *viz.*, a horse, a boar, a youth and a man, seem to correspond with Kalki, Varâha, Vâmana and Râma amongst the ten Avatâras mentioned in the Purâṇic literature. This shows that the conception of the ten Avatâras was, at any rate, Indo-Iranian in origin, and it is no doubt interesting to follow it up and trace its development on the Indian soil. The Matsya, the Kûrma, the Varâha, the Nârasiṁha, the Vâmana and, as we have now seen, the Râma Avatâra can be more or less traced to the Ṛig-Veda. But it would require much patient research to thoroughly investigate these matters, and I cannot do more than to throw out such hints as have occurred to me, and ask the reader to take them for what they are worth. If the Arctic theory is established, it will throw a good deal of new light not only on the Vedic but also on the Purâṇic mythology, and it will then be necessary to revise, in some cases entirely recast, the current explanations of both. But the work as stated previously cannot be undertaken in a book which is mainly devoted to the examination of evidence in support of the new theory.

We have now discussed most of the Vedic legends likely to throw any light on the main point of our inquiry. There are many other incidents, which can be better explained on the Arctic theory than at present. For instance, we can now well understand why Mitra and Varuṇa were originally conceived as two correlated deities; for according to our theory they would represent half-year-long light and darkness in the Paradise of the Aryan race, and Varuṇa can then be very well described as "embracing the nights," (*kṣhapaḥ pari ṣhasvaje*, VIII, 41, 3). But we cannot go into all these points in this place. What I have said is, I think, sufficient to convince any one that there are a number of incidents in the Vedic myths, which are inexplicable on the theory of a diurnal struggle between light and darkness, or the conquest of spring over winter, or of the storm-god over clouds. Thus we have not been able as yet to explain why Vṛitra was killed once a year, why the waters and the light were described as being released simultaneously by killing Vṛitra, or why Indra's fight with Shambara was said to have commenced on the 40th day of *Sharad*, or why the fight was said to be conducted in the *parâvat* regions, why Dîrghatamas was described as having grown old in the 10th *yuga*, why Mârtâṇḍa was cast away as a dead son, why Trita, or the Third, was said to have fallen into a pit, or again why Viṣhṇu's third stride was said to be invisible. We now find that not only all these but many more incidents in the Vedic myths are satisfactorily accounted for, and the legends in their turn directly lead us to the Arctic theory. The legends of Indra and Vṛitra, of Saptavadhri, of Aditi and her seven flourishing and one still-born son, of Sûrya's wheel and of Dîrghatamas, are again found to contain express passages which indicate seven or ten months' period of sunshine at the place, where these legends originated; and unless we are prepared to say that all these may be accidental coincidences, we cannot, I think, legitimately withhold our assent to a theory which explains so many facts, and incidents, hitherto ignored, neglected or misunderstood, in an easy, natural and intelligible manner. I do not mean to say that the Arctic theory would entirely dispense with the necessity of the Dawn, the Storm or the Vernal theory. All that I contend for is that the Arctic theory explains a number of legendary or traditional facts hitherto hopelessly given up as inexplicable and that in the interpretation of Vedic myths it furnishes us with a weapon far more powerful and effective than either the Dawn, the Storm or the Vernal theory. In short, from a mythological point of view alone, there is ample ground to recommend it to our acceptance side by side with, and, in some cases, even in substitution of the old theories. In addition to this it has been already shown in previous chapters that the new theory rests on direct and independent statements of facts, contained in the Ṛig-Veda, about the duration and nature of the dawn, days and nights, seasons, months and the year in the home of the ancient fathers of the Vedic Ṛishis; and that the Avestic and Roman traditions fully corroborate our conclusion. We have further seen that the theory is perfectly consistent with the latest results of geological and archæological researches. Shall we then still withhold our assent to the only theory which explains so many facts, legends, and incidents, in a natural and intelligent way and which throws such a flood of light on the ancient history of the Aryan race, simply because it seems to be rather uncouth at the first sight? The rules of logic and scientific research will not justify us in doing so, and I fully rely on them for the eventual success or failure of the theory I have endeavoured to prove in these pages.

CHAPTER XI.

THE AVESTIC EVIDENCE.

Nature of Avestic evidence stated —Different views of scholars regarding its character —Necessity of re-examining the subject —An abstract of the first Fargard of the Vendidad —Sixteen lands created by Ahura Mazda with their modern equivalents &c.—Airyana Vaejo, the first created land represents the Paradise of the Iranians —Different views regarding its position —Darmesteter, Spiegel and others locate it in the east ; Haug and Bunsen in the far north —Darmesteter's argument examined —Airyana Vaejo cannot be determined from the position of Vanguhi —Identification of Rangha with the Caspian Sea or the westernmost river doubtful —Rangha is probably the same as Rasâ in the Rig-Veda X, 75, 6 —Unsoundness of Darmesteter's reasoning —The position of the Airyana Vaejo must be determined from its special characteristics found in the Avesta —The passage where ten months winter is said to be such a characteristic cited —Ten months winter first introduced into the happy land by Angra Mainyu —Indicates that before the fiend's invasion there must have been ten months summer and two months winter in the land —Sudden change in the Polar climate fully confirmed by latest geological researches —Two months winter necessarily synchronous with long Arctic night —The tradition about seven months summer and five months winter also refers to the original climate in the Airyana Vaejo —Mentioned in the Bundahish —Not inconsistent with the tradition of ten months summer recorded in the original passage —Both possible in the Arctic regions —Similar statements in the Rig-Veda —Coincidence between seven months summer, the legend of Aditi, and the date of Indra's fight with Shambara, pointed out —Summary of the second Fargard —Yima's Vara in the Airyana Vaejo —Annual sun-rise and a year-long day therein —Shows that the Airyana Vaejo must be located near the North Pole and not to the east of Iran —The account too graphic to be imaginary or mythical —Represents the advent of the Glacial epoch in the land —It is the oldest human testimony to the advent of the Ice-age, destroying the Arctic home —Special importance of the Avestic evidence pointed out —Fully corroborated by scientific evidence —Migration from Airyana Vaejo rendered necessary by glaciation —Sixteen lands in the first Fargard therefore represent successive stages of migration to Central Asia —Establishes the historical character of the first Fargard —The legend of deluge in the Shatapatha Bráhmana —Probably refers to the same event as the Avestic legends —Other Vedic passages indicating the northern origin of Indian Aryas —Conclusion to be drawn from the Vedic and Avestic evidence combined.

In dealing with the Vedic evidence, both direct and circumstantial, we have by way of comparison quoted or referred to some Avestic legends or myths in the foregoing chapters. But the Avesta contains some important passages directly bearing upon the question of the original Aryan home in the far north, and migrations therefrom to the regions watered by the Oxus, the Jaxartes or the Indus; and it is necessary to discuss these passages in a separate chapter, because they not only confirm and supplement the conclusions we have previously arrived at by the examination of the Vedic evidence, but constitute, what may be called, independent evidence pointing out to the same result. As regards the antiquity of the Avesta, it is superfluous to adduce any proofs in this place; for it is admitted by scholars that the Vedas and the Avesta are but two branches of the same parent stream, though the latter may not be as well preserved as the former. To use a Vedic phrase, the sacred books of the Bráhmans and the Parsis are the twin books of the Aryan race; and they can, therefore, be safely taken to supplement each other whenever it is necessary and possible to do so. This character of the two books is well exhibited with regard to the subject in hand. We have seen that while there are a number of passages in the Vedic literature, which speak of long dawns, continuous darkness, or a sacrificial session of ten months, we have no text or legend which directly refers to the home in the far north or to the cause or causes which forced the ancient Aryans to abandon their primeval home and migrate southwards. But fortunately for us, the Avesta, though not generally as well preserved as the Vedas, contains a passage which supplies the omission in a remarkable way ; and we mean to discuss this passage at some length in this chapter. The Avestic legends and traditions quoted in the foregoing chapters show that a day and a night of six months each were known to the ancestors of the Iranians, and that the appointed time for the appearance of Tishtrya before the worshipper, after his fight with Apaosha, varied from one to a hundred nights, thus indicating that a long darkness extending over a hundred nights was also known to the forefathers of the worshippers of Mazda. The stoppage of the flow of waters and of the movement of the sun in winter, as described in the Farvardîn Yasht, have also been referred to ; and it is shown that the custom of keeping a dead body in the house for two nights, three nights or a month long in winter, until the floods begin to flow, must be ascribed to the absence of sunlight during the period when the floods as well as light were shut up in the nether world by the demons of darkness. All these traditions have their counterparts in the Vedic literature. But the Avestic tradition regarding the original home in the far north and its destruction by snow and ice stands by itself, though in the light of the Vedic evidence discussed in the previous chapters, we can now clearly show that it has a historical basis and that it preserves for us a distinct reminiscence, howsoever fragmentary, of the ancient Aryan home. This tradition is contained in the first two Fargards or chapters of the Vendidad, or the law book of the Mazda-yasnians. They have no connection with the subsequent chapters of the book, and appear to be incorporated into it simply as a relic of old historical or traditional literature. These two Fargards have not failed to attract the attention of Zend scholars ever since the discovery of the

Avesta by Anquetil; and many attempts have been made not only to identify the places mentioned therein, but to draw historical conclusions therefrom. Thus Heeren, Rhode, Lassen, Pictel, Bunsen, Haug and others have recognized in these accounts of the Vendidad, a half historical, half mythical reminiscence of the primeval home and the countries known to the followers of the Avesta, when these Fargards were composed. Professor Spiegel at first took the same view as Rhode, but has latterly retracted his opinion. On the other hand, Kiepert, Breal, Darmesteter and others have shown that no historical conclusion can be drawn from the description contained in the first two chapters of the Vendidad; and this view seems to be now mainly accepted. But it must be borne in mind that this view was formulated at a time when the Vedic evidence in support of the Arctic theory, set forth in the previous chapters, was entirely unknown, and when the existence of an Arctic home in ancient times was not regarded as probable even on geological grounds, man being believed to be post-Glacial and the Arctic regions always unsuited for human habitation. The recent discoveries in Geology and Archæology have, however, thrown a flood of new light on the subject; and if the interpretation of the Vedic traditions noticed in the previous chapters is correct, it will, I think, be readily admitted that a reconsideration of the Avestic tradition from the new standpoint is a necessity and that we should not be deterred from undertaking the task by the recent verdict of Zend scholars against the views of Bunsen and Haug regarding the historical character of the first two Fargards of the Vendidad.

The first Fargard of the Vendidad is devoted to the enumeration of sixteen lands created by Ahura Mazda, the Supreme God of the Iranians. As soon as each land was created Angra Mainyu, the evil spirit of the Avesta, created different evils and plagues to invade the land and made it unfit for human habitation. There were thus sixteen creations of Ahura Mazda, and sixteen counter-creations of Angra Mainyu; and the first Fargard of the Vendidad contains a description of all these creations, and counter-creations, stating in detail how each good land was created by Ahura Mazda and how Angra Mainyu rendered it unfit for human residence by creating some evil or plague therein. The Fargard is too long to be quoted here in full; and I, therefore, borrow Muir's abstract of the same prepared from the versions of Spiegel and Haug, inserting in some places Darmesteter's renderings with the aid of his translation of the Vendidad in the Sacred Books of the East Series. The paragraphs are marked first according to Darmesteter, and then according to Spiegel by figures within brackets.

1, 2, (1-4):—"Ahura Mazda spake to the holy Zarathustra: 'I formed into an agreeable region that which before was nowhere habitable. Had I not done this, all living things would have poured forth after Airyana Vaêjo.'"

3, 4, (5-9):—"I, Ahura Mazda, created as the first best region, Airyana Vaêjo, of the good creation, (or, according to Darmesteter, by the good river Dâitya). Then Angra Mainyu, the destroyer, formed in opposition to it, a great serpent and winter [or snow], the creation of the Daêvas. There are there ten months of winter, and two of summer."

5, (13, 14):—"I, Ahura Mazda, created as the second best region, Gaû (plains), in which Sughdha is situated. Thereupon in opposition to it, Angra Mainyu, the death-dealing, created a wasp which is death to cattle and fields."

6, (17, 18):—"I, etc., created as the third best region, Môuru, the mighty, the holy."

[Here, and in most of the following cases the counter-creations of Angra Mainyu are omitted.]

7, (21, 22):—"I, etc., created as the fourth best region, the fortunate Bâkhdhi, with the lofty banner."

8, (25, 26):—" I, etc., created as the fifth best region, Nisaya, [situated between Môuru and Bâkhdhi.]."

9. (29, 30) :—" I, etc., created as the sixth best region, Harôyu, abounding in the houses [or water]."

10, (33-36) :—" I, etc., created as the seventh best region, Vaêkereta where Dujak is situated (or, according to Darmesteter, of evil shadows). In opposition to it, Angra Mainyu, the destroyer, created the Pairika Khnathaiti, who clung to Keresâspa,"

11, (37, 38) :—" I, etc., created as the eighth best region Urva, full of pastures."

12, (41, 42) :—" I, etc., created as the ninth best region, Khnenta (a river) in Vehrkâna."

13, (45, 46) :—" I, etc., created as the tenth best region, the fortunate Harahvaiti."

14, (49, 50) :—" I, etc., created as the eleventh best region, Haêtumant, the rich and shining."

16, (59, 60) :—"I, etc., created as the twelfth best region, Ragha, with three fortresses [or races]."

17, (63,64) :—" I, etc., created as the thirteenth best region, Chakhra, the strong."

18, (67, 68) :—" I, etc., created as the fourteenth, best region, Varena, with four corners ; to which was born Thraêtaona, who slew Azi Dahâka."

19, (72, 73) :—" I, etc., created as the fifteenth best country, Hapta Hendu [from the eastern to the western Hendu]. In opposition, Angra Mainyu created untimely evils, and pernicious heat [or fever]."

20, (76, 77) :— " I, etc., created as the sixteenth and best, the people who live without a head on the floods of Rangha (or according to Haug 'on the seashore ')."

21, (81) :— " There are besides, other countries, fortunate, renowned, lofty, prosperous and splendid."

Spiegel, Haug and other scholars have tried to identify

the sixteen lands mentioned in this description, and the following tabular statement sums up the results of the investigations of these scholars in this direction. The letters S, H, and D, stand for Spiegel, Haug and Darmesteter.

	Zend Name.	*Old Persian.*	*Greek.*	*Modern.*	Angra Mainyu's evils therein.
1	AiryanaVaêjo	Iran Vêjo	...	...	Severe winter and snow.
2	Sughdha	Suguda	Sogdiana	Samarkand	Cattle wasp and fly.
3	Môuru	Margu	Margiana	Merv	Sinful lust.
4	Bâkhdhi	Bâkhtri	Bactria	Balkh	Devouring ants or beasts.
5	Nisâya	...	Nisæa	...	Unbelief.
6	Harôyu (Sans. *Sharayu*)	Haraiva	Areia	Herat, (the basin of Hari river)	Mosquito, Poverty.
7	Vaêkereta	...	...	Cabul (S) Segestan (H)	Pairikâs, (Parîs).
8	Urva	...	...	Cabul (H) Land around Ispahan (D)	Evil defilement, Pride, or Tyranny.
9	Khnenta, in Vehrkâna	Varkâna	Hyrcania	Gurjân (S) Kandahar (H)	Unnatural sin.
10	Harahvaiti (Sans. *Sarasvatî*)	Harauvati	Arakhosia	Harût	Burial of the dead.
11	Haêtumant (Sans. *Setumat*)	...	Etumandros	Helmend	Wizards, Locusts.
12	Ragha	Raga	Ragai	Rai	Unbelief, Hereticism.
13	Chakhra (Sans. *Chakra*)	...	...	A Town in Khorasan (?)	Cremation of the dead.
14	Varena (Sans. *Varuna*)	...	...	Ghilan (H) ?	Despotic foreign rule.
15	Hapta Hendu (Sans. *Sapta-Sindhu*)	Hindavas	Indoi	Panjaub	Excessive heat.
16	Rangha (Sans. *Rasá*)	...	...	Caspian Sea (H). Arvastân-i-Rûm or Mesopotamia (D)	Winter, earthquake.

The old Persian and Greek names in the above table are taken from the inscriptions of the Achæmenian kings and the works of Greek writers after the overthrow of the Achæmenian dynasty by Alexandar the Great. They show that at least 10 out of 16 lands can be still identified with certainty; and if so, we can safely say that the account in the first Fargard is real and not mythical. But with regard to the land mentioned first in the list, there has been a difference of opinion amongst Zend scholars. The Airyana Vaêjo is the first created happy land, and the name signifies that it was the birth-land (Vaêjo = seed, Sans. *bija*) of the Aryans (Iranians), or the Paradise of the Iranian race. Was this a mythical region or a real country representing the original home of the Aryans, and if it was a real country where was it situated? This is the first question which we have to answer from the evidence contained in the first two Fargards of the Vendidad; and secondly, we have to decide whether the sixteen lands mentioned above were the successive countries occupied by the ancestors of the Iranian race in their migrations from the original home in the north. The Fargard says nothing about migration. It simply mentions that so many lands were created by Ahura Mazda and that in opposition thereto Angra Mainyu, the evil Spirit of the Avesta, created so many different evils and plagues which rendered the lands unfit for human residence. It is inferred from this that the Fargard does not contain an account of successive migrations, but merely gives us a description of the countries known to the ancestors of the Iranians at the time when the Fargards were composed. In other words, the chapter is geographical and not historical, containing nothing but a specification of the countries known to the Iranians at a particular time; and it is argued that it would be converting geography into history to take the different countries to represent the successive stages of migrations from the primeval home, when not a word about migration is found in the original text. Professor Darmesteter further observes that as the enumeration of the sixteen lands begins with Airyana Vaêjo by the river Vanguhi Dâitya and ends with Rangha, which corresponds with the Vedic Rasâ, a mythical river that divides the gods from the fiends, and that as the Vanguhi and the Rangha were originally the celestial rivers that came down from heaven (like the two heavenly Gânges) to surround the earth, the one in the east and the other in the west, (Bundahish, XX), the Airyana Vaêjo and the Rangha must be taken to denote the eastern and the western boundaries of the countries known to the ancient Iranians at the time when the Fargard was composed. Spiegel also takes the same view, and places Airyana Vaêjo "in the farthest east of the Iranian plateau, in the region where the Oxus and Jaxartes take their rise;" and Darmesteter seems to quote with approval the identification of the Rangha or the sixteenth land, in the commentary on the Vendidad, with Arvastân-i-Rûm or Roman Mesopotamia. The whole Fargard is thus taken to be a geographical description of the ancient Iran, and Professor Darmesteter at the end of his introduction to the Fargard observes "It follows hence no historical conclusion can be drawn from this description: it was necessary that it should begin with the Vanguhi and end with the Rangha. To look to it for an account of geographical migrations is converting cosmology into history." Bunsen and Haug, on the other hand, maintain that the Airyana Vaêjo represents the original home of the Iranians in the far north, and the countries mentioned in the Fargard must, therefore, be taken to represent the lands through which the Aryans passed after leaving their ancient home. The first question which we have, therefore, to decide is whether the Airyana Vaêjo was merely the easternmost boundary of the ancient Iran, or whether it was the *primeval* abode of the Iranians in the far north. In the former case we may take the Fargard to be merely a chapter on ancient geography; while if it is found impossible to locate the Airyana Vaêjo except in the far north, the countries from Samarkand and Sughdha to Hapta Hendu or the Panjaub mentioned in the Fargard would naturally represent the route taken by the ancient Iranians in their migrations from the ancient home. Everything thus depends upon the view that we take of the situation of the Airyana Vaêjo; and we shall, therefore, first see if there is anything in the Avestic description of the land which will enable us to determine its position with certainty.

It may be observed at the outset that the river Vanguhi is not mentioned in the Fargard along with the Airyana Vaêjo. The original verse speaks only of the "good *dâitya* of Airyana Vaêjo," but it is doubtful if "*dâitya*" denotes a river in this place. The Zend phrase *Airyanem Vaêjô vanghuyâô dâityayô*, which Darmesteter translates as "the Airyana Vaêjo, by the good (*vanghuhi*) river Dâitya," is understood by Spiegel to mean "the Airyana Vaêjo of the good creation," while Haug takes it as equivalent to "the Airyana Vaêjo of good capability." It is, therefore, doubtful if the Dâitya river is mentioned along with the Airyana Vaêjo in this passage.[1] But even supposing that Darmesteter's rendering is correct, he gives us no authority for identifying Dâitya with Vanguhi. The Bundahish (XX, 7 and 13) mentions Vêh (Vanguhi) and Dâîtîk (Dâitya) as *two* distinct rivers, though both seem to be located in the Aîrân-vêj (Airyana Vaêjo). We cannot again lose sight of the fact that it is not the Vanguhi (Vêh) alone that flows through the Airyana Vaêjo, but that the Rangha (Arag) has the same source and flows through the same land, *viz.*, the Airyana Vaêjo. Thus in the very beginning of Chapter XX of the Bundahish, we read that the Arag and the Vêh

1. See Dr. West's note on Bundahish XX, 13. The original passage mentions the Dâitîk river coming out from Aîrân vêj; but Dr. West observes that this may not be a river though the phrase (in the Avesta) has, no doubt, led to locating the river Dâitîk in Aîrân-vêj.

are the chief of the eighteen rivers, and that they "flow forth from the north, part from Albûrz *and* part from the Albûrz of Auhar-mazd; one towards the west, that is the Arag; and one towards the east, that is the Vêh river." The Bundahish (VII, 15) further informs us that the Vêh river flows out from the same source as the Arag river, and Dr. West in a footnote observes that both these rivers flow out from "the north side of the Arêdvîvsûr (Ardvi Sûra Anâhita) fountain of the sea, which is said to be on the lofty Hûgar (Hukairya), a portion of Albûrz." Even according to Bundahish, the Vanguhi is, therefore, the eastern and the Rangha the western river, in the northern part of Albûrz; or, in other words, they represent two rivers in a country, situated in the north, one flowing towards the east, and one to the west, in that region. It would, therefore, be, to say the least, unsafe to infer from this that the Airyana Vaêjo represents the eastern-most country, because the name Vêh or Vanguhi was in later times attached to the easternmost river in Irân. For by parity of reasoning, we can as well place the Airyana Vaêjo in the far west, in as much as the name Arag or Rangha was given, as stated by Darmesteter himself, in later times to the western-most river.

It is again a question why Rangha should be identified with the Caspian Sea, or some western river in Iran. The Fargard does not say anything about the situation of Rangha. It simply states that the fifteenth land created by Ahura Mazda was Hapta Heṇdu, and the sixteenth was on the floods of Rangha. Now if Hapta Heṇdu is identified with Sapta Sindhu, or the Panjaub, why take a big and a sudden jump from the Panjaub to the Caspian Sea, to find out the Rangha river. Rangha is Sanskrit Rasâ, and in the Ṛig-Veda (X, 75, 6) a terrestrial river, by name Rasâ, is mentioned along with the Kubhâ, the Krumu and the Gomatî, which are all known to be the affluents of the Indus. Is it not, therefore, more likely that Rangha may be the Vedic Rasâ, a tributary of the Indus? If the context is any guide to the determination of the sense of ambiguous words, the mention of Hapta Heṇdu, as the fifteenth land, shows that Rasâ the sixteenth must be sought for somewhere near it, and the point is pretty well settled when we find Rasâ actually mentioned in the Ṛig-Veda along with some other tributaries of the Indus. The identification of Rangha with the westernmost river is, therefore, at best doubtful, and the same may be said of Vanguhi, which by-the-by is not mentioned in the Fargard at all. But Darmesteter's reasoning does not stop here. On the strength of this doubtful identification he would have us believe that the *ancient* land of the Airyana Vaêjo was situated in the same region where the river named Vanguhi, or Vêh, in *later* times was said to flow. But the reasoning is obviously erroneous. The names of the two rivers Vanguhi and Rangha in the primeval home may have been subsequently transferred to the real rivers in the new settlement; but we cannot infer therefrom that the country through which these *new* rivers flowed was the *original* site of the Airyana Vaêjo. It is a well-known fact that persons migrating from their motherland to new countries often name the places they come across after the names of places familiar to them in their motherland. But on that account no one has ventured to place England in America or Australia; and it is strange how such a mistake should have been committed by Zend scholars in the present case. For even if a province or country in Central Asia had been named Airyana Vaêjo, we could not have located the original home in that province; just as the abode of Varuṇa cannot be placed in the land named Varena, which is the Zend equivalent of Varuṇa. The whole of Darmesteter's reasoning must, therefore, be rejected as unsound and illogical, and but for the preconceived notion that the original home of the Iranians cannot be placed in the far north, I think no scholar would have cared to put forward such guesses. There are express passages in the Avesta, which describe in unmistakable terms the climatic characteristics of the Airyana Vaêjo, and so far as I am aware, no valid reason has yet been assigned why we should treat this description as mythical and have recourse to guess-work for determining the position of the primeval home. Thus at the beginning of the first Fargard, we are told that the Airyana Vaêjo was the first good and happy creation of Ahura Mazda, but Angra Mainyu converted it into a land of ten months winter and two months summer, evidently meaning that at the time when the Fargard was composed it was an ice-bound land. The winter of ten months' duration, therefore, naturally points to a position in the far north, at a great distance beyond the Jaxartes; and it would be unreasonable to ignore this description which is characteristic only of the Arctic regions, and, relying on doubtful guesses, hold that the Airyana Vaêjo was the easternmost boundary of the ancient Iran. As the passage, where the ten months' winter is described as the present principal climatic characteristic of the Airyana Vaêjo, is very important for our purpose, I give below the translations of the same by Darmesteter, Spiegel and Haug:—

VENDIDAD, FARGARD I.

Darmesteter.	*Spiegel.*	*Haug and Bunsen.*
3. The first of the good lands and countries, which I, Ahura Mazda, created, was the Airyana Vaêjo, by the good river Dâitya.	5. The first and best of regions and places have I created, I who am Ahura Mazda;	3. As the first best of regions and countries I, who am Ahura Mazda, created Airyana Vaêjo of good capability; thereupon in opposition, to him Angra Mainyus, the death-dealing, created a mighty serpent and snow, the work of the Daêvas.
Thereupon came Angra Mainyu, who is all death, and he counter-created by his witchcraft the serpent in	6. The Airyana Vaêjo of the good creation. 7. Then Añgra Mainyus, who is full of death, created an opposition to the same; 8. A great Serpent	

Darmesteter.	*Spiegel.*	*Haug and Bunsen.*
the river and winter, a work of the Daêvas.	and Winter, which the Daêvas have created.	
4. There are ten winter months there, two summer months ;° and those are cold for the waters, cold for the earth, cold for the trees. Winter falls there, with the worst of its plagues.	9. Ten winter months are there, two summer months, 10. And these are cold as to the water, cold as to the earth, cold as to the trees. 11. After this to the middle of the earth, then to the heart of the earth, 12. Comes the winter ; then comes the most evil.	4. Ten months of winter are there, two months of summer. [Seven months of summer are there ; five months of winter there were ; the latter are cold as to water, cold as to earth, cold as to trees; there (is)—midwinter, the heart of winter; there all around falls deep snow; there is the direst of plagues.]†
° *N. B.*—Darmesteter states in a note that after summer months the Vendidad Sâdah adds, "It is known that [in the ordinary course of nature] there are seven months of summer and five of winter."		† *N. B.*—According to Haug the whole of the passage within brackets is a later addition.

It will be seen from the above translations that they all agree in the main points, *viz.*, (1) that the Airyana Vaêjo was the first good land created by Ahura Mazda, (2) that severe winter and snow were first introduced into it by Angra Mainyu, and (3) that after the invasion of Angra Mainyu there were ten winter months and two summer months in that land. The only difference between the three versions is that while Darmesteter and Spiegel regard the last sentence "And these are cold for the waters, etc." as a part of the original text Haug regards it as a subsequent addition. All the translators again agree in holding that the statement "Seven months of summer are there and five months of winter" is a later insertion. But we shall take up this question afterwards. For the present we are concerned with the statement that "*Ten months of winter are there, two months of summer,*" and it will be seen that there is no difference on this point in the three renderings given above. Another important fact mentioned in the passage is that the prolonged duration of winter was the result of Angra Mainyu's counter-action, meaning thereby that before the invasion of Angra Mainyu different climatic conditions prevailed in that region. This view is further strengthened by the consideration that the Iranians could never have placed their Paradise in a land of severe winter and snow. Bunsen has, therefore, rightly observed that the Airyana Vaêjo was originally a perfect country and had a very mild climate, until the hostile deity created a powerful serpent and snow, so that only two months of summer remained while winter prevailed during ten. In short, the passage in question speaks of a sudden change in the climate of the original home, a change that converted the paradise into a kind of ice-bound land with long and severe winters. If we, therefore, want to know what the land was like before the invasion of Angra Mainyu, we must reverse the climatic conditions that obtained after the invasion, and suppose that this cradle of the Iranian race was situated in the extreme north where long cool summers of ten months and short mild winters of two months originally prevailed. It was Angra Mainyu who altered this genial climate by means of glaciation and rendered it unbearable to man. The description of the two summer months after the invasion, *viz.*, that "These were cold as to the water, cold as to the earth, cold as to the trees," shows that after glaciation even the summer climate was unsuited for human habitation.

We have stated above that the passage in question indicates a sudden change in the climate of the Airyana Vaêjo, converting ten months summer and two months winter into ten months severe winter and two months cold summer. Thirty or forty years ago such a statement or proposition would have been regarded not only bold, but impossible or almost insane, for the geological knowledge of the time was not sufficiently advanced to establish the existence of a mild climate round about the North Pole in ancient times. It was probably this difficulty which stared Zend scholars in the face when they declined to place the Airyana Vaêjo in the far north, in spite of the plain description clearly indicating its northernmost position. Happily the recent discoveries in Geology and Archæology have not only removed this difficulty by establishing, on scientific grounds, the existence of a warm and genial climate near the North Pole in inter-glacial times, but have proved that the Polar regions were invaded, at least twice, by glaciation which destroyed their genial climate. Thus it is now a settled scientific fact that the Arctic regions were once characterised by warm and short winters and genial and long summers, a sort of perpetual spring, and that this condition of things was totally upset or reversed by the advent of the Glacial period which made winters long and severe and summers short and cold. The description of the climatic changes introduced by Angra Mainyu into the Airyana Vaêjo is, therefore, just what a modern geologist would ascribe to the Glacial epoch; and when the description is so remarkably and unexpectedly corroborated by the latest scientific researches, I fail to see on what ground we can lightly set it aside as mythical or imaginary. If some Zend scholars have done so in the past, it was because geological knowledge was not then sufficiently advanced to establish the probability of the description contained in the Avesta. But with new materials before us which go to confirm the Avestic description of the Airyana Vaêjo in every detail, we shall be acting unwisely if we decline to revise the conclusions of Zend scholars arrived at some years ago on insufficient materials. When we look at the question from this point of view, we have to place the site of the Airyana Vaêjo in the Arctic regions, where alone we can have a winter of ten months *at the present day*. We can escape from such a conclusion only by denying the possibility that the passage in question contains any traditional account of the ancient home of the Iranians; and this course seems to have been adopted by some Zend scholars of the day. But with the Vedic evidence, set forth and discussed in the previous chapters, before us, we need not have any of those apprehensions which have hitherto led many Zend scholars to err on the side of caution and moderation. We have seen that there are strong grounds for holding that the ancient Indo-European year was a year of ten months followed by a long night of two months; in other words, it was a year of ten summer months and two winter months, that is, exactly of the same kind as the one which prevailed in the Airyana Vaêjo before the happy land was invaded by the evil spirit. The word for summer in Zend is *hama*, the same as Sanskrit *samâ*, which means "a year" in the Ṛig-Veda. The period of ten summer months mentioned in the Avesta would, therefore, mean a year of ten months' sunshine, or of ten *mânushâ yugâ*, followed by a long wintry night of two months as described in the previous chapters. It may be urged that the Vendidad does not say that the two winter months were all dark, and we have, therefore, no authority for converting two winter months into two months of continuous darkness. A little reflection will, however, show that the objection is utterly untenable. In order to have a winter of ten months at the present day, we must place the Airyana Vaêjo in the Arctic regions; and once we do so, a long night of one, two or three months follows as a matter of course. This long night will now fall in the middle of the winter of ten months; but before the last Glacial epoch, or the invasion of Angra Mainyu, when there was a summer of ten months in the Arctic regions, the duration of the long night and that of the winter of two months must have been co-extensive. That is an important difference in the description of the paradise of the Aryans, as it is at present and as it was before the last Glacial epoch. The long night characterised these regions before the Glacial period as it does at present. But when the winters were short they corresponded with, and were confined only to, the long night; while at the present day, since the winter in the Arctic regions lasts for ten months, the long night falls in the middle of such winter. The description of the Airyana Vaêjo in the Vendidad, therefore, naturally leads us to infer that ten months sunshine or summer followed by two months dark winter represented the climatic conditions of the place before the invasion of Angra Mainyu, who converted summer into winter and *vice versa*, by introducing ice and snow into the land. We have already referred to the maximum period of a hundred nights during which Tishtrya fought with Apaosha, and to the custom of keeping the dead bodies in the house for two nights, three nights or a month long in winter, until waters and light, which stood still in winter, again began to flow or come up, showing that the period was one of continuous darkness. These passages taken in conjunction with the aforesaid description of the Airyana Vaêjo clearly establish the fact that the paradise of the Iranians was situated in the extreme north or almost near the North Pole, and that it was characterised by long delightful summers, and short and warm but dark winters, until it was rendered unfit for human habitation by the invasion of Angra Mainyu, or the advent of the Glacial epoch, which brought in severe winter and snow causing the land to be covered with an icecap several hundreds of feet in thickness.

There is one more point which deserves to be noticed in this connection. We have seen that to the description of the Airyana Vaêjo quoted above, the old Zend commentators have added what is believed to be an inconsistent statement, *viz.*, that "There are seven months of summer and five of winter therein." Dr. Haug thinks that the paragraph "The latter are cold as to water etc." is also a later addition, and must, therefore, be taken with the "five months of winter." But both Spiegel and Darmesteter, as well as the commentator, are of opinion that the phrases "And these are cold as to the water etc." form a part of the original text, and must, therefore, be taken to refer to the two summer months; and this view seems to be more reasonable, for a later insertion, if any, is more likely to be a short one than otherwise. The only addition to the original text thus seems to be the statement "It is known that there are seven months of summer and five of winter;" and this must be taken as referring to the climatic conditions which obtained in the Airyana Vaêjo before the invasion of Angra Mainyu, for the latter reduced the duration of summer only to two months, which again were cold to the water, the earth and the trees. It has been shown above that as the Airyana Vaêjo was originally a happy land, we must suppose that the first climatic conditions therein were exactly the reverse of those which were introduced into it by Angra Mainyu; or, in other words, a summer of ten months and a winter of two months must be said to have originally prevailed in this happy land. But the Zend commentators have stated that there were seven months of summer and five of winter therein; and this tradition appears to have been equally old, for we read in the Bundahish (XXV, 10–14) that "on the day Aûharmazd (first day) of Âvân the winter acquires strength and enters into the world,...and on the auspicious day Atarô of the month Dîn (the ninth day of the tenth month) the winter arrives, with much cold, at Aîrân-vêj, and until the end, in the auspicious month Spendarmad, winter advances through the whole world; on this account they kindle a fire everywhere on the day Âtarô of the month Dîn, and it forms an indication that the winter *has* come." Here the five months of winter in the Airyana Vaêjo are expressly mentioned to be Avân, Âtarô, Dîn, Vohûman and Spendarmad; and we are told that Rapîtvîn Gâh is not celebrated during this period as Rapîtvîn goes under-ground during winter and comes up from below the ground in summer. The seven months of summer are similarly described in the same book as extending "from the auspicious day Aûharmazd (first) of the month Farvardîn to the auspicious day Anîrân (last) of the month Mitrô," (XXV, 7). It seems from this account that the tradition of seven months summer and five months winter in the Airyana Vaêjo was an old tradition, and the Bundahish, in recording it, gives us the climatic conditions in the ancient home and not, as supposed by some, those which the writer saw in his own day. For in the twentieth paragraph of the same chapter twelve months and four seasons are enumerated, and the season of winter is there said to comprise only the last three months of the year, *viz.*, Dîn, Vohûman and Spendarmad. I have shown elsewhere that the order of months in the ancient Iranian calendar was different from the one given in the Bundahish. But whatever the order may be, the fact of the prevalence of seven months summer and five months winter in the Airyana Vaêjo seems to have been traditionally preserved in these passages; and the old Zend commentators on the Vendidad appear to have incorporated it into the original text, by way of, what may be called, a marginal note, in their anxiety to preserve an old tradition. We have thus two different statements regarding the climatic conditions of the Airyana Vaêjo before it was invaded by Angra Mainyu: one, that there were ten months of summer and two of winter, the reverse of the conditions introduced by Angra Mainyu; and the other, traditionally preserved by the commentators, *viz.*, that there were seven summer months and five winter months therein. It is supposed that the two statements are contradictory; and contradictory they undoubtedly are so long as we do not possess the true key to their interpretation. They are inconsistent, if we make the Airyana Vaêjo the easternmost boundary of the ancient Iran;

but if the paradise is placed in the circumpolar regions in the far north the inconsistency at once disappears, for then we can have seven months summer and ten months summer at the same time in the different parts of the original home of the Iranians. We have seen in the discussion of the Vedic evidence that the legend of Aditi indicates seven months summer or sun-shine, and the legend of the Dashagvas a sacrificial session, or a period of sun-shine, of ten months. It has also been pointed out that between the North Pole and the Arctic circle the sun is above the horizon for any period longer than seven and less than twelve months according to the latitude of the place. There is, therefore, nothing strange, extraordinary or inconsistent, if we get two statements in the Avesta regarding the duration of summer in the primeval home; and we need not assume that the commentators have added the statement of seven months summer simply because the description of two months summer and ten months winter did not appear to them suitable to the first land of blessing. It is not possible that they could have misunderstood the original text in such a way as to suppose that the climatic conditions introduced by Angra Mainyu were the conditions which obtained originally in the Airyana Vaêjo. We must, therefore, reject the explanation which tries to account for this later insertion on the ground that it was made by persons who regarded the description in the original as unsuited to the first created happy land. If the original text is properly read and interpreted, it gives us a summer of ten months in the Airyana Vaêjo before Angra Mainyu's invasion, and the statement regarding the summer of seven months refers to the same place and time. We have the same thing in the Ṛig-Veda where the sun is once represented as having seven rays and once as having ten rays, meaning seven months and ten months of sun-shine, both of which are possible only in the Arctic regions. The two Avestic traditions stated above must, therefore, be taken to represent the Arctic climatic conditions prevailing in the ancient home in the far north; and the correctness of the explanation is proved by the discussion in the foregoing chapters. With regard to the custom of kindling a fire on the ninth day of Dîn or the tenth month, noticed in the Bundahish, it seems to me that instead of taking it to be an indication that winter "*has* come," it is better to trace its origin to the commencement of winter at that time in some part of the original home; for if a fire is to be kindled there is greater propriety in kindling it to commemorate the commencement of winter rather than the expiry of two out of five winter months. If the custom is so interpreted, it will imply that a year of nine months and ten days was once prevalent in some part of the Aryan home, a conclusion well in keeping with the ancient Roman year of ten months. But apart from this suggestion, there is a striking coincidence between the Vedic and the Avestic tradition in this respect. According to the Bundahish (XXV, 20), the year is divided into four seasons of three months each, Farvarḍîn, Arḍavahisht and Horvadaḍ constituting the season of the spring; Tîr, Amerôdaḍ and Shatvaîrô the summer; Mitrô, Âvân and Âtarô the autumn; and Dîn, Vohûman and Spendarmaḍ, the winter. The fortieth day of *Sharad* or autumn would, therefore, represent the tenth day (Abân) of Avân; and the Vedic statement discussed in the ninth chapter, that Indra's fight with Shambara commenced "on the fortieth day of *Sharad*" agrees well (only with a difference of ten days) with the statement in the Bundahish that the winter in the Airyana Vaêjo commenced with the month of Âvân the second month in autumn. We have thus a very close resemblance between the Vedic and the Avestic tradition about the end of summer in the original Arctic home; and the corresponding Roman and Greek traditions have been previously noticed. In short, a year of seven or ten months sun-shine can be traced back to the Indo-European period; and since its double character can be explained only by placing the original home in the circumpolar regions, we are inevitably led to the conclusion that the Airyana Vaêjo must also be placed in the same region. The Avestic account is by itself plain and intelligible, and the apparent inconsistencies would have been explained in a natural way long ago, if Zend scholars had not created unnecessary difficulties by transferring the site of this Paradise to the east of the ancient Iran. Under these circumstances it is needless to say which of the two theories regarding the position of the Airyana Vaêjo is correct; for no one would accept a hypothesis which only enhances the confusion, in preference to one which explains every thing in a natural and satisfactory manner.

We have so far discussed the passage in the first Fargard which describes the climate of the Airyana Vaêjo. The passage, even when taken by itself, is quite intelligible on the Arctic theory; but in ascertaining the original climate of the Airyana Vaêjo we supposed that it was the reverse of the one introduced by the invasion of Angra Mainyu. The second Fargard of the Vendidad, which is similar in character to the first, contains, however, a passage, which does away with the necessity of such assumption, by giving us a graphic description of the actual advent of ice and snow which ruined the ancient Iranian Paradise. This Fargard is really a supplement to the first and contains a more detailed account of the Airyana Vaêjo and a description of the paradisiacal life enjoyed there before Angra Mainyu afflicted it with the plague of winter and snow. This is evident from the fact that the coming of the severe winter is foretold in this Fargard and Yima is warned to prepare against it; while in the first Fargard the happy land is described as actually ruined by Angra Mainyu's invasion. Darmesteter divides this Fargard into two parts, the first comprising the first twenty (or according to Spiegel forty-one) paragraphs, and the second the remaining portion of the Fargard. In the first part Ahura Mazda is said to have asked king Yima, the ruler of the Airyana Vaêjo, who is called *sruto Airyênê vaêjahê*, 'famous in Airyana Vaêjo', to receive the law from Mazda; but Yima refused to become the bearer of the law, and he was, therefore, directed by Ahura Mazda to keep his people happy and make them increase. Yima is accordingly represented as making his men thrive and increase by keeping away death and disease from them, and by thrice enlarging the boundaries of the country which had become too narrow for its inhabitants. Whether this fact represents a gradual expansion of the oldest Aryan settlements in the Arctic home we need not stop to inquire. The second part of the Fargard opens with a meeting of the celestial gods called by Ahura Mazda, and "the fair Yima, the good shepherd of high renown in the Airyana Vaêjo," is said to have attended this meeting with all his excellent mortals. It was at this meeting that Yima was distinctly warned by Ahura Mazda that fatal winters were going to fall on the happy land and destroy everything therein. To provide against this calamity the Holy One advised Yima to make a Vara or enclosure, and remove there the seeds of every kind of animals and plants for preservation. Yima made the Vara accordingly, and the Fargard informs us that in this Vara the sun, the moon and the stars "*rose but once a year*," and that "*a year seemed only as a day*" to the inhabitants thereof. The Fargard then closes with the description of the happy life led by the inhabitants of this Vara of which Zarathushtra and his son Urvatadnara are said to be the masters or overseers.

Yima's Vara here described is something like Noah's ark. But there is this difference between the two that while the Biblical deluge is of water and rain, the Avestic deluge is of snow and ice; and the latter not only does not conflict with geological evidence but is, on the contrary, fully and unexpectedly confirmed by it. Secondly, the description that "a year seemed only as a day" to the inhabitants of this Vara, and that the sun and stars "rose only once a year therein," serves, in an unmistakable manner, to fix the geographical position of this Vara in the region round about the North Pole; for nowhere on the surface of the earth can we have a year-long day-and-night except at the Pole. Once the position of Yima's Vara is thus fixed the position of the Airyana Vaêjo is at once determined; for Yima's Vara, as stated in the Mainyô-i-khard, must obviously be located in the Airyana Vaêjo. Here is, therefore, another argument for locating the Aïryana Vaêjo in the extreme north and not to the west of the ancient Iran, as Spiegel, Darmesteter and others have done. For whether Yima's Vara be real or mythical, we cannot suppose that the knowledge of a year-long day and of the single rising of the sun during the whole year was acquired simply by a stretch of imagination, and that it is a mere accident that it tallies so well with the description of the Polar day and night. The authors of the Fargard may not have themselves witnessed these phenomena, but there can be no doubt that they knew these facts by tradition; and if so, we must suppose that their remote ancestors must have acquired this knowledge by personal experience in their home near the North Pole. Those that locate the Airyana Vaêjo in the extreme east of the Iranian highlandtry to account for ten months winter therein by assuming that a tradition of a decrease in the earth's temperature was still in the mind of the author of this Fargard, or that the altitude of the table-land, where the Oxus and the Jaxartes take their rise, was far higher in ancient times than at present, thereby producing a cold climate. Both these explanations are however artificial and unsatisfactory. It is true that a high altitude produces a cold climate; but in the present instance the climate of the Airyana Vaêjo was mild and genial before the invasion of Angra Mainyu, and we must, therefore, suppose that the Iranian table-land was not elevated at first, until Angra Mainyu upheaved it and produced a cold climate. But the present altitude of the plateau is not so great as to produce a winter of ten months, and this requires us again to assume the submergence of this land after the invasion of Angra Mainyu. Unfortunately there is no geological evidence forthcoming to support the upheaval and submergence of this land in the order mentioned above. But even if such evidence were forthcoming, the explanation would still fail to account why the inhabitants of Yima's Vara in the Airyana Vaêjo regarded a year as a single day, a description, which is true only at the North Pole. All attempts to locate the primitive Airyana Vaêjo in a region other than the circumpolar country must, therefore, be abandoned. The names of mythical rivers and countries may have been transferred in later times to real terrestrial rivers and provinces; but if we were to settle the position of the primitive rivers or countries by a reference to these new names, we can as well locate the Airyana Vaêjo between the Himâlaya and the Vindhya mountains in India, for in later Sanskrit literature the land lying between these two mountains is called the Âryâvarta or the abode of the Aryans. The mistake committed by Darmesteter and Spiegel is of the same kind. Instead of determining the position of the Airyana Vaêjo from the fact that a winter of ten months is said to have been introduced therein by Angra Mainyu, and that a year seemed only as a day to the inhabitants thereof, they have tried to guess it from the uncertain data furnished by the names of rivers in Iran, though they were aware of the fact that these names were originally the names of mythical rivers and were attached to the real rivers in Iran only in later times, when a branch of the

Aryan race went over to and settled in that country. Naturally enough this introduced greater confusion into the account of the Airyana Vaêjo instead of elucidating it, and scholars tried to get out of it by supposing that the whole account is either mythical, or is, at best, a confused reminiscence of the ancient Iranian home. The recent scientific discoveries have, however, proved the correctness of the Avestic traditions, and in the light thrown upon the subject by the new materials there is no course left but to reject the erroneous speculations of those Zend scholars that make the Airyana Vaêjo the eastern boundary of ancient Iran.

But the most important part of the second Fargard is the warning conveyed by Ahura Mazda to Yima that fatal winters were going to fall on the land ruled over by the latter, and the description of glaciation by which the happy land was to be ruined. The warning is in the form of a prophecy, but any one who reads the two Fargards carefully can see that the passage really gives us a description of the Glacial epoch witnessed by the ancestors of the Iranians. We give below the translation of the passage both by Darmesteter and Spiegel.

VENDIDAD, FARGARD II.

Darmesteter.	*Spiegel.*
22. And Ahura Mazda spake unto Yima saying, "O fair Yima, son of Vîvanghat! Upon the material world the fatal winters are going to fall, that shall bring the fierce, foul frost; upon the material world the fatal winters are going to fall, that shall make snow-flakes fall thick, even an	46. Then spake Ahura Mazda to Yima: "Yima the fair, the son of Vivañhâo, 47. Upon the corporeal world will the evil of winter come: 48. Wherefore a vehement, destroying frost will arise. 49. Upon the corporeal world will the evil of winter come: 50. Wherefore snow will fall

Darmesteter.	*Spiegel.*
aredvi deep on the highest tops of mountains.	in great abundance, 51. On the summits of the mountains, on the breadth of the heights.
23. And all the three sorts of beasts shall perish, those that live in the wilderness, and those that live on the tops of the mountains, and those that live in the bosom of the dale, under the shelter of stables.	52. From three (places), O Yima, let the cattle depart, 53. If they are in the most fearful places, 54. If they are on the tops of the mountains, 55. If they are in the depths of the valleys, 56. To secure dwelling places.
24. Before that winter, those fields would bear plenty of grass for cattle: now with floods that stream, with snows that melt, it will seem a happy land in the world, the land wherein footprints even of sheep may still be seen.	57. Before this winter the country produced pasture ; 58. Before flow waters, behind is the melting of the snow. 59. Clouds, O Yima, will come over the inhabitated regions, 60. Which now behold the feet of the greater and smaller cattle :
25. Therefore make thee a Vara, long as a riding-ground, on every side of the square, and thither bring the seeds of sheep and oxen, of men, of dogs, of birds, and of red blazing fires.	61. Therefore make thou a circle of the length of a race-ground to all four corners. 62. Thither bring thou the seed of the cattle, of the beasts of burden, and of men, of dogs, of birds, and of the red burning fires.

Can anything, we ask, be more clear and distinct than the above description of the advent of the Glacial epoch in the happy land over which Yima ruled, and where a year was equivalent to a single day? There is no reference to Angra Mainyu in this passage which describes in the form of a prophecy the evils of glaciation, much in the same manner as a modern geologist would describe the progress of the ice-cap during the Glacial period. Ahura Mazda tells Yima that fierce and foul frost will fall on the material world, and even the tops of the highest mountains will be covered with or rather buried in snow which will destroy all living beings whether on the tops of the mountains or in the valleys below. The snow, it is said, would fall *aredvi* deep, which Spiegel translates by the phrase 'in great abundance,' while Darmesteter, quoting from the commentary, explains in a footnote that "even where it (the snow) is least, it will be one Vîtasti two fingers, that is, fourteen fingers deep." A cubit of snow, at the lowest, covering the highest tops of the mountains and the lowest depths of the valleys alike cannot but destroy all animal life; and I do not think that the beginning of the Ice-age can be more vividly described. With this express passage before us ascribing the ruin of the happy land to the invasion of ice and winter, we should have no difficulty whatsoever in rightly interpreting the meaning of the invasion of Angra Mainyu described in the beginning of the first Fargard. It is no longer a matter of inference that the original genial climate of the Airyana Vaêjo was rendered inclement by the invasion of winter and snow, afterwards introduced into the land. The above passage says so in distinct terms, and the description is so graphic that we cannot regard it as mythical or imaginary. Add to it the fact that the recent geological discoveries have established the existence of at least two Glacial periods, the last of which closed and the post-Glacial period commenced, according to American geologists, not later than about 8000 B. C. When the Avestic traditions regarding the destruction of the primeval Arctic home by glaciation is thus found to be in complete harmony with the latest geological researches, there is no reason, except prejudice, why we should not regard the Avestic account as a correct reminiscence of an old real historical fact? The author of the Fargards in question cannot be supposed to have given us by imagination such a graphic account of a phenomenon, which is brought to light or discovered by the scientists only during the last forty or fifty years. Darmesteter in his translation of the Fargards observes in a footnote that the account of glaciation is the result of a mythical misunderstanding by which winter was thought to be the counter-creation of Irân Vêj. This passed off very well twenty years ago; but the phenomenon of glaciation in the Ice-age is now better understood, and we cannot accept guesses and conjectures of scholars regarding the meaning of a passage in the Avesta which describes the glaciation of the Iranian paradise. It only proves how the ancient records, howsoever express and distinct they may be, are apt to be misunderstood and misinterpreted owing to our imperfect knowledge of the climatic or other conditions or surroundings amongst which the ancestors of our race lived in remote ages. But for such a misunderstanding, it was not difficult to perceive that the Airyana Vaêjo, or the original home of the Airyan race, was situated near the North Pole, and that the ancestors of our race abandoned it not out of "irresistible impulse," or "overcrowding," but simply because it was ruined by the invasion of snow and ice brought on by the Glacial epoch. In short, the Avestic tradition, as recorded in this Fargard, is the oldest documentary evidence of the great climatic convulsion, which took place several hundreds of years ago, and the scientific evidence of which was discovered only during the last forty or fifty years. It is, therefore, a matter of regret that the importance of this tradition should have been so long misunderstood or overlooked.

It will be seen from the foregoing discussion that the traditional evidence preserved in the first two Fargards of the

Vendidad is especially important for our purpose. The Dawn-hymns in the Ṛig-Veda supply us with the evidence of a long continuous dawn of thirty days in the ancient home, and there are passages in the Vedas which speak of a long continuous night of six months or of shorter duration, and a year of seven or ten months. It can also be shown that several Vedic myths and deities bear an unmistakable stamp of their Arctic origin. But, as stated before, in the whole Vedic literature there is no passage which will enable us to determine the time when the Polar regions were inhabited, or to ascertain the reason why they were abandoned. For that purpose we drew upon geology which has recently established the fact that the climate of the circumpolar regions, which is now so cold as to render the land unsuited for human habitation, was mild and genial before the last Glacial period. It followed, therefore, that if the Vedic evidence pointed to an Arctic home, the forefathers of the Aryan race must have lived therein *not after* but *before* the last Glacial epoch. But the traditions preserved in the Avesta dispense with the necessity of relying on geology for this purpose. We have now direct traditional evidence to shew (1) that the Airyana Vaêjo had originally a good climate, but Angra Mainyu converted it into a winter of ten and a summer of two months, (2) that the Airyana Vaêjo was so situated that the inhabitants of Yima's Vara therein regarded the year only as a day, and saw the sunrise only once a year, and (3) that the happy land was rendered uninhabitable by the advent of a Glacial epoch which destroyed all life therein. It is true, that but for recent geological discoveries these statements, howsoever plain and distinct, would have remained unintelligible, or regarded as improbable by scholars, who would have always tried, as Darmesteter has already done, to put some artificial or unnatural construction upon these passages to render the same comprehensible to them. We cannot, therefore, deny that we are indebted to these scientific discoveries for enabling us to determine the true meaning of the Avestic traditions, and to clear the mist of misinterpretation that has gathered round them. But nevertheless, the value of this traditional testimony is not thereby impaired in any way. It is the oldest traditional record, preserved by human memory, of the great catastrophe which overtook the northern portion of Europe and Asia in ancient times, and obliged the Aryan inhabitants of the Arctic regions to migrate southwards. It has been preserved during thousands of years simply as an ancient record or tradition, though its meaning was not intelligible, until at last we now see that the accuracy of the account is fully and unexpectedly borne out by the latest scientific researches. There are very few instances where science has proved the accuracy of the ancient semi-religious records in this way. When the position of the Airyana Vaêjo and the cause of its ruin are thus definitely settled both by traditional and scientific evidence, it naturally follows that the sixteen lands mentioned in the first Fargard of the Vendidad must be taken to mark the gradual diffusion of the Iranians from their ancient home to the country of the Rasâ and the seven rivers; or, in other words, the Fargard must be regarded as historical and not geographical as maintained by Spiegel and Darmesteter. It is true that the first Fargard does not say anything about migration. But when the site of the Airyana Vaêjo is placed in the extreme north, and when we are told in the second Fargard that the land was ruined by ice, no specific mention of migration is needed, and the fact that the sixteen lands are mentioned in a certain specific order is naturally understood, in that case, to mark the successive stages of migration of the Indo-Iranian people. It is not contended that every word in these two Fargards may be historically correct. No one would expect such a rigid accuracy in the reminiscences of old times traditionally preserved. It is also true that the Airyana Vaêjo has grown into a sort of mythical land in the later Parsi literature, somewhat like Mount Meru, the seat of Hindu gods, in the Purâṇas. But for all that we cannot deny that in the account of the Airyana Vaêjo in the first two Fargards of the Vendidad we have a real historical reminiscence of the Arctic cradle of the Iranian or the Aryan races, and that the Fargard gives us a description of the countries through which the Indo-Iranians had to pass before they settled in the Hapta Hendu or on the floods of Rangha, at the beginning of the post-Glacial period.

This story of the destruction of the original home by ice may well be compared with the story of deluge found in the Indian literature. The oldest of these accounts is contained in the Shatapatha Brâhmaṇa (I, 8,1, 1-10), and the same story is found, with modifications and additions, in the Mahâbhârata (Vana-Parvan, Ch. 187), and in the Mâtsya, the Bhâgavata and other Purāṇas. All these passages are collected and discussed by Muir in the first Volume of his Original Sanskrit Texts (3rd Ed. pp. 181-220); and it is unnecessary to examine them at any length in this place. We are concerned only with the Vedic version of the story and this appears in the above mentioned passage in the Shatapatha Brâhmaṇa. A fish is there represented as having fallen into the hands of Manu along with water brought for washing in the morning. The fish asked Manu to save him, and in return promised to rescue Manu from a flood (*aughaḥ*) that would sweep away (*nirvoḍhâ*) all creatures. The Brâhmaṇa does not say when and where this conversation took place, nor describes the nature of the calamity more fully than that it was a flood. Manu preserved the fish first in a jar, then in a trench, and lastly, by carrying him to the ocean. The fish then warns Manu that in such and such a year (not definitely specified) the destructive flood will come, and advises him to construct a ship (*nâvam*) and embark in it when the flood would arise. Manu constructs the ship accordingly, and when the flood rises, embarks in it, fastens its cable (*pâsham*) to the fish's horn and passes over (*ati-dudrâva*) to "this northern mountain" (*etam uttaram girim*) by which phrase the commentator understands the Himavat or the Himâlaya mountain to the north of India. The fish then asks Manu to fasten the ship to a tree, so that it may gradually descend, without going astray, along with the subsiding water; and Manu acts accordingly. We are told that it is on this account that the northern mountain has received the appellation of *Manor-ava-sarpaṇam* or 'Manu's descent.' Manu was the only person thus saved from the deluge; and desirous of offspring he sacrificed with the *Pâka-yajña*, and threw butter, milk, and curds as oblations into the waters. Thence in a year rose a woman named Iḍâ, and Manu living with her begot the offspring, which is called Manu's off-spring (*prajâtiḥ*). This is the substance of the story as found in the Shatapatha Brâhmaṇa, and the same incident is apparently referred to in the Atharva Veda Saṁhitâ (XIX, 39, 7-8), which says that the *kushṭha* plant was born on the very spot on the summit of the Himavat, the seat of the 'Gliding down of the ship' (*nâva-prabhraṁshanam*), the golden ship with golden tackle that moved through the heaven. In the Mahâbhârata version of the legend this peak of the Himâlaya is said to be known as Nau-bandhanam, but no further details regarding the place or time are given. The Mâtsya Purâṇa, however, mentions Malaya, or the Malabar, as the scene of Manu's austerity, and in the Bhâgavata, Satyavrata, king of Draviḍa, is said to be the hero of the story. Muir has compared these accounts, and pointed out the differences between the oldest and the later versions of the story, showing how it was amplified or enlarged in later times. We are, however, concerned with the oldest account; and so far as it goes, it gives us no clue for determining the place whence Manu embarked in the ship. The deluge again appears to be one of water, and not of ice and snow as described in the Avesta. Nevertheless it seems that the Indian story of deluge refers to the same catastrophe as is described in the Avesta and not to any local deluge of water or rain. For though the Shatapatha Brâhmaṇa mentions only a flood (*aughaḥ*), the word *prâleya*, which Pâṇinî (VII, 3, 2) derives from *pralaya* (a deluge), signifies 'snow,' 'frost,' or 'ice' in the later Sanskrit literature. This indicates that the connection of ice with the deluge was not originally unknown to the Indians, though in later times it seems to have been entirely overlooked. Geology informs us that every Glacial epoch is characterised by extensive inundation of the land with waters brought down by great rivers flowing from the glaciated districts, and carrying an amount of sand or mud along with them. The word *aughaḥ*, or a flood, in the Shatapatha Brâhmaṇa may, therefore, be taken to refer to such sweeping floods flowing from the glaciated districts, and we may suppose Manu to have been carried along one of these in a ship guided by the fish to the sides of the Himâlaya mountain. In short, it is not necessary to hold that the account in the Shatapatha Brâhmaṇa refers to the water-deluge pure and simple, whatever the later Purâṇas may say; and if so, we can regard the Brahmanic account of deluge as but a different version of the Avestic deluge of ice. It was once suggested that the idea of deluge may have been introduced into India from an exclusively Semitic source; but this theory is long ago abandoned by scholars, as the story of the deluge is found in such an ancient book as the Shatapatha Brâhmaṇa, the date of which has now been ascertained to be *not later* than 2500 B. C., from the fact that it expressly assigns to the Kṛittikâs, or the Pleiades, a position in the due east. It is evident, therefore, that the story of the deluge is Aryan in origin, and in that case the Avestic and the Vedic account of the deluge must be traced to the same source. It may also be remarked that Yima, who is said to have constructed the Vara in the Avesta, is there described as the son of Vîvanghat; and Manu, the hero in the Indian story, though he receives no epithet in the account of the deluge in the Shatapatha Brâhmaṇa, is very often described in the Vedic literature as the son of Vivasvat (*Vaivasvata*), the Iranian Vîvanghat, (Shat. Brâh. XIII, 4, 3, 3; Ṛig. VIII, 52, 1). Yama is also expressly called *Vaivasvata* in the Ṛig-Veda (X, 14, 1). This shows that in spite of the fact that Yima is the hero in one account and Manu in the other, and that one is said to be the deluge of ice and the other of water, we may regard the two accounts as referring to the same geological phenomenon.[1] The Avestic account is, however, more specific than that in the Shatapatha Brâhmaṇa, and as it is

1. The story of the deluge is found also in other Aryan mythologies. The following extract from Grote's History of Greece (Vol. I, Chap. 5) gives the Greek version of the story and some of the incidents therein bear striking resemblance to the incidents in the story of Manu :—

"The enormous iniquity with which earth was contaminated—as Apollodôrus says, by the then existing brazen race, or as others say, by the fifty monstrous sons of Lykaôn—provoked Zeus to send a general deluge. An unremitting and terrible rain laid the whole of Greece under water, except the highest mountain-tops, whereon a few stragglers found refuge. Deukaliôn was saved in a chest or ark, which he had been forewarned by his father Promêtheus to construct. After floating for nine days on the water, he at length landed on the summit of Mount Parnasses. Zeus having sent Hermês to him, promising to grant whatever he asked, he prayed that men and companions might be sent to him in his solitude; accordingly Zeus directed both him and Pyrrha (his wife) to cast stones over their heads: those cast by Pyrrha became women, those by Deukaliôn men. And thus the "stony race of men" (if we may be allowed to translate an etymology which the Greek language presents exactly, and which has not been disdained by Hesiod, by Pindar, by Epicharmas, and by Virgil) came to tenant the soil of Greece. Deukaliôn on landing from the ark sacrificed a grateful offering to Zeus Phyxios, or the God of escape; he also erected altars in Thessaly to the twelve great gods of Olympus."

In commenting upon the above story Grote remarks that the reality of this deluge was firmly believed throughout the historical ages of Greece, and even Aristotle, in his meteorological work, admits and reasons upon it as an unquestionable fact.

corroborated, almost in every detail, by the scientific evidence regarding the advent of the Glacial epoch in early times, it follows that the tradition preserved in the two Fargards of the Vendidad is older than that in the Shatapatha Brâhmaṇa. Dr. Haug has arrived at a similar conclusion on linguistic grounds. Speaking about the passage in the Vendidad he says "the original document is certainly of high antiquity and is undoubtedly one of the oldest of the pieces which compose the existing Vendidad." The mention of Hapta Heṇdu, a name not preserved even in the later Vedic literature, is said also to point to the same conclusion.

We may here refer to certain passages cited by Muir in his Original Sanskṛit Texts (3rd Ed. Vol. II. pp 322-329) to show that the reminiscences of the northern home have been preserved in the Indian literature. He first refers to the expression *shatam himâḥ*, or 'a hundred winters,' occurring in several places in the Ṛig-Veda (I, 64, 14; II, 33, 2; V, 54, 15; VI, 48, 8), and remarks that though the expression *sharadaḥ shatam*, or 'a hundred autumns,' also occurs in the Ṛig-Veda (II, 27, 10; VII, 66, 16), yet *shatam himâḥ* may be regarded as a relic of the period when the recollection of the colder regions from which the Vedic Aryas migrated had not yet been entirely forgotten. The second passage quoted by him is from the Aitareya Brâhmaṇa (VIII, 14) which says "wherefore in this northern region all the people who dwell beyond the Himavat, (called) the Uttara Kurus and the Uttara Madras are consecrated to the glorious rule (Vairâjyam)." The Uttara Kurus are again described in the same Brâhmaṇa (VIII, 23) as the land of gods which no mortal may conquer, showing that the country had come to be regarded as the domain of mythology. The Uttara Kurus are also mentioned in the Râmâyaṇa (IV, 43, 38) as the abode of those who performed the meritorious works, and in the Mahâbhârata (Sabhâ-Parvan, Ch. 28) Arjuna is told "Here are the Uttara Kurus whom no one attempts to combat." That the Uttara Kurus were not a fabulous land is shown by the fact that a mountain, a people and a city called Ottorocorra is mentioned by Ptolemy, and Lassen thinks that Megasthenes had the Uttara Kurus in view when he referred to the Hyperboreans. Muir concludes this section with a passage from the Sâṅkhyâyana or the Kaushîtakî Brâhmaṇa (VII, 6) where Pathyâ Svasti, or the goddess of speech, is said to know the northern region (*udîchîm disham*), and we are told that "Hence in the northern region speech is better known and better spoken, and it is to the north that men go to learn speech." Muir thinks that some faint reminiscence of an early conncetion with the north may be traced in these passages. But none of them are conclusive, nor have we any indication therein of the original home being in the Arctic regions, as we have in the case of the Vedic passages discussed previously which speak of the long, continuous dawn and night, or a year of ten months. We may, however, take the passages cited by Muir as corroborative evidence and they have been referred to here in the same light. It is upon the Vedic passages and legends examined in the previous chapters and the Avestic evidence discussed above that we mainly rely, for establishing the existence of the primeval Aryan home in the Arctic regions; and when both these are taken together we get direct traditional testimony for holding that the original home of the Aryan races was situated near the North Pole and not in Central Asia, that it was destroyed by the advent of the Glacial epoch, and that the Indo-Iranians, who were compelled to leave the country, migrated southwards, and passing through several provinces of Central Asia eventually settled in the valleys of the Oxus, the Indus, the Kubhâ and the Rasâ, from which region we see them again migrating, the Indians to the east and the Persians to the west at the early dawn of the later traditional history.

CHAPTER XII.

COMPARATIVE MYTHOLOGY.

The value of Comparative Mythology as corroborative evidence —Its use in the present case —The ancient calendars of the European Aryan races —The plurality of Dawns in the Lettish, the Greek and the Celtic mythology —The ancient Roman year of ten months and Numa's reform thereof —Plutarch's view —Improbability of Lignana's theory pointed out —The ancient Celtic year —Closed with the last day of October and marked the commencement of winter and darkness —The winter feast celebrated on the day —The mid-summer feast of Lugnassad on the first of August —The commencement of summer on the first of May —The date of the battle of Moytura —Similar duration of the Old Norse year —Comparison with the ancient Greek calendar —All indicate six months' light and six months' darkness —Corroboration derived from comparative philology —Two divisions of the year in primeval times —The Maid of Nine Forms in the Celtic mythology —The Nine paces of Thor in the Norse legend —Compared with the Vedic Navagvas and Vifra Navaza in the Avesta —Balder's home in the heavens —Indicates the long Arctic day —The Slavonic story of Ivan and his two brothers —Continuous night in Ivan's home —Comparison with the Vedic legend of Trita —The Slavonic winter demon —The story of Dawn and Gloaming in the Finnish mythology —Indicates a long day of four weeks —Celtic and Teutonic legends representing the Sun-god's annual struggle with darkness —Baldur and Hodur, Cuchulainn and Fomori —Temporary sickness and indisposition of gods and heroes —Prof. Rhys' views thereon —The affliction indicates winter darkness —Celtic and Teutonic myths indicating long continuous day and night —All point to a primeval home in the Arctic region —Recent ethnological researches in favour of European home referred to —Indicate northern Germany or Scandinavia —The necessity of going still farther North —Prof. Rhys suggests Finland or White Sea —Not inconsistent with the theory which seeks to make the North Pole the home of the *whole* human race —Prof. Rhys' method and conclusion —Primeval

Arctic home established alike by the traditions of the eastern and western Aryas —Its relation with the general theory about the cradle of the human race at the North Pole explained.

We propose in this chapter to examine whether and how far the conclusions we have deduced from the Vedic and the Avestic evidence are corroborated by the myths and traditions of the European branches of the Aryan race. It is true that the evidence, collected in the foregoing chapters, is so general in character that it will have to be taken into account, even if the traditions of other races are found to conflict with it in any way. In other words, it has nothing specially Asiatic in it and without further corroboration we can, therefore, safely say that the original home of the Indo-Iranians, before the last Glacial epoch, must also be the home of the other Aryan people in those remote times. But still we may usefully examine the traditions of other Aryan races, and see if the latter have preserved any reminiscences of the original home, either in their ancient calendar or in their other ancient myths or legends. Of course the evidence cannot be expected to be as reliable as that found in the Veda or the Avesta, but still it has its own value for corroborative purposes. The history of comparative mythology and philology shows that when Vedic literature and language became accessible to European scholars, quite a new light was thrown thereby on the Greek and the Roman mythology; and it is not unlikely that the discovery of the Vedic and the Avestic evidence, in favour of the Arctic home may similarly serve to elucidate some points in the legendary literature of the Aryan races in Europe. But the subject is so vast that it cannot be treated in a single chapter of this book, nor do I possess the necessary means to undertake the task. I shall, therefore, content myself with a statement of such facts as plainly indicate the reminiscence of an ancient Arctic home in the traditional literature of the Greek, Roman, Celtic, Teutonic and Slavonic branches of the Aryan race; and I may here state that I am greatly indebted for this purpose to that learned and masterly work, *The Hibbert Lectures*, by Prof. Rhys, *On the origin and growth of religion as illustrated by Celtic Heathendom.*

Following the order adopted in the discussion of the Vedic evidence, we shall first take up the question of the ancient calendar and see if the traditions preserved by the western Aryan races about the ancient year point out to any Arctic characteristics, such as the long dawn, the long day, the long night, or an annual period of sunshine of less than twelve months' duration. We have seen that the Dawn is very often spoken of in the plural in the Ṛig-Veda and that a group of thirty Dawn-Sisters is actually described as moving round and round with one mind and in the same enclosure without being separated from each other, a phenomenon which is peculiar only to the Arctic regions. This Vedic account of the Dawn does not stand by itself. Thus in the Lettish mythology, the Dawn is called *diewo dukte*, or the sky-daughter or the god-daughter, much in the same way as the Uṣhas is called *divo duhitâ* in the Ṛig-Veda; "and the poets of the Lets speak likewise of many beautiful sky-daughters, or god-daughters *diewo dukruzeles*."[1] Prof. Max Muller further informs us that in the Greek mythology we can "easily find among the wives of Hêrakles, significant names, such as Auge (sun-light), Xanthis (yellow), Chrysêis (golden), Iole (violet), Aglaia (resplendent), and Eône, which cannot be separated from Eos, dawn."[2] The same story appears again in the Celtic mythology where Cuchulainn, the Sun-hero, is described as having a wife, who is variously named as Emer, Ethne Ingubai. Upon this Prof. Rhys observes that "it may be that the myth pictured the dawn not as one but as many to all of whom the Sun-god made love in the course of the three

1. Max Muller's Contributions to the Science of Mythology, p. 432.
2. *Id.* p. 722.

hundred and more days of the year."[1] It has been shown previously that the description of the Vedic Dawns, as a closely united band, precludes us from regarding them as three hundred and more dawns of the year; and that the only inference we can draw from a closely united group of dawns is that it represents the long and continuous Arctic dawn divided into a number of parts of twenty-four hours each for convenience. The description of the dawn in the Lettish mythology does not seem to be so full as that in the Vedas and by itself it may not be sufficient to indicate the Polar dawn; but considering the fact that the dawn is described as sky-daughter and spoken of in the plural by the poets of the Lets and the poets of the Ṛig-Veda alike, we may safely extend to the Lettish mythology the conclusion we have drawn from the more detailed description of the Dawn in the Ṛig-Veda, and the same may be said of the Celtic and the Greek stories of the Dawn given above.

In treating of the *Gavâm-ayanam* and the corresponding legend of the Dashagvas, a reference has already been made to the Greek legend of Hêlios, who is described as having 350 oxen and as many sheep, obviously representing a year of 350 days and nights, and to the Roman tradition about *December* being the tenth and the last month of the year as denoted by its etymology. Prof. Lignana in his essay on *The Navagvas and the Dashagvas of the Ṛig-Veda*, published in the proceedings of the seventh International Congress of the Orientalists, 1886, however, remarks that the passage of Plutarch in the life of Numa, where this tradition is mentioned, does not support the view that the Romans originally counted not more than ten months. It is true that Plutarch mentions an alternative story of Numa's altering the order of months "making March the third which was the first, January first which was the eleventh of Romulus, and February the second

1. Rhys' Hibbert Lectures p. 458.

which was the twelfth and the last." But immediately afterwards Plutarch says, "Many, however, assert that two months of January and February were added by Numa, whereas before they had reckoned ten months in the year"; and in the next paragraph gives his own opinion, "That the Roman year contained at first ten months only and not twelve, we have a proof in the name of the last; for they still call it *December*, or the tenth month; and that March was first is also evident, because the fifth from it was called *Quintilis*, the sixth *Sextilis*, and so the rest in their order."[1] I have referred to this passage previously and shown that Plutarch's reasoning about the order of the months as indicated by their numerical names cannot be lightly set aside. If January and February were the last two months in the ancient calendar of the Romans, we should have to assume that the numerical order from *Quintilis* to *December* was abruptly given up after *December*, which does not seem probable. It is, therefore, more reasonable to hold that Numa actually added two months to the old year, and that the story of the transposition of the two months of January and February from the end to the beginning of the year was a later suggestion put forward by those who knew not how to account for a year of ten months, or 304 days only. But besides Plutarch, we have also the testimony of Macrobius, who, as stated before, tells us that Romulus had a year of ten months only. There can, therefore, be little doubt about the existence of a tradition of the ancient Roman year of ten months, and we now see that it is thoroughly intelligible by comparison with the annual sacrificial *sattras* of ten months mentioned in the Vedic literature. The names of the Roman months from *Quintilis* to *December* further show that the months of the year had no special names in ancient times, but were named simply in their numerical order, a fact which

1. *Vide* Langhorne's Translation of Plutarch's Lives, published by Ward, Lock and Co. London, pp. 53, 54.

accounts for the absence of common names for the months of the year in different Aryan languages.

The evidence regarding the ancient year of Celts, Teutons and Greeks is not however so definite, though it may be clearly shown that in each case the year was marked by a certain period of cold and darkness, indicating the Arctic origin of the ancient calendar. Speaking of the ancient Celtic year Prof. Rhys observes, "Now as the Celts were in the habit formerly of counting winters, and of giving precedence in their reckoning to night and winter over day and summer, I should argue that the last day of the year in the Irish story of Diarmait's death meant the eve of November or All-halloween, the night before the Irish *Samhain*, and known in Welsh as *Nos Galan-gaeaf*, or the Night of the Winter Calends. But there is no occasion to rest on this alone, for we have the evidence of Cormac's Glossary that the month before the beginning of winter was the last month, so that the first day of the first month of winter was also the first day of the year."[1] Various superstitious customs are then alluded to, showing that the eve of November was considered to be the proper time for prophecy or the appearance of goblins ; and the Professor then closes the discussion regarding the above-mentioned last day of the Celtic year with the remark that "It had been fixed upon as the time of all others, when the Sun-god whose power had been gradually falling off since the great feast associated with him on the first of August, succumbed to his enemies, the powers of darkness and winter. It was their first hour of triumph after an interval of subjection, and the popular imagination pictured them stalking abroad with more than ordinary insolence and aggressiveness ; and if it comes to giving individuality and form to the deformity of darkness, to describe it as a sow, black or grisly, with neither ears nor tail, is not perhaps very readily surpassed as

1. Rhys' Hibbert Lectures, p. 514.

an instance of imaginative aptitude."[1] This shows that the ancient Celtic year closed with the season of autumn and the beginning of winter which corresponded with the last day of October, or the eve of November, and was marked by festivals which indicated the victory of darkness over light. As regards the middle of the year or summer in the Celtic traditions, the same authority further informs us that "The Lammas fairs and meetings forming the Lugnassad in ancient Ireland marked the victorious close of the sun's contest with the powers of darkness and death, when the warmth and light of that luminary's rays, after routing the colds and blights, were fast bringing the crops to maturity. This, more mythologically expressed, was represented as the final crushing of Fomori and Fir Bolg, the death of their king and the nullifying of their malignant spells, and as the triumphant return of Lug with peace and plenty to marry the maiden Erinn and to enjoy a well-earned banquet, at which the fairy host of dead ancestors was probably not forgotten. Marriages were solemnized on the auspicious occasion; and no prince, who failed to be present on the last day of the fair, durst look forward to prosperity during the coming year. The Lugnassad was the great event of the summer half of the year, which extended from the calends of May to the calends of Winter. The Celtic year was more thermometric than astronomical, and the Lugnassad was so to say its summer solstice, whereas the longest day was, so far as I have been able to discover, of no special account."[2] The great feast of the Lugnassad thus marked the middle of the year or summer, and it was held at the beginning of August. Therefore, "the First of May must, according to Celtic ideas, have been the right season for the birth of the summer Sun-god";[3] and this is confirmed by the story of Gwin and Gwythur, who fought for the same damsel, and be-

1. Rhys' Hibbert Lectures, pp. 516-17. 2. *Ibid.* pp. 418-19.
3. *Ibid.* p. 546.

tween whom peace was made on the condition that they were to fight for the damsel "on the Calends of May every year thenceforth till the Day of Doom, and he who should prove victorious on the Day of Doom was to take the Damsel to wife."[2] This is interpreted by Prof. Rhys to mean that "the Sun-god would recover his bride at the beginning of summer after his antagonist had gained possession of her at the beginning of winter";[1] and he compares the legend to the story of Persephone, daughter of Zeus carried away by Pluto, who was, however, able to retain her at his side only for six months in the year. We might also cite in this connection the legend of Demeter or Mother Earth, who is said to rejoice for six months in the presence of Proserpine, the green herb, her daughter, and for six months regret her absence in dark abodes beneath the earth. The ancient Celtic year thus seems to have been divided into two halves, one representing the six summer months, and the other, which commenced on the eve of November, the six months of winter darkness. But what is still more remarkable is that just as the Ṛig-Veda gives us the exact date of the commencement of the battle between Indra and Shambara, so Celtic myths record the exact date of the first battle of Moytura and also of the fight between Labraid of the Swift Hand on the Sword, king of an Irish Hades, whom Cuchulainn goes to assist, and his enemies called the Men of Fidga. They were fought on the eve of November, "when the Celtic year began with the ascendency of the powers of darkness."[2] Prof. Rhys further points out that the ancient Norse year was similar in character. The great feast of the Norsemen occupied three days called the Winter Nights, and began on the Saturday falling on or between the 11th and the 18th of October; and according to Dr. Vigfusson this feast marked the beginning of the ancient year of the Norsemen. The old Norse year thus appears to have been shorter by a few

1. Rhys' Hibbert Lectures, p. 562. 2. *Ibid* p. 460.

days than the Celtic one; but Prof. Rhys accounts for this difference on the ground "that winter, and therefore the year commences earlier in Scandinavia than in the continental centre from which the Celts dispersed themselves."[1]

As regards the ancient Greek calendar, Prof. Rhys has shown that the old year ended with the festival of Apaturia and the new one began with the Chalceia, an ancient feast in honour of Hephæstus and Athene, the exact date being the *énu kai nea* of the month of Pyanepsion, that is, approximately the last day of October. Prof. Rhys then compares the Celtic feast of the Lugnassad with the Greek festival named Panathenæa, and the feast on the Calends of May with the Athenian Thargelia, and concludes his comparison of the Celtic and the Greek calendar by observing that "a year which was common to Celts with Greeks is not unlikely to have once been common to them with some or all other branches of the Aryan family."[2]

This shows that the ancient Aryan races of Europe knew of six months' day and six months' night, and their calendars were the modifications of this Arctic division of the year. Comparative philology, according to Dr. Schrader, leads us to the same conclusion. Speaking of the ancient division of the year he says:—"Nearly everywhere in the chronology of the individual peoples a division of the year into two parts can be traced. This finds linguistic expression in the circumstance that the terms for summer, spring, and winter have parallel suffix formations. As in the primeval period **jhi-m* and **sem-* existed side by side, so in Zend *zima* and *hama* correspond to each other, in Armenian *amarn* and *jmern*, in Teutonic *sum-ar* and *wint-ar*, in Celtic *gam* and *sam*, in Indian *vasanta* and *hemanta*. There is absolutely no instance, in which one and the same language shows identity of suffixes in the names of the *three* seasons of the year. In Slavonic, also, the year is divi-

1. Rhys' Hibbert Lectures, p. 676. 2. *Id*. p. 521.

ded into two principal divisions, summer (*lêto*) and winter (*zima*); and finally evident traces of old state of things are not wanting in Greek and Latin."[1] Dr. Schradar further remarks that the separate conceptions of winter and summer were combined in one whole even in primitive times; but there is no word for a year common to all or most of the Aryan languages, and it is not unlikely that the names of summer or winter were used to denote the return of the seasons more frequently than the conception of winter and summer combined into one whole. As the length of summer, or the period of sunshine, as contrasted with the period of darkness, varied from six to twelve months in the Arctic regions the conception of a year of twelve months was perhaps less suited for practical reckoning in the primeval home than the conception of so many months' summer or so many months' winter taken singly, and this explains why in the Ṛig-Veda we have the expression "*mânushâ yugâ* and *kṣhapaḥ*" to denote the whole year.

In discussing the legend of the Navagvas and the Dashagvas we have shown that the numerals incorporated in their names must be interpreted as referring to the number of months during which they completed their annual sacrifices, and that Prof. Lignana's view that they refer to the months of pregnancy is not only improbable but opposed to the express Vedic texts which tell us that the Navagvas and the Dashagvas completed their sacrifices in ten months. Let us now see if there are corresponding personages in other Aryan mythologies. Prof. Lignana has pointed out the resemblance between the Navagvas and the Novemsides of the Romans. The comparison is no doubt happy, but there is nothing in the cult of the Novemsides which gives us a clue to the original meaning of the word. We know nothing beyond the fact that Novemsides (also spelt Novemsiles) were certain Latin gods, who ac-

1. Schrader's Prehistoric Antiquities of Aryan Peoples, translated by Jevons, Part IV, Ch. VI, p. 302.

cording to the double etymology (*novem*, nine, or *novus*, new) were taken for nine Muses, or for gods newly introduced, as after the conquest of a place in contrast with the old gods of the country. But the Celtic tradition of the Maid of Nine Forms is much more explicit, inasmuch as it is distinctly connected with the sun-hero Cuchulainn. The story is thus narrated by Rhys: Conchobar had a passing fair daughter called Fedelm of the nine forms, for she had so many fair aspects, each of which was more beautiful, as we are told, than the others; and when "Cuchulainn had, at the news of the approach of the enemy from the west, advanced with his father to the frontier of the realm, he suddenly hastened away in the evening to a place of secret meeting, where he knew Fedelm to have a bath got ready for him in order to prepare him for the morrow and his first encounter with the invading army."[1] This reminds us of the assistance rendered by the Navagvas and the Dashagvas to Indra by means of Soma sacrifices performed by them and which sacrifices are said to have invigorated Indra and prepared him for his fight with the powers of darkness, represented by Vṛitra, Vala, Shambara and other demons. The Maid of Nine Forms is therefore a Celtic paraphrase of the Nine-going sacrificers in the Ṛig-Veda. Prof. Rhys considers Fedelm to be a sort of Athene with nine forms of beauty, and refers to the story of Athene weaving a peplos for her favourite Hêrakles, or causing springs of warm water to gush forth from the ground, to supply him at the end of the day with a refreshing bath.[2] But this comparison does not explain why there should be nine forms of beauty in either case. The mystery is, however, cleared up, if we suppose these legends to refer to the nine months of sunshine at the end of which the setting sun-god is refreshed or invigorated for his struggle with the demons of darkness by the acts or services of the Nine-going sacrificers or the Maid of Nine Forms.

1. Rhys' Hibbert Lectures, pp. 630-1. 2. *Id.* pp. 378-9.

In the Norse literature we are told that Thor, the son of Earth, slays the World-dragon, walks nine paces and dies of the venom of the Serpent.* If the slaying of the dragon be understood, as remarked by Prof. Rhys, to mean the conquest of the Sun-hero over the powers of darkness, and the death of Thor be taken to represent the sinking of the summer-sun below the horizon, we have here a clear statement that Thor, the Sun-hero, walked nine paces during the time that intervened between the end of winter and the end of summer. These nine paces could not be nine days or nine years; and there is therefore no alternative but to hold that the legend refers to the nine months' life of the Sun-god before he succumbed to the powers of darkness. The Avestic story of Vafra, or, according to Spiegel, Vifra Navâza (Yt. V, 61) belongs, I think, to the same class. He is said to have been flung up in the air, in the shape of a bird by Thraêtaona and was flying for three days and three nights towards his own house, but could not turn down. At the end of the third night when the beneficent dawn came dawning up, he prayed unto Ardvi Sûra Anâhita to help him, promising to offer Haomas and meat by the brink of the river Rangha. Ardvi Sûra Anâhita listening to his prayer is then said to have brought him to his house safe and unhurt. Vifra Navâza in this legend is very likely Vipra Navagva of the Ṛig-Veda. We have seen that the Navagvas and seven *Vipras* are mentioned together in the Ṛig-Veda (VI, 22, 2) and that the Ashvins, who are called *Vipra-vâhasâ* in (V, 74, 7), are said to have resided for three days and three nights in the distant region. It is not unlikely, therefore, that the story of the Navagvas, who go to help Indra in the world of darkness after completing their sacrificial session of nine months, may have been combined with the story of the Ashvins in the Avestic legend of Vifra Navâza, Sanskrit

* Rhys' Hibbert Lectures, p. 616.

krit *Vipra* being changed into Avestic *Vifra* and Navagva into Navâza.

The above legends from the Greek, Celtic and Norse literatures show that a long winter-darkness was not unknown to the ancestors of the Aryan races in Europe, who have preserved distinct reminiscences of a year of ten or six months' sun-shine, and that the Navagvas and the Dashagvas of the Ṛig-Veda have again their parallels in the mythology of other Aryan races, though the resemblance may not be as obvious in the one as in the other case. A year of six months' or ten months' sunshine necessarily implies a long continuous day and a long continuous night, and distinct references to these Arctic characteristics of day and night are found in Norse and Slavonic legends. Thus the Norse Sun-god Balder is said to have dwelt in a place in heaven called Breidablik or Broadgleam, the most blessed of all lands, where nought unclean or accursed could abide. Upon this Prof. Rhys observes, "It is remarkable that Balder had a dwelling place in the heavens, and this seems to refer to the Arctic summer when the sun prolongs his stay above the horizon. The pendant to the picture would naturally be his staying as long in the nether world."[1] This corresponds exactly with the Vedic description of the sun's unyoking his carriage and making a halt in the mid of the heaven, discussed in the sixth chapter. The story of three brothers in the Slavonic literature also points out to the same conclusion. We are told that "Once there was an old couple who had three sons. Two of them had their wits about them, but the third, Ivan, was a simpleton. Now in the land in which Ivan lived, there was never any day but *always night*. This was a snake's doing. Well, Ivan undertook to kill that snake. Then came a third snake with twelve heads, Ivan killed it and destroyed the heads and im-

1. Rhys' Hibbert Lectures, p. 536.

mediately there was light throughout the whole land."[1] This reminds one of the story of Trita in the Ṛig-Veda previously described. Trita's abode is said to be in the distant region, and we have interpreted it to mean the nether world of darkness, an interpretation which amongst others is fully borne out by the story of Ivan and his two brothers. But the dark power takes a distinctive Russian appearance in the awful figure of Koshchei, the deathless,—a fleshless skeleton who squeezes heroes to death in his bony arms. He carries off a princess; after seven years the hero reaches his under-ground palace and is hidden; but is discovered by Koshchei who typifies winter in this case. All these legends clearly indicate a dark winter of some months' duration, or the long winter-night of the Arctic regions. There are other stories in which the Sun-hero is said to have been detained in a place of darkness; but it is not necessary to refer to them in this place. For comparison I shall only refer briefly to a legend in the Finnish mythology, which, though not Aryan in origin, may yet serve to throw some light on the subject under consideration. In the mythology of the Finns, the Dawn is called Koi and "Koi, the Dawn (masc.), and Ammarik, the Gloaming (fem.), are said to have been entrusted by Vanna-issa, the Old Father, with lighting and extinguishing every morning and evening the torch of the day. As a reward for their faithful services Vanna-issa would allow them to get married. But they preferred to remain bride and bride-groom, and Vanna-issa had nothing more to say. He allowed them, however, to meet at midnight during four weeks in summer. At that time Ammarik hands the dying torch to Koi, who revives it with his breath."[2] If this legend has any meaning it signifies the cessation of extinguishing the torch of the day during four weeks in summer. Koi and Ammarik both leave

1. Poor's Comparative Mythology, p. 390. 2. Max Muller's Contributions to the Science of Mythology, pp. 267-8.

their places and arrange to meet at midnight but without extinguishing the torch. This means a long day of four weeks, and as it must have a long night of four weeks to match it the story points out to a period of eleven months' sun-shine, and an Arctic night of four weeks.

From the legends mentioned, or referred to, or described above, it may be easily seen that many traces of the Arctic calendar are still discernible in the mythology of the western Aryan races like Celts, Teutons, Lets, Slavs, Greeks and Romans. Long dawns or a number of dawns, long days, long nights, dark winters, are all alluded to more or less explicitly in these myths, though none of these legends refers directly to the position of the primeval home and the cause of its destruction. But this omission or defect is removed by the evidence contained in the Veda and the Avesta ; and when the European legends are viewed in the light of the Indo-Iranian traditions they clearly point to the existence of a primeval home near the North Pole. There are a number of other legends in the Celtic and Teutonic literatures which describe the victory of sun-hero over the demons of darkness every year, similar in character to the victory of Indra over Vṛitra, or to the achievements of the Ashvins, the physicians of the gods. Thus in the Norse mythology, Hodur, the blind god of winter, is represented as killing Balder or Baldur, or the god of summer, and Vali the son of Odin and Rind is said to have avenged his brother's death afterwards. The encounters of Cuchulainn, the Celtic Sun-god, with his enemies, the Fomori or the Fir Bolg, the Irish representatives of the powers of darkness, are of the same character. It may also be remarked that according to Prof. Rhys the world of waters and the world of darkness and the dead are identical in Celtic myths, in the same way as the world of water, the abode of Vṛitra and the world of darkness are shown to be in the Vedic mythology. The strange custom of *couvade*, by which the whole population of Ireland is described as being laid up in confinement or indisposed so as to be unable to defend their country against the invasion of Ailill and Medle with their Fir Bolg, excepting Cuchulainn and his father, again indicates, according to Prof. Rhys, a sort of decline in the power of gods like that witnessed in the case of the winter-sun ; in other words, it was an indisposition or inactivity of the same sort which amounts in the Norse Edda to nothing less than actual death of the Anses at the hands of the powers of evil. This temporary affliction or the indisposition of the gods forms the subject of many other legends. But we have no space to narrate all of them, and shall, therefore, only quote here the conclusion, which Prof. Rhys has been forced to adopt, regarding the meaning of these myths after a critical examination of the different Celtic and Teutonic legends. Speaking of Gods, Demons and Heroes, in the last lecture of his learned work, he thus sums up his views regarding the myths describing the encounters between Gods or Sun-heroes and the powers of darkness :—

"All that we have thus far found with regard to the contest of the gods and their allies against the powers of evil and theirs, would seem to indicate that they were originally regarded as yearly struggles. This appears to be the meaning of the fore-knowledge as to the final battle of Moytura, and as to the exact date of the engagement on the Plain of Fidga in which Cuchulainn assists Labraid of the Swift Hand on the sword, a kind of Celtic *Zeus*, or Mars-Jupiter, as the ruler of an Elysium in the other world. It was for a similar reason that the northern Sibyl could predict that, after the Anses had been slain by Swart, aided by the evil brood, Balder would come to reign, when all would be healed, and the Anses would meet again in the Field of Ith. Nor can the case have been materially different with the Greek gods, as proved by the allusion to the prophecy about the issue of the war with the giants.

And this was not all; for we are told that the Cretans represented *Zeus* as born and bred and also buried in their island, a view sometimes formally regarded as confirming the character ascribed to them for lying; but that deserves no serious consideration, and the Cretans in their mysteries are supposed to have represented the god going through the stages of his history every year. A little beyond the limits of the Greek world a similar idea assumed a still more remarkable form, namely, among the Phrygians, who are said by Plutarch to have believed their god (like the Purâṇic Vishṇu) to sleep during the winter and resume his activity during summer. The same author also states that the Paphlagonians were of opinion that the gods were shut up in a prison during winter and let loose in summer. Of these peoples, the Phrygians at least appear to have been Aryan, and related by no means distantly to the Greeks; but nothing could resemble the Irish *couvade* of the Ultonion heroes more closely than the notion of the Phrygian god hibernating. This, in its turn, is not to be severed from the drastic account of the *Zeus* of the Greek Olympus reduced by Typho to a sinewless mass and thrown for a time into a cave in a state of utter helplessness. Thus we seem to be directed to the north as the orginal home of the Aryan nations; and there are other indications to the same effect, such as Woden's gold ring Draupnir, which I have taken to be symbolic of the ancient eight-day week: he places it on Balder's pile, and with him it disappears for a while into the nether world, which would seem to mean the cessation for a time of the vicissitude of day and night, as happens in midwinter within the Arctic Circle. This might be claimed as exclusively Icelandic, but not if one can show traces, as I have attempted, of the same myth in Ireland. Further, a sort of complement to it is supplied by the fact that Cuchulainn, the Sun-hero, is made to fight several days and nights without having any sleep, which though fixed at the wrong season of the year in the epic tale in its present form, may probably be regarded as originally referring to the sun remaining above the horizon continuously for several days in summer. Traces of the same idea betray themselves in Balder's son Forseti or the Judge, who, according to a passage in old Norse literature, sits long hours at his court settling all causes in his palace of Glitnir in the skies. These points are mentioned as part of a hypothesis I have been forced to form for the interpretation of certain features of Aryan mythology; and that hypothesis, to say the least of it, will not now be considered so wild as it would have been a few years ago; for the recent researches of the students of language and ethnology have profoundly modified their views, and a few words must, at this point, be devoted to the change that has come over the scene."[1]

Prof. Rhys then goes on to briefly describe how the views of mythologists and philologists regarding the primeval home of the Aryan race have been modified by the recent discoveries in Geology, Archæology and Craniology, and how the site of that home has been shifted from the plains of Central Asia to the northern parts of Germany or even to Scandinavia not only on ethnological but also on philological grounds. As we have discussed the subject previously, we omit this portion of Prof. Rhys' remarks and quote the concluding paragraph which runs as follows:—

"Thus the voice of recent research is raised very decidedly in favour of Europe, though there is no complete unanimity as to the exact portion of Europe, to regard as the early home of the Aryans; but the competition tends to lie between North Germany and Scandinavia, especially the south of Sweden. This last would probably do well enough as the country in which the Aryans may have consolidated and organized themselves before beginning to send forth their excess of population to conquer the other lands now possessed by nations

1. Rhys' Hibbert Lectures, pp. 631-3.

speaking Aryan languages. Nor can one forget that all the great states of modern Europe, except that of the sick man, trace their history back to the conquest of the Norsemen who set out from the Scandinavian land, which Jordanis proudly calls *officina gentium* and *vagina nationum. But I doubt whether the teachings of evolution may not force us to trace them still further towards the North*: in any case, the mythological indications to which your attention has been called, point, if I am not mistaken, *to some spot within the Arctic Circle*, such, for example, as the region where Norse legend placed the Land of Immortality, somewhere in the north of Finland and the neighbourhood of the White Sea. There would, perhaps, be no difficulty in the way of supposing them to have thence in due time descended into Scandinavia, settling, among other places, at Upsala, which has all the appearance of being a most ancient site, lying as it does on a plain dotted with innumerable burial mounds of unknown antiquity. This, you will bear in mind, has to do only with the origin of the early Aryans, and not with that of the human race generally ; but it would be no fatal objection to the view here suggested, if it should be urged that the mythology of nations beside the Aryans, such as that of the Paphlagonians, in case of their not being Aryan, point likewise to the north; for it is not contended that the Aryans may be the only people of northern origin. Indeed, I may add, that a theory was not long ago propounded by a distinguished French savant, to the effect that the entire human race originated on the shores of the Polar Sea at a time when the rest of the northern hemisphere was too hot to be inhabited by man. M. de Saporta, for that is the learned writer's name, explains himself in clear and forcible terms ; but how far his hypothesis may satisfy the other students of this fascinating subject I cannot say. It may, however, be observed in passing that it need not disconcert even the most orthodox of men, for it supposes all the races of mankind traceable to a single non-simian origin, and the Bible leaves it an open question where exactly and when the Garden of Eden flourished."[1]

I have very little to add to the views expressed in the above passages; in fact Prof. Rhys has left us little to be done so far as Celtic and Teutonic myths are concerned. The way in which he proceeds to analyze the legends and show that they all point to a primeval home in the Arctic regions is at once interesting and instructive. He first clears the ground by ascribing the different prophecies occurring in the legends not to any fore-knowledge on the part of the poet, but to the simple fact that the events spoken of were of annual occurrence, and as they were known to recur regularly it was not difficult to adopt the language of prophecy and predict the happening of these events in future. He then collects a number of facts which go to prove that gods and heroes were afflicted with some disability or distress at certain intervals of time, which rendered them incapable to carry on the annual struggle with the powers of evil and darkness. The only physical phenomena corresponding to such distress of the solar hero, or the sun, are his daily setting, the decay of his powers in winter and his disappearing below the horizon for some months in the Polar regions. As the struggle between the Sun-god and his enemies is, as stated above, determined to be annual, the daily setting of the sun does not come within the range of the possible explanations of the temporary distress of the sun-god. Out of the two remaining physical phenomena, the decay of sun's power in winter would have answered the purpose, had there been no legends or myths which indicated the cessation of the vicissitude of day and night for some time. I have pointed out before how Prof. Max-Muller, who has followed the same method of interpreta-

1. Rhys' Hibbert Lectures, pp. 636-7.

tion in his discussion of the achievements of the Ashvins, has failed to grasp the real meaning of the Ashvins' legends by disregarding the statements which distinctly speak of the proteges of the Ashvins as dwelling or labouring in darkness. Prof. Rhys is more cautious in this respect, and is anxious to account for all the incidents in the legends if they could possibly be accounted for on any theory. The result is that he has been gradually led, or we might even say forced, to adopt the theory of the ancient Arctic home of the Aryan people inasmuch as all the different incidents in the legends under consideration can be accounted for only by this theory. In short, Prof. Rhys has done for the Celtic and Teutonic myths what we have endeavoured to do in this book in regard to the Vedic and Avestic traditions. This has considerably lightened our labour in regard to the examination of Celtic and Teutonic myths from our point of view, and our thanks are due to Prof. Rhys for the same. But we feel sure that if the Vedic evidence and facts stated and discussed in the foregoing chapters had been known to the learned Professor before he wrote his work, he would have expressed himself still more confidently regarding the inference to be drawn from the traces of Arctic origin discernible in Teutonic myths; but even as it is, the value of his testimony stands very high in the decision of the question before us. It is the testimony of an expert given after a critical and careful examination of all Celtic and Teutonic myths, and after comparing them with similar Greek traditions; and when this testimony falls in so completely with the conclusions we have drawn from an independent consideration of the Vedic and Avestic myths, our results may, so to say, be regarded as doubly proved. It has already been shown that the results of comparative philology also support, or, at any rate, are not inconsistent with our conclusions. The theory of the Asiatic home may be said to have been now abandoned on linguistic or etymological grounds, but it has not yet been proved that the neolithic Aryan races of Europe were autochthonous in the countries where their remains are now found. Therefore the question of the original home of the Aryan people is still an open question, and we are free to draw any conclusion regarding the ancient home from a legitimate consideration of the traditional evidence before us. Prof. Rhys has well described the situation by observing that the teachings of evolution may force us to look for the original home still farther north in the Arctic regions. In fact we have to go to a latitude which will give us seven months' sunshine, or a hundred nights' continuous darkness, or thirty days' continuous dawn. The question whether the home of other nations, beside the Aryan, can be traced to the North Pole, has been ably discussed by Dr. Warren on his *Paradise Found*, or the Cradle of the Human Race at the North Pole. It is an important question from an anthropological point of view; but its very comprehensiveness precludes us from collecting evidence from the traditional literatures of the different human races living on the surface of this earth. It is true that we sometimes derive help from the discussion of the broader questions at first; but for all practical purposes it is always desirable to split up the inquiry into different sections, and when each section has been thoroughly investigated to combine the results of the different investigators and see what conclusions are common to all. Our inquiry of the original Aryan home is, therefore, not only not inconsistent with the general theory about the cradle of the human race at the North Pole, but a necessary complement to it ; and it matters little whether it is undertaken as an independent inquiry as we have done, or as a part of the general investigation. Any how ours is a limited task, namely, to prove that the original home of the Aryan people was situated in the Arctic regions before the last Glacial epoch and that the oldest ancestors of the Aryan race had to abandon it owing to its destruction by ce and snow of the Glacial period. The Vedic and the Avestic passages, quoted in the previous chapters, directly point to such a home in primeval times, and we now see that the testimony of scholars, like Prof. Rhys, who have independently examined the Celtic, Teutonic and other mythologies of the European branches of the Aryan race, fully bears out the conclusion we have deduced from the Indo-Iranian traditions. We have also seen that our view is supported by the latest scientific researches, and is not inconsistent with the results of comparative philology. We may, therefore, take it as established that the original home of the Aryan people was in the far north, in regions round about the North Pole, and that we have correctly interpreted the Vedic and the Avestic traditions which had long remained mis-interpreted or mis-understood.

CHAPTER XIII.

THE BEARING OF OUR RESULTS ON THE HISTORY OF PRIMITIVE ARYAN CULTURE AND RELIGION.

Proofs of the theory of the Arctic home summed up —They clearly indicate a Polar home, but the exact spot in the Arctic regions, that is, north of Europe or Asia, still undeterminable —An Arctic home possible only in inter-Glacial times according to geology —Ancient Vedic chronology and calendar examined —The interval between the commencement of the Post-Glacial era and the Orion period cannot, according to it, be so great as 80,000 years —Supported by the moderate estimate of the American geologists —Purânic chronology of *yugas, manvantaras* and *kalpas* —Rangâchârya's and Aiyer's views thereon —Later Purânic system evolved out of an original cycle of four yugas of 10,000 years, since the last deluge —The theory of '*divine* years' unknown to Manu and Vyâsa —Adopted by later writers who could not believe that they lived in the Krita age —The original tradition of 10,000 years since the last deluge fully in accord with Vedic chronology —And also with the American estimate of 8,000 B. C. for the beginning of the Post-Glacial period —All prove the existence of a Polar Aryan home before 8,000 B. C. —Trustworthiness of the ancient traditions and the method of preserving them —The theory of the Polar origin of the whole human race not inconsistent with the theory of the Arctic Aryan home —Current views regarding primitive Aryan culture and religion examined —Primitive Aryan man and his civilisation cannot now be treated as Post-Glacial —Certain destruction of the primeval civilization and culture by the Ice Age —Short-comings or defects in the civilisation of the Neolithic Aryan races in Europe must, therefore, be ascribed to a post-diluvian relapse into barbarism —Life and calendar in the inter-Glacial Arctic home —*Devayâna* and *Pitriyâna* and the deities worshipped during the period —The ancient sacrifices of the Aryan race —The degree of civilisation reached by the undivided Aryans in their Arctic home —The results of Comparative Philology stated —The civilisation disclosed by them

must be taken to be the *minimum* or the *lowest*, that can be predicated of the undivided Aryans —The culture of the undivided Aryans higher than the culture of the Stone or the Metal age —Use of metal coins among them highly probable —Beginnings of the Aryan language, or the differentiation of human races according to colour or language still untraceable —The origin of Aryan man and religion lost in geological antiquity —Theological views regarding the origin and character of the Vedas summarised —Differently supported by writers on the different schools of philosophy —Patanjali's and Vyâsa's view that the Vedas were lost in the last deluge and repromulgated *in substance*, if not in *form*, at the beginning of the new age —The four periods into which the Post-Glacial era may be divided on astronomical grounds —Compared with the characteristics of the four yugas given in the Aitareya Brâhmana —Theological and historical views regarding the origin &c. of the Vedas stated in parallel columns and compared —Vedic texts, showing that the *subject matter* of the hymns is ancient though the *language* may be new, cited —Vedic deities and their exploits all said to be ancient —Improbability of Dr. Muir's suggested reconciliation —Vedas, or rather Vedic religion, shown to be inter-Glacial in *substance* though post-Glacial in *form* —Concluding remarks.

We have now completed our investigation of the question of the original home of the ancestors of the Vedic Aryans from different stand-points of view. Our arguments, it will be seen, are not based on the history of culture, or on facts disclosed by linguistic palæontology. The evidence, cited in the foregoing chapters, mainly consists of direct passages from the Vedas and the Avesta, proving unmistakably that the poets of the Ṛig-Veda were acquainted with the climatic conditions witnessible only in the Arctic regions, and that the principal Vedic deities, such as the revolving Dawn, the Waters captivated by Vṛitra, the Ashvins the rescuers of the afflicted gods and Sûrya, Indra the deity of a hundred sacrifices, Vishṇu the vast-strider, Varuṇa the lord of night and the ocean, the Âditya brothers or the seven monthly sun-gods, Trita or the Third, and others, are clothed with attributes which clearly betray their

Arctic origin. In other words, all the *differentiæ*, mentioned in the third chapter as characteristic of the Polar and Circum-Polar regions, are met with in the Ṛig-Veda in such a way as to leave no doubt regarding the conclusion to be drawn from them. A day or a night of six months, and a long continuous dawn of several days' duration with its revolving splendours, not to mention the unusually long Arctic day and night or a year of less than twelve months' sunshine, were all known to the Vedic bards, and have been described by them not mythologically or metaphorically but directly in plain and simple words, which, though misinterpreted so long, can, in the light thrown upon the question by recent scientific researches, be now rightly read and understood. In fact the task, which I set to myself, was to find out such passages, and show how in the absence of the true key to their meaning, they have been subjected to forced construction, or ignored and neglected, by Vedic scholars both Indian and foreign, ancient and modern. I do not mean, however, to underrate, on that account, the value or the importance of the labours of Indian Nairuktas like Yâska, or commentators like Sâyaṇa. Without their aid we should have, it is readily admitted, been able to do little in the field of the Vedic interpretation; and I am fully aware of the service they have rendered to this cause. There is no question that they have done their best in elucidating the meaning of our sacred books; and their claims on the grateful remembrance of their services by future generations of scholars will ever remain unchallenged. But if the Vedas are really the oldest records of our race, who can deny that in the light of the advancing knowledge regarding primitive humanity, we may still discover in these ancient records facts and statements which may have escaped the attention of older scholars owing to the imperfect nature, in their days, of those sciences which are calculated to throw further light on the habits and environments of the oldest ancestors of our race? There is, therefore, nothing strange if some of the passages in the Ṛig-Veda and the Avesta disclose to us ideas which the ancient commentators could not and did not perceive in them; and I would request the reader to bear this in mind in comparing the interpretations and explanations proposed by me in the foregoing chapters with the current interpretations of these passages by eastern or western Vedic scholars.

But our conclusions do not rest merely on the interpretation of passages which, if rightly construed, disclose climatic characteristics peculiar to the Arctic regions; though this evidence is, by itself, sufficient to prove our hypothesis. We have seen that in the sacrificial literature of the Vedic people as well as in their mythology there are many indications which point to the same conclusion; and these are fully corroborated by the ancient traditions and legends in the Avesta and also by the mythologies of the European branches of the Aryan race. A sacrificial session of ten months held by the Dashagvas, or an annual *sattra* of the same duration, compared with the oldest Roman year ending in December or the tenth month, are the principal instances on the point; and they have been fully discussed in the foregoing chapters. I have also shown that the knowledge of the half-year-long day or night is not confined to the traditions of the eastern Aryas, but is common also to the European branches of the Aryan race. The tradition preserved in the Vendidad about the ancient Iranian Paradise in the far north, so that a year was equal to a day to the inhabitants thereof, and its destruction by snow and ice burying the land under a thick ice-cap, again affords the most striking and cogent proof of the theory we have endeavoured to prove in these pages. Thus if the traditions of the western Aryas point out, according to Prof. Rhys, to Finland or the White Sea as the original home of the Aryan people, the Vedic and the Avestic traditions carry us still farther to the north; for a continuous dawn of thirty days is possible only within a few degrees of the North Pole. But though the latitude of the original home can be thus ascertained more or less definitely, yet there is unfortunately nothing in these traditions which will enable us to determine the longitude of the place, or, in other words, whether the original home of the Aryan race was to the north of Europe or Asia. But considering the fact that the traditions of the original Polar home are better preserved in the sacred books of the Brahmins and the Parsis, it is not unlikely that the primeval home was located to the north of Siberia rather than to the north of Russia or Scandinavia. It is, however, useless to speculate on the point without further proof. The Vedic and the Avestic evidence clearly establish the existence of a primeval Polar home, the climate of which was mild and temperate in ancient times, before it was invaded by the Glacial epoch; and with this result we must rest content, until we get sufficient new materials to ascertain the exact position of the Aryan home within the Arctic regions.

We commenced the book with a summary of the results of the latest geological and archæological researches regarding the history of primitive humanity and the invasion of northern Europe and Asia by a series of glacial epochs in the Quarternary era. This discussion was prefixed to the book with the object of clearing up certain misapprehensions regarding the early history of our planet based on knowledge derived from older geological works, when man was believed to be post-glacial; and it will now be seen that our theory of the primeval Arctic home of the Aryan races is in perfect accord with the latest and most approved geological facts and opinions. A primeval Arctic home would have been regarded an impossibility, had not science cleared the ground by establishing that the antiquity of man goes back to the Tertiary era, that the climate of the Polar regions was mild and temperate in inter-glacial times, and that it was rendered cold and inclement by the advent of the Glacial epoch. We can now also understand why attempts to prove the existence of an Arctic home by discovering references to severe winter and cold in the Vedas did not succeed in the past. The winter in the primeval home was originally, that is, in inter-glacial times, neither severe nor inclement, and if such expressions as "a hundred winters" (*shatam himâḥ*) are found in the Vedic literature, they cannot be taken for reminiscences of severe cold winters in the original home; for the expression came into use probably because the year in the original home closed with a winter characterised by the long Arctic night. It was the advent of the Ice Age that destroyed the mild climate of the original home and converted it into an ice-bound land unfit for the habitation of man. This is well expressed in the Avesta which describes the Airyana Vaêjo as a happy land subsequently converted by the invasion of Angra Mainyu into a land of severe winter and snow. This correspondence between the Avestic description of the original home and the results of the latest geological researches, at once enables us to fix the age of the Arctic home, for it is now a well-settled scientific fact that a mild climate in the Polar regions was possible only in the inter-glacial and not in the post-glacial times.

But according to some geologists 20,C00 or even 80,000 years have passed since the close of the last Glacial epoch; and as the oldest date assigned to the Vedic hymns does not go beyond 4500 B. C., it may be contended that the traditions of the Ice Age, or of the inter-glacial home, cannot be supposed to have been accurately preserved by oral transmission for thousands of years that elapsed between the commencement of the post-Glacial era and the oldest date of the Vedic hymns. It is, therefore, necessary to examine the point a little more closely in this place. In my *Orion* or *Researches into the antiquity of the Vedas*, I have shown that while the Taittirîya Saṁhitâ and the Brâhmaṇas begin the Nakshatras with the Krittikâs or the Pleiades, showing that the vernal equinox then coincided with the aforesaid asterism (2500 B. C.), the Vedic literature contains traces of Mriga or Orion being once the first of the Nakshatras and the hymns of the Rig-Veda, or at least many of them, which are undoubtedly older than the Taittirîya Saṁhitâ, contain reference to this period, that is, about 4500 B. C. approximately. It is also pointed out that there are faint traces of the same equinox being once in the constellation of Punarvasû, presided over by Aditi, which was possible in about 6000 B. C. I have in my later researches tried to push back this limit by searching for the older zodiacal positions of the vernal equinox in the Vedic literature, but I have not found any evidence of the same. My attention was, however, directed more and more to passages containing traces of an Arctic calendar and an Arctic home, and I have been gradually led to infer therefrom that at about 5000 or 6000 B. C., the Vedic Aryas had settled on the plains of Central Asia, and that at the time the traditions about the existence of the Arctic home and its destruction by snow and ice, as well as about the Arctic origin of the Vedic deities, were definitely known to the bards of these races. In short, researches in Vedic chronology and calendar do not warrant us in placing the advent of the last Glacial epoch, which destroyed the ancient Aryan home, at a time several thousands of years previous to the Orion period; and from what has been stated in the first two chapters of the book, it will be seen that this estimate well agrees with the conclusions of American geologists, who, from an examination of the erosion of valleys and similar other well-ascertained facts, assign to the close of the last Glacial epoch a date not older than about 8000 B. C. We might even go further and say that ancient Vedic chronology and calendar furnish an independent corroboration of the moderate view of the American geologists;

and when two independent lines of research unexpectedly lead us to the same result, we may very well reject, at least in the present state of our knowledge, the extravagant speculations of Croll and his followers, and, for all practical purposes, adopt the view that the last Glacial epoch closed and the post-Glacial period commenced at about 8000 B. C. From this to the Orion period is an interval of about 3000 years, and it is not at all improbable that the traditions of the ancient home should have been remembered and incorporated into hymns whose origin can be clearly traced to that period. In short, the Vedic traditions, far from being contradictory to the scientific evidence, only serve to check the extravagant estimates regarding the age of the last Glacial epoch; and if the sober view of American geologists be adopted, both geology and the traditions recorded in the ancient books of the Aryan race will be found alike to point out to a period not much older than 8000 B. C. for the commencement of the post-Glacial era and the compulsory migration of the Aryan races from their Arctic home.

And not only Vedic but also Purâṇic chronology, properly understood, leads us to the same conclusion. According to the Purâṇas the earth and the whole universe are occasionally subjected to destruction at long intervals of time, the earth by a small and the universe by a grand deluge. Thus we are told that when the god Brahmâ is awake during *his* day the creation exists; but when at the end of the day he goes to sleep, the world is destroyed by a deluge, and is re-created when he awakes from his sleep and resumes his activity the next morning. Brahmâ's evening and morning are thus synonymous with the destruction and the re-creation of the earth. A day and a night of Brahmâ are each equal to a period of time called a *Kalpa*, and a *Kalpa* is taken for a unit in measuring higher periods of time. Two *Kalpas* constitute a nycthemeron (day-and-night) of Brahmâ, and $360 \times 2 = 720$ *Kalpas* make his year, while a hundred such years constitute his life-time, at the end of which a grand deluge overtakes the whole universe including Brahmâ. Now according to the Code of Manu and the Mahâbhârata the four yugas of Kṛita, Tretâ, Dvâpara and Kali form a yuga of gods, and a thousand such yugas make a *Kalpa* or a day of Brahmâ of 12,000,000 years, at the end of which a deluge destroys the world. The Purâṇas, however, have adopted a different method of computation. The four yugas of Kṛita, Tretâ, Dvâpara and Kali are there said to constitute a Mahâ-yuga; 71 such Mahâ-yugas constitute a Manvantara, and 14 Manvantaras make a *Kalpa*, which, according to this method of counting, contains 4,320,000,000 years. The difference between the durations of a *Kalpa* according to these two methods is due to the fact that the years making up the four yugas of Kṛita, Tretâ, Dvâpara and Kali are considered to be *divine* in the latter, while they are obviously human in Manu and the Mahâbhârata. For further details the reader is referred to the late Mr. S. B. Dixit's *History of Indian Astronomy* in Marâṭhi, Prof. Raṅgâchârya's essay on *Yugas*, and Mr. Aiyer's *Chronology of Ancient India*, a book, in which the question of yugas and especially that of the beginning of the Kali yuga, is subjected to a searching and exhaustive examination. The Hindu writers on astronomy seem to have adopted the same system, except Âryabhaṭṭa, who holds that 72, and not 71, Mahâ-yugas make a Manvantara, and that a Mahâ-yuga is divided into four equal parts which are termed Kṛita, Tretâ, Dvâpara and Kali. According to this chronological system, we are, at present, in the 5003rd year (elapsed) of the Kali yuga of the 28th Mahâ-yuga of the 7th (Vaivasvata) Manvantara of the current Kalpa; or, 1,972,949,003 years have, in other words, elapsed since the deluge which occurred at the beginning of the present or the Shveta-vârâha Kalpa. This estimate is, as observed by Prof. Raṅgâchârya, quite beyond the limit admitted by modern geology; and it is not unlikely that Hindu astronomers, who held the view that the sun, the moon, and all the planets were in a line at the beginning of the Kalpa, arrived at this figure by mathematically calculating the period during which the sun, the moon and all the planets made an integral number of complete revolutions round the earth. We need not, however, go into these details, which, howsoever interesting, are not relevant to the subject in hand. A cycle of the four yugas, *viz.*, Kṛita, Tretâ, Dvâpara and Kali, is, it will be seen, the basis of this chronological system, and we have therefore to examine more critically what this collection of four yugas, otherwise termed a Mahâ-yuga, really signifies and whether the period of time originally denoted by it was the same as it is said to be at present.

Prof. Raṅgâchârya and especially Mr. Aiyer have ably treated this subject in their essays, and I agree in the main with them in their conclusions. I use the words 'in the main' deliberately, for though my researches have independently led me to reject the hypothesis of '*divine* years,' yet there are certain points which cannot, in my opinion, be definitely settled without further research. I have shown previously that the word *yuga* is used in the Ṛig-Veda to denote 'a period of time,' and that in the phrase *mânushâ yugâ* it cannot but be taken to denote 'a month.' *Yuga* is, however, evidently used to denote a longer period of time in such expressions as *Devânâm prathame yuge* in the Ṛig-Veda, X, 72, 3; while in the Atharva Veda VIII, 2, 21, which says "We allot to thee a hundred, ten thousand years, two, three, (or) four *yugas*," a *yuga* evidently means a period of not less than 10,000 years;[1] and Mr. Aiyer is right in pointing out that the omission of the word 'one' in the above verse is not accidental. According to this view a

1. Atharva Veda, VIII, 2, 21,—शतं तेऽयुतं हायनान्द्वे युगे त्रीणि चत्वारि कृण्मः।

yuga may be taken to have, at the longest, denoted a period of 10,000 years in the days of the Atharva Veda Saṁhitâ. Now it is found that Manu and the Mahâbhârata both assign 1000, 2000, 3000 and 4000 years to the four yugas of Kali, Dvâpara, Tretâ and Kṛita respectively. In other words, the durations of Dvâpara, Tretâ and Kṛita are obtained by doubling, trebling and quadrupling the duration of Kali; and taking into consideration that Kṛita (which Mr. Aiyer compares with Latin *quatuor*) means 'four' in Sanskrit literature, the names of the yugas may perhaps be derived from this fact. We are, however, concerned with the duration of the four yugas, and adding up the numbers given above, we obtain 10,000 years for a cycle of four yugas, or a *Mahâ-yuga*, according to the terminology explained above. Manu and Vyâsa, however, add to this 10,000 another period of 2,000 years, said to represent the Sandhyâ or the Sandhyâṁsha periods intervening between the different *yugas*. Thus the Kṛita age does not pass suddenly into Tretâ, but has a period of 400 years interposed at each of its ends, while the Tretâ is protected from the contact of the preceding and the succeeding yuga by two periods of 300 years each, the Dvâpara of 200 and the Kali of 100 years. The word *Sandhyâ* denotes the time of the dawn in ordinary literature; and Mr. Aiyer points out that as the period of the dawn and the gloaming, or the morning and the evening twilight, is each found to extend over three out of thirty *ghatis* of a day, so one-tenth of the period of each yuga is assigned to its *Sandhyâ* or the period of transition into another yuga; and that it is not improbable that these supplementary periods were subsequent amendments. The period of 10,000 years for a cycle of the four yugas is thus increased to 12,000, if the *Sandhyâ* periods are included in it, making Kṛita comprise 4800, Tretâ 3600, Dvâpara 2400 and Kali 1200 years. Now at the time of the Mahâbhârata or the Code of Manu, the Kali yuga had already set in; and if the yuga contained no more than 1,000, or, including the Sandhyâs, 1200 *ordinary* years, it would have terminated about the beginning of the Christian era.[1] The writers of the Purâṇas, many of which appear to have been written during the first few centuries of the Christian era, were naturally unwilling to believe that the Kali yuga had passed away, and that they lived in the Kṛita yuga of a new Mahâ-yuga; for the Kṛita yuga meant according to them a golden age, while the times in which they lived showed signs of degeneration on all sides. An attempt was, therefore, made to extend the duration of the Kali yuga by converting 1000 (or 1200) ordinary human years thereof into as many *divine* years, a single *divine* year, or a year of the gods, being equal to 360 human years. A Vedic authority for such an interpretation was found in the text from the Taittirîya Brâhmaṇa, which, we have quoted and discussed previously, *viz.*, "That which is a year is a day of the gods." Manu and Vyâsa simply assign 1000 years to the Kali yuga. But as Manu, immediately after recording the duration of the *yugas* and their *Sandhyâs*, observes "that this period of 12,000 years is called the yuga of the gods," the device of converting the ordinary years of the different yugas into as many divine years was, thereby, at once rendered plausible; and as people were unwilling to believe that they could be in a yuga other than the Kali, this solution of the difficulty

---

1. Compare Manu, I, 69-71. In the Mahâbhârata the subject is treated in two places, once in the Shânti-Parvan, Chap. 231, and once in the Vana-Parvan, Chap. 188, V. 21-28, (Cal. Ed.). The following verses are taken from the latter place:—आदितो मनुजव्याघ्र कृत्स्नस्य जगतः क्षये। चत्वार्याहुः सहस्राणि वर्षाणां तत्कृतं युगम् ॥ तस्य तावच्छती संध्या संध्यांशश्च तथाविधः। त्रीणि वर्षसहस्राणि त्रेतायुगमिहोच्यते ॥ तस्य तावच्छती संध्या संध्यांशश्च ततः परं। तथा वर्षसहस्रे द्वे द्वापरं परिमाणतः ॥ तस्यापि द्विशती संध्या संध्यांशश्च तथाविधः ॥ सहस्रमेकं वर्षाणां तथा कलियुगं स्मृतं । तस्य वर्षशतं संधिः संध्यांशश्च ततः परं ॥ संधिसंध्यांशयोस्तुल्यं प्रमाणमुपधारय। क्षीणे कलियुगे चैव प्रवर्तति कृतं युगं ॥ एषा द्वादशसाहस्री युगाख्या परिकीर्तिता। एतत्सहस्रपर्यंतमहर्ब्राह्ममुदाहृतम् ॥ The first line clearly states that the Kṛita yuga commences after the deluge. Cf. Muir O. S. T., Vol. 1, 45-48.

was universely adopted, and a Kali of 1200 ordinary years was at once changed, by this ingenious artifice, into a magnificent cycle of as many divine, or 360 × 1200 = 432,000 ordinary years. The same device converted, at one stroke, the 12,000 ordinary years of a Mahâ-yuga into as many divine, or 360 × 12,000 = 4,320,000 ordinary years, affecting in a similar way the higher cycles of time like Manvantaras and Kalpas. How the beginning of the Kali yuga was thrown back, by astronomical calculations, to 3102 B. C., when this hypothesis of 'divine years' was adopted, is a separate question by itself; but not being pertinent to the subject in hand we need not go into it in this place. Suffice it to say that where chronology is invested with semi-religious character, artifices or devices, like the one noticed above, are not unlikely to be used to suit the exigencies of the time; and those who have to investigate the subject from a historical and antiquarian point of view must be prepared to undertake the task of carefully sifting the data furnished by such chronology, as Prof. Rangâchârya and Mr. Aiyer have done in their essays referred to above.

From a consideration of the facts stated above it will be seen that so far as the Code of Manu and the Mahâbhârata are concerned, they preserve for us a reminiscence of a cycle of 10,000 years comprising the four yugas, the Kṛita, the Tretâ, the Dvâpara and the Kali; and that the Kali yuga of one thousand years had then already set in. In other words, Manu and Vyâsa obviously speak only of a period of 10,000, or, including the Sandhyâs, of 12,000 ordinary or human (not divine) years, from the beginning of the Kṛita to the end of the Kali yuga; and it is remarkable that in the Atharva Veda we should find a period of 10,000 years apparently assigned to one yuga. It is not, therefore, unlikely that the Atharva Veda takes the Kṛita, the Tretâ, the Dvâpara and the Kali together, and uses the word *yuga* to denote the combined duration of all these in the passage referred to above.

Now considering the fact that the Kṛita age is said to commence after a *pralaya* or the deluge, Manu and Vyâsa must be understood to have preserved herein an old tradition that about 10,000 years before their time (supposing them to have lived at the beginning of the Kali age of 1200 years), the new order of things commenced with the Kṛita age; or, in other words, the deluge which destroyed the old order of things occurred about 10,000 years before their time. The tradition has been very much distorted owing to devices adopted in later times to make the traditional chronology suit the circumstances of the day. But still it is not difficult to ascertain the original character of the tradition; and when we do so, we are led to conclude that the beginning of the new order of things, or, to put it more scientifically, the commencement of the current post-Glacial era was, according to this tradition, not assigned to a period older than 10,000 years before the Christian era. We have shown that researches in Vedic chronology do not allow us to carry back the date of the post-Glacial era beyond this estimate, for traditions of the Arctic home appear to have been well understood by the bards of the Ṛig-Veda in the Orion period. It is, therefore, almost certain that the invasion of the Arctic Aryan home by the last Glacial epoch did not take place at a time older than 10,000 B. C. The American geologists, we have seen, have arrived at the same conclusion on independent scientific grounds; and when the Vedic and the Purâṇic chronology indicate nearly the same time,—a difference of one or two thousand years, in such cases does not matter much,—we may safely reject the extravagant estimates of 20,000 or 80,000 years, and adopt, for all practical purposes, the view that the last Glacial epoch closed and the post-Glacial period commenced at about 8,000, or, at best, about 10,000 B. C.

We have now to consider how the tradition about the existence of the original home at the North Pole and its destruction by snow and ice of the Glacial epoch, and other cognate reminiscences were preserved until they were incorporated into the law-book of the Mazdayasnians and the hymns of the Ṛig-Veda. That a real tradition is preserved in these books is undoubted, for we have seen that an examination of the traditions preserved by the European branches of the Aryan race have led Prof. Rhys to the same conclusion; and those who know the history of the preservation of our sacred books will see nothing improbable herein. In these days of writing and printing, we have no need to depend upon memory, and consequently we fail to realise what memory, kept under the strictest discipline, is capable of achieving. The whole of the Ṛig-Veda, nay, the Veda and its nine supplementary books, have been preserved by the Brahmins of India, letter for letter and accent for accent, for the last 3000 or 4000 years at least; and priests who have done so in recent times may well be credited with having faithfully preserved the traditions of the ancient home, until they were incorporated into the sacred books. These achievements of disciplined memory may appear marvellous to us at present; but, as stated above, they were looked upon as ordinary feats when memory was trusted better than books, and trained and cultivated with such special care as to be a faithful instrument for transmitting along many generations whatever men were most anxious to have remembered. It has been a fashion to cry down the class of priests who make it their sole profession to cultivate their memory by keeping it under strict discipline and transmit by its means our sacred writings without the loss of a single accent from generation to generation. They have been described, even by scholars like Yâska, as the carriers of burden, and compared by others to parrots who repeat words without understanding their meaning. But the service, which this class has rendered to the cause of ancient history and religion by preserving the oldest traditions of the race, is invaluable; and looking to the fact that a specially disciplined memory was needed for such preservation, we cannot but gratefully remember the services of those whose hereditary devotion to the task, we might say, the sacred religious task, rendered it possible for so many traditions to be preserved for thousands of years. Paṇḍits might analyse and explain the Vedic hymns more or less elaborately or correctly; but for that reason, we cannot forget that the very basis of their labours would have been lost long ago, had the institution of priests who made disciplined memory their exclusive business in life not been in existence. If the institution has outlived its necessity,—which is doubtful, for the art of writing or printing can hardly be trusted to the same extent as disciplined memory in such matters,—we must remember that religious institutions are the hardest to die in any country in the world.

We may, therefore, safely assert that Vedic and Avestic traditions, which have been faithfully preserved by disciplined memory, and whose trustworthiness is proved by Comparative Mythology as well as by the latest researches in Geology and Archæology, fully establish the existence of an Arctic home of the Aryan people in inter-glacial times; and that after the destruction of this home by the last Glacial epoch the Aryan people had to migrate southwards and settle at first in the northern parts of Europe or on the plains of Central Asia at the beginning of the post-Glacial period, that is about 8000 B. C. The antiquity of the Aryan race is thus carried back to interglacial times, and its oldest home to regions round about the North Pole, where alone a long dawn of thirty days is possible. Whether other human races, beside the Aryan, lived with them in the circum-polar country is a question which does not fall within the purview of this book. Dr. Warren, in his *Paradise Found*, has cited Egyptian, Akkadian, Assyrian, Babylonian, Chinese and even Japanese traditions indicating the existence of an Arctic home of these races in ancient times; and from a consideration of all these he arrives at the conclusion that the cradle of the *whole human race* must be placed in the circum-polar regions, a conclusion in which he is also supported by other scholars. But, as observed by Prof. Rhys, it is no fatal objection to the view we have endeavoured to prove in these pages that the mythologies of nations, beside the Aryan, also point to the North Pole as their original home; for it is not contended that the Aryans may be the only people of northern origin. On the contrary, there are grounds to believe that the five races of men (*pañcha janâḥ*) often mentioned in the Ṛig-Veda may have been the races which lived with the Aryans in their original home, for we cannot suppose that the Vedic Aryas after their dispersion from the original home met only with five races in their migrations, or were divided only into five branches. But the question is one which can be finally decided only after a good deal of further research; and as it is not necessary to mix it up with the question of the original home of the Aryans, we may leave it out for the present. If the North Pole is conclusively shown to be the cradle of the human race hereafter, it would not affect in the least the conclusion we have drawn in these pages from a number of definite Vedic and Avestic traditions, but if the existence of the Aryan home near the North Pole is proved, as we have endeavoured to do in the foregoing pages, by independent testimony, it is sure to strengthen the probability of the northern home of the whole human race; and as the traditions of the Aryan people are admittedly better preserved in the Veda and the Avesta than those of any other race, it is safer and even desirable to treat the question of the primeval Aryan home independently of the general problem taken up by Dr. Warren and other scholars. That the Veda and the Avesta are the oldest books of the Aryan race is now conceded by all, and we have seen that it is not difficult to ascertain, from traditions contained therein, the site of the Aryan Paradise, now that we begin to search for it in the light thrown upon the subject by modern scientific researches.

But if the fact of an early Aryan home in the far north is once established by indisputable traditional evidence, it is sure to revolutionise the existing views regarding the primitive history or religion of the Aryan races. Comparative philologists and Sanskritists, who looked for the primeval home "somewhere in Central Asia," have advanced the theory that the whole progress of the Aryan race, intellectual, social or moral, from primeval savagery to such civilisation as is disclosed by the Vedic hymns, was effected on the plains of Central Asia. It was on these plains, we are told, that our oldest ancestors, gazed upon the wonders of the dawn or the rising sun with awe and astonishment, or reverentially watched the storm-clouds hovering in the sky to be eventually broken up by the god of rain and thunder, thereby giving rise to the worship of natural elements and thus laying down the foundations of later Aryan mythology. It was on these plains that they learnt the art of weaving, the products of which superseded the use of hides for clothing, or constructed their chariots, or trained their horses, or discovered the use of metals like gold and silver. In short, all the civilisation and culture which Comparative Philology proves on linguistic grounds to have been common to the different Aryan races before their separation is regarded to have first originated or developed on the plains of Central Asia in post-Glacial times. Dr. Schrader, in his *Pre-historic Antiquities of the Aryan Peoples*, gives us an exhaustive summary of facts and arguments regarding primitive Aryan culture and civilisation which can be deduced from Linguistic Palæology, or Comparative Philology, and as a repertory of such facts the book stands unrivalled. But we must remember that the results of Comparative Philology, howsoever interesting and instructive they may be from the linguistic or the historical point of view, are apt to mislead us if we know not the site of the original home, or the time when it was inhabited or abandoned by the ancestors of our race. Comparative Philology may teach us that cow was an animal known and domesticated before the Aryan separation, or that the art of weaving was known in those old days, because the words 'cow' and 'weave' can be traced in all the Aryan languages. But it is now found that equations like these do not help us much in definitely ascertaining where the united Aryans lived and when they separated; while recent researches in Archæology and Anthropology have exhibited the improbability of a Central Asian home of the Aryan races and successive migrations therefrom to European countries. The hypothesis of a Central Asian home is, therefore, now almost abandoned; but strange to say, that those, who maintain that Europe was inhabited at the beginning of the Neolithic age by the ancestors of the races who now inhabit the same regions, are prepared to leave undetermined the question whether these races originated in Europe or went there from some other land. Thus Canon Taylor, in his *Origin of the Aryans*, confidently advises us that we need not concern ourselves with the arguments of those who assert that Europe was inhabited by the ancestors of the existing races even in the Palæolithic period; for, says he, "philologists will probably admit that within the limits of the Neolithic age, it would be possible to find sufficient time for the evolution and the differentiation of the Aryan languages."[1] In the last chapter of the same book we are further informed that the mythologies of the different branches of the Aryan race must have been developed after their separation, and that resemblances, like Dyaus-pitar and Jupiter, or Varuṇa and Uranus, must be taken to be merely verbal and not mythological in their origin. In short, the

1. See Taylor's Origin of the Aryans, p. 57.

advocates of the Central Asian as well as of the northern European home of the Aryans are both unwilling to carry back the beginning of the Aryan civilisation beyond post-glacial times, and we are told that Aryan mythology and religion cannot, therefore, claim any higher antiquity.

All such guesses and speculations about the origin of the Aryan race and its civilisation will have now to be revised in the new light thrown upon the subject by the theory of the Arctic home in pre-Glacial times. We cannot now maintain that primitive Aryans were a post-Glacial race, or that they advanced from barbarism to civilisation in the Neolithic period either in Central Asia or in the northern parts of Europe; nor is it possible to argue that because the mythologies of the different branches of the Aryan race do not disclose the existence of common deities, these mythologies must be taken to have developed after the separation of the Aryan races from their common home. Thus for instance, we are told that though the word *Uṣhas* occurs in Zend as *Uṣhangh*, and may be compared to Greek *Eos*, Latin *Aurora*, Lithuanian *Auszra*, Teutonic *Asustrô* and Anglo-Saxon *Eostra*, yet it is only in the Vedic mythology that we find Uṣhas raised to the dignity of the goddess of the morning; and from this we are asked to infer that the worship of the dawn was developed only on the Indian soil. The theory of the Arctic home, however, makes it impossible to argue in this way. If Vedic deities are clothed with attributes which are unmistakably polar in their origin,—and in the case of Uṣhas, the polar character has been shown to be unquestionable,—we cannot hold that the legends pertaining to these deities were developed on the plains of Central Asia. It was impossible for the Indian priests to conceive or picture the splendours of the dawn in the way we meet with in the Ṛig-Veda; for it has been shown that the evanescent dawn, with which they were familiar, is quite dissimilar in character to the Arctic dawn, the subject of the

Vedic hymns. And what applies to the dawn can be predicated as well of other deities and myths, *e.g.*, of Indra and Vṛitra or the captive Waters, of Vishṇu hibernating for four months in a year, or of Trita or the Third going down in a well, or of the Ashvins rescuing or saving the gods from the temporary affliction to which they were again and again subjected. These very names may not be found in the Celtic or the Teutonic mythology, but an examination of the latter has been found to disclose the same polar characteristics which are possessed by Vedic deities or myths; and so long as this fundamental coincidence exists between the two, it is unreasonable to contend that the mythologies of the different branches of the Aryan race had no common origin, or that the resemblances between the names of the deities are more linguistic than mythological. The destruction of the ancient Aryan home by glaciation and deluge introduces a new factor in the history of the Aryan civilisation; and any short-comings or defects in the civilisation of the Aryan races, that are found to have inhabited the northern parts of Europe in the beginning of the Neolithic age, as distinguished from the civilisation of the Asiatic Aryan races, must now be accounted for as the result of a natural relapse into barbarism after the great catastrophe. It is true that ordinarily we cannot conceive a race that has once launched on a career of progress and civilisation suddenly retrograding or relapsing into barbarism. But the same rule cannot be applied to the case of the continuation of the ante-diluvian civilisation into post-diluvian times. In the first place very few people could have survived a cataclysm of such magnitude as the deluge of snow and ice; and those that survived could hardly be expected to have carried with them all the civilisation of the original home, and introduced it intact in their new settlements, under adverse circumstances, amongst the non-Aryan tribes in the north of Europe or on the plains of Central Asia. We must also bear in mind the fact that the climate of northern Europe and Asia, though temperate at present, must have been very much colder after the great deluge, and the descendants of those who had to migrate to these countries from the Polar regions, born only to a savage or nomadic life, could have, at best, preserved only fragmentary reminiscences of the ante-diluvian culture and civilisation of their forefathers living in the once happy Arctic home. Under these circumstances we need not be surprised if the European Aryas are found to be in an inferior state of civilisation at the beginning of the Neolithic age. On the contrary the wonder is that so much of the ante-diluvian religion or culture should have been preserved from the general wreck, caused by the last Glacial epoch, by the religious zeal and industry of the bards or priests of the Iranian or the Indian Aryas. It is true that they looked upon these relics of the ancient civilisation, as a sacred treasure entrusted to them to be scrupulously guarded and transmitted to future generations. Yet considering the difficulties with which they had to contend, we cannot but wonder how so much of the ante-diluvian civilisation, religion, or worship was preserved in the Veda or the Avesta. If the other Aryan races have failed to preserve these ancient traditions so well, it would be unreasonable to argue therefrom that the civilisation or the culture of these races was developed after their separation from the common stock.

It has been shown previously that the climate of the Arctic regions in the inter-Glacial period was so mild and temperate as to be almost an approach to a perpetual spring, and that there was then a continent of land round about the Pole, the same being submerged during the glacial epoch. The primitive Aryans residing in such regions must, therefore, have lived a happy life. The only inconvenience experienced by them was the long Arctic night; and we have seen how this phenomenon has served to give rise to various myths or legends describing the struggle between the powers of light and darkness. The occurrence of the Arctic night, its tiresome length, and the long expected morning light on the horizon after some months were, naturally enough, the most important facts which attracted the attention of our primeval forefathers, and it is no wonder if they believed it to be the greatest exploit of their gods when the beneficent dawn came dawning up, after several months of darkness, from the nether world of aerial waters, inaugurating a new yearly round of sacrifices, festivals, or other religious or social ceremonies. It was the beginning of the Devayâna, when the powers of light celebrated their victory over the demons of darkness, and the Child of the Morning, the Kumâra, the leader of the army of gods, walked victoriously along the Devayâna path commencing the cycle of human ages, or *mânushâ yugâ*, as mentioned in the Rig-Veda. The Pitṛiyâna, or the walk of the Manes, corresponded with the dark winter, the duration of which extended in the original home from two to six months. This was the period of rest or repose during which, as observed previously, people refrained even from disposing the bodies of the dead owing to the absence of sunshine. All social and religious ceremonies or feasts were also suspended during this period as the powers of darkness were believed to be in the ascendant. In short, the oldest Aryan calendar was, as remarked by Dr. Schrader, divided into two parts, a summer of seven or ten months and a corresponding winter of five or two months. But it seems to have been an ancient practice to reckon the year by counting the recurrence of summers or winters rather than by combining the two seasons. It is thus that we can account for a year of seven or ten months in old times, or annual sacrificial *sattras* extending over the same period. This calendar is obviously unsuited to places to the outh of the Arctic circle; and the Aryans had, therefore, to change or reform the same, as was done by Numa, in post-glacial times, when, expatriated from their mother land, they settled in the northern parts of Europe and Central Asia. But the reminiscence of the Devayâna as a special period of sacrifices and ceremonies was tenaciously preserved, and even nowit is looked upon as a season of special religious merit. We can, on this theory, easily explain why the Gṛihya-Sûtras attach special importance to the *Uttarâyaṇa* from a ceremonial point of view, and why death during the *Dakṣhiṇâyana* is regarded as inauspicious. How the inter-glacial year of seven or ten months was changed to a year of twelve months in postglacial times, and how the equinoctial division which obtained at first on the analogy of the Devayâna and the Pitṛiyâna, was subsequently altered to the solstitial one, the old meaning of the word *Uttarâyaṇa* undergoing (*Orion*, p. 25 *f.*) a similarchange, are questions, which, though important in the history of the Aryan calendar, are not relevant in this place; and we shall, therefore, proceed with the subject in hand. It is urged by some writers that though the worship of natural elements is found to obtain in several ancient Indo-European religions, yet its beginnings cannot be supposed to go back to the time of the common origin of the related peoples. Dr. Schrader has ably refuted this view in the concluding pages of his book on the pre-historic antiquities of Aryan peoples; and the theory of the Arctic home powerfully supports Dr. Schrader in his conclusions. "If we put aside everything unsafe and false," observes Dr. Schrader, "that Comparative Mythology and History of Religion has accumulated on this subject, we are solely, from the consideration of perfectly trustworthy material, more and more driven, on all sides, to assume that the common basis of ancient European religions was a worship of the powers of Nature practised in the Indo-European period."

1. See Dr. Schrader's Pre His. Antiqui. Ary. Peoples, translated by Jevons, p. 418.

The fact that the Vedic deities like Uṣhas, the Âdityas, the Ashvins or the Vṛitrahan are found invested with Polar characteristics, further goes to confirm the conclusion based on linguistic grounds, or common etymological equations for sky, morning, fire, light or other natural powers. In short, whatever be the stand-point from which we view the subject in question, we are led to the conclusion that the shining sky (*Dyaus pitâ*), the sun (*Sûrya*), the fire (*Agni*), the Dawn (*Uṣhas*), the storm or thunder (*Tanyatu*) had already attained to the dignity of divine beings or gods in the primeval period; and etymological equations like Sanskrit *yaj*, Zend *yaz* and Greek *azomai*, show that these gods were worshipped and sacrifices offered to them to secure their favour even in primeval times. Whether this worship originated, or, in other words, whether the powers of nature were invested with divine honours only in inter-glacial times, or in times anterior to it, cannot, as stated above, be ascertained from the materials in our hands at present. But this much is beyond question that the worship of these elements, as manifestations of divine power, had already become established amongst the undivided Aryans in the Arctic home, and the post-diluvian Aryan religions were developed from this ancient system of worship and sacrifices. We have seen that the Ṛig-Veda mentions the ancient sacrificers of the race like Manu, Aṅgirases, Bhṛigus and others, and the fact that they completed their sacrificial sessions in seven, nine or ten months proves that they were the sacrificers of the undivided Aryans in their Arctic home. It was these sacrificers who performed the sacrifices of the people during a summer of seven or ten months and worshipped the matutinal deities with offerings in primeval times. But when the sun went down below the horizon, these sacrificers naturally closed their sessions and made their offerings *only* to Vṛitrahan, the chief hero in the struggle with the demons of darkness, in order that he may, invigorated by their offerings, eventually bring back the light of the dawn to these worshippers. I do not mean to assert that an elaborate system of sacrifices existed in inter-glacial times; but I do maintain that sacrifice was the main ritual of the primeval Aryan religion, and that it is a mistake to suppose that it originated or was invented only in post-glacial times. I have dwelt at some length on the question of ancient religious worship and ritual in this place because the theory of the Arctic home very well exposes, in my opinion, the fallacious character of many of the existing views on this subject.

A people, who had come to worship the powers of Nature as manifestations of divine will and energy, who had a well-developed language of their own, and who had already evolved a legendary literature out of the Arctic conditions of the year in their congenial home near the North Pole, may well be expected to have made a good advance in civilisation. But we have at present very few means by which we can ascertain the exact degree of civilisation attained by the undivided Aryans in their primitive home. Comparative Philology tells us that primitive Aryans were familiar with the art of spinning and weaving, knew and worked in metals, constructed boats and chariots, founded and lived in cities, carried on buying and selling, and had made considerable progress in agriculture. We also know that important social or political institutions or organisations, as for instance, marriage or the laws of property, prevailed amongst the forefathers of our race in those early days; and linguistic palæontology furnishes us with a long list of the fauna and the flora known to the undivided Aryans. These are important linguistic discoveries, and taking them as they are, they evidently disclose a state of civilisation higher than that of the savages of the Neolithic age. But in the light of the Arctic theory we are naturally led to inquire if the culture of the primitive Aryans was confined only to the level disclosed by Comparative Philology, or whether it was of a higher type than the one we can predicate of them simply on linguistic grounds. We have seen above that in the case of the mythological deities and their worship the Polar character of many of the deities at once enables us to assign them to the primitive period even when their names are not found in all the Aryan languages; and the results of Comparative Philology regarding primitive Aryan culture will have to be checked and revised in the same way. The very fact that after compulsory dispersion from their mother land the surviving Aryans, despite the fragmentary civilisation they carried with them, were able to establish their supremacy over the races they came across in their migrations from the original home at the beginning of the post-Glacial period, and that they succeeded, by conquest or assimilation, in Aryanising the latter in language, thought and religion under circumstances which could not be expected to be favourable to them, is enough to prove that the original Aryan civilisation must have been of a type far higher than that of the non-Aryan races, or than the one found among the Aryan races that migrated southward after the destruction of their home by the Ice Age. So long as the Aryan races inhabiting the northern parts of Europe in the beginning of the Neolithic age were believed to be autochthonous there was no necessity of going beyond the results of Comparative Philology to ascertain the degree of civilisation attained by the undivided Aryans. But now we see that the culture of the Neolithic Aryans is obviously only a relic, an imperfect fragment, of the culture attained by the undivided Aryans in their Arctic home; and it would, therefore, be unreasonable to argue that such and such civilisation, or culture cannot be predicated of the undivided Aryans simply because words indicating the same are found only in some and not in all the Aryan languages. In other words, though we may accept the results of Comparative Philology so far as they go, we shall have to be more cautious hereafter in inferring that such and such a thing was not known to the primitive Aryans because common etymological equations for the same cannot be discovered in all the Aryan languages. We have, it is true, no means of ascertaining how much of the original civilisation was lost in the deluge, but we cannot, on that account, deny that some portion of it must have been irrecoverably lost in the great cataclysm that destroyed the original home. Under these circumstances all that we can safely assert is that the degree of culture disclosed by Comparative Philology is the *lowest* or the *minimum* that can be predicated of the undivided Aryans. It is important to bear this reservation in mind because undue importance is sometimes attached to the results of Comparative Philology by a kind of reasoning which appeared all right so long the question of the site of the original home was unsettled. But now that we know that Aryan race and religion are both inter-Glacial and their ultimate origin is lost in geological antiquity, it does not stand to reason to suppose that the inter-Glacial Aryans were a race of savages. The archæologists, it is true, have established the succession of the ages of Stone, Bronze and Iron; and according to this theory the Aryan race must have once been in the Stone age. But there is nothing in archæology which requires us to place the Stone age of the Aryan races in post-Glacial times; and when Comparative Philology has established the fact that undivided Aryans were acquainted with the use of metals, it becomes clear that the degree of civilisation reached by the undivided Aryans in their Arctic home was higher than the culture of the Stone age or even that of the age of metals. I have referred in the first chapter of the book to the opinion of some eminent archæologists that the metal age was introduced into Europe from other countries either by commerce or by the Indo-European race going there from outside, and the theory of the Arctic home with its inter-Glacial civilisation lends support to this view.

I might in passing here refer to an instance which illustrates the danger of relying exclusively on Comparative Philology in this respect. Dr. Schrader has shown that copper, at any rate, was known to the primitive Aryans; and he admits the possibility that this metal may, in isolated cases, have been employed in the manufacture of weapons like fighting knives or lance-heads. But we are told that there are linguistic difficulties which prevent us from assuming that gold and silver were known in the primitive period. On an examination of the subject it will, however, be seen that in cases like these the philologist relies too much on his own methods or follows them too rigidly. For instance *khalkos* (copper or bronze) is mentioned by Homer as a medium of exchange (Il. vii, 472); and Comparative Philology discloses two etymological equations, one derived from the root **mei* (Sans. *me*) denoting 'barter,' and the other derived from the Sanskrit *krî*, Greek *priamai*, meaning purchase. The Ṛig-Veda (VIII, 1, 5) also mentions a measure of value called *shulka*, and, as the word is used in later Sanskrit literature to denote a *small* payment made at a toll-house, it is not unlikely that *shulka* originally meant a small coin of copper or bronze similar in character to the *khalkos* mentioned by Homer. Now it is true that ordinarily Greek *kh*, is represented by *h* in Sanskrit, and that if this rule be rigidly applied to the present case it would not be possible to phonetically identify *khalkos* with *shulka*. Philologists have, therefore, tried to compare *khalkos* with Sanskrit *hrîku* or *hlîku*. But, as remarked by Dr. Schrader, the connection seems to be altogether improbable. *Hrîku* is not a Vedic word, nor does it mean copper or bronze. Despite the phonetic difficulty,—and the difficulty is not so serious as it seems to be at the first sight, for Sanskrit *sh* is represented by *k* in Greek, and this *k* sometimes gives place to the aspirated *kh*,—I am, therefore, inclined to identify *khalkos* with *shulka*; and if this is correct, we must conclude that undivided

Aryans were familiar with some metal, either copper or bronze, as a medium of exchange. There are many other points similar in character. But it is impossible to go further into this subject in this place. I only want to point out the reservation with which we shall have now to accept the results of Comparative Philology in forming our estimate of the degree of culture reached by the primitive Aryans, and show that when the primitive Aryan culture is carried back to the inter-Glacial age, the hypothesis that primitive Aryans were hardly better than the savage races of the present day at once falls to the ground. If the civilisation of some Aryan races in the Neolithic age appears to be inferior or imperfect it must, therefore, be, as observed above, ascribed to relapse or retrogression after the destruction of the ancient civilisation by the Ice Age, and the necessarily hard and nomadic life led by the people who survived the cataclysm. The Asiatic Aryans, it is true, were able to preserve a good deal more of the original religion and culture, but it seems to be mainly due to their having incorporated the old traditions into their religious hymns or songs; and made it the exclusive business of a few to preserve and hand down with religious scrupulosity these prayers and songs to future generations by means of memory specially trained and cultivated for the purpose. But even then how difficult the task was can be very well seen from the fact that a greater portion of the hymns and songs originally comprised in the Avesta has been lost; and though the Veda is better preserved, still what we have at present is only a portion of the literature which is believed on good grounds to have once been in existence. It may seem passing strange that these books should disclose to us the existence of an original Arctic home so many centuries after the traditions were incorporated into them. But the evidence in the foregoing pages shows that it is a fact; and if so, we must hold that the Neolithic Aryan people in Europe were not, as

Prof. Max Muller thinks, progressive, but, for the time at least, necessarily retrogressive savages working only with such residua of the ante-diluvian civilisation as were saved from its general wreck.[1]

But though the Vedic or Aryan people and their religion and culture can thus be traced to the last inter-glacial period, and though we know that the degree of culture attained by the primitive Aryans was of a higher type than some scholars seem to be willing to assign to them, yet there are many points in the primitive Aryan history which still remain unsolved. For instance, when and where the Aryan race was differentiated from other human races, or how and where the Aryan speech was developed, are important questions from the anthropological point of view, but we have, at present, no means to answer the same satisfactorily. It is quite possible that other human races might have lived with the Aryans in their home at this time; but the Vedic evidence is silent on this point. The existence of the human race is traced by geologists to the Tertiary era; and it is now geologically certain that the gigantic changes wrought on this globe by glacial epochs were witnessed by man. But anthropology does not supply us with any data from which we can ascertain when, where, or how the human race came to be differentiated according to colour or language. On the contrary, it is now proved that at the earliest date at which human remains have been found, the race was already divided into several sharply distinguished types; and this, as observed by Laing, leaves the question of man's ultimate origin completely open to speculation, and enables both monogenists and polygenists to contend for their respective views with plausible arguments and without fear of being refuted by facts.[2] The evidence, set forth in the foregoing pages, does not enable us to

1. Max Muller's Last Essays, pp. 172 *ff.*
2. Laing's Human Origins, pp. 404-5.

solve any of these questions regarding the ultimate origin of the human race or even of the Aryan people or their language and religion. We have nothing in this evidence for ascertaining how far the existence of the Aryan race can be traced back to pre-glacial, as distinguished from inter-glacial times; or whether the race was descended from a single pair (monogeny) or plurality of pairs (polygeny) in the remotest ages. The traditional evidence collected by us only warrants us in taking back the Aryan people and their civilisation from the Temperate zone in post-glacial to the Arctic regions in inter-glacial times. It is true that Aryans and their culture or religion cannot be supposed to have developed all of a sudden at the close of the last inter-glacial period, and the ultimate origin of both must, therefore, be placed in remote geological times. But it is useless to speculate on this question without further evidence, and in the present state of our knowledge we must rest content with the result that though Aryan race or religion can be traced to the last interglacial-period yet the ultimate origin of both is still lost in geological antiquity.

I cannot conclude this chapter without briefly examining the bearing of our results on the views entertained by Hindu theological scholars regarding the origin, character and authority of the Vedas. It is a question which has been discussed with more or less acuteness, subtlety, or learning ever since the days of the Brâhmaṇas ; and from a purely theological point of view I do not think there remains anything to be now said upon it. Again for the purposes of scientific investigation it is necessary to keep the theological and the antiquarian aspect of the question quite distinct from each other. Yet when our investigation, conducted on strict scientific lines, is completed, we may usefully compare our conclusions with the theological views and see how far they harmonise or clash with each other. In fact no Hindu who reads a book like the present, can avoid making such a comparison; and we shall be lightening his task by inserting in this place a few remarks on this subject. According to the view held by Hindu theologians, the Vedas are eternal (*nitya*), without a beginning (*anâdi*), and also not created by a human author (*a-paurusheya*); and we are told that these attributes have been predicated of our sacred books from the most ancient times known to our divines or philosophers. The whole of the third Volume of Dr. Muir's *Original Sanskrit Texts* is devoted to the discussion of this subject, a number of original passages and arguments bearing on which are there collected, including Sâyaṇa's lucid summary in the introduction to his commentary on the Ṛig-Veda; and more recently the late Mahâmahopâdhyâya Râjârâma Shâstri Bodas, the editor of the Bombay edition of the Ṛig-Veda, has done the same in a Sanskrit pamphlet, the second edition of which is now published by his son, Mr. M. R. Bodas, of the Bombay High Court Bar. I shall, therefore, give in this place only a summary of the different views of Hindu theologians, without entering into the details of the controversy which can be studied from the above books. The question before us is whether the Vedic hymns, that is, not only the words of the hymns but also the religious system found or referred to therein, are the compositions of the Ṛishis to whom they are assigned in the Anukramaṇikâs, or the ancient Indexes of the Veda, in the sense in which the Shâkuntala is a composition of Kâlidâsa; or whether these hymns existed from times immemorial, in other words, whether they are eternal and without a beginning. The hymns themselves are naturally the best evidence on the point. But, as shewn by Dr. Muir in the second chapter (pp. 218-86) of the Volume above mentioned, the utterances of the Vedic Ṛishis on this point are not unanimous. Thus side by side with passages in which the Vedic bards have expressed their emotions, hopes or fears, or prayed for worldly comforts and victory over their enemies, condemning evil practices like gambling with dice (X, 34), or have described events, which on their face seem to be the events of the day; side by side with passages where the poet says that he has made (*kṛi*), generated (*jan*), or fabricated (*takṣh*) a new (*navyasî* or *apûrvya*) hymn, much in the same way as a carpenter fashions a chariot (I, 47, 2; 62, 13; II, 19, 8; IV, 16, 20; VIII, 95, 5; X, 23, 6; 39, 14; 54, 6; 160, 5; &c.); or with hymns in which we are plainly told that they are composed by so and so, the son of so and so, (I, 60, 5; X, 63, 17; 67, 1; &c.), there are to be found in the Ṛig-Veda itself an equally large number of hymns where the Ṛiṣhis state in unmistakable terms that the hymns sung by them were the results of inspiration from Indra, Varuṇa, Soma, Aditi, or some other deity; or that the Vedic verses (*ṛichaḥ*) directly emanated from the Supreme Puruṣha, or some other divine source; or that they were given by gods (*devatta*), or generated by them and only seen or perceived (*pashyât*) by the poets in later times, (I, 37, 4; II, 23, 2; VII, 66, 11; VIII, 59, 6; X, 72, 1; 88, 8; 90, 9; &c.). We are also told that Vâch (Speech) is *nityâ* or eternal (VIII, 75, 6, also cf. X, 125); or that the gods generated the divine Vâch and also the hymns (VIII, 100, 10; 101, 16; X, 88, 8). The evidence of the Vedic hymns does not, therefore, enable us to decide the question one way or the other; but if the composition of the hymns is once ascribed to human effort, and once to divine inspiration or to the gods directly, it is clear that at least some of these old Ṛiṣhis believed the hymns to have been sung under inspiration or generated directly by the goddess of speech or other deities. We may reconcile the former of these views with the passages where the hymns are said to be *made* by human effort, on the supposition that the poets who sang the hymns believed themselves to be acting under divine inspiration. But the explanation fails to account for the statement that the Ṛik, the Yajus, and the Sâman, all emanated from the Supreme Purusha or the gods; and we must, therefore, conclude that the tradition about the eternity of the Vedas, or their divine origin is as old as the Veda itself. Accordingly, when we come to the Brâhmaṇas and the Upanishads, we naturally find the same view prevailing. They tell us that the Ṛig-Veda proceeded from Agni (fire), the Yajur-Veda from Vâyu (wind), and the Sâma-Veda from Sûrya (the sun), and that these three deities got their warmth from Prajâpati who practised *tapas* for the purpose, (Shat. Brâh. XI, 5, 8, 1 *ff*; Ait. Brâh. V, 32-34; Chân. Up. IV, 17, 1); or that the Vedas are the breathings of the Supreme Being (Bṛih. Up. II, 4, 10); or that Prajâpati by means of the eternal Vâch created the Vedas and everything else in this world; and the same view is met with in the Smṛitis like those of Manu (I, 21-23) and others, or in the Purâṇas, several extracts from which are given by Dr. Muir in the volume above referred to. It is admitted that the Vedas, with other things, are destroyed, at the end of a Kalpa, by the deluge (*pralaya*) which overtakes the world at the time. But we are told that this does not affect the question of the eternity of the Vedas, as they are re-promulgated at the beginning of the new Kalpa by Brahmâ himself after the grand deluge, and by the Ṛishis, who survive, after minor deluges. The authority generally quoted in support of this view is a verse from the Mahâbhârata (Shânti-Parvan, Chap. 210, v. 19) which says, "The great Ṛishis, empowered by Svayambhû (the self-born), formerly obtained, through *tapas* (religious austerity), the Vedas and the Itihâsas, which had disappeared at the end of the (preceding) *Yuga*."[1] The Ṛishis are, therefore, called the *seers* and not

1. The verse is as follows :—युगान्तेऽन्तर्हितान् वेदान् सैतिहासान् महर्षयः । लेभिरे तपसा पूर्वमनुज्ञाता स्वयंभुवा ॥ Bhavabhûti, Utt. 1, 15, similarly says in another connection :—ब्रह्मर्षयो ब्रह्महिताय तप्त्वा । परःसहस्राः शरदस्तपांसि ॥ एतान्यपश्यन् गुरवः पुराणाः । स्वान्येव तेजांसि तपोमयानि ॥ Also Cf. Ṛig. VIII, 59, 6, quoted *infra*.

the *makers* of the Vedic hymns; and the personal designation of some Shâkhâs, branches or recensions of the Vedas, as Taittirîya, Kâṭhaka, &c., as well as the statements in the Vedic hymns, which say that so and so has *made* or *generated* such and such a hymn, are understood to mean that the particular Shâkhâ or hymn was perceived, and *only perceived*, by the particular Ṛiṣhi or poet. It is not, however, till we come to the works of the authors and expositors of the different schools of Hindu philosophy (*darshanas*) that we find the doctrine of the eternity of the Vedas subjected to a searching examination; and, as remarked by Dr. Muir, one who reads the discussions of these writers cannot fail to be struck "with the acuteness of their reasoning, the logical precision with which their arguments are presented, and the occasional liveliness and ingenuity of their illustrations."[1] They all bear witness to the fact that so far as tradition went,—an unbroken tradition of great antiquity,—there was no remembrance of the Vedas having been ever composed by or ascribed to any human author; and taking into consideration the learning and the piety of these scholars, their testimony must be regarded as an unimpeachable proof of the existence of such a tradition, which was considered ancient several centuries before the Christian era. But though a tradition whose high antiquity can be so well established deserves to be seriously considered in our investigations regarding the character of the Vedas, yet it is, after all, a negative proof, showing, it may be urged, nothing more than no human author of the Veda has been known from times beyond the memory of all these ancient scholars. Jaimini, the author of Mîmâṁsâ Sutras, therefore, further deduces (I, 1, 5) the eternity of the Vedas from the relation or connection between words and their meanings, which he holds to be eternal (*autpattika*) and not conventional. A word is defined to be an aggregate of letters in a particular

1. Muir, O. S. T., Vol. III, p. 58.

order, and its sense is said to be conveyed by these letters following each other in a definite succession. But Grammarians are not satisfied with this view, and maintain that the sense of a word is not expressed by the aggregate of its constituent letters which are transient, but by a certain super-sensuous entity, called *sphoṭa* (*i. e.*, manifester, from *sphuṭ*), which supervenes the aggregate of the letters as soon as they are pronounced, and reveals their meaning. Jaimini denies that there are words in the Vedas which denote any transient objects, and as the Vedic words and their sense are eternal, it follows, according to him, that the Vedas are self-demonstrative, or that they shine, like the sun, by their own light, and are, therefore, perfect and infallible. If particular parts of the Vedas are designated after some Ṛishis, it does not, we are told, prove those sages to have been their authors, but merely the teachers who studied and handed them down. Bâdarâyaṇa, as interpreted by Shaṅkarâchârya (I, 3, 26-33), the great leader of the Vedânta School, accepts the doctrine of the eternity of sound or words, but adds that it is the species to which the word belongs, and not the word itself, that is eternal or indestructible, and, therefore, though the names of deities, like Indra and others, which are all created and hence liable to destruction, are mentioned in the Veda, it does not affect the question of its eternity as the species to which Indra and others are said to belong is still eternal. In short, Vedic names and forms of species are eternal, and it is by remembering these that the world is created by Brahmâ at the beginning of each Kalpa, (Maitr. Up., VI, 22). The Veda is, therefore, the original WORD the source from which every thing else in the world emanated, and as such it cannot but be eternal; and it is interesting, as pointed out by Prof. Max Muller in his *Lectures on Vedânta Philosophy*, to compare this doctrine with that of Divine *Logos* of the Alexandrian Schools in the West. The Naiyâyikas, on the other hand, deny the doctrine of the eternity of sound or word, but hold that the authority of the Vedas is established by the fact of their having emanated from competent (*âpta*) persons who had an intuitive perception of duty (*sâkshâtkṛita-dharmâṇaḥ*, as Yâska puts it), and whose competence is fully proved by the efficacy of such of the Vedic injunctions as relate to mundane matters, and can, therefore, be tested by experience; while the author of the Vaisheṣhika Sûtras clearly refers (I, 1, 3) the Veda to Îshvara or God as its framer. The Sâṅkhyas (Sâṇkhya Sûtras, V, 40-51) agree with the Naiyâyikas in rejecting the doctrine of the eternity of the connection of a word with its meaning; and though they regard the Veda as *paurusheya* in the sense that it emanated from the Primeval Purusha, yet they maintain that it was not the result of a conscious effort on the part of this Purusha, but only an unconscious emanation from him like his breathing. According to this view the Veda cannot be called eternal in the same sense as the Mîmâṁsakas have done, and, therefore, the texts which assert the eternity of the Vedas, are said to refer merely to "the unbroken continuity of the stream of homogeneous succession," (*Veda-nityatâ-vâkyâni cha sajâtîyânupûrvi-pravâhânuchcheda-parâṇi*).[1] Patanjali, the great grammarian, in his gloss on Pâṇini IV, 3, 101, solves the question by making a distinction between the *language* (the succession of words or letters, *varṇânupûrvi*, as we find it in the present texts) of the Vedas and their *contents* (*artha*), and observing that the question of the eternity of the Vedas refers to their sense which is eternal or permanent (*artho nityaḥ*), and not to the order of their letters, which has not always remained the same (*varṇânupûrvi anityâ*), and that it is through this difference

1. Cf. Vedântaparibhâṣhâ, Âgama-parichchheda, p. 55, quoted in Mahâmahopâdhyâya Jhalkikar's Nyâya-kosha, 2nd Ed. p. 736, *s. v.* वेद :— सर्गाद्यकाले परमेश्वरः पूर्वसर्गसिद्धवेदानुपूर्वीसमानानुपूर्वीकं वेदं विरचितवान् न तु तद्विजातीयं वेदम् ।

in the latter respect that we have the different versions of Kaṭhas, Kalâpas, Mudakas, Pippalâdas and so on. This view is opposed to that of the Mîmâṁsakas who hold both sense and order of words to be eternal. But Patanjali is led to reject the doctrine of the eternity of the order of words, because in that case we cannot account for the different versions or Shâkhâs of the same Veda, all of which are considered to be equally authoritative though their verbal readings are sometimes different. Patanjali, as explained by his commentators Kaiyyaṭa and Nâgoji Bhaṭṭa, ascribes this difference in the different versions of the Veda to the loss of the Vedic texts in the *pralayas* or deluges which occasionally overtake the world, and their reproduction or repromulgation, at the beginning of each new age, by the sages, who survived, according to their remembrance.[1] Each *manvantara* or age has thus a Veda of its own which differs only in expression and not in sense from the ante-diluvian Veda, and that different recensions of co-ordinate authority of the same Veda are due to the difference in the remembrance of the Ṛishis whose names are associated with the different Shâkhâs, and who repromulgate, at the beginning of the new age, the knowledge inherited by them, as a sacred trust, from their forefathers in the preceding Kalpa. This view substantially accords with that of Vyâsa as recorded in the verse from the Mahâbhârata quoted above. The later expositors of the different schools of philosophy have further developed these views of the Sûtra-writers and criticised or defended the doctrine of the self-demonstrated authority of the scriptural texts (*shabda-pramâṇa*) in various ways. But we cannot

1. Patanjali's words are,—ननु चोक्तं न हि च्छन्दांसि क्रियन्ते नित्यानि च्छन्दांसीति। यद्यप्यर्थो नित्यो या त्वसौ वर्णानुपूर्वी साऽनित्या। तद्भेदाच्चैतद्भवति काठकं कालापकं मौदकं पैप्पलादकमिति॥ Nâgoji Bhaṭṭa in his gloss quotes the verse—प्रतिमन्वन्तरं चैषा श्रुतिरन्याऽभिधीयते ; and observes that धाता यथापूर्वमकल्पयत् (Ṛig. X,190, 3) does not require us to assume that order of words was the same in the new Kalpa. See Muir O. S. T., Vol. III, pp. 96-97.

go into their elaborate discussions in this place; nor is it necessary to do so, for eventually we have to fall back upon the view of Vyâsa and Patanjali, mentioned above, if the destruction of the Vedas during each *pralaya*, and its repromulgation at the commencement of the new age is admitted.

Such, in brief, are the views entertained by Hindu orthodox theologians, scholars and philosophers in regard to the origin, character and authority of the Vedas; and on comparing them with the results of our investigation, it will be found that Patanjali's and Vyâsa's view about the antiquity and the eternity of the Vedas derives material support from the theory of the Arctic home which we have endeavoured to prove in the foregoing pages on strict scientific and historical grounds. It has been shown that Vedic religion and worship are both inter-glacial; and that though we cannot trace their ultimate origin, yet the Arctic character of the Vedic deities fully proves that the powers of Nature represented by them had been already clothed with divine attributes by the primitive Aryans in their original home round about the North Pole, or the Meru of the Purâṇas. When the Polar home was destroyed by glaciation, the Aryan people that survived the catastrophe carried with them as much of their religion and worship as it was possible to do under the circumstances; and the relic, thus saved from the general wreck, was the basis of the Aryan religion in the post-Glacial age. The whole period from the commencement of the post-Glacial era to the birth of Buddha may, on this theory, be approximately divided into four parts :—

10000 or 8000 B. C.—The destruction of the original Arctic home by the last Ice Age and the commencement of the post-Glacial period.

8000–5000 B. C.—The age of migration from the original home. The survivors of the Aryan race roamed over the northern parts of Europe and Asia in search of lands suitable for new settlements. The vernal equinox was then in the constellation of Punarvasû, and as Aditi is the presiding deity of Punarvasû, according to the terminology adopted by me in *Orion*, this may, therefore, be called the Aditi or the Pre-Orion Period.

5000–3000 B. C.—The Orion Period, when the vernal equinox was in Orion. Many Vedic hymns can be traced to the early part of this period and the bards of the race seem to have not yet forgotten the real import or significance of the traditions of the Arctic home inherited by them. It was at this time that first attempts to reform the calendar and the sacrificial system appear to have been systematically made.

3000–1400 B. C.—The Kṛittikâ Period, when the vernal equinox was in the Pleiades. The Taittirîya Saṁhitâ and the Brâhmaṇas, which begin the series of nakṣhatras with the Kṛittikâs, are evidently the productions of this period. The compilation of the hymns into Saṁhitâs also appears to be a work of the early part of this period. The traditions about the original Arctic home had grown dim by this time and very often misunderstood, making the Vedic hymns more and more unintelligible. The sacrificial system and the numerous details thereof found in the Brâhmaṇas seem to have been developed during this time. It was at the end of his Period that the Vedâṅga-jyotiṣha was originally composed, or at any rate the position of the equinoxes mentioned therein observed and ascertained.

1400–500 B. C.—The Pre-Buddhistic Period, when the Sûtras and the Philosophical systems made their appearance.

These periods differ slightly from those mentioned by me in *Orion*; but the change is needed in consequence of the theory of the Arctic home which carries back the beginning of the Pre-Orion or the Aditi Period to the commencement of the present post-Glacial era. In the language of the Purâṇas the first period after the close of the Ice Age (8000-5000 B. C.) may be called the Kṛita Yuga, or the age of wandering, as the Aitareya Brâhmaṇa (VII, 15) describes it to be. It was the period when the Aryan races, expatriated from their mother land, roamed over the northern parts of Europe and Asia in search of new homes. It is doubtful if the Brâhmaṇa meant as much when it described Kṛita to be the age of wandering. But nevertheless it is interesting to notice the new light thrown upon the characteristics of the four Yugas mentioned in the Brâhmaṇa. Thus we are told that "Kali is lying, Dvâpara is slowly moving, Tretâ is standing up, and Kṛita is wandering."[1] Dr. Haug understands this stanza to refer to the game of dice, and other scholars have proposed different interpretations. But in the light of the Arctic theory we may as well suppose that the different stages of life through which the Aryan races had to pass in post-Glacial times, from wandering in search of homes to final settlement in some lands of their choice, are here described, somewhat after the manner of the Avestic account of the sixteen ancient lands created by Ahura Mazda, and invaded in succession by Angra Mainyu. But even apart from this verse, we can very well see that during the first of the above periods the Aryan races had no fixed home, and many must have been the settlements made and abandoned by them before they permanently settled in congenial lands. I have already stated above that Aryan religion and worship are both inter-glacial; and that Vedic religion and ritual is a post-Glacial development of such relics of the ancient religion as were preserved from the general wreck caused by the Ice Age; and this affords in my opinion a safe basis to compare our results with the

1. Ait. Brâh. VII, 15,—कलिः शयानो भवति संजिहानस्तु द्वापरः । उत्तिष्ठँस्त्रेता भवति कृतं संपद्यते चरन् ॥

theological views mentioned above. We may not be able to fix definitely when each hymn of the Ṛig-Veda was sung; but we may safely say that those who survived the catastrophe, or their immediate descendants, must have incorporated into hymns the religious knowledge they had inherited as a sacred trust from their forefathers at the first opportunity, that is, soon after they were able to make at least temporary settlements. The hymns cannot, therefore, be supposed to promulgate a new religion consciously or unconsciously evolved on the plains of Central Asia in post-Glacial times; and the Polar character of the Vedic deities removes every doubt on the point. How far the language of the hymns, as we have them at present, resembled the ante-diluvian forms of speech is a different question; and according to Patanjali and Vyâsa, we are not here concerned with the words or the syllables of the hymns, which, it is admitted, have not remained permanent. We have to look to the subject matter of the hymns; and there is no reason to doubt either the competency or the trustworthiness of the Vedic bards to execute what they considered to be their sacred task or duty, *viz.*, that of preserving and transmitting, for the benefit of future generations, the religious knowledge they had inherited from their ante-diluvian forefathers. It was by an agency similar to this that the hymns have been preserved accent for accent, according to the lowest estimate, for the last 3000 or 4000 years; and what is achieved in more recent times can certainly be held to have been done by the older bards in times when the traditions about the Arctic home and religion were still fresh in their mind. We may also observe that the hymns were publicly sung and recited, and the whole community, which must be supposed to have been interested in preserving its ancient religious rites and worship, must have keenly watched the utterances of these Ṛishis. We may, therefore, safely assert that the religion of the primeval Arctic home was correctly preserved in the form of traditions by the disciplined memory of the Ṛishis until it was incorporated first into crude as contrasted with the *polished* hymns (*su-uktas*) of the Ṛig-Veda in the Orion period, to be collected later on in Maṇḍalas and finally into Saṁhitâs; and that the subject matter of these hymns is inter-glacial, though its ultimate origin is still lost in geological antiquity. Without mixing up the theological and historical views we may, therefore, now state the two in parallel columns as follows:—

Theological view.	*Historical view.*
1. The Vedas are eternal (*nitya*), beginning-less (*anâdi*), and not made by man (*a-paurushеya*).	1. The Vedic or the Aryan religion can be proved to be inter-glacial; but its ultimate origin is still lost in geological antiquity.
2. The Vedas were destroyed in the deluge, at the end of the last Kalpa.	2. Aryan religion and culture were destroyed during the last Glacial period that invaded the Arctic Aryan home.
3. At the beginning of the present Kalpa, the Ṛishis, through *tapas*, reproduced in substance, if not in form, the ante-diluvian Vedas, which they carried in their memory by the favour of god.	3. The Vedic hymns were sung in post-Glacial times by poets, who had inherited the knowledge or contents thereof in an unbroken tradition from their ante-diluvian forefathers.

On a comparison of the two columns it will be found that the tradition about the destruction and the reproduction of the Vedas, recorded by Vyâsa in the Mahâbhârata verse referred to above, must be taken to have been founded substantially on a historical fact. It is true that according to the Purâṇic chronology the beginning of the current Kalpa is placed several thousands of years before the present time; but if, according to the estimates of some modern geologists, the post-Glacial period is, even now, said to have commenced some 80,000 years ago, if not earlier, we need not be much surprised at the Purâṇic estimate, especially when, as stated above, it is found to disclose a real tradition of 10,000 years assigned to a cycle of the four yugas, the first of which began with the new Kalpa, or, in the language of geology, with the present post-Glacial period. Another point wherein the two views may be said to differ is the beginning-less-ness (*anâditva*) of the Vedas. It is impossible to demonstrate historically or scientifically that Vedic religion and worship is *absolutely* without a beginning. All that we can say is that its beginning is lost in geological antiquity, or that the Vedic religion is as old as the Aryan language or the Aryan man himself. If theologians are not satisfied with the support which this scientific view accords to their theory about the eternity of the Vedas, the scientific and the theological views must stand, as they are, distinct from each other, for the two methods of investigation are essentially different. It is for this reason that I have stated the views in parallel columns for comparison without mixing them up. Whether the world was produced from the original WORD, or the Divine Logos, is a question which does not fall within the pale of historical investigation; and any conclusions based upon it or similar other doctrines cannot, therefore, be treated in this place. We may, however, still assert that for all practical purposes the Vedic religion can be shown to be beginningless even on strict scientific grounds.

A careful examination of the Ṛig-Vedic hymns will show that the Vedic Ṛishis were themselves conscious of the fact that the subject matter of the hymns sung by them was ancient or ante-diluvian in character, though the expressions used were their own productions. We have already referred before to the two sets of Vedic passages, the first expressly saying that the hymns were *made*, *generated* or *fashioned* like a chariot by the Ṛishis to whom they are ascribed, and the other stating in equally unmistakable terms that the hymns were *inspired*, *given* or *generated* by gods. Dr. Muir attempts to reconcile these two contradictory views by suggesting that the different Ṛishis probably held different views; or that when both of them can be traced to the same author, he may have expressed the one at the time when it was uppermost in his mind, and the other at another; or that the Vedic Ṛishis or poets had no very clearly defined ideas of inspiration, and thought that the divine assistance of which they were conscious did not render their hymns the less truly the producation of their own mind.[1] In short, the existence of a human is not supposed to be incompatible with that of the super-human element in the composition of these hymns. But it will be seen that the above reconciliation is at once weak and unsatisfactory. A better way to reconcile the conflicting utterances of the Ṛishis would be to make a distinction between the *expression*, *language*, or *form* on the one hand, and the *contents*, *substance*, or the *subject matter* of the hymns on the other; and to hold that while the *expression* was human, the *subject matter* was believed to be ancient or superhuman. There are numerous passages in the Ṛig-Veda where the bards speak of ancient poets (*pûrve ṛishayaḥ*), or ancient hymns (I, 1, 2; VI, 44, 13; VII, 29, 4; VIII, 40, 12; X, 14, 15; &c.); and Western scholars understand by these phrases the poets or hymns of the past generations of Vedic bards, but not anterior to the post-Glacial times. But there are clear indications in the hymns themselves which go to refute this view. It is true that the Vedic bards speak of ancient and modern hymns; but they often tell us that though the hymn is new (*navyasi*), yet the god or the deity to whom it is addressed is old (*pratna*), or ancient, (VI, 22, 7; 62, 4; X,

1. See Muir O. S. T., Vol. III, pp. 274-5.

91, 13; &c.) This shows that the deities whose exploits were sung in the hymns were considered to be ancient deities. Nay, we have express passages where not only the deities but their exploits are said to be ancient, evidently meaning that the achievements spoken of in the hymns were traditional and not witnessed by the poet himself; thus, in I, 32, 1, the poet opens his song with a clear statement that he is going to sing those exploits of Indra which were achieved at first (*prathamâni*) or in early times, and the adjectives *pûrvyâṇi* and *pûrvîḥ* are applied to Indra's exploits in I, 11, 3, and I, 61, 13. The achievements of the Ashvins are similarly said to be *pûrvyâṇi* in I, 117, 25; and the long list of the exploits given in this hymn clearly shows that the poet is here rather summarising the exploits traditionally known to him than enumerating events witnessed by himself or by his forefathers in the near past. This is also evident from the fact that the ancient Ṛishis mentioned in the hymns, like the Aṅgirases or Vasiṣhṭha, are believed to have been invested with supernatural powers (VII, 33, 7-13), or to have lived and conversed with (I, 179, 2), or shared in the enjoyments of the gods (*Devânâm sadhamâdaḥ*, VII, 76, 4). They are also said to be the earliest guides (*pathikṛit*, X, 14, 15) for future generations. It is impossible to suppose that Vedic poets could have ascribed such superhuman character to their ancestors in the near past; and we are, therefore, led to the conclusion that the ancestors here spoken of were the ante-diluvian ancestors (*naḥ pûrve pitaraḥ*) who completed their sacrifices in the Arctic year of 7 or 10 months. And what is true of the ancestors applies as well to the ancient deities mentioned in the hymns. I have pointed out previously that the legend of Aditi and her sons is expressly stated to be a legend of the past age (*pûrvyam yugam*); and the same thing may be predicated of the legends of Indra, the Ashvins or the other deities whose exploits are described in the Ṛig-Veda as *pûrvyâṇi* or *prathamâni*, that is, old or ancient. In short, the ancient hymns, poets, or deities, mentioned in the Ṛig-Veda must be referred to a by-gone age and not to post-Glacial times. The Arctic character of these deities, it may be further observed, is intelligible only on this view. The Vedic bards may well be credited with having composed, or fashioned new songs or hymns; but the question still remains whether the subject matter of these hymns was of their own creation, and the fact that the deities have been called ancient in contradistinction with the songs offered to them (VI, 62, 4), and are clothed with Polar attributes, at once enables us to solve the question by answering that though the wording of the hymns was new, their subject matter was old, that is, traditionally handed down to the poet from remote ages. Thus in a hymn of the tenth Maṇḍala (X, 72, 1-2), the poet desiring to celebrate the births or the origin of gods, thus begins his hymn, "Let us, from the love of praise, celebrate, in recited hymns, the births of gods,—any one of us who in this later age may *see* them, (*yaḥ pashyâd uttare yuge*)." Here we have a distinct contrast between the births of gods on the one hand and the poet who may *see* the hymn in the later age on the other, evidently meaning that the subject matter of the hymn is an occurrence of the former age (*yuga*), and that the poet celebrates as he *perceives* or *sees* it in the later age. The view that the Vedic hymns, or rather their contents, were *perceived* and *not made* by the Ṛishis, derives material support from this statement. A similar expression is also found in VIII, 59, 6, which says "Indra and Varuṇa! I have *seen* (*abhi apashyam*) through *tapas* that which *ye formerly gave* to the Ṛishis, wisdom, understanding of speech, sacred lore (*shrutam*), and all the places which the sages created when performing sacrifices."[1] The notion about the perception of the sub-

1. Ṛig. VIII, 59, 6,—इंद्रावरुणा यदृषिभ्यो मनीषां वाचो मतिं श्रुतमदत्त-मग्रे । यानि स्थानान्यसृजंत धीरा यज्ञं तन्वानास्तपसाभ्यपश्यम् ॥

ject matter of the Vedic hymns is here referred to almost in the same terms in which it is expressed by Vyâsa in the Mahâbhârata verse quoted above; and with such express texts before us, the only way to reconcile the conflicting statements about the human and the superhuman origin of the hymns is to refer them to the *form* and the *matter* of the hymns respectively, as suggested by Patanjali and other scholars. Dr. Muir notices a passage (VIII, 95, 4–5) where the poet is said to have "generated (*ajîjanat*) for Indra the *newest* exhilerating hymn (*navîyasîm mandrâm giram*), springing from an intelligent mind, an *ancient* mental product (*dhiyam pratnâm*), full of sacred truth."[1] Here one and the same hymn is said to be both new and old at the same time; and Dr. Muir quotes Aufrecht to show that *gir*, that is, *expression* or *wording*, is here contrasted with *dhî* or *thought*, obviously showing that an old thought (*pratnâ dhîḥ*) has been couched in new language (*navîyasî gîḥ*) by the bard to whom the hymn is ascribed. In other words, the hymn is ancient in substance though new in expression,—a conclusion to which we have been already led on different grounds. We may also cite in this connection the fact that amongst the different heads into which the contents of the Brâhmaṇas have been classified by Indian divines, we find one which is termed *Purâ-kalpa* or the rites or traditions of a by-gone age, showing that even the Brâhmaṇas are believed to contain ante-diluvian stories or traditions. The statement in the Taittirîya Saṁhitâ that "The priests, in old times, were afraid that the dawn would not terminate or ripen into sunshine," is quoted by Sâyaṇa as an example of *Purâ-kalpa*, and we have seen before that this can be explained only by supposing it to refer to the Arctic dawn,—an incident witnessible by man only in the inter-glacial times. If the Brâhmaṇas can be thus shown to contain or refer to the facts of a by-gone age, *a fortiori* the

1. See Muir O. S. T., Vol. III, p. 239.

Vedas may, very well, be said to do the same. Thus from whatever side we approach the question, we are irresistibly led, by internal as well as external evidence, to the conclusion that the subject matter of the Vedic hymns is ancient and inter-glacial, and that it was incorporated into the Vedic hymns in post-Glacial times by Ṛishis who inherited the same in the shape of continuous traditions from their inter-glacial forefathers.

There are many other points in Vedic interpretation, or in Vedic and Purâṇic mythology, which are elucidated, or, we may even say, intelligently and rationally explained for the first time, by the theory of the Arctic home in inter-glacial times. For instance, we can now easily account for the disappointment of those Western scholars, who, when the Vedas became first known to them, expected to find therein the very beginnings of the Aryan civilisation or the out-pourings of the Aryan mind as it first became impressed with awe and wonder by the physical phenomena or the workings of natural elements and looked upon them as divine manifestations. Our theory now shows very clearly that though the Vedas are the oldest records of the Aryan race, yet the civilisation, or the characteristics and the worship of the deities mentioned therein did not originate with the Vedic bards, but was derived by them from their inter-glacial forefathers and preserved in the forms of hymns for the benefit of posterity; and if any one wants to trace the very beginnings of the Aryan civilisation he must go back beyond the last Glacial period, and see how the ancestors of the Aryan race lived and worked in their primeval Polar home. Unfortunately we have very few materials for ascertaining the degree of this civilisation. But we think we have shewn that there are grounds to hold that the inter-glacial Aryan civilisation and culture must have been of a higher type than what it is usually supposed to be;

and that there is no reason why the primitive Aryans should not be placed on an equal footing with the prehistoric inhabitants of Egypt in point of culture and civilisation. The vitality and superiority of the Aryan races, as disclosed by their conquest, by extermination or assimilation, of the non-Aryan races with whom they came in contact in their migrations in search of new lands from the North Pole to the Equator, if not to the farther south, is intelligible only on the assumption of a high degree of civilisation in their original Arctic home; and when the Vedas come to be further examined in the light of the Arctic theory, we may certainly expect to discover therein many other facts, which will further support this view, but which are still hidden from us owing to our imperfect knowledge of the physical and social surroundings amidst which the ancestors of the Vedic Ṛishis lived near the North Pole in times before the last Glacial epoch. The exploration of the Arctic regions which is being carried on at present, may also help us hereafter in our investigation of the beginnings of the Aryan civilisation. But all these things must be left to be done by future investigators when the theory of the Arctic home of the Aryans comes to be generally recognised as a scientific fact. Our object at present is to show that there is enough evidence in the Veda and the Avesta to establish the existence of an Arctic home in inter-Glacial times; and the reader, who has followed us in our arguments, set forth in the preceding pages, will at once perceive that the theory we have endeavoured to prove, is based on a solid foundation of express texts and passages traditionally preserved in the two oldest books of the Aryan race, and that it is amply fortified by independent corroboration received from the latest results of the correlative sciences, like Geology, Archæology, Linguistic Palæology, Comparative Mythology and Astronomy. In fact, the idea of searching for the evidence of an Arctic home in the Vedas may be said to have been stimulated, if not suggested, by the recent advances made in these sciences, and it will be seen that the method, adopted by us in working it up, is as rigid as it ought to be. It is now several centuries since the science of Vedic exegetics was founded by Indian Nairuktas; and it may seem surprising that traces of an Arctic home in the Vedas should remain undiscovered so long. But surprises like these are out of place in investigations of this kind, where one must be prepared to accept the results proved, in the light of advancing knowledge, by the strictest rules of logic and scientific research. It is these rules that we have taken for our guide, and if the validity of our conclusions be tested by this standard, we hope it will be found that we have succeeded in discovering the true key to the interpretation of a number of Vedic texts and legends hitherto given up as hopeless, ignored or misunderstood. In these days of progress, when the question of the primitive human culture and civilisation is approached and investigated from so many different sides, the science of Vedic interpretation cannot stand isolated or depend exclusively on linguistic or grammatical analysis; and we have simply followed the spirit of the time in seeking to bring about the co-ordination of the latest scientific results with the traditions contained in the oldest books of the Aryan race,—books which have been deservedly held in the highest esteem and preserved by our ancestors, amidst insurmountable difficulties, with religious enthusiasm ever since the beginning of the present age.

FINIS.

GENERAL INDEX.

INDEX OF VEDIC PASSAGES.

ṚIG-VEDA.

(In the case of passages to which † mark is prefixed a new meaning or construction is suggested.)

Maṇḍala I.

Maṇḍala VIII.

(Vâlakhilyas are counted in this Maṇḍala as hymns 49—59 both inclusive.)

Maṇḍala IX.

TAITTIRÎYA SAṀHITÂ.

(The references are to Kâṇḍa, Prapâṭhaka, Anuâvka, and Varga.)

VÂJASANEYI SAṀHITÂ.

SÂMA-VEDA SAṀHITÂ.

ATHARVA-VEDA SAṀHITÂ

AITAREYA BRÂHMAṆA.

KAUSHÎTAKÎ BRÂHMAṆA.

TAITTIRÎYA BRÂHMAṆA.

SHATAPATHA BRÂHMAṆA.

TÂṆḌYA BRÂHMAṆA.

SHADVIṀSHA BRÂHMANA.

TAITTIRIYA ÂRAṆYAKA.

UPANISHADS.

INDEX OF THE AVESTIC PASSAGES.

(The references are to S. B. E. Series translation of the Zend Avesta in three parts.)

VENDIDAD.

YASHTS.

YASNA.

Scheme of Trans-literation.

अ	आ	इ	ई	उ	ऊ	ऋ	ॠ	ए	ऐ	
a	â	i	î	u	û	ṛi	ṛî	e	ai	
ओ	औ	ं	ः	क	ख	ग	घ	ङ		
o	au	ṁ	ḥ	k	kh	g	gh	ṅ		
च	छ	ज	झ	ञ	ट	ठ	ड	ढ	ण	
ch	chh	j	jh	ñ	ṭ	ṭh	ḍ	ḍh	ṇ	
त	थ	द	ध	न	प	फ	ब	भ	म	
t	th	d	dh	n	p	ph	b	bh	m	
य	र	ल	व	श	ष	स	ह	ळ	क्ष	ज्ञ
y	r	l	v	sh	ṣh	s	h	ḷ	kṣh	jñ

ERATTA.

Page	13,	*Line*	22,	*for*	earlier,	*read*	later,
,,	69,	,,	31,	,,	नमोत्तम	,,	नगोत्तम
,,	70,	,,	2,	,,	concerned we,	,,	concerned, we
,,	,,	,,	18,	,,	That	,,	that
,,	77,	,,	10,	,,	case	,,	cases
,,	83,	,,	8,	,,	out of	,,	out of the
,,	84,	,,	28,	,,	स्वाहोदि	,,	स्वाहोदे
,,	85,	,,	5,	,,	due-lighted	,,	dew-lighted
,,	99,	,,	9,	,,	followers	,,	follower
,,	106,	,,	20,	,,	III, 61, 2,	,,	III, 61, 3,
,,	153,	,,	4,	,,	X, 72, 2-3	,,	X, 72, 8-9
,,	158,	,,	32,	,,	X, 119, 3	,,	X, 189, 3
,,	167,	,,	26,	,,	V, 4, 7	,,	V, 47, 5.
,,	168,	,,	4,	,,	Nanagvas	,,	Navagvas
,,	,,	,,	12,	,,	VIII, 64, 6	,,	VIII, 75, 6
,,	169,	,,	11,	,,	IV, 5, 1	,,	IV, 6, 1
,,	179,	,,	21,	,,	X, 139, 6	,,	X, 138, 6
,,	207,	,,	20,21,	,,	*Ayus*	,,	*Âyus*
,,	247,	,,	6,	,,	II, 11, 19,	,,	II, 11, 9
,,	,,	,,	14,	,,	I, 57, 6,	,,	I, 54, 10
,,	,,	,,	19,	,,	I, 34, 10	,,	I, 54, 10
,,	250,	,,	3,	*after*	*effects*	*insert*	(*Sâkam*, in VI, 30, 5)
,,	255,	,,	15,	*for*	I, 108, 8	*read*	I, 100, 8
,,	259,	,,	27,	,,	X, 152, 5	,,	X, 152, 4
,,	263,	,,	20,	,,	I, 23, 18	,,	II, 23, 18
,,	267,	,,	11,	,,	Wallace	,,	Wallis
,,	290,	,,	19,	,,	134, 11	,,	I, 34, 11
,,	302,	,,	8,	,,	*Shatâritram*	,,	*Shatâritrâm*
,,	314,	,,	3,	,,	X, 97, 1	,,	X, 37, 1
,,	328,	,,	15,	,,	VIII, 63, 9	,,	VIII, 100, 12
,,	345,	,,	4,	,,	VII, 4, 1	,,	VIII, 4, 1
,,	377,	,,	27,	,,	highlandtry	,,	highland try
,,	383,	,,	25,	,,	sunrise	,,	sun rise
,,	447,	,,	23,	,,	100, 10	,,	100, 11
,,	448,	,,	11,	,,	Chân.	,,	Chhân.
,,	452,	,,	34,	,,	that order	,,	that the order